EAST/WEST  NETWORK, INC.

THE BEST RESTAURANTS IN AMERICA

Introduction by

Jacques Pépin

A Fireside/East/West Network Book
Published by Simon & Schuster, Inc.
NEW YORK

THE BEST RESTAURANTS IN AMERICA
Was Developed and Produced by

Hebert & Associates, Inc., 9701 Wilshire Boulevard, Beverly Hills, CA 90212

Raymond E. Hebert, Jr., President and Publisher

Carol Olivier, Editor and Project Director

Karen McBride, Art Director and Book Designer

Diner's Dictionary and Wine Vintage Guide compiled by
Rita Leinwand, Noted Food Writer and Cookbook Author

Typesetting and Graphic Production by
Catered Graphics, Inc., Chatsworth, CA 91311

Richard M. Ray, President

Miriam Boucher, Copywriting and Editorial Supervision

A Fireside Book
Published by Simon & Schuster, Inc.
Simon & Schuster Building
Rockefeller Center
1230 Avenue of the Americas
New York, New York 10020

FIRESIDE and colophon are registered trademarks of Simon & Schuster, Inc.

Manufactured in the United States of America

10 9 8 7 6 5 4 3 2 1

ISBN: 0-671-60446-5

Contents

Introduction

During the last few years, I have traveled more than 40 weeks a year and have witnessed and enjoyed the incredible interest in food and the expansion of restaurants all over the country.

No less than 10 years ago, a traveler would go from the East Coast to the West Coast and back again, discussing and debating the merits of the eating establishments of both coasts while ignoring the rest of the country, which was essentially a gastronomic wasteland. In the last few years, the situation has changed in a swift and most dramatic way. Although there are still many restaurants that cater indifferent, tired, and stale food coupled with careless and mediocre service, significant changes are taking place.

Good, honest, imaginative establishments run by young, enthusiastic, and demanding chefs are sprouting up all over the land. Yet, even with the best intentions and talent, a restaurateur is helpless without dedicated and interested customers. There can be no good cooking or great chefs without patronage, and public interest is paramount to successful restaurants.

This is the important change of the last few years: The clientele is here and so is the good food. But, how does one find out about the other? Restaurant guides are usually sketchy and often obsolete by the time they are used. Moreover, they are frequently elitist, not reflecting the taste and point of view of the ordinary traveler.

In a democratic society such as ours, the people's choice is the only proper and acceptable alternative. A vote of confidence given to an establishment by its own patrons does reflect the situation adequately and it works as well in the reverse situation, when the restaurant is found to be inferior. In short, it guarantees the democratic process and assures objective criticism.

By asking you, its world traveler readers, for your recommendations, EAST/WEST NETWORK has done just that. More than 100,000 of you responded to its inquiry, generously sharing your outstanding, good, and even mediocre dining experiences. The result is a comprehensive, extensive, and objective guide loaded with the latest information and recommending only the restaurants that you, the travelers, like to visit.

It is not possible for a few critics to visit, taste the food, and judge thousands of restaurants throughout the United States and then to keep the criticism current and accurate. However, travelers can easily supply the necessary and proper information for such a book and keep it current. You have committed yourselves, deciding upon the restaurants and supplying the recommendations. THE BEST RESTAURANTS IN AMERICA is your guide. Enjoy it!

Jacques Pépin

About the Best Restaurants in America

East/West Network, the publishers of inflight magazines including *United, Eastern Review, Pan Am Clipper, Northwest Orient, Republic, Southwest Airlines Spirit, Western's World, PSA,* and *Ozark,* gratefully acknowledges the help of over 100,000 of its readers and frequent fliers for their participation in the publication-wide survey that led to the development of THE BEST RESTAURANTS IN AMERICA. The results of that survey, after careful months of follow-up research, have enabled us to bring you the most comprehensive guide to fine dining available today. Now you will know where to entertain clients or just enjoy your vacation dining at only THE BEST RESTAURANTS IN AMERICA. You might even discover a delightfully new dining experience right in your own city. We know that this guide will bring you many pleasurable dining delights as you visit the various restaurants selected by your fellow travelers.

As you can imagine with the thousands of fine restaurants throughout the United States, it was no simple task to present to you only the very best ones. Our primary criteria for the restaurants selected were the judgments of our discerning world travelers who participated in our survey. The thoughts and opinions of these people, whose tastes have been honed in their travels, form the basis for this guide. They have discovered for us, those restaurants serving only the very finest cuisine in an atmosphere of comfort and style, from casual to elegant. As a result, you will find you want to toss this essential traveling companion into your suitcase before you head out the door on your next trip. You will also find it essential to have this guide at home as a handy reference for the very best restaurants in your own city.

As is the nature of the restaurant business, however, there can be openings and closings at a rather rapid rate. With that in mind, we have made every effort to ensure the accuracy of this guide by continuing to review each city up until press time. Obviously, as careful as we have been, any one of the restaurants listed could have undergone major changes regarding ownership, food quality, ambiance, or price and, of course, we cannot assume responsibility for these changes.

We invite you to enjoy your dining tour of the 28 featured cities included in this guide. The pleasure of dining in THE BEST RESTAURANTS IN AMERICA is now yours!

Raymond E. Hebert, Jr. — Publisher
Carol Olivier — Editor

Use of the Guide

Your fellow travelers have rated each restaurant according to food, service, ambiance, and price. They were rated on a Four Star system as shown below. The information about each restaurant is presented concisely and there are convenient location-coded maps corresponding to the number after each restaurant name.

F - Food, S - Service, A - Ambiance

★ ★ ★ ★	The Very Best
★ ★ ★	Excellent
★ ★	Good
★	Fair

P - Price (Entrée only, excluding wine, spirits, tax, and tips.)

★ ★ ★ ★	Very Expensive — $20.00 and over
★ ★ ★	Expensive — $15.00 to $20.00
★ ★	Moderate — $10.00 to $15.00
★	Inexpensive — Under $10.00

Credit Card Code

AE American Express
CB Carte Blanche
DC Diners Club
MC Master Card
V   Visa

"All major credit cards" indicates all of the above.

Atlanta

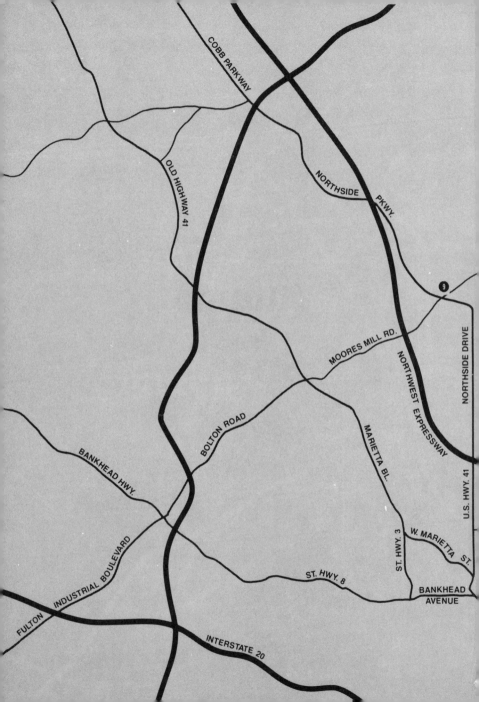

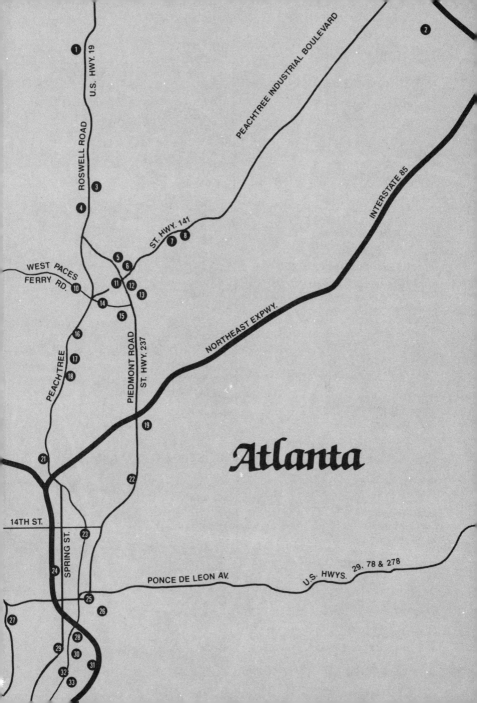

THE ABBEY 25

163 Ponce de Leon Avenue
Atlanta, GA
(404) 876-8532

Continental

F ★ ★ ★ ½
S ★ ★ ★ ½
A ★ ★ ★ ½
P ★ ★ ★ ½

Jacket required
Valet and lot parking
All major credit cards
Full bar
Reservations required

Dinner: Nightly 6:00PM-11:00PM

A landmark church, circa 1915, resplendent with stained glass windows and a 40-foot vaulted ceiling, is now the home of The Abbey. Meticulously prepared continental dishes are quietly served by waiters in monk's robes.

ANTHONY'S 13

3109 Piedmont Road, N.E.
Atlanta, GA
(404) 262-7379

American/Continental

F ★ ★ ★ ½
S ★ ★ ★ ½
A ★ ★ ★ ½
P ★ ★ ★ ★

Jacket required
Valet parking
All major credit cards
Full bar
Reservations required

Dinner: Mon.-Sat. 6:00PM-12:00AM
Closed Sunday

A. J. Anthony's restaurant occupies a 13-room restored antebellum plantation home, built in 1797, that is an historical landmark. Duckling, veal, fresh Maine lobster, quail, and a host of other choice entrées are included on the eclectic bill of fare.

BONE'S STEAK AND 12
SEAFOOD

3130 Piedmont Road, N.E.
Atlanta, GA
(404) 237-2663

American

F ★ ★ ★
S ★ ★ ★
A ★ ★ ★
P ★ ★ ★ ½

No dress restrictions
Valet parking
All major credit cards
Full bar
Reservations recommended

Lunch: Mon.-Fri. 11:30AM-2:30PM
Dinner: Sun.-Thurs. 6:00PM-11:00PM
Fri. & Sat. 6:00PM-12:00AM

Dedicated to providing the highest quality of food and service, Bone's is acclaimed for prime aged beef, live Maine lobster (flown in daily), and fresh seafood from the Gulf and Atlantic coasts. The décor is reminiscent of a New York steakhouse.

BOSTON SEA PARTY 4

3820 Roswell Road
Atlanta, GA
(404) 233-1776

American/Seafood

F ★ ★ ★ ½
S ★ ★ ½
A ★ ★ ★ ½
P ★ ★ ★ ★

Good taste in dress required
Lot parking
All major credit cards
Full bar
Reservations not required

Dinner: Mon.-Thurs. 6:00PM-10:00PM
Fri.& Sat. 5:30PM-11:00PM
Sun. 5:30PM-9:00PM

One of Atlanta's oldest buildings now serves as the unique setting for the Boston Sea Party. Fresh oysters, smoked salmon, caviar, Alaskan snow crab legs, salads, and soups precede your choice of a lobster or filet entrée.

THE BRASS KEY 17

2355 Peachtree Road, N.E.
Atlanta, GA
(404) 233-3202

Continental

F ★ ★ ★
S ★ ★ ★ ½
A ★ ★ ★ ½
P ★ ★ ★

Jacket required, no jeans
Lot parking
All major credit cards
Full bar
Reservations recommended

Lunch: Mon.-Fri. 11:30AM-2:30PM
Dinner: Mon.-Sat. 6:00PM-10:00PM
Closed Sunday

Enjoy dining in a setting of subdued elegance established with charming old-world European décor. Smoked trout, bouillabaisse, and sturgeon are included in the classic continental cuisine.

BUGATTI 27

Omni International Hotel
1 Omni International
Atlanta, GA
(404) 659-0000

Italian

F ★ ★ ★ ½
S ★ ★ ★
A ★ ★ ★
P ★ ★ ★ ½

Jacket required
Valet parking
All major credit cards
Full bar
Reservations recommended

Lunch: Mon.-Fri. 11:30AM-2:00PM
Dinner: Mon.-Sat. 6:00PM-11:00PM
Sun. 6:30PM-11:00PM
Brunch: Sun. 11:00AM-3:00PM

Emulating a New York City club atmosphere, Bugatti brings you a warmly masculine setting for dining. Chefs from Northern Italy prepare their native regional dishes with a knowing hand.

COACH & SIX 21

1776 Peachtree Street, N.W.
Atlanta, GA
(404) 872-6666

American

F ★ ★ ★ ½
S ★ ★ ★
A ★ ★ ★ ½
P ★ ★ ★ ½

Jacket required
Valet parking
All major credit cards
Full bar
Reservations required

Lunch: Sun.-Fri. 11:30AM-2:30PM
Dinner: Sun.-Fri. 6:00PM-11:00PM
Sat. 6:00PM-12:00AM

Retreat to the sanctity of Coach & Six's private British clublike atmosphere to quietly enjoy the candle light, fresh flowers, and the fine collection of original Impressionist oil paintings. Menu highlights include prime steaks, chops, Maine lobster, and fresh seafood.

COUNTRY PLACE   23

1197 Peachtree Street
Atlanta, GA
(404) 881-0144

American

F ★ ★ ★ ½
S ★ ★ ★ ½
A ★ ★ ★ ½
P ★ ★ ★

Good taste in dress required
Lot parking
AE, DC, MC, V
Full bar
Reservations not required

Lunch: Sun.-Fri. 11:00AM-2:30PM
Dinner: Sun.-Thurs. 5:30PM-12:00AM
Fri.& Sat. 5:30PM-12:30AM

Portuguese tile walls and a plethora of foliage plants and fresh flowers create a bright, cheerfully provincial Mediterranean atmosphere at the Country Place. The house specialty is a 3/4-pound steak, soy-marinated and enhanced with herbs.

DAILEY'S   32

17 International Boulevard, N.E.
Atlanta, GA
(404) 681-3303

American/Continental

F ★ ★ ★ ½
S ★ ★ ★ ½
A ★ ★ ★ ½
P ★ ★ ★

No dress restrictions
Lot parking
All major credit cards
Full bar
Reservations not required

Lunch: Mon.-Fri. 11:00AM-3:30PM
Sat. 11:30AM-3:30PM
Dinner: Sun.-Thurs. 5:30PM-11:00PM
Fri.& Sat. 5:30PM-12:00AM

Dailey's occupies a spacious renovated warehouse and is a lively, good-time place attracting a convention and business crowd. There is live entertainment in the piano lounge and a varied menu with entrées designed to appeal to every mood and taste.

DIPLOMAT   29

230 Spring Street
Atlanta, GA
(404) 525-6375

American/Continental

F ★ ★ ★
S ★ ★ ★
A ★ ★ ★
P ★ ★ ½

Jacket and tie required, no jeans
Valet parking
All major credit cards
Full bar
Reservations required

Lunch/
Dinner: Mon.-Thurs. 11:30AM-11:00PM
Fri. 11:30AM-12:00AM
Sat.& Sun. 6:00PM-12:00AM

The Diplomat, a pleasant stroll from downtown hotels, offers you the choice of dining in the sophisticated Embassy Room, where nouvelle and continental cuisine is featured, or in the more casual Palm Room, specializing in American meals.

THE FISH MARKET   6

3393 Peachtree Road, N.E.
Atlanta, GA
(404) 262-3165

Seafood

F ★ ★ ★ ½
S ★ ★ ★ ½
A ★ ★ ★ ½
P ★ ★ ★

Jacket required
Lot parking
All major credit cards
Full bar
Reservations required for dinner

Lunch: Mon.-Sat. 11:30AM-2:30PM
Dinner: Mon.-Sat. 6:00PM-10:30PM
            Closed Sunday

The Fish Market is Atlanta's "ultimate in chic." Hand-painted columns, antiques, crystal chandeliers, and a wealth of hanging greenery form an elegant backdrop for innovatively prepared fresh seafood.

GENE & GABE'S   22

1578 Piedmont Avenue, N.E.
Atlanta, GA
(404) 874-6145

Italian

F ★ ★ ★
S ★ ★ ★
A ★ ★ ★
P ★ ★ ★

Good taste in dress required
Lot and street parking
All major credit cards
Full bar
Reservations required

Dinner: Nightly 6:00PM-12:00AM

Patterned after a sophisticated New York street front restaurant, you will find bright red tablecloths and a cheerful ambiance here. Milk-fed veal and fresh fish dishes are featured.

GOJINKA   2

5269-3 & 4 Buford Highway
Doraville, GA
(404) 458-0558

Japanese

F ★ ★ ★ ½
S ★ ★ ★
A ★ ★ ★
P ★ ★

Good taste in dress required
Lot parking
All major credit cards
Full bar
Reservations not required

Dinner: Mon.-Sat. 6:00PM-10:00PM
            Closed Sunday

Exquisitely prepared sushi, sashimi, tempura, sukiyaki, teriyaki, negimayaki, and homemade tofu dishes distinguish the broad menu at Gojinka. The food presentation is an art in itself here, and you will find both the service and ambiance in the finest Oriental tradition.

HEDGEROSE   15
HEIGHTS INN

490 East Paces Ferry Road
Atlanta, GA
(404) 233-7673

International

F ★ ★ ★ ½
S ★ ★ ★ ½
A ★ ★ ★
P ★ ★ ★ ½

Jacket required
Lot parking
All major credit cards
Full bar
Reservations required

Dinner: Tues.-Sat. 6:30PM-10:00PM
            Closed Sunday and Monday

The warm peach and green color scheme of this small, intimate inn is echoed by the lush plants and fresh flowers. The cuisine is prepared with a decidedly French influence, and served with continental flair.

HUGO'S   33

Hyatt Regency Atlanta
265 Peachtree Street, N.E.
Atlanta, GA
(404) 577-1234

French

F ★ ★ ★ ★
S ★ ★ ★ ½
A ★ ★ ★ ½
P ★ ★ ★

Jacket and tie required
Valet parking
All major credit cards
Full bar
Reservations required

Dinner: Nightly 6:00PM-10:30PM

Hugo's epitomizes elegance and classic good taste. Fresh roses grace the tables and a harpist adds musical enchantment. Chefs, whose skills were honed in European kitchens, prepare classic French entreés such as Sweetbreads Financière and Veal Oskar.

LA GROTTA   16
RISTORANTE ITALIANO

2637 Peachtree Road, N.E.
Atlanta, GA
(404) 231-1368

Italian

F ★ ★ ★ ★
S ★ ★ ★ ★
A ★ ★ ★ ★
P ★ ★ ★ ½

Jacket and tie required
Valet parking
All major credit cards
Full bar
Reservations required

Dinner: Tues.-Sat. 6:00PM-10:30PM
          Closed Sunday and Monday

Classic Northern Italian cuisine featuring homemade pastas, unusual antipastos, veal specialties, and fresh seafood is prepared and served with gusto in this attractive restaurant with its rustic, candlelit elegance and enticing dining terrace.

THE LARK AND THE DOVE   1

5788 Roswell Road, N.E.
Atlanta, GA
(404) 256-2922

American

F ★ ★ ★
S ★ ★ ★
A ★ ★ ★
P ★ ★ ★

Good taste in dress required
Valet and lot parking
All major credit cards
Full bar
Reservations not required

Lunch: Daily 11:30AM-2:30PM
Dinner: Nightly 6:00PM-11:30PM

On the "Atlanta's Best" list, The Lark & The Dove is renowned for prime rib and superior steaks as well as fresh seafood, veal dishes, steamed vegetables, Caesar's Salad, Bananas Foster, and specialty coffees, all done tableside.

LENNOX'S   18

2225 Peachtree Street, N.E.
Atlanta, GA
(404) 233-5450

Cajun

F ★ ★ ★
S ★ ★ ★
A ★ ★ ★
P ★ ★ ½

No dress restrictions
Lot parking
All major credit cards
Full bar
Reservations not required

Dinner: Mon.-Thurs. 6:00PM-11:00PM
          Fri. & Sat. 6:00PM-12:00AM
          Sun. 6:00PM-10:00PM

This jaunty restaurant with its New Orleans jazz club décor will keep your feet tapping to the live New Orleans or Cajun music played nightly. Owner Lennox Gavin presents cuisine focused on such specialties as blackened redfish and crawfish dishes.

MIDNIGHT SUN   30

Peachtree Center
225 Peachtree Street, N.E.
Atlanta, GA
(404) 577-5050

Continental

F ★ ★ ★
S ★ ★ ★
A ★ ★ ★
P ★ ★ ★

Jacket required
Valet parking
All major credit cards
Full bar
Reservations required

Lunch: Mon.-Fri. 11:30AM-2:30PM
Dinner: Nightly 6:30PM-10:00PM

Built around an impressive marble fountain/atrium that is open to the sky, the Midnight Sun has a handsome decor, an exceptional wine list, and delectable contemporary continental cuisine that is out of the ordinary.

NAKATO   19

1893 Piedmont Road
Atlanta, GA
(404) 873-6582

Japanese

F ★ ★ ★
S ★ ★ ★
A ★ ★ ★
P ★ ★ ★

No dress restrictions
Lot parking
All major credit cards
Full bar
Reservations required

Dinner: Mon.-Thurs. 5:30PM-10:30PM
Fri.& Sat. 5:30PM-11:00PM
Sun. 5:00PM-10:00PM

Nakato features separate rooms, each decorated with superb Oriental restraint, for different menus. The atmosphere is congenial and the presentation and preparation of the food beautifully executed.

NIKOLAI'S ROOF   28
& TOWERS

Atlanta Hilton Hotel
255 Courtland Street
Atlanta, GA
(404) 659-2000

Russian/Continental

F ★ ★ ★ ★
S ★ ★ ★ ★
A ★ ★ ★ ★
P ★ ★ ★ ★

Jacket and tie required
Valet parking
All major credit cards
Full bar
Reservations required

Dinner: Nightly seatings at
6:30PM & 9:30PM

Sited on top of the Hilton Hotel, you are afforded a sweeping view of Atlanta and its environs while dining like royalty on a five-course pre fixe dinner selected from a menu that rotates every l0 days.

103 WEST   10

103 West Paces Ferry Road
Atlanta, GA
(404) 233-5993

Continental

F ★ ★ ★ ½
S ★ ★ ★ ½
A ★ ★ ★ ½
P ★ ★ ★ ½

Jacket required, no denims
Valet parking
All major credit cards
Full bar
Reservations recommended

Dinner: Mon.-Sat. 5:00PM-1:00AM
Closed Sunday

An opulent old-world setting with crystal chandeliers and rich brocade wallpaper is the stage upon which 103 West presents its classic continental dishes prepared with innovative flair.

PANO'S AND PAUL'S 9

1232 West Paces Ferry Road, N.W.
Atlanta, GA
(404) 261-3662

American/Continental

F ★ ★ ★ ½
S ★ ★ ★ ★
A ★ ★ ★ ½
P ★ ★ ★ ½

Jacket required, no denims
Lot parking
All major credit cards
Full bar
Reservations recommended

Dinner: Mon.-Thurs. 6:00PM-10:00PM
Fri.& Sat. 6:00PM-11:00PM
Closed Sunday

The romantic elegance of the Victorian era is reflected in the décor at Pano's and Paul's. Owner Pano Karatassos offers a comprehensive menu with a variety of fresh seafood, veal, beef, lamb, and nightly specials.

THE PATIO RESTAURANT 5

3349 Piedmont Road, N.E.
Atlanta, GA
(404) 237-5878

Continental

F ★ ★ ★ ½
S ★ ★ ★ ½
A ★ ★ ★ ½
P ★ ★ ★

Jacket and tie required
Lot parking
All major credit cards
Full bar
Reservations required

Lunch: Mon.-Fri. 11:30AM-2:30PM
Dinner: Nightly 6:00PM-11:00PM

Regency antiques, fresh flowers, fine china and appointments, and a gallery of contemporary art create a rich environment in this small, intimate restaurant. Country style European cuisine offers you such choices as fresh trout, oysters, prime beef, and veal entrées.

PEASANT UPTOWN 8

3500 Peachtree Road, N.E.
Atlanta, GA
(404) 261-6341

Continental

F ★ ★ ★
S ★ ★ ★
A ★ ★ ★
P ★ ★ ★

Good taste in dress required
Lot parking
All major credit cards
Full bar
Reservations not required

Lunch: Mon.-Sat. 11:30AM-2:30PM
Dinner: Nightly 5:30PM-12:00AM
Brunch: Sun. 11:00AM-2:30PM

Relax in a country garden courtyard setting highlighted by an antique-enhanced 100-foot-high greenhouse that lets the sun and moon shine in. The continental menu encompasses a broad range of well prepared dishes that are presented by a friendly staff.

PIERRE'S RUE DE PARIS   14

315 East Paces Ferry Road
Atlanta, GA
(404) 261-9600

French

F ★ ★ ★ ½
S ★ ★ ★ ½
A ★ ★ ★ ½
P ★ ★ ★ ★

Jacket required
Valet parking
All major credit cards
Full bar
Reservations recommended

Lunch: Mon.-Fri. 11:30AM-2:30PM
Dinner: Nightly 6:00PM-12:00AM

Enjoy award-winning epicurean food in a French country inn setting decorated with priceless antiques. Entrées include beef, lamb, veal, seafood, and poultry dishes, with many meals served tableside from carts. The wine list is widely acclaimed.

PITTYPAT'S PORCH   31

25 International Boulevard, N.W.
Atlanta, GA
(404) 525-8228

Southern/Seafood

F ★ ★ ★
S ★ ★ ★
A ★ ★ ★
P ★ ★ ★

No dress restrictions
Lot parking
All major credit cards
Full bar
Reservations not required

Dinner: Mon.-Sat. 4:00PM-12:00AM
Closed Sunday

Leisurely dining becomes a fine art when you visit Pittypat's Porch with its antebellum ambiance and gracious service. An appetizer buffet and salad bar, complete with shrimp and oysters, preludes superb southern specialties and fresh seafood entrées.

THE PLEASANT PEASANT   26

555 Peachtree Street
Atlanta, GA
(404) 874-3223

French

F ★ ★ ★
S ★ ★ ★
A ★ ★ ★
P ★ ★ ½

Good taste in dress required
Lot parking
All major credit cards
Full bar
Reservations not required

Dinner: Sun.-Thurs. 5:30PM-12:00AM
Fri. & Sat. 5:30PM-1:00AM

The Pleasant Peasant resides in an 1890s building converted into a New York style bistro with a tile floor, brick walls, and a tin ceiling. You'll dine in cozy comfort in the midst of plants and flowers. The French provincial country food is robust, hearty, and authentically prepared.

THE RITZ-CARLTON   7
DINING ROOM

The Ritz-Carlton Hotel
3434 Peachtree Road, N.E.
Atlanta, GA
(404) 237-2700

Continental

F ★ ★ ★ ½
S ★ ★ ★ ½
A ★ ★ ★ ½
P ★ ★ ★ ½

Jacket and tie required, dresses only
Valet, lot, and street parking
All major credit cards

Full bar
Reservations recommended

Lunch: Mon.-Fri. 11:30AM-2:30PM
Dinner: Mon.-Thurs. 6:00PM-10:30PM
Fri. & Sat. 6:00PM-11:00PM
Closed Sunday

Vintage wines, a refined atmosphere, luxurious décor, and such extravagant touches as Hutschenreuther China, lure a discerning clientele to this fine restaurant. The continental menu features fresh seafood and aged meats perfectly prepared on mesquite grills.

SIDNEY'S 3

4225 Roswell Road
Atlanta, GA
(404) 256-2339

International

F ★ ★ ★ ½
S ★ ★ ★ ½
A ★ ★ ½
P ★ ★ ★

No dress restrictions
Lot parking
All major credit cards
Full bar
Reservations recommended

Dinner: Mon.-Sat. 6:00PM-10:30PM
Closed Sunday

For the past 12 years, warm, family style hospitality has been enjoyed by diners visiting Sidney's charming cottage, where country French and Jewish cuisine attracts an international clientele. Fresh fish, veal, and duckling are house specialties.

SUN DIAL 24

Westin Peachtree Plaza Hotel
210 Peachtree Street
Atlanta, GA
(404) 659-0099

American

F ★ ★ ★ ½
S ★ ★ ★ ★
A ★ ★ ★
P ★ ★ ★ ½

Good taste in dress required
Valet parking
All major credit cards
Full bar
Reservations required

Lunch: Daily 11:30AM-2:30PM
Dinner: Nightly 6:00PM-11:00PM

A glorious view of Atlanta, from this revolving 73-story high restaurant, and superb aged steaks and hickory-smoked prime rib, help account for the Sun Dial's loyal clientele. The service is smooth, luncheon menu ample, and fixed-price dinners excellent.

TROTTERS 11

3215 Peachtree Road, N.E.
Atlanta, GA
(404) 237-5988

American

F ★ ★ ★
S ★ ★ ★
A ★ ★ ★
P ★ ★ ★

No dress restrictions
Valet parking
All major credit cards
Full bar
Reservations recommended

Lunch: Mon.-Fri. 11:30AM-2:30PM
Dinner: Sun.-Thurs. 6:00PM-11:00PM
Fri. & Sat. 6:00PM-12:00AM
Brunch: Sun. 11:30AM-2:30PM

You'll take delight in Trotters' 1920s Country Club atmosphere with its unusual harness-racing motif, enhanced by Currier & Ives prints. Emphasis is on freshness of ingredients (the herbs are grown on the grounds) in all dishes that include veal, charcoal-grilled seafood, and homemade pastas.

Baltimore

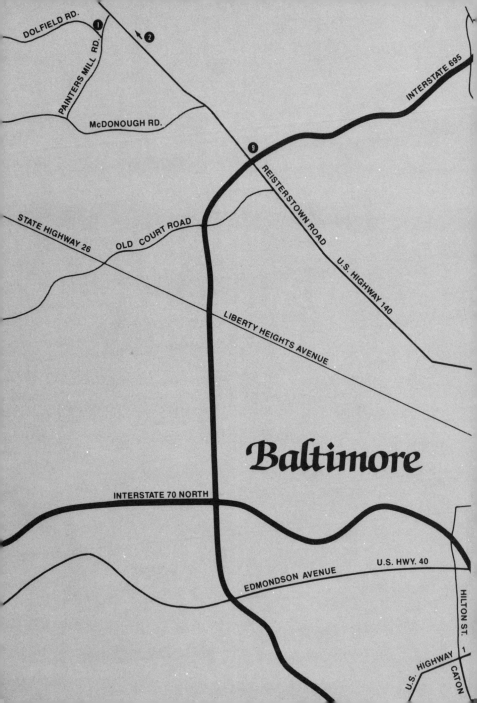

BAMBOO HOUSE 3

26 Yorktown Plaza
Cockeysville, MD
(301) 666-9550

Chinese

F ★ ★ ★ ½
S ★ ★ ★ ½
A ★ ★ ★ ½
P ★ ★ ½

Good taste in dress required
Lot parking
AE, MC, V
Full bar
Reservations required

Lunch: Sun.-Fri. 11:30AM-3:00PM
Dinner: Nightly 5:00PM-11:00PM

A rich mélange of modern French décor with restrained touches of the Orient creates a high-fashion setting at the Bamboo House. Mandarin and Szechwan style Chinese cuisine includes a range of dishes from mildly spiced to very peppery. The Peking Duck is a perennial favorite.

THE BRASS ELEPHANT 12

924 North Charles Street
Baltimore, MD
(301) 547-8480

Italian

F ★ ★ ★ ★
S ★ ★ ★ ½
A ★ ★ ★ ★
P ★ ★ ★

Jacket and tie required
Lot parking
AE, MC, V
Full bar
Reservations required

Dinner: Mon.-Thurs. 5:30PM-9:30PM
Fri. & Sat. 5:30PM-11:00PM
Sun. 5:00PM-9:00PM

Primo Italian cuisine prepared with finesse and served with aplomb is yours to enjoy at The Brass Elephant. Located in a meticulously restored Victorian townhouse, circa 1860, the restaurant is lavishly appointed with teak and oak woods, crystal, and marble.

CAFÉ DES ARTISTES 10

1501 Sulgrave Avenue
Baltimore, MD
(301) 664-2200

French

F ★ ★ ★ ½
S ★ ★ ★
A ★ ★ ★
P ★ ★ ★ ½

Jacket required
Valet parking
All major credit cards
Full bar
Reservations required

Lunch: Mon.-Sat. 11:30AM-2:30PM
Dinner: Sun.-Thurs. 5:30PM-10:00PM
Fri. & Sat. 5:30PM-11:00PM

Bask in the warm, comfortable ambiance of this elegant dining room, decorated with French posters, flickering candles, and fresh flowers. The wine cellar is lavishly stocked to complement the wide range of classic French entrées and innovative daily specials.

CAPRICCIO 22

242 South High Street
Baltimore, MD
(301) 685-2710

Italian/French

F ★ ★ ★ ½
S ★ ★ ★
A ★ ★ ★
P ★ ★ ½

Jacket required
Street parking
All major credit cards
Full bar
Reservations required

Lunch: Mon.-Fri. 11:30AM-2:30PM
Dinner: Sun.-Thurs. 5:00PM-11:00PM
         Fri. & Sat. 5:00PM-1:00AM

A trio of snug, intimate dining rooms and a friendly pub room, all decorated with modern paintings, form a pleasant haven for savoring Northern Italian and French cuisine. You'll find the pasta is freshly homemade and the classic dishes are prepared and served respectfully.

CHESAPEAKE, THE ORIGINAL   13

1701 North Charles Street
Baltimore, MD
(301) 837-7711

American

F ★ ★ ★
S ★ ★ ★
A ★ ★ ½
P ★ ★ ★

Jacket required at dinner
Valet and lot parking
AE, DC, MC, V
Full bar
Reservations recommended

Lunch/
Dinner: Sun.-Fri. 11:30AM-11:00PM
         Sat. 5:00PM-12:00AM

For five decades the Chesapeake has been acclaimed for its traditional Maryland seafood and prime charcoal steaks. Food preparation and service is consistently good; salads are created tableside. The ample wine cellar is an award winner.

CHIAPPARELLI'S   23

237 South High Street
Baltimore, MD
(301) 539-1786

Italian

F ★ ★ ★
S ★ ★ ★
A ★ ★ ½
P ★ ★

Good taste in dress required
Lot and street parking
All major credit cards
Full bar
Reservations recommended

Lunch/
Dinner: Sun.-Thurs. 11:00AM-11:00PM
         Fri. 11:00AM-1:00AM
         Sat. 11:00AM-2:00AM

Famous for "Baltimore Best" house salad and clams casino, Chiapparelli's specializes in creatively prepared veal and seafood dishes. The atmosphere is redbrick warm and friendly; the service invariably good. Located in the famous "Little Italy" district near the harborplace.

COUNTRY FARE INN   1

100 Painters Mill Road
Owings Mills, MD
(301) 363-3131

French

F ★ ★ ★ ½
S ★ ★ ★
A ★ ★ ★
P ★ ★ ½

No dress restrictions
Lot parking
AE, MC, V
Full bar
Reservations recommended

Lunch: Mon.-Fri. 11:30AM-2:00PM
Dinner: Mon.-Thurs. 5:30PM-9:30PM
Fri. & Sat. 5:30PM-10:00PM
Sun. 4:00PM-8:30PM

Housed in a beautifully restored historic home, built in 1767 for Samuel Owings, this inn entices you with a menu featuring fresh seafood, veal, duck, beef, and such seasonal specialties as venison and Maryland soft crabs. The Wine Cellar Pub invites after-dinner conviviality.

CROSSROADS 11

Crosskeys Inn
5100 Falls Road
Baltimore, MD
(301) 532-6900

French

F ★ ★ ★
S ★ ★ ★
A ★ ★ ★
P ★ ★ ★

No dress restrictions
Lot parking
All major credit cards
Full bar
Reservations recommended

Lunch: Mon.-Fri. 11:30AM-2:30PM
Dinner: Mon.-Sat. 5:30PM-11:00PM
Closed Sunday

Exuding an atmosphere of warm hospitality, this intimate eatery is lavished with wall tapestries that create a distinctive décor. Seafood is the specialty of the house, and a seafood platter is offered that has been widely acclaimed.

DANNY'S 14

1201 North Charles Street
Baltimore, MD
(301) 539-1393

French/American

F ★ ★ ★ ½
S ★ ★ ★ ½
A ★ ★ ★ ½
P ★ ★ ★

Jacket required
Lot and street parking
All major credit cards
Full bar
Reservations recommended

Lunch/
Dinner: Mon.-Fri. 11:30AM-11:00PM
Sat. 5:00PM-12:00AM
Closed Sunday

Family owned and operated for 23 years, Danny's is an inviting, elegant restaurant where owner-chef Danny Dickman does magic things with Chesapeake Bay seafood, Maine lobster, crab cakes, prime beef, and continental specialties such as Scotch-smoked salmon, Dover sole, and Beef Wellington.

8 EAST 19

Tremont Hotel
8 East Pleasant Street
Baltimore, MD
(301) 576-1200

French

F ★ ★ ★ ½
S ★ ★ ★
A ★ ★ ★ ½
P ★ ★ ½

Jacket and tie preferred
Valet, lot, and street parking
All major credit cards
Full bar
Reservations recommended

Lunch: Mon.-Fri. 11:30AM-2:30PM
Dinner: Nightly 5:30PM-10:30PM

Fashioned in the manner of a New York style café in the '20s, this chic dining room has won awards for its unique design. Lobster, seafood, fettuccine, and Veal Chanteloupe are among the wide range of entrées offered.

GIANNI'S   24

Harbor Place
201 East Pratt Street
Baltimore, MD
(301) 837-1130

Italian/American

F ★ ★ ★ ½
S ★ ★ ★
A ★ ★ ★
P ★ ★ ½

Good taste in dress required
Lot and garage parking
AE, MC, V
Full bar
Reservations recommended

Lunch: Mon.-Fri. 11:30AM-3:00PM
          Sat. 11:30AM-4:00PM
Dinner: Mon.-Thurs. 5:00PM-10:00PM
          Fri. & Sat. 5:00PM-11:00PM
          Sun. 3:30PM-8:00PM
Brunch: Sun. 11:00AM-3:30PM

At Gianni's you will enjoy a spectacular view of Baltimore Harbor, and a beautifully designed art déco décor. Fresh local seafood, prepared à la Northern Italy and Maryland styles is a highlight of the menu, as are the 20 fresh pastas, and Maryland-style crab bisque.

HARVEY HOUSE   16

920 North Charles Street
Baltimore, MD
(301) 539-3110

Continental

F ★ ★ ★
S ★ ★ ★
A ★ ★ ½
P ★ ★ ½

Good taste in dress required
Lot and street parking
All major credit cards
Full bar
Reservations required on weekends

Lunch/
Dinner: Mon.-Thurs. 11:00AM-11:00PM
          Fri. & Sat. 11:00AM-12:00AM
          Closed Sunday

Near theaters, galleries, and sporting events, this restaurant has delighted patrons for three decades with its hearty, prepared-to-order meals. The menu is extensive, emphasizing prime rib, steaks, and fresh local seafoods. Good vintage wines are available.

HAUSSNER'S   25

3242 Eastern Avenue
Baltimore, MD
(301) 327-8365

German/American

F ★ ★ ★ ½
S ★ ★ ★ ½
A ★ ★ ★ ½
P ★ ★ ★

Good taste in dress required
Street parking
AE, MC, V
Full bar
Reservations not required

Lunch/
Dinner: Tues.-Sat. 11:00AM-11:00PM
          Closed Sunday and Monday

Family owned and operated since 1926, this establishment is as famous for its fine art collection as it is for the scope of its menu — which lists over 50 seafood items and more than 40 meat dishes, all prepared to order. All baked goods are home-made — the desserts are delectable.

HERSH'S ORCHARD INN   8

1528 East Joppa Road
Baltimore, MD
(301) 823-0384

Continental

F ★ ★ ★
S ★ ★ ★
A ★ ★ ★
P ★ ★ ½

Good taste in dress required; no jeans,
T-shirts, tennis shoes, or cut-offs
Valet and lot parking
AE, MC, V
Full bar
Reservations recommended

Lunch/
Dinner: Daily 11:30AM-11:00PM

A long-time favorite of sports and entertainment personalities, this spot offers a
six-page menu with something to please
every taste. Prime beef, fresh seafood,
veal, poultry, and lamb are all prepared
and served with distinction.

THE KING'S 30
CONTRIVANCE

10150 Shaker Drive
Columbia, MD
(301) 995-0500

French

F ★ ★ ★ ½
S ★ ★ ★ ½
A ★ ★ ★ ½
P ★ ★ ★

Jacket required
Valet and lot parking
AE, MC, V
Full bar
Reservations required

Lunch: Mon.-Fri. 11:30AM-2:00PM
Dinner: Mon.-Sat. 5:30PM-9:30PM
Sun. 4:00PM-9:00PM

Turn back the clock to another era and dine
regally in this turn-of-the-century Colonial
mansion that nestles in five acres of
wooded land. Owner Paul Bukovsky offers
meticulously prepared French cuisine
served with professional polish in the restaurant's seven gracious dining rooms.

LA PROVENCE 21

9 Hopkins Plaza
Baltimore, MD
(301) 837-6600

French/Italian

F ★ ★ ★ ½
S ★ ★ ★
A ★ ★ ★
P ★ ★ ★ ½

Jacket and tie required
Lot parking
AE, MC, V
Full bar
Reservations required

Lunch: Daily 11:30AM-2:30PM
Dinner: Nightly 5:00PM-9:30PM

Whether you opt for the French haute
cuisine served in the dining room, or venture into the Bistro with its French provincial ambiance and Italian-style cooking,
you'll find dining here is an exhilarating
experience. The Bistro's after-theater specials, served until 10:30PM on the
weekends also lure a lively crowd.

MAISON MARCONI 18

106 West Saratoga Street
Baltimore, MD
(301) 752-9286

Continental

F ★ ★ ★ ★
S ★ ★ ★
A ★ ★ ★
P ★ ★ ★

Jacket required
Street parking
MC, V
Full bar
Reservations not required

Lunch: Tues.-Sat. 12:00PM-3:30PM
Dinner: Tues.-Sat. 5:00PM-8:00PM
Closed Sunday and Monday

The timeless charm of traditional Baltimore is reflected in the décor and in the old converted row house this restaurant occupies. The regional seafood and French and Italian specialties that round out the menu have earned the praise of Baltimore residents for more than 60 years.

MILTON INN 4

14833 York Road
Sparks, MD
(301) 771-4366

Continental

F ★ ★ ★ ½
S ★ ★ ★ ½
A ★ ★ ★ ½
P ★ ★ ★ ½

Jacket and tie required in main dining room
Lot parking
All major credit cards
Full bar
Reservations required on weekends

Lunch: Mon.-Fri. 12:00PM-2:30PM
Dinner: Mon.-Thurs. 6:00PM-10:00PM
          Fri. & Sat. 6:00PM-11:00PM
          Closed Sunday

Originally a Quaker meeting house, then the oldest Pub in the county, the historic home of Milton Inn dates from 1740. The present owner, Eleanora E. Allori, carries on the family tradition, presenting well prepared continental cuisine, including fresh Maryland seafood, the long-time house specialty.

PEERCE'S DOWNTOWN 6

225 North Liberty Street
Baltimore, MD
(301) 727-0910

French

F ★ ★ ★ ½
S ★ ★ ★ ½
A ★ ★ ★
P ★ ★ ★

Jacket preferred, required on weekends; no jeans
Valet parking
AE, MC, V
Full bar
Reservations required

Lunch: Mon.-Fri. 11:30AM-2:00PM
Dinner: Mon.-Fri. 5:30PM-9:00PM
          Sat. 5:30PM-10:00PM
          Closed Sunday

A sophisticated, New York style restaurant, elegant and Victorian in aura, Peerce's takes pride in its formal French service and meticulously prepared classic French cuisine.

PEERCE'S PLANTATION 7

12450 Dulaney Valley Road
Phoenix, MD
(301) 252-3100

French/Continental

F ★ ★ ★ ½
S ★ ★ ★ ½
A ★ ★ ★ ½
P ★ ★ ½

Jacket required at dinner
Valet and lot parking
AE, MC, V
Full bar
Reservations required

Lunch: Mon.-Sat. 11:30AM-3:00PM
Dinner: Mon.-Thurs. 5:00PM-10:00PM
          Fri. & Sat. 5:00PM-11:00PM
          Sun. 1:00PM-9:00PM

This southern antebellum style dining room that overlooks Loch Raven Reservoir provides a delightful setting for sipping Mint Juleps in summer, or fireside dining in winter. Superb pâtés, and veal and fresh fish entrées are specialties of the house.

THE PEPPERMILL   5

1301 York Road
Baltimore, MD
(301) 583-1107

American

F ★ ★ ★ ½
S ★ ★ ★
A ★ ★ ★
P ★ ★ ½

Good taste in dress required
Lot parking
All major credit cards
Full bar
Reservations not required

Lunch: Mon.-Sat. 11:00AM-3:00PM
Dinner: Sun.-Thurs. 4:00PM-10:00PM
         Fri. & Sat. 4:00PM-12:00AM

Sited in the ground floor of an office building, The Peppermill brings a casual, open,
airy ambiance to the Baltimore dining
scene. Fresh cut meats and fresh seafood are featured. They are well prepared
and nicely served. You'll also find appealing daily specials augmenting the extensive menu.

PHILLIPS HARBORPLACE   27

301 Light Street, Space #1
Baltimore, MD
(301) 685-6600

Seafood

F ★ ★ ★ ½
S ★ ★ ★ ½
A ★ ★ ★ ½
P ★ ★

No dress restrictions
Street parking
All major credit cards
Full bar
Reservations not required

Lunch/
Dinner: Daily 11:00AM-11:00PM

This casual and fun dining spot has been
dispensing warm hospitality and the
highest quality fresh Maryland seafoods
to a large and loyal clientele, for the past 28
years. A sing-along piano bar adds to the
general enjoyment.

PIMLICO   9

1777 Reisterstown Road
Baltimore, MD
(301) 486-6776

American/Chinese

F ★ ★ ★ ½
S ★ ★ ★
A ★ ★ ½
P ★ ★ ★

Good taste in dress required
Valet and lot parking
AE, DC, MC, V
Full bar
Reservations recommended

Lunch/
Dinner: Sun.-Fri. 11:30AM-11:30PM
         Sat. 11:30AM-12:30AM

Pimlico's has been happily transplanted to
a large and grand new site from a location
it had occupied for 33 years, and the
eclectic and lengthy menu for which the
restaurant is renowned now includes a
separate Chinese culinary department.
You'll find something here to please every
mood and palate. Music nightly.

THE PRIME RIB   15

1101 North Calvert Street
Baltimore, MD
(301) 539-1804

American

F ★ ★ ★ ★
S ★ ★ ★ ★
A ★ ★ ★ ½
P ★ ★ ★ ½

Jacket required
Valet parking
All major credit cards
Full bar
Reservations not required

Dinner: Nightly 5:00PM-2:00AM

This sleek, sophisticated restaurant is decorated with gold-sconced, black vinyl walls displaying risque art déco prints. Owner C. P. BeLer specializes in fresh seafood and prime beef, offering you such entrées as Jumbo-Lump Crab Imperial, and a huge rib of beef. You'll also find a good California cabernet wine list.

RUDY'S 2900   2

2900 Baltimore Boulevard
Finksburg, MD
(301) 833-5777

Continental

F ★ ★ ★
S ★ ★ ★
A ★ ★ ½
P ★ ★ ½

Jacket required
Valet parking
AE, MC, V
Full bar
Reservations required

Lunch: Mon.-Fri. 11:30AM-2:30PM
Dinner: Mon.-Thurs. 5:30PM-10:00PM
          Fri. & Sat. 5:30PM-11:00PM
          Sun. 4:00PM-9:00PM

A quaint French Provincial country inn setting complements the innovative and classic cuisine at Rudy's, which offers you a tempting array from pasta to flounder to Weiner Schnitzel. Co-owners Rudi Paul, Maître d', and Rudi Speckamp, chef, emphasize freshness of ingredients, and adroit tableside service.

THE RUSTY SCUPPER   28

Inner Harbor
402 Key Highway
Baltimore, MD
(301) 727-3678

American

F ★ ★ ★ ½
S ★ ★ ★
A ★ ★ ★
P ★ ★ ½

Good taste in dress required
Lot parking
All major credit cards
Full bar
Reservations recommended

Lunch: Mon.-Sat. 11:30AM-2:30PM
Dinner: Mon.-Thurs. 5:00PM-10:00PM
          Fri. & Sat. 5:00PM-11:00PM
          Sun. 3:00PM-9:00PM
Brunch: Sun. 11:00AM-3:00PM

Designed with glass on all sides, The Rusty Scupper affords you a panoramic view of the city, while surrounding you with a woodsy plant-filled ambiance. Local seafood is featured — steaks and prime rib equally good. Contemporary in concept, yet rich in warmth and charm.

SABATINO'S   29

901 Fawn Street
Baltimore, MD
(301) 727-9414

Italian/American

F ★ ★ ★ ½
S ★ ★ ★
A ★ ★ ★
P ★ ★

Good taste in dress required
Street parking
MC, V
Full bar
Reservations required

Lunch/
Dinner: Daily 11:30AM-3:00AM

Expect to find a little bit of Italy right in Baltimore when you dine at Sabatino's. The setting is lovely with an art déco feel. The bill of fare offers a wide range of choices, but special emphasis is placed on dishes prepared in the manner of the central region of Italy.

TIO PEPE RESTAURANTE   17

10 East Franklin Street
Baltimore, MD
(301) 539-4675

Spanish

F ★ ★ ★ ½
S ★ ★ ★ ½
A ★ ★ ★
P ★ ★ ★ ½

Jacket required at dinner
Street parking
AE, MC, V
Full bar
Reservations required

Lunch: Mon.-Fri. 11:30AM-2:30PM
Dinner: Mon.-Thurs. 5:00PM-10:30PM
          Fri. & Sat. 5:00PM-11:30PM
          Sun. 4:00PM-10:30PM

Tio Pepe occupies the basements of two townhouses, converted into nine dining rooms lavishly decorated with Spanish ceramics, mantillas, and paintings. Regionally influenced Spanish cuisine is served.

TRELLIS GARDEN RESTAURANT   26

Hyatt Regency-Baltimore
300 Light Street
Baltimore, MD
(301) 528-1234

American/Continental

F ★ ★ ★
S ★ ★ ★
A ★ ★ ★
P ★ ★ ★

Jacket and tie required
Lot parking
All major credit cards
Full bar
Reservations recommended

Lunch: Mon.-Fri. 11:30AM-2:00PM
Dinner: Sun.-Thurs. 6:00PM-10:00PM
          Fri. & Sat. 6:00PM-11:00PM

A shimmering indoor lake plus lush greenery creates an atmosphere of natural elegance for your dining pleasure at Trellis Garden. You'll find specialties such as Veal Medallions and local seafood including crab, scallops, and swordfish.

TUG'S   20

222 St. Paul Street
Baltimore, MD
(301) 244-7300

American

F ★ ★ ★
S ★ ★ ★
A ★ ★ ★
P ★ ★ ½

Good taste in dress required
Lot parking
All major credit cards
Full bar
Reservations recommended

Breakfast: Daily 6:30AM-9:30AM
Lunch: Mon.-Fri. 11:30AM-2:30PM
Dinner: Sun.-Thurs. 5:30PM-10:00PM
          Fri. & Sat. 5:30PM-11:00PM

A 20-foot piece of etched glass depicting Baltimore's Inner Harbor dominates the décor at this seafood lover's favorite new haunt. Specialties to look for here are the bouillabaisse and Veal Oscar. There is a large assortment of fresh seafood from which to choose.

Boston

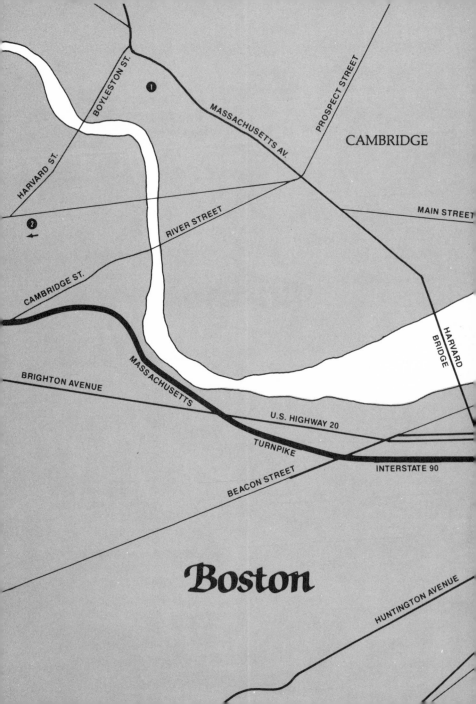

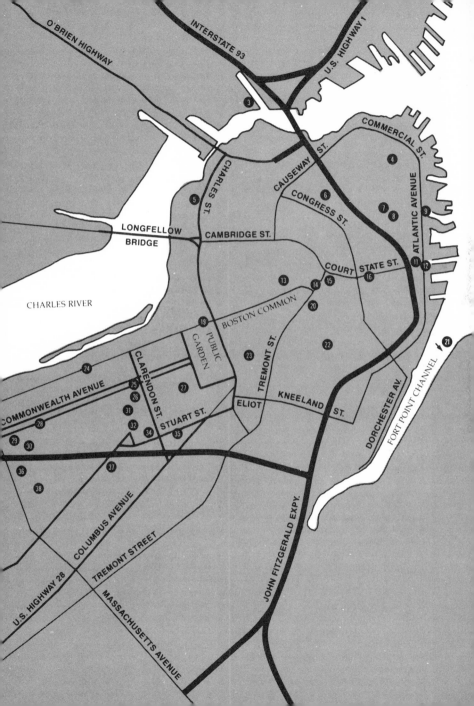

ANTHONY'S PIER 4   21

140 Northern Avenue
Boston, MA
(617) 423-6363

Seafood

F ★ ★ ★ ½
S ★ ★ ★
A ★ ★ ★
P ★ ★ ★

Jacket required
Valet and lot parking
All major credit cards
Full bar
Reservations not required

Lunch/
Dinner: Mon.-Fri. 11:30AM-11:00PM
          Sat. 12:30PM-11:00PM
          Sun. 12:30PM-10:30PM

Dine at the end of a pier, surrounded by nostalgic mementos of early sailing days at this spacious establishment. Lobster, seafoods, and fresh fish highlight the menu which also includes steaks and chops.

APLEY'S   36

Sheraton Boston Hotel
39 Dalton Street
Boston, MA
(617) 236-2000

American/Continental

F ★ ★ ★ ½
S ★ ★ ★ ½
A ★ ★ ★ ½
P ★ ★ ★ ★

Jacket and tie required
Lot parking
All major credit cards
Full bar
Reservations recommended

Dinner: Mon.-Sat. 6:00PM-10:00PM
          Closed Sunday

Apley's is an impressive often honored two-level restaurant with an air of ultra

elegance. You'll dine on fine china surrounded with crystal and sterling and the lilting strains of live harp music. Veal medallions, filet of lamb, and tournedos of beef are among your entrée choices.

BAY TOWER ROOM   16

60 State Street
Boston, MA
(617) 723-1666

Continental

F ★ ★ ★ ½
S ★ ★ ★ ½
A ★ ★ ★ ½
P ★ ★ ★ ½

Jacket and tie required
Lot parking
All major credit cards
Full bar
Reservations recommended

Dinner: Mon.-Sat. 5:00PM-10:00PM
          Closed Sunday

This dramatic multi-leveled restaurant perches 33 stories high giving you a sweeping view of the Boston waterfront and harbor. The continental cuisine is augmented by regional seafood entrées.

BOODLE'S RESTAURANT   38

Back Bay Hilton
Dalton at Belvedere
Boston, MA
(617) 236-1100

English Grill

F ★ ★ ★
S ★ ★ ★
A ★ ★ ★
P ★ ★ ★

Good taste in dress required
Valet parking
All major credit cards
Full bar
Reservations recommended

Breakfast: Daily 7:00AM-11:00AM
Lunch: Daily 11:30AM-2:30PM
Dinner: Nightly 5:00PM-11:00PM

A mellow, masculine atmosphere greets you at Boodle's, where reproductions of paintings and prints from Queen Victoria's house feature prominently in the décor. The menu typifies the selections offered in a fine English grill.

CAFÉ BUDAPEST   24

90 Exeter Street
Boston, MA
(617) 266-1979/734-3388

Hungarian

F ★ ★ ★ ½
S ★ ★ ★ ½
A ★ ★ ★ ★
P ★ ★ ★ ★

Jacket and tie required
Lot and street parking
All major credit cards
Full bar
Reservations recommended

Lunch: Mon.-Sat. 12:00PM-3:00PM
Dinner: Sun.-Thurs. 5:00PM-10:30PM
          Fri. & Sat. 5:00PM-12:00AM

Owner Edith Ban has created a romantic old-world setting with three dining rooms, each decorated differently, in which to offer authentic home-style Hungarian dishes.

CAFÉ PLAZA   32

Copley Plaza Hotel
138 Saint James Avenue
Boston, MA
(617) 267-5300

Continental

F ★ ★ ★ ½
S ★ ★ ★ ½
A ★ ★ ★ ★
P ★ ★ ★ ★

Jacket and tie required
Valet parking
All major credit cards
Full bar
Reservations required

Breakfast: Daily 7:00AM-10:00AM
Lunch: Mon.-Fri. 12:00PM-2:00PM
Dinner: Nightly 5:30PM-10:30PM

Formal and opulent, Café Plaza has a high sculptured ceiling, walls of oak paneling, Waterford crystal chandeliers, and marble floors. Pheasant, swordfish, and Veal Kidney Dijonnaise are among the continental entrées you will find on the menu. Dinner is served accompanied by classical piano music.

CASA ROMERO   29

30 Gloucester Street
(Side entrance in alley way)
Boston, MA
(617) 536-4341

Mexican

F ★ ★ ★ ½
S ★ ★ ★
A ★ ★ ★
P ★ ★ ½

No dress restrictions
Street parking
All major credit cards
Full bar
Reservations not required

Dinner: Sun.-Thurs. 5:00PM-10:00PM
          Fri. & Sat. 5:00PM-11:00PM

Casa Romera, deftly tucked away with an alley entrance, offers you a surprisingly romantic setting decorated with ceramic tile tables and Mexican artwork. Traditional Mexican cuisine is featured, complemented by gourmet dishes with a Spanish influence.

COPLEY'S   34

Copley Plaza Hotel
138 Saint James Avenue
Boston, MA
(617) 267-5300

American

F ★ ★ ★ ½
S ★ ★ ★ ½
A ★ ★ ★ ½
P ★ ★ ★ ½

Good taste in dress required
Valet parking
All major credit cards
Full bar
Reservations not required

Lunch: Daily 11:00AM-3:00PM
Dinner: Nightly 5:30PM-11:30PM

A lush Edwardian décor rich with British memorabilia; and your choice of a trophy room, library, or wine room motif makes dining at Copley's a special delight. Fresh fish from local waters, carpetbagger steak, curry, and clams casino share the bill of fare with other stellar entrées.

DAVIO'S   28

269 Newbury Street
Boston, MA
(617) 262-4810

Italian

F ★ ★ ★
S ★ ★ ★
A ★ ★ ★
P ★ ★ ★

Jacket required
Valet parking
All major credit cards
Full bar
Reservations required

Lunch: Mon.-Sat. 11:30AM-3:00PM
Dinner: Nightly 5:00PM-11:00PM

A subterranean setting decorated with brick, brass, and crushed velvet creates an intimate, romantic aura for savoring such hearty Northern Italian dishes as Scaloppine di Vitello Sorrentino, Spaghettini Carbonara, and Cuori di Filetto Bordolese.

DEVON ON THE   23 COMMON

150 Boylston Street
Boston, MA
(617) 482-0722

Continental/Creole

F ★ ★ ★ ½
S ★ ★ ★ ½
A ★ ★ ★
P ★ ★ ½

Jacket and tie preferred
in the main dining room
Valet parking
All major credit cards
Full bar
Reservations required

Café:
Lunch/
Dinner: Mon.-Sat. 11:00AM-12:00AM
Upstairs Dining Room:
Dinner: Mon.-Sat. 5:30PM-10:00PM
            Closed Sunday

Continental cuisine with mesquite-grill cookery is featured in the high-fashion dining room you will find upstairs at this trendy new restaurant. The downstairs café, with its more relaxed ambiance, is devoted to creole and cajun cuisine.

DURGIN PARK   8

30 North Market Street
Boston, MA
(617) 227-2038

American

F ★ ★ ★ ½
S ★ ★ ½
A ★ ★ ½
P ★ ★

No dress restrictions
Street parking
Credit cards not accepted
Full bar
Reservations not required

Lunch/
Dinner: Daily 11:30AM-11:00PM
          Sun. 12:00PM-9:00PM

Hearty Yankee-style fare and family seating have earned a special niche for Durgin Park, and a loyal following. Expect to enjoy fresh fish, prime rib, Indian pudding, real mashed potatoes, fresh vegetables, and freshly made apple pan dowdy.

FELICIA'S   4

145A Richmond Street
Boston, MA
(617) 523-9885

Italian

F ★ ★ ★ ½
S ★ ★ ★
A ★ ★ ★
P ★ ★

Good taste in dress required
Street parking
AE, CB, DC
Beer/Wine
Reservations not required

Dinner: Mon.-Thurs. 5:00PM-10:00PM
          Fri. & Sat. 4:30PM-10:30PM
          Sun. 2:00PM-9:30PM

For thirty years Felicia's has served as a romantic retreat for discerning diners who enjoy good Northern Italian cooking. House specialties include Chicken Verdicchio, Lasagna Verdi, Shrimp Toscano, and Meat or Seafood Cannelloni.

GENJI   30

327 Newbury Street
Boston, MA
(617) 267-5656

Japanese

F ★ ★ ★
S ★ ★ ★
A ★ ★ ★
P ★ ★

Good taste in dress required
Valet and lot parking
All major credit cards
Full bar
Reservations required on weekends

Lunch: Mon.-Fri. 12:00PM-2:30PM
          Sat. 12:00PM-3:00PM
Dinner: Mon.-Thurs. 5:30PM-10:30PM
          Fri. & Sat. 5:30PM-11:00PM
          Sun. 5:00PM-10:00PM

Decorated in the manner of a Japanese garden and tea room, Genji is a wonderful spot to sample sushi with its delicate texture and flavors, enjoy the graceful Japanese tea ceremony, and feast royally on adroitly prepared classic Japanese cuisine.

HAMPSHIRE HOUSE   19

84 Beacon Street
Boston, MA
(617) 227-9600

Continental

F ★ ★ ★
S ★ ★ ★
A ★ ★ ★ ½
P ★ ★ ★

Jackets required, no jeans or sneakers
Lot and street parking
Valet parking Wed.-Sat.
All major credit cards
Full bar
Reservations recommended

Lunch: Daily 11:45AM-2:30PM
Dinner: Nightly 5:30PM-10:30PM

Return to the elegance of yore when dining at Hampshire House, which occupies the first floor of a turn-of-the-century Beacon Hill mansion, overlooking a spacious public garden. Heritage Boston fare is augmented with dishes such as Veal Marsala, Chicken Verdicchio, and Shrimp Scampi.

HARBOR TERRACE   11

Marriott Hotel
296 State Street
Boston, MA
(617) 227-0800

Seafood

F ★ ★ ★ ½
S ★ ★ ★ ½
A ★ ★ ★
P ★ ★ ★

Good taste in dress required
Valet parking
All major credit cards
Full bar
Reservations required

Breakfast: Daily 6:30AM-11:30AM
Lunch: Daily 11:30AM-2:00PM
Dinner: Nightly 5:30PM-10:00PM
Brunch: Sun. 10:00AM-2:30PM

An expansive harbor view from all the tables in this two-level restaurant, and a terrace for summer service make this a spot favored by Bostonians who enjoy the wide range of beautifully prepared and served featured seafood specialties.

JASPER   9

240 Commercial Street
Boston, MA
(617) 523-1126

American

F ★ ★ ★
S ★ ★ ★
A ★ ★ ★
P ★ ★ ★ ★

Good taste in dress required
Valet and lot parking
All major credit cards
Full Bar
Reservations required

Dinner: Mon.-Thurs. 6:00PM-10:00PM
          Fri. & Sat. 6:00PM-11:00PM
          Closed Sunday

Jasper White, chef/owner, creates his own interpretation of the new American cuisine in this spacious, warmly elegant waterfront restaurant. House specialties include lobster sausage with cabbage, tortellini with rabbit sauce, and rack of lamb with grilled leeks.

JIMMY'S HARBORSIDE   21

242 Northern Avenue
Boston, MA
(617) 423-1000

Seafood

F ★ ★ ★
S ★ ★ ★
A ★ ★ ½
P ★ ★ ★

Jacket preferred
Valet parking
All major credit cards
Full bar
Reservations required

Lunch/
Dinner: Mon.-Sat. 11:30AM-9:30PM
          Closed Sunday

Jimmy's has been providing customers with a grand view of the fish pier and historic harbor, and serving them choice seafood, for nearly 60 years. House specialties include a rich creamy fish chowder, finnan haddie, shrimp Charles, and lobster.

JOE TECCE'S   3

61 North Washington Street
Boston, MA
(617) 742-6210

Italian

F ★ ★ ★ ½
S ★ ★ ★
A ★ ★ ½
P ★ ★ ½

Good taste in dress required
Lot and street parking
AE, DC
Full bar
Reservations required for eight
or more people

Lunch: Mon.-Fri. 11:30AM-3:30PM
Dinner: Mon.-Sun. 4:00PM—11:00PM

You'll find a bit of Italy in the '30s, including an indoor sidewalk café, when you dine at Joseph Tecce's family run restaurant. Renowned for their antipasto, Steak Mafia, and Mrs. Tecce's Baked Stuffed Shells, the classic Italian cuisine is skillfully prepared and presented.

LE BOCAGE   2

72 Bigelow Avenue
Watertown, MA
(617) 923-1210

French

F ★ ★ ★ ½
S ★ ★ ★ ½
A ★ ★ ★
P ★ ★ ★ ★

No dress restrictions
Lot and street parking
AE, DC, MC, V
Full Bar
Reservations not required

Dinner: Mon.-Sat. 6:00PM-11:00PM
Closed Sunday

At French country-style Le Bocage, owner Enzo Danesi offers a prix fixe menu that changes daily to reflect the availability of fresh ingredients. Food preparation is handled with meticulous care and the service is quick and courteous in this warm, intimate dining spot.

LEGAL SEAFOODS   35

Park Plaza Hotel
35 Columbus Street
Boston, MA
(617) 426-4444

Seafood

F ★ ★ ★ ½
S ★ ★ ★
A ★ ★ ½
P ★ ★ ½

Good taste in dress required
Lot parking
AE, DC, MC, V
Full bar
Reservations not required

Lunch/
Dinner: Sun.-Thurs. 11:00AM-10:00PM
Fri. & Sat. 10:30AM-11:00PM

No limit to your catch at Legals where one of the area's largest selection of fresh seafoods is featured. You can enjoy such diverse delights as mussels au gratin, baked stuffed lobster, salmon flown in from the West Coast, and rainbow trout from Idaho at this friendly eatery.

L'ESPALIER   26

30 Gloucester Street
Boston, MA
(617) 262-3023

French

F ★ ★ ★ ½
S ★ ★ ★ ½
A ★ ★ ★
P ★ ★ ★ ★

Jacket and tie required
Valet parking
All major credit cards
Wine
Reservations required

Dinner: Mon.-Sat. 6:00PM-10:00PM
Closed Sunday

L'Espalier is located in a beautiful 19th century townhouse with high ceilings and handsome wood paneling and moldings. Here the owner-chef combination of Mancef Meddeb and Donna Doll present their interpretation of French cuisine, prepared in the nouvelle manner.

LOCKE-OBER 20

3 Winter Place
Boston, MA
(617) 542-1340

Continental

F ★ ★ ★ ½
S ★ ★ ★
A ★ ★ ★
P ★ ★ ★ ½

Jacket and tie required
Valet parking
All major credit cards
Full bar
Reservations required

Lunch: Mon.-Fri. 11:00AM-3:00PM
         Sat. 12:00PM-3:00PM
Dinner: Mon.-Fri. 3:00PM-10:00PM
         Sat. 3:00PM-10:30PM
         Closed Sunday

Established in 1875, Locke -Ober has successfully presented quality food in a resplendent Victorian setting ever since. Lobster Savannah, baked oysters, Filet of Beef Mirabeau, and roast duckling are among the palate-pleasing entrées.

MAISON ROBERT 15

Boston's Historic Old City Hall
45 School Street
Boston, MA
(617) 227-3370/227-3371

French

F ★ ★ ★ ½
S ★ ★ ★ ½
A ★ ★ ★ ½
P ★ ★ ★ ½

Upstairs: Jacket and tie required
Downstairs: No dress restrictions
Valet parking
All major credit cards
Full bar
Reservations recommended

Lunch: Mon.-Fri. 11:30AM-2:30PM
Dinner: Mon.-Fri. 5:30PM-10:30PM
         Sat. 6:00PM-10:30PM
         Closed Sunday

Housed in Boston's old city hall, this French eatery, owned and managed by Chef Lucien Robert, offers you a choice of two restaurants serving gourmet quality food—the chic Bonhomme Richard on the 1st floor, and Ben's Café at ground level, where you may dine on the outdoor terrace in the summer.

MAÎTRE JACQUES 5

10 Emerson Place
Boston, MA
(617) 742-5480

French/Continental

F ★ ★ ★ ½
S ★ ★ ★ ½
A ★ ★ ★
P ★ ★ ★

Jacket and tie required
Lot parking
All major credit cards
Full bar
Reservations required

Lunch: Mon.-Fri. 11:45AM-2:45PM
Dinner: Mon.-Thurs. 6:00PM-10:00PM
          Fri. 6:00PM-10:30PM
          Sat. 6:00PM-11:00PM
          Closed Sunday

This well designed contemporary restaurant with its formal, continental air, faces on the Charles River and Park. You'll find lamb, duck, veal, and a daily fresh fish special all included on the menu. Your food will be well prepared and presented with professional polish.

MICHAEL'S 12
WATERFRONT

85 Atlantic Avenue
Boston, MA
(617) 367-6425

Continental/American

F ★ ★ ★ ½
S ★ ★ ★
A ★ ★ ★ ½
P ★ ★ ★

Good taste in dress required
Valet parking
AE, CB, MC, V
Full bar
Reservations required

Dinner: Mon.-Thurs. 5:30PM-10:30PM
          Fri. & Sat. 6:00PM-11:00PM
          Sun. 4:30PM-9:00PM

Beamed ceilings, wooden floors, Oriental carpets, and overflowing book shelves create the illusion of dining in an elegant, beautifully appointed library. The bill of fare is rich and varied, and includes such dishes as twin lobsters and Steak au Poivre, among the myriad continental and American entrées offered.

PARKER'S 14

The Parker House
60 School Street
Boston, MA
(617) 227-8600

American

F ★ ★ ★ ½
S ★ ★ ★ ★
A ★ ★ ★ ½
P ★ ★ ★ ★

Jacket required
Valet parking
All major credit cards
Full bar
Reservations recommended

Lunch: Daily 11:30AM-2:30PM
Dinner: Nightly 5:30PM-10:30PM

Located in one of the city's grandest historic hotels, Parker's projects an image of stately Boston elegance. You'll be treated to exemplary service and a wide choice of cuisine ranging from steamed Dover sole to succulent roast rack of lamb.

POLONAISE 27

384 Boylston Street
(Second Floor)
Boston, MA
(617) 247-9249

Continental

F ★ ★ ★ ½
S ★ ★ ★
A ★ ★ ★
P ★ ★ ★ ½

Good taste in dress required
Street parking
All major credit cards
Beer/Wine
Reservations required

Lunch: Tues.-Sat. 11:30AM-2:00PM
Dinner: Tues.-Thurs. 5:30PM-10:00PM
          Fri. & Sat. 5:30PM-11:00PM
          Closed Sunday and Monday

Spacious and attractive, this second-floor dining room is handsomely decorated with contemporary Polish tapestries. Co-owners Grace Grybko and Grazyna Slanda offer seasonal menus featuring Polish specialties.

RITZ-CARLTON 25
DINING ROOM

Ritz-Carlton Hotel
15 Arlington Street
Boston, MA
(617) 536-5700

French

F ★ ★ ★ ½
S ★ ★ ★ ★
A ★ ★ ★ ★
P ★ ★ ★ ★

Jacket and tie required
Lot parking
All major credit cards
Full bar
Reservations required

Breakfast: Mon.-Sat. 7:00AM-10:00AM
Lunch: Mon.-Sat. 11:00AM-3:00PM
Dinner: Nightly 5:30PM-12:00AM
Brunch: Sun. seatings at
          11:00AM & 1:00PM

A sophisticated, formal setting, with a delightful view of the public gardens, and a long history of superb food and service have made the Ritz-Carlton Dining Room a landmark institution. Such gustatory delights as braised sweetbreads, lobster whiskey and Dover Sole Meunière highlight the menu.

ST. BOTOLPH   37

99 St. Botolph Street
Boston, MA
(617) 266-3030

Continental

F ★ ★ ★
S ★ ★ ★
A ★ ★ ★
P ★ ★ ★

Good taste in dress required
Valet parking
All major credit cards
Full bar
Reservations required

Lunch: Mon.-Fri. 12:00PM-2:30PM
Dinner: Sun.-Thurs. 6:00PM-10:30PM
          Fri. & Sat. 6:00PM-12:00AM
Brunch: Sun. 11:00AM-3:00PM

Dining here lets you enjoy a mellow, contemporary atmosphere, while appreciating the beauty of the restored 19th century brick townhouse. Daily fresh fish specials, duckling, lamb, and veal chops, and an excellent selection of seafoods offer entrée selections guaranteed to delight the most discriminating palate.

SCHROEDER'S   22

8 High Street
Boston, MA
(617) 426-1234

Continental

F ★ ★ ★ ½
S ★ ★ ★ ½
A ★ ★ ★ ½
P ★ ★ ★ ½

No dress restrictions
Free valet parking
All major credit cards
Full bar
Reservations not required

Lunch: Mon.-Fri. 11:30AM-3:00PM
Dinner: Tues.-Fri. 3:00PM-9:30PM
          Sat. 5:00PM-10:00PM
          Closed Sunday

Schroeder's occupies what was once the lobby of one of Boston's oldest banks. In this handsome, spacious setting, tuxedoed career waiters politely serve you fine continental cuisine prepared in the award-winning kitchen. Plan to linger, as you'll find dining here is richly rewarding.

SEASONS   10

Bostonian Hotel
Faneuil Hall Marketplace
Boston, MA
(617) 523-3600

American

F ★ ★ ★ ½
S ★ ★ ★ ½
A ★ ★ ★
P ★ ★ ★ ★

Jacket preferred, no jeans
Valet parking
All major credit cards
Full bar
Reservations required

Breakfast: Daily 7:00AM-10:30AM
Lunch: Mon.-Fri. 11:30AM-2:30PM
          Sat. & Sun. 12:00PM-3:00PM
Dinner: Mon.-Fri. 6:00PM-9:30PM
          Sat. & Sun. 6:00PM-10:30PM

This sleek, contemporary restaurant, with walls of glass and a pleasant view, offers you a seasonally changing menu, and an attractive ambiance. Rack of lamb and duckling are included on the bill of fare which presents regional American classic dishes.

THOMPSON'S CHOWDER HOUSE   10

Faneuil Hall Marketplace
Boston, MA
(617) 227-9660

American

F ★ ★ ★
S ★ ★ ★
A ★ ★ ★
P ★ ★ ★

Good taste in dress required
Street parking
All major credit cards
Full bar
Reservations not required

Lunch/
Dinner: Daily 11:00AM-10:30PM

You'll find three floors of dining excellence at Ben Thompson's chowder house, each with its own picturesque décor. Your options are the "seafood" level which includes a raw seafood bar; a floor devoted to sandwiches and other informal fare; and a gourmet dining room with a range of entrées to satisfy every taste.

TIGERLILIES   13

23 Joy Street
Boston, MA
(617) 523-0609

American

F ★ ★ ★
S ★ ★ ★
A ★ ★ ★ ½
P ★ ★ ½

Good taste in dress required
Street parking
All major credit cards
Beer/Wine
Reservations recommended

Lunch: Mon.-Fri. 11:30AM-3:00PM
Dinner: Mon.-Thurs. 5:00PM-10:00PM
          Fri. & Sat. 5:00PM-10:30PM
Brunch: Sun. 11:30AM-2:30PM

As charming as a romantic hideaway, Tigerlilies gives you the choice of dining in a 1920s garden, complete with a pool, or in either of two dining rooms with cozy fireplaces. The American nouvelle cuisine changes regularly but always features fresh daily prepared pasta, fish, beef, and chicken entrées, and vegetarian specialties.

TOP OF THE HUB   31

Prudential Center
800 Boylston Street
Boston, MA
(617) 536-1775

Seafood

F ★ ★ ★
S ★ ★ ★
A ★ ★ ★
P ★ ★ ★

Good taste in dress required
Lot parking
All major credit cards
Full bar
Reservations required

Lunch: Mon.-Fri. 11:30AM-2:30PM
         Sat. 12:00PM-3:00PM
Dinner: Mon.-Thurs. 5:30PM-9:30PM
         Fri. & Sat. 5:30PM-10:30PM
         Closed Sunday

This elegant restaurant lets you enjoy a panoramic view of Boston and savor some of the region's most exceptional seafood. A rich bouillabaisse, and scallops prepared with mushrooms and chablis are two of the many specialties for which Top of The Hub is renowned.

UNION OYSTER HOUSE   6

41 Union Street
Boston, MA
(617) 227-2750

American

F   ★ ★ ★ ½
S   ★ ★ ½
A   ★ ★ ★
P   ★ ★ ½

No dress restrictions
Street parking
All major credit cards
Full bar
Reservations not required

Lunch/
Dinner: Sun.-Thurs. 11:00AM-9:30PM
         Fri. & Sat. 11:00AM-10:00PM

Boston's oldest restaurant, established in 1826, Union Oyster House occupies a building that is over 300 years old. Enjoy visiting this historical site, stop by the oyster bar, and dine on sumptuous New England seafood specialties or charbroiled prime meats.

VILLA FRANCESCA   7

150 Richmond
Boston, MA
(617) 367-2948

Italian

F   ★ ★ ★
S   ★ ★ ★
A   ★ ★ ★
P   ★ ★ ½

Good taste in dress required
Street parking
AE, CB, DC
Beer/Wine
Reservations not required

Dinner: Mon.-Thurs. 5:00PM-10:30PM
         Fri. & Sat. 5:00PM-11:00PM
         Sun. 4:00PM-10:00PM

Owner William Ranauro has created an inviting old world ambiance at Villa Francesca with its antique furnishings and cheerful red checked tablecloths. Here, you can relax in casual comfort and feast on the classically prepared Northern Italian style cuisine.

VOYAGERS   1

45½ Mt. Auburn Street
Cambridge, MA
(617) 354-1718

International

F   ★ ★ ★ ½
S   ★ ★ ★
A   ★ ★ ★
P   ★ ★ ★ ½

Good taste in dress required
Lot parking
All major credit cards
Full bar
Reservations required

Dinner: Tues.-Thurs. & Sun. 6:00PM-
         9:30PM
         Fri. & Sat. 6:00PM-10:00PM
         Closed Monday

Gourmet food of many ethnic persuasions, an intimate setting given sparkle by a colorful roof garden, and the dulcet tones of harp and harpsichord music combine to make dining here an extraordinary experience. The menu changes daily; the extensive wine list remains a constant joy.

Chicago

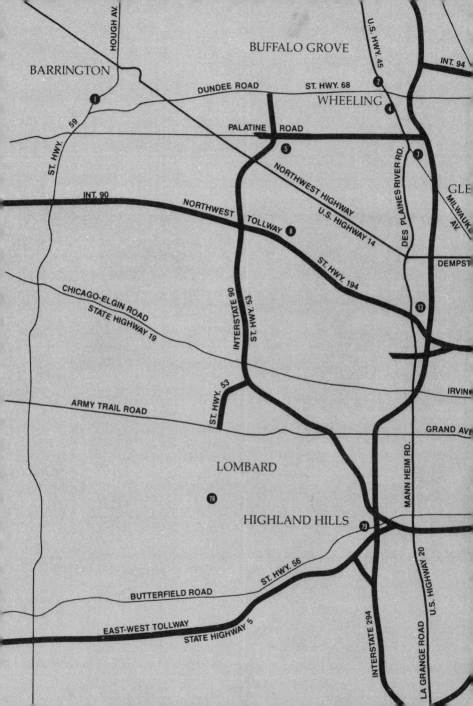

THE ABACUS 31

2619 North Clark Street
Chicago, IL
(312) 477-5251

Chinese

```
F  ★  ★  ★  ½
S  ★  ★  ½
A  ★  ★  ½
P  ★  ★  ½
```

Good taste in dress required
Lot parking
All major credit cards
Full bar
Reservations required

Dinner: Nightly 5:00PM-12:00AM
Brunch: Sun. 11:30AM-3:00PM

Sampling the Mandarin, Cantonese, Shanghai, and Szechwan cuisine available at The Abacus turns your visit into an exciting dining adventure. Try such exotic dishes as Sour Hot Soup, Peking Duck, Mongolian Beef, Shanghai Lobster, and their famous Abacus Egg Roll.

ALOUETTE 3

440 Green Bay Road
Highwood, IL
(312) 433-5600

French

```
F  ★  ★  ★  ½
S  ★  ★  ★
A  ★  ★  ★
P  ★  ★  ½
```

No dress restrictions
Lot parking
All major credit cards
Full bar
Reservations required

Lunch: Tues.-Fri. 11:30AM-2:00PM
Dinner: Tues.-Fri. & Sun.
         5:00PM-10:00PM
         Sat. 5:00PM-11:00PM
         Closed Monday

Rife with French country charm, this restaurant is a serene retreat where gourmets gather to pay tribute to well prepared nouvelle cuisine. The menu changes to offer seasonal bounty and there are innovative daily specials. Expect the freshest ingredients prepared masterfully.

AMBRIA 24

2300 Lincoln Park West
Chicago, IL
(312) 472-5959

French

```
F  ★  ★  ★  ★
S  ★  ★  ★  ★
A  ★  ★  ★  ½
P  ★  ★  ★  ★
```

Jacket required, no denims
Valet parking
All major credit cards
Full bar
Reservations required

Dinner: Mon.-Thurs. 6:00PM-9:30PM
         Fri. & Sat. 6:00PM-10:30PM
         Closed Sunday

The art-nouveau décor and the nouvelle cuisine at Ambria complement each other, both contributing to your dining enjoyment. The regular menu that features light, imaginatively prepared dishes is balanced by specials that change daily.

ARMANDO'S 54

735 North Rush Street
Chicago, IL
(312) 337-7672

Italian

```
F  ★  ★  ★
S  ★  ★  ★
A  ★  ★  ★
P  ★  ★  ★
```

Good taste in dress required
Valet parking
All major credit cards
Full bar
Reservations not required

Lunch/
Dinner: Mon.-Fri. 11:00AM-1:00AM
           Sat. & Sun. 12:00PM-1:00AM

When your heart is set on enjoying authentically prepared traditional Italian dishes, pay a visit to Armando's. It's comfortable and roomy, with an old-fashioned, candlelit ambiance that's as pleasing as the pasta, the specialty dishes, and the friendly service.

ARNIE'S   35

1050 North State Street
Chicago, IL
(312) 266-4800

Continental

F ★ ★ ★
S ★ ★ ★
A ★ ★ ★
P ★ ★ ★

Jacket required
Lot parking
All major credit cards
Full bar
Reservations recommended

Lunch: Mon.-Fri. 11:30AM-2:30PM
Dinner: Mon.-Fri. 5:00PM-12:00AM
           Sat. 5:30PM-1:00AM
           Sun. 5:30PM-10:00PM
Brunch: Sun. 10:30AM-2:30PM

A place to "see and be seen," Arnold Morton's restaurant appeals to a sophisticated clientele with its art déco setting, nightly music, and quality food. Specialties of the house include Pasta Primavera, Sicilian Veal Chops, rack of lamb, steaks, and fresh fish.

THE ATRIUM   5

3223 West Algonquin Road
Rolling Meadows, IL
(312) 259-7070

American/Continental

F ★ ★ ★ ½
S ★ ★ ★
A ★ ★ ★
P ★ ★ ½

Good taste in dress required
Valet and lot parking
All major credit cards
Full bar
Reservations recommended

Lunch/
Dinner: Mon.-Thurs. 11:00AM-12:00AM
           Fri. 11:00AM-1:00AM
           Sat. & Sun. 5:30PM-1:00AM
Brunch: Sun. 11:30AM-2:30PM

If variety be the spice of life, The Atrium offers you a full measure, for the luncheon menu offers 46 items ranging from sandwiches to lobster tail, and the gourmet dinner menu includes steaks, seafoods, rack of lamb, and prime rib.

THE BAKERY   38

2218 North Lincoln Avenue
Chicago, IL
(312) 472-6942

American/Continental

F ★ ★ ★ ½
S ★ ★ ★ ½
A ★ ★ ★
P ★ ★ ★ ★

Good taste in dress required
Street parking
All major credit cards
Full bar
Reservations recommended

Dinner: Tues.-Sat. 5:00PM-11:00PM
Closed Sunday and Monday

This family run restaurant is urbane and polished, but not pretentious. Owner/chef Louis Szathmary offers prix fixe dinners featuring seasonal specialties and classics such as Beef Wellington. Multilingual, tuxedoed waiters, silver service, crisp white linens, and fresh flowers lend a continental air.

THE BARN OF   1
BARRINGTON

1415 South Barrington Road
Barrington, IL
(312) 381-8585

Continental

F ★ ★ ★
S ★ ★ ★
A ★ ★ ★
P ★ ★ ½

Jacket required
Lot parking
All major credit cards
Full bar
Reservations required

Lunch: Mon.-Fri. 11:00AM-2:30PM
Dinner: Tues.-Sat. 5:00PM-10:30PM
Sun. 4:00PM-10:30PM
Brunch: Sun. 10:30AM-2:00PM

The transformation of a 120 year old barn into an elegant European-style castle, created a marvelous setting for The Barn. You'll find polished and professional service, and a menu of continental favorites that caters to every taste.

BASTILLE   60

21 West Superior
Chicago, IL
(312) 787-2050

French

F ★ ★ ★ ½
S ★ ★ ★
A ★ ★ ★
P ★ ★ ½

Good taste in dress required
Valet and lot parking
AE, MC, V
Full bar
Reservations required

Lunch: Mon.-Fri. 11:30AM-3:00PM
Dinner: Mon.-Thurs. 5:00PM-10:30PM
Fri. & Sat. 5:00PM-11:00PM
Sun. 5:00PM-10:00PM

George Badonsky's Bastille has an aura that echoes the bistros of France. It's filled with old French posters, and exudes a warm, friendly atmosphere. The country French menu always includes fresh fish among its hearty dishes. Vintage wines and gracious service are both yours to enjoy.

BENIHANA OF TOKYO   45

166 East Superior Street
Chicago, IL
(312) 664-9643

Japanese

F ★ ★ ★
S ★ ★ ★
A ★ ★ ★ ½
P ★ ★ ★

Good taste in dress required
Lot parking
All major credit cards
Full bar
Reservations recommended

Dinner: Mon.-Thurs. 5:30PM-10:30PM
Fri. & Sat. 5:30PM-11:30PM
Sun. 4:00PM-10:00PM

Skilled chefs perform their dramatic culinary rituals tableside at Benihana, and seated family style, you become an involved observer as your dinner is prepared on the hibachi tables. This fascinating bit of showmanship produces a bevy of satisfying, succulent morsels served sizzling from the grill.

THE BERGHOFF   76

17 West Adams Street
Chicago, IL
(312) 427-3170

German/Continental

F ★ ★ ★ ½
S ★ ★ ★ ½
A ★ ★ ★
P ★ ★

No dress restrictions
Street parking
AE, MC, V
Full bar
Reservations not required

Lunch/
Dinner: Mon.-Thurs. 11:00AM-9:30PM
           Fri. & Sat. 11:00AM-10:00PM
           Closed Sunday

The Berghoff has been a Chicago Loop landmark since l898, renowned for its oak paneled, turn-of-the-century décor and consistently fine food. Traditional German fare is featured — the extensive menu also includes seasonal specialties, fresh seafood, and aged steaks.

BIGGS   64

1150 North Dearborn Parkway
Chicago, IL
(312) 787-0900

French/Continental

F ★ ★ ★ ½
S ★ ★ ★ ½
A ★ ★ ★ ½
P ★ ★ ★ ★

Jacket required
Valet parking
All major credit cards
Wines/Liqueurs
Reservations recommended

Dinner: Nightly 5:00PM-10:30PM

At Biggs you recapture the grandeur of bygone days. Housed in a restored Victorian mansion, there are eight dining rooms, each with its own fireplace. The menu tends to the eclectic, with many daily specials including game dishes and lightly sauced entrées.

BILLY'S   57

936 North Rush Street
Chicago, IL
(312) 943-7080

Italian

F ★ ★ ★ ½
S ★ ★ ★ ½
A ★ ★ ★
P ★ ★ ★

Good taste in dress required
Street parking
All major credit cards
Full bar
Reservations required

Dinner: Mon.-Sat. 5:00PM-2:00AM
           Closed Sunday

Gourmet Italian food, an art déco ambiance, the music of a small combo, and pleasing service make your dinner at Billy's a special affair. Steaks and chops are offered, and their interpretations of classic Veal Piccante and Chicken Vesuvio are noteworthy.

BINYON'S   72

327 South Plymouth Court
Chicago, IL
(312) 341-1155

American

F ★ ★ ★
S ★ ★ ★
A ★ ★ ½
P ★ ★

No dress restrictions
Valet, lot, and street parking
All major credit cards
Full bar
Reservations not required

Lunch/
Dinner: Mon.-Sat. 11:30AM-10:00PM
Closed Sunday

The legendary Binyon's, a vital part of "loop" history, is a family owned restaurant serving Chicagoans for 135 years. Patronized by judges, politicians, and sports celebrities who relish the turtle soup, classic American cooking, and hearty daily specials.

BLACKHAWK   58

110 East Pearson Street
Chicago, IL
(312) 943-3300

American

F ★ ★ ★ ½
S ★ ★ ★ ½
A ★ ★ ★
P ★ ★ ½

Jacket preferred
Lot parking
All major credit cards
Full bar
Reservations recommended

Lunch/
Dinner: Mon.-Sat. 11:30AM-10:00PM
Sun. 5:00PM-10:00PM

The Mediterranean décor and intimate feeling found here carry on the tradition of the original Blackhawk on Wabash. Prime rib and steaks are prepared to order and there are fresh fish specials daily. Explore the salad bar — it's an award winner.

BONES   12

7110 North Lincoln Avenue
Lincolnwood, IL
(312) 677-3350

American/Barbecue

F ★ ★ ★ ½
S ★ ★ ★ ½
A ★ ★
P ★ ★

No dress restrictions
Street parking
All major credit cards
Full bar
Reservations not required

Lunch/
Dinner: Mon.-Thurs. 11:30AM-11:00PM
Fri. & Sat. 11:30AM-12:00AM
Sun. 3:00PM-10:00PM

The tantalizing aroma of hickory-smoked barbecue permeates the friendly, neighborhood-bar atmosphere at Bones. Slow-cooked ribs and chicken, beef and pork sandwiches, choice steaks, and fresh fish specialties win accolades from a loyal clientele.

CAFÉ LA CAVE   13

2733 Mannheim Road
Des Plaines, IL
(312) 827-7818

Continental

F ★ ★ ★ ½
S ★ ★ ★ ½
A ★ ★ ★ ½
P ★ ★ ★

Jacket required
Valet parking
All major credit cards

Full bar
Reservations required

Lunch/
Dinner: Mon.-Fri. 11:30AM-1:00AM
        Sat. 5:00PM-2:00AM
        Sun. 5:00PM-1:00AM

Café La Cave offers you the option of being seated in the main dining room in Louis XIV elegance, or requesting a table in the romantic second room that resembles a cozy cave. Steak Diane (cooked tableside), baby rack of lamb, and fresh fish are featured entrées.

CAFÉ PROVENCAL   11

1625 Hinman Avenue
Evanston, IL
(312) 475-2233

French

F ★ ★ ★ ½
S ★ ★ ★ ½
A ★ ★ ★
P ★ ★ ★ ½

Jacket required
Street parking
All major credit cards
Full bar
Reservations recommended

Dinner: Mon.-Sat. from 6:00PM
        Closed Sunday

A flower-filled dining room with chintz curtains, panelled walls, and a large fireplace, give Café Provencal a warm, welcoming feeling. Owner-chef Leslee Reis uses only the freshest ingredients in the creative country French cuisine, so the menu changes with the seasons.

CAPE COD ROOM   50

Drake Hotel
140 East Walton Place
Chicago, IL
(312) 787-2200

Seafood

F ★ ★ ★ ★
S ★ ★ ★
A ★ ★ ★
P ★ ★ ★ ★

Jacket preferred
Valet parking
All major credit cards
Full bar
Reservations required

Lunch/
Dinner: Daily 12:00PM-11:30PM

Cozy and colorful with checked tablecloths and hanging copper pots, the Cape Cod Room has been acclaimed for more than half a century for the quality and selection of fresh seafood and fish in which it specializes.

CARLOS   3

429 Temple Avenue
Highland Park, IL
(312) 432-0770

French

F ★ ★ ★ ½
S ★ ★ ★
A ★ ★ ★ ½
P ★ ★ ★ ★

Jacket and tie preferred
Valet parking
All major credit cards
Full bar
Reservations required

Dinner: Mon.-Wed.-Thurs.-Sun.
        Seatings at 5:30PM & 8:00PM
        Fri. & Sat. Seatings at
        5:30PM & 9:00PM
        Closed Tuesday

Small and intimate, Carlos caters to gourmets who lean toward the nouvelle style of French cuisine. Seasonal daily specials augment the standard menu that includes duck, Maine lobster, and fresh fish. The wine list is extensive; the desserts irresistible.

CARLUCCI   18

2215 North Halsted Street
Chicago, IL
(312) 281-1220

Italian

F ★ ★ ★
S ★ ★ ★
A ★ ★ ½
P ★ ★ ½

Good taste in dress required
Valet and street parking
AE, MC, V
Full bar
Reservations not required

Dinner: Nightly 6:00PM-11:00PM

The lustrous mahogany bar and table tops, soft lighting, and muted wall tones give Joe Carlucci's restaurant a warm, comfortable aura. Traditional dishes from the many regions of Italy are featured, providing you with a fine selection of interesting entrées.

CARSON'S THE   14 15 33 78
PLACE FOR RIBS

612 North Wells and
5970 North Ridge
Chicago, IL
(Suburban locations in Lombard and Skokie)
(312) 275-5000

American/Barbecue

F ★ ★ ★
S ★ ★ ★ ½
A ★ ★ ½
P ★ ★ ½

Good taste in dress required, no shorts
Valet and lot parking
All major credit cards
Full bar
Reservations not required

Lunch/
Dinner: Daily 11:00AM-12:00AM

Widely acclaimed as "The Place for Ribs" in the Chicago area, Carson's does a brisk restaurant and take-out business. They are noted for their barbecued baby back ribs — sticky with baked-on sweet-spicy sauce. Steaks, prime rib, chicken, and fish are also featured

CHESTNUT STREET GRILL   27

845 North Michigan Avenue
Chicago, IL
(312) 280-2720

American

F ★ ★ ★
S ★ ★ ★
A ★ ★ ½
P ★ ★ ★

No dress restrictions
Street and in-building parking
All major credit cards
Full bar
Reservations not required

Lunch/
Dinner: Mon.-Thurs. 11:30AM-10:30PM
          Fri. & Sat. 11:30AM-11:30PM
          Sun. 4:30PM-9:30PM
Brunch: Sun. 11:00AM-3:00PM

The turn-of-the-century architecture and décor makes a dramatic foil for the contemporary display kitchen at this restaurant, where you can watch your fresh seafood, steaks, and chops charcoal-grilled to perfection over mesquite wood. The desserts and wine list are both deserving of your attention.

CHEZ PAUL   56

660 North Rush Street
Chicago, IL
(312) 944-6680

French

F ★ ★ ★ ½
S ★ ★ ★ ½
A ★ ★ ★ ½
P ★ ★ ★ ★

Jacket required
Street parking
All major credit cards
Full bar
Reservations recommended

Lunch: Mon.-Fri. 12:00PM-3:00PM
Dinner: Sun.-Thurs. 5:30pm-10:30PM
        Fri. & Sat. 5:30PM-11:00PM

Occupying the Robert Hall McCormick 19th-century mansion, Chez Paul offers food as sophisticated as the setting is romantic. Salmon en Crôute, Canard Rôti à L'Orange, and Filet au Poivre Flambé Armagnac typify your choice of entrées.

CIEL BLEU   63

Mayfair Regent Hotel
181 East Lake Shore Drive
Chicago, IL
(312) 951-2864/5 or 787-8500

French

F ★ ★ ★ ½
S ★ ★ ★ ★
A ★ ★ ★ ★
P ★ ★ ★ ★

Jacket and tie required at dinner
Valet parking
AE, DC, MC, V
Full bar
Reservations required

Lunch: Daily 11:30AM-2:00PM
Dinner: Nightly 6:00PM-10:00PM

Dine in luxurious ease, while overlooking Oak Street Beach and Lake Michigan, in the 19th floor location of Ciel Bleu. Well known for "La Cuisine du Marche," you'll savor sumptuous food, served with aplomb, under the guidance of Maître d' Pierre Robert.

THE COTTAGE   83

525 Torrence Avenue
Calumet City, IL
(312) 891-3900

Continental

F ★ ★ ★ ★
S ★ ★ ★
A ★ ★ ★
P ★ ★ ★

No dress restrictions
Free lot parking
MC, V
Full bar
Reservations recommended

Dinner: Tues.-Fri. 6:00PM-10:00PM
        Sat. 5:00PM-11:00PM
        Sun. 4:00PM-9:00PM

Maître d' Gerald J. Buster, and chef Carolyn Buster, a husband and wife team, have imbued The Cottage with the mark of their personalities. Continental cuisine with French accents is prepared with skill and artistry using fresh and seasonal ingredients. European-trained waiters provide smooth service.

CRICKETS   53

100 East Chestnut Street
Chicago, IL
(312) 280-2100

Continental

F ★ ★ ★ ½
S ★ ★ ★ ½
A ★ ★ ★ ½
P ★ ★ ★ ½

Jacket and tie required, no jeans
Valet parking
All major credit cards
Full bar
Reservations required

Breakfast: Daily 7:00AM-10:30AM
Lunch: Daily 12:00PM-2:00PM
Dinner: Nightly 6:00PM-10:30PM

Casual and comfortable, corporate logos and other business memorabilia give Crickets a definite clublike atmosphere. The wide menu includes Rack of Lamb with Chutney, Medallions of Veal Basilic, and Roast Quail in Potato Basket, among other continental entrées.

DIANNA'S OPAA   82

212 South Halsted
Chicago, IL
(312) 332-1225

Greek

F ★ ★ ★
S ★ ★ ★
A ★ ★ ½
P ★ ★

Good taste in dress required
Lot parking
All major credit cards
Full bar
Reservations required

Lunch/
Dinner: Daily 11:30AM-2:00AM

Festive and cheerful, Petros Kogeonos' restaurant resembles a town square in Greece tucked under a Chicago roof. Customers sing, dance, and feast on the flavorful cuisine. A combination platter lets you sample lots of Greek dishes, and the menu offers a different specialty every day.

DON ROTH'S   66
RIVER PLAZA

405 North Wabash Avenue
Chicago, IL
(617) 527-3100

Creole

F ★ ★ ★
S ★ ★ ★
A ★ ★
P ★ ★ ★

Jacket preferred
Lot parking
All major credit cards
Full bar
Reservations required

Lunch/
Dinner: Daily 11:30AM-10:00PM

This handsome split-level dining room offers you a gorgeous view overlooking the Chicago River and the city skyline. The traditional Creole dishes are supplemented by beef and fish choices prepared New Orleans cajun style — different and delicious.

DON ROTH'S WHEELING   2

61 North Milwaukee
Wheeling, IL
(312) 537-5800

American

F ★ ★ ★
S ★ ★ ★
A ★ ★
P ★ ★ ★

Good taste in dress required
Lot parking
All major credit cards
Full bar
Reservations required

Lunch: Mon.-Fri. 11:30AM-2:30PM
Dinner: Mon.-Thurs. 5:30PM-10:30PM
          Fri. 5:00PM-11:00PM
          Sat. 5:00PM-12:00AM
          Sun. 4:00PM-9:00PM

Don Roth has transformed a rustic 130-year-old farmhouse into a cozy restaurant with a Spanish décor and a warm, intimate feeling. There's an outdoor patio for summer dining and winter viewing. A salad bar and raw fish bar are popular adjuncts to the menu that emphasizes seafood.

DORO'S   59

871 Rush Street
Chicago, IL
(312) 266-1414

Continental/Italian

F ★ ★ ★ ½
S ★ ★ ★ ½
A ★ ★ ★ ½
P ★ ★ ★

Jacket required
Valet parking
All major credit cards
Full bar
Reservations required

Lunch/
Dinner: Daily 11:30AM-11:00PM

Sports and show business celebrities have adopted Doro's, and so will you when you discover its elegant décor, lively piano bar lounge, and sinfully good food. All pastas are made in-house, seafoods are treated with care, and steaks, veal, and chicken meticulously prepared.

ELI'S THE PLACE   49
FOR STEAK

215 East Chicago Avenue
Chicago, IL
(312) 642-1393

American

F ★ ★ ★ ½
S ★ ★ ★
A ★ ★ ½
P ★ ★ ★ ★

Jacket required
Garage parking
AE, DC
Full bar
Reservations required

Lunch: Mon.-Fri. 11:00AM-2:30PM
Dinner: Mon.-Sat. 4:00PM-11:00PM
          Closed Sunday

Join the parade of celebrities to Eli Schulman's friendly, intimate dining room, and feast on your choice of Eli's Famous Liver, steak, prime rib, fish, Shrimp Marc, or other entrées offered. The service is prompt; the piano bar popular.

EUGENE'S   43

1255 North State Parkway
Chicago, IL
(312) 944-1445

American/Continental

F ★ ★ ★ ½
S ★ ★ ★
A ★ ★ ★
P ★ ★ ★

Jacket required, no denims; no dress restrictions on Sunday
Valet parking
All major credit cards
Full bar
Reservations recommended

Dinner: Nightly 4:30PM-2:00AM

Expect casual elegance in a clubby atmosphere at Eugene's — plus an extensive wine list, wide cognac collection, and pleasantly formal service. This house is renowned for its Fettuccine and Crab, prime dry-aged beef, and good selection of fresh seafood.

FLORENTINE ROOM   74

Italian Village
71 West Monroe Street
Chicago, IL
(312) 332-7005

Italian

F ★ ★ ★ ½
S ★ ★ ½
A ★ ★ ★
P ★ ★ ★

Jacket required
Valet parking
AE, CB, DC
Full bar
Reservations recommended

Lunch: Mon.-Fri. 11:30AM-2:30PM
Dinner: Mon.-Fri. 5:00PM-10:00PM
          Sat. 5:00PM-12:00AM
          Closed Sunday

A seasonally changing menu, extraordinary wine list, friendly waiters, and a décor featuring Florentine family crests attracts a stellar clientele to the Florentine Room. The imaginatively prepared veal, seafood, game, and beef specialties are memorable.

FROGGY'S   3

306 Greenbay Road
Highwood, IL
(312) 433-7080

French

F   ★ ★ ★
S   ★ ★ ★
A   ★ ★ ★
P   ★ ★ ½

No dress restrictions
Street parking
CB, DC, MC, V
Full bar
Reservations not required

Lunch: Mon.-Fri. 11:30AM-2:00PM
Dinner: Mon.-Thurs. 5:00PM-10:00PM
          Fri. & Sat. 5:00PM-11:00PM
          Closed Sunday

Chicago connoisseurs keep Froggy's business brisk. Imaginative food preparation is the secret of the cuisine's success. The menu changes monthly, featuring the freshest seasonal ingredients. Contented diners return regularly to discover the new and exciting specialties being featured.

GENE & GEORGETTI   69

500 N. Franklin
Chicago, IL
(312) 527-3718

American/Italian

F   ★ ★ ★ ½
S   ★ ★ ½
A   ★ ★ ★
P   ★ ★ ★

No dress restrictions
Valet, lot, and street parking
AE, CB, DC
Full bar
Reservations not required

Lunch/
Dinner: Mon.-Thurs. 11:30AM-12:30AM
          Fri. & Sat. 11:30AM-1:00AM
          Closed Sunday

A landmark restaurant in business for 43 years, Gene & Georgetti occupies a 100-year-old building that historically has been a saloon. Noted for steak, prepared to perfection, and other classic specialties such as Chicken Vesuvio, and liver with bacon and onions.

GEORGE BADONSKY'S   40
MAXIM'S DE PARIS

1300 Astor Street
Chicago, IL
(312) 943-1111

French

F   ★ ★ ★ ½
S   ★ ★ ★ ½
A   ★ ★ ★
P   ★ ★ ★ ★

Jacket and tie required
Valet parking
AE, CB, MC, V
Full bar
Reservations recommended

Dinner: Mon.-Thurs. 6:30PM-9:00PM
Fri. & Sat. 6:30PM-9:30PM
Closed Sunday

A sparkling spinoff of its illustrious Parisian ancestor, this Maxim's features rich woods, mirrors, burgundy wallpaper, and art nouveau décor. Against this handsome backdrop, classic French dishes are offered, including specialties such as Veal Orloff and Sole Albert.

GIANNOTTI'S 80

7711 West Roosevelt
Forest Park, IL
(312) 366-1199

Italian/American

F ★ ★ ★
S ★ ★ ★
A ★ ★ ½
P ★ ★

Good taste in dress required
Valet parking
All major credit cards
Full bar
Reservations required

Lunch/
Dinner: Mon.-Thurs. 11:00AM-
12:00AM
Fri. & Sat.11:00AM-1:00AM
Sun. 2:00PM-11:00PM

Although the décor at Giannotti's is old-world elegant, the ambiance is warm and homey with a blazing fireplace and a semi-private balcony area. You have a choice of the giant Fiesta Dinner (for 3 or more), seven-course meals, or any of the many innovative entrées on the menu.

GOLDEN OX 41

1578-80 North Clybourn Avenue
Chicago, IL
(312) 664-0780

German/Continental

F ★ ★ ★ ½
S ★ ★ ★ ½
A ★ ★ ★
P ★ ★ ½

Good taste in dress required
Valet parking
All major credit cards
Full bar
Reservations recommended

Lunch/
Dinner: Mon.-Sat. 11:00AM-11:00PM
Sun. 3:00PM-8:30PM

Old world charm and savory German dishes distinguish this half-a-century old restaurant. Traditional menu favorites are Zwiebelfleisch, Wiener Schnitzel, Sauerbraten, crisp young roast duckling, fresh potato pancakes, and homemade strudel.

GORDON 48

500 North Clark Street
Chicago,IL
(312) 467-9780

French

F ★ ★ ★ ★
S ★ ★ ★ ½
A ★ ★ ★
P ★ ★ ★ ½

Jacket required
Lot and street parking
All major credit cards
Full bar
Reservations required

Lunch: Mon.-Fri. 11:30AM-2:00PM
Dinner: Sun.-Thurs. 5:30PM-10:00PM
Fri. & Sat. 5:30PM-11:30PM
Brunch: Sun. 11:00AM-3:00PM

Gordon's sleek décor provides a sophisticated setting for exploring the well thought out, changing menu, and superb cooking. Fresh seafood is served with light natural sauces; and innovative grilled pork medallions with date mousse, spinach and chutney sauce typify the nouvelle house specialties.

GREEK ISLANDS 81

200 South Halsted Street
Chicago, IL
(312) 782-9855

Greek

F ★ ★ ★ ½
S ★ ★ ★ ½
A ★ ★ ½
P ★ ★

No dress restrictions
Valet parking
All major credit cards
Full bar
Reservations not required

Lunch/
Dinner: Sun.-Thurs. 11:00AM-12:00AM
         Fri. & Sat. 11:00AM-1:00AM

When you venture to this large five-room restaurant, you will find attractive Greek décor and paintings, seafood specialties cooked in the Greek manner, and tantalizing appetizers such as taramosalata and tzatziki, as well as a range of hearty traditional Greek dishes.

HOUSE OF HUNAN 62

535 North Michigan Avenue
Chicago, IL
(312) 329-9494

Chinese

F ★ ★ ★
S ★ ★ ★
A ★ ★ ★
P ★ ★ ★

Good taste in dress required
Lot parking
AE, DC, MC, V
Full bar
Reservations required

Lunch/
Dinner: Daily 11:30AM-10:30PM

At House of Hunan you can explore the tastes and textures of the various styles of Chinese cuisine, as dishes from many Provinces are featured. The menu includes some 20 appetizers and several dozen entrées. The helpful staff can guide you in selecting dishes from rather bland to fiery, spiced to please your individual palate.

IRELAND'S 65

500 North La Salle Street
Chicago, IL
(312) 337-2020

Seafood

F ★ ★ ★
S ★ ★ ★
A ★ ★ ½
P ★ ★ ½

Good taste in dress required, no shorts
Valet parking
All major credit cards
Full bar
Reservations recommended

Lunch: Mon.-Fri. 11:00AM-4:00PM
Dinner: Nightly from 5:00PM to closing

Established in 1906, Ireland's is a Chicago tradition, specializing in the freshest fish, prepared to order. Steaks, live lobster, and an extensive salad bar are also available. Try the oyster bar for clams, oysters, and other scrumptious seafood treats.

JIMMY'S PLACE 16

3420 North Elston Avenue
Chicago, IL
(312) 539-2999

French

F ★ ★ ★ ½
S ★ ★ ★
A ★ ★ ★
P ★ ★ ★ ★

No dress retrictions
Free lot parking
All major credit cards
Full bar
Reservations required

Lunch: Mon.-Fri. 11:30AM-2:00PM
Dinner: Mon.-Sat. 5:00PM-9:30PM
Closed Sunday

An operatic motif, reflecting owner Jimmy Rohr's musical taste, decorates the setting in which French nouvelle cuisine reigns supreme. The menu changes monthly and includes fresh fish dishes, veal, and rack of lamb. The wine list reflects the quality of the food.

JOVAN 47

1660 North La Salle Street
Chicago, IL
(312) 944-7766

French

F ★ ★ ★ ½
S ★ ★ ★ ½
A ★ ★ ★
P ★ ★ ★ ½

Good taste in dress required
Valet parking
All major credit cards
Full bar
Reservations not required

Dinner: Mon.-Sat. 5:30PM-10:00PM
Closed Sunday

An understated sophistication permeates Jovan, from the muted wall tones to the quality of service, and the varied cuisine. Classic French fare is balanced with American and continental flavors. Great emphasis is placed on the use of seasonally fresh ingredients in all dishes.

JW'S 55

540 North Michigan Avenue, 4th Floor
Chicago, IL
(312) 836-0100

French

F ★ ★ ★
S ★ ★ ★
A ★ ★ ★
P ★ ★ ★

Jacket required
Valet and lot parking
All major credit cards
Full bar
Reservations not required

Lunch: Mon.-Fri. 11:30AM-2:00PM
Dinner: Mon.-Sat. 6:00PM-10:00PM
Closed Sunday

JW's offers you fine traditional French cuisine served graciously in an atmosphere of old world charm. The menu spans a range of gourmet dishes, many classically prepared, others touched with innovative ingredients and refreshing food combinations.

KON TIKI PORTS 77

Hotel Continental
505 North Michigan Avenue
Chicago, IL
(312) 527-4286

Polynesian

F ★ ★ ★ ½
S ★ ★ ★ ½
A ★ ★ ★ ½
P ★ ★ ½

Good taste in dress required
Lot parking
AE, DC, MC, V
Full bar
Reservations required

Lunch: Mon.-Fri. 11:30AM-4:00PM
Dinner: Nightly 4:00PM-11:15PM

Five differently decorated sections, replicating Polynesian "Ports," have given diners a tantalizing taste of tropic adventure for the last 23 years, at this exotic eatery. Chef Bing, with the restaurant since it opened, consistently produces delicious Polynesian cuisine.

LA CHEMINÉE   42

1161 North Dearborn Street
Chicago, IL
(312) 642-6654

French

F ★ ★ ★
S ★ ★ ★
A ★ ★ ★
P ★ ★ ★ ½

Good taste in dress required
Valet parking
All major credit cards
Full bar
Reservations required

Dinner: Mon.-Sat. 5:30PM-12:00AM
          Sun. 4:30PM-10:30PM

Strolling musicians, glowing candles, fresh flowers, and a good wine cellar all contrive to make dinner at La Cheminée a thoroughly romantic evening. The French country cooking encompasses a wide range of classic favorites with a chef's special being offered daily.

LA STRADA   67
RISTORANTE

North Michigan Avenue at Randolph
Chicago, IL
(312) 565-2200

Italian

F ★ ★ ★ ½
S ★ ★ ★
A ★ ★ ★
P ★ ★ ★

Jacket and tie required
Valet parking
All major credit cards
Full bar
Reservations required

Lunch: Mon.-Fri. 11:30AM-2:30PM
Dinner: Mon.-Fri. 5:00PM-10:30PM
          Sat. 5:00PM-11:00PM
          Closed Sunday

Glass-domed La Strada provides a luxurious staging for enjoying primo Italian cuisine. The menu features such dishes as Piccata di Vitello, Saltimbocca Romano, Costoletta di Vitello Milanese, plus specials of the day. The wine list is excellent.

LA TOUR   51

Park Hyatt Hotel
800 Michigan Avenue
Chicago, IL
(312) 280-2222

French

F ★ ★ ★ ½
S ★ ★ ★ ½
A ★ ★ ★ ½
P ★ ★ ★ ★

Jacket and tie required at dinner, no jeans
Valet parking
All major credit cards
Full bar
Reservations required

Breakfast: Mon.-Sat. 7:30AM-10:30AM
Lunch: Mon.-Sat. 11:30AM-2:30PM
Dinner: Nightly 6:00PM-9:30PM
Brunch: Sun. 11:00AM-2:30PM

A unique setting, overlooking the historic Michigan Avenue water tower, coupled with an elegant décor enhanced with flickering candles and fresh flowers gives La Tour a lovely ambiance. Nouvelle French cuisine, with naturally reduced sauces that accent, rather than obscure, ingredient flavors is featured.

LAWRY'S THE PRIME RIB   52

100 East Ontario Street
Chicago, IL
(312) 787-5000

American

F ★ ★ ★ ½
S ★ ★ ★ ½
A ★ ★ ★
P ★ ★ ★

Jacket preferred, no shorts
Valet parking
All major credit cards
Full bar
Reservations recommended

Lunch: Mon.-Fri. 11:30AM-2:00PM
Dinner: Mon.-Thurs. 5:00PM-11:00PM
          Fri. & Sat. 5:00PM-12:00AM
          Sun. 3:00PM-10:00PM

The old McCormick mansion is the historic home of this elegantly decorated restaurant. Roast prime rib of beef, carved to your specifications at tableside, is the featured dinner entrée. The luncheon menu offers a wide choice of well prepared dishes.

LE FRANÇAIS   4

269 South Milwaukee Avenue
Wheeling, IL
(312) 541-7470

French

F ★ ★ ★ ★
S ★ ★ ★ ★
A ★ ★ ★ ★
P ★ ★ ★ ★

Jacket and tie required, no denims
Valet parking
All major credit cards
Full bar
Reservations required

Dinner: Tues.-Sun. Seatings at
          6:00PM and 9:00PM
          Closed Monday
          Closed in January

Owner-chef Jean Banchet prepares culinary masterpieces with great virtuosity that are served with élan in Le Français' elegantly appointed country inn setting. An à la carte menu and daily specials reflect high quality standards and the seasonal availability of all ingredients.

LE PERROQUET   32

70 East Walton Place
Chicago, IL
(312) 944-7990

French

F ★ ★ ★ ★
S ★ ★ ★ ½
A ★ ★ ★
P ★ ★ ★ ★

Jacket and tie required
Garage parking next door
AE, CB, DC
Full bar
Reservations required

Lunch: Mon.-Fri. 12:00PM-3:00PM
Dinner: Mon.-Sat. 6:00PM-12:00AM
          Closed Sunday

A third floor private entrance gives you the illusion of dining in a chic Parisian restaurant when you visit Le Perroquet. Honored with many awards, the nouvelle cuisine offers items such as Aiguillettes of Mallard Breast, Arlequin of Halibut, and Tian D'Agneau aux Herbes.

L'ESCARGOT ON   21
HALSTED

2925 North Halsted Street
Chicago, IL
(312) 528-5522

French

F ★ ★ ★ ½
S ★ ★ ★ ½
A ★ ★ ★
P ★ ★ ★ ★

No dress restrictions
Lot parking
All major credit cards
Full bar
Reservations recommended

Dinner: Mon.-Sat. 5:00PM-10:30PM
Closed Sunday

A refreshing oasis for lovers of fine French food, with its soft lighting and mellow décor, here you will find chef Lucien Verge's marvelous provencial-style cooking served with polished flair. Cassoulet Toulousain is a much touted house specialty.

L'ESCARGOT ON MICHIGAN   36

701 North Michigan Avenue
Chicago, IL
(312) 337-1717

French

F ★ ★ ★ ½
S ★ ★ ★ ½
A ★ ★ ★
P ★ ★ ★

No dress restrictions
Lot parking
All major credit cards
Full bar
Reservations recommended

Breakfast: Daily 7:00AM-10:30AM
Lunch: Daily 11:30AM-2:30PM
Dinner: Nightly 5:00PM-10:30PM

Bright, airy, and hospitable, with fresh flowers and crisp linens, L'Escargot features French provincial food prepared with great care. You will find fresh fish daily and a bounty of seasonal specialties. The wine list is ample — the service unobtrusive.

MALLORY'S ON WELLS   25

1400 North Wells Street
Chicago, IL
(312) 944-5404

American/Continental

F ★ ★ ★
S ★ ★ ★
A ★ ★ ½
P ★ ★ ½

Good taste in dress required
Lot and street parking
All major credit cards
Full bar
Reservations recommended

Lunch/
Dinner: Daily 11:00AM-11:00PM

Alan Mallory's restaurant offers you a choice of many well prepared and served menu items, presented in an inviting, casual setting. There are grilled pork chops, calves liver, strip steaks, omelettes, pastas, and dishes with ethnic touches, to satisfy diverse palates.

MILLER'S PUB & GRILL   68

23 East Adams Street
Chicago, IL
(312) 922-7446

American

F ★ ★ ★
S ★ ★ ★
A ★ ★ ★
P ★ ★ ★

Good taste in dress required
Lot parking

All major credit cards
Full bar
Reservations recommended

Lunch/
Dinner: Daily 11:00AM-3:30AM

A celebrity crowd has been drawn to the Gallios brothers' busy eatery for the past 35 years. The Canadian baby back barbecued ribs served here are legendary, and the steaks, chops, and Greek and Italian dishes all have their own loyal devotees.

MORTON'S   17

1050 North State Street
Chicago, IL
(312) 266-4820

American

F ★ ★ ★ ½
S ★ ★ ★
A ★ ★ ★
P ★ ★ ★ ½

Jacket preferred
Lot parking
All major credit cards
Full bar
Reservations not required

Dinner: Mon.-Thurs. 5:30PM-12:00AM
           Fri. & Sat. 5:30PM-1:00AM
           Closed Sunday

At Arnold Morton's steakhouse, a unique "living menu" is wheeled to your table and you choose your own entrée, fresh vegetable, and baked potato. Prime steaks and chops, Maine lobster, veal, fresh fish, and prime rib are standing favorites on the bill of fare.

NANTUCKET COVE   30

1000 North Lake Shore Drive
Chicago, IL
(312) 943-1600

American

F ★ ★ ★
S ★ ★ ★ ½
A ★ ★ ★ ½
P ★ ★ ★

No dress restrictions
Valet parking
AE, MC, V
Full bar
Reservations recommended

Dinner: Sun.-Thurs. 5:30PM-10:30PM
           Fri. & Sat. 5:30PM-11:30PM

You'll have the feeling you've journeyed to a New England fishing village when you dine at Nantucket Cove. Expect to choose from a large selection of fresh seafood and steaks, served with professional polish in an authentically decorated setting.

NICK'S FISHMARKET   39

One First National Plaza
Chicago, IL
(312) 621-0200

Seafood

F ★ ★ ★ ½
S ★ ★ ★ ½
A ★ ★ ★
P ★ ★ ★ ★

Jacket required
Valet parking
All major credit cards
Full bar
Reservations required

Lunch: Mon.-Fri. 11:30AM-3:00PM
Dinner: Mon.-Thurs. 5:30PM-11:30PM
           Fri. & Sat. 5:30PM-12:00AM
           Closed Sunday

Nick's does things on a grand scale, from the over-sized booths with their dimmer light switches, to the broad selection of seafood offered. Mahi-mahi and opakapaka from Hawaii, California abalone, and whole baby salmon are all available — cooked with care and nicely served.

THE 95TH   75

John Hancock Center
172 East Chestnut Street
Chicago, IL
(312) 787-9596

American

F ★ ★ ★ ½
S ★ ★ ★ ½
A ★ ★ ★ ½
P ★ ★ ★ ½

Jacket required at dinner, no denims
Adjacent garage parking
All major credit cards
Full bar
Reservations recommended

Lunch: Mon.-Fri. 11:30AM-2:30PM
Dinner: Nightly from 5:30PM
Brunch: Sun. 11:30AM-2:30PM

Enjoy the magnificent view of the city from the top of the Hancock building while dining in this posh establishment. Beautiful appointments, exemplary service, and gourmet contemporary American cuisine that changes with the seasons make dining here a sublime experience.

PALM   28

Mayfair Regent Hotel
181 East Lake Shore Drive
Chicago, IL
(312) 944-0135

Continental/American

F ★ ★ ★
S ★ ★ ★
A ★ ★ ★
P ★ ★ ★ ★

No dress restrictions
Valet parking
All major credit cards
Full bar
Reservations required

Lunch/
Dinner: Mon.-Fri. 11:30AM-10:45PM
          Sat. 5:00PM-10:45PM
          Closed Sunday

Brash and bustling, Palm, with its sawdust-covered floors and celeb-cartoon décor is a lively spin-off of a New York City chain. King-sized steaks and lobsters are featured — other menu items worthy of exploring include northern Italian specialties.

PRINTER'S ROW   73

550 South Dearborn
Chicago, IL
(312) 461-0780

American

F ★ ★ ★
S ★ ★ ★
A ★ ★ ★
P ★ ★ ★

Good taste in dress required
Lot parking
All major credit cards
Full bar
Reservations recommended

Lunch/
Dinner: Mon.-Thurs. 11:30AM-10:00PM
          Fri. & Sat. 5:30PM-11:00PM
          Closed Sunday

Soft lighting, walnut wood, a grey and burgundy color scheme, and colorful fresh flowers form a warm aura at Printer's Row. Here ingredients are used imaginatively to produce tantalizing entrées such as Country Lamb Stew with fresh Thyme, and Ragóut of Sweetbreads with Sorrel and Cream.

THE PUMP ROOM 19

Ambassador East Hotel
1301 North State Parkway
Chicago, IL
(312) 266-0360

Continental

F ★ ★ ★ ½
S ★ ★ ★ ½
A ★ ★ ★ ½
P ★ ★ ★

Jacket required at dinner, no jeans
Valet and lot parking
All major credit cards
Full bar
Reservations recommended

Breakfast/
Lunch/
Dinner: Daily 7:00AM-2:00AM

The muted beauty of mahogany wood, mirrors, candle light, and fresh flowers create a mood of understated elegance at The Pump Room. "Booth One" is favored by celebrities; selections from the varied menu are savored by all. You'll find devilishly good desserts and an ample wine list to add to your dining pleasure.

THE RITZ-CARLTON 29
THE DINING ROOM

160 East Pearson Street
Chicago, IL
(312) 266-1000, Ext. 4223

French

F ★ ★ ★ ★
S ★ ★ ★ ★
A ★ ★ ★ ★
P ★ ★ ★ ★

Jacket and tie required
Lot parking
All major credit cards
Full bar
Reservations required

Lunch: Mon.-Fri. 12:00PM-2:30PM
Dinner: Mon.-Sat. 6:00PM-11:00PM
          Sun. 6:00PM-10:00PM
Brunch: Sun. 10:30AM-2:00PM

Imbued with an innate sense of grandeur, The Ritz-Carlton offers marvelous food and fabulous service. A fixed-price three-course luncheon menu, and five-course dinner menu are augmented with à la carte alternatives. Both desserts and the wine list are impressive.

R.J. GRUNTS 22

2056 Lincoln Park West
Chicago, IL
(312) 929-5363

American

F ★ ★ ★
S ★ ★ ★
A ★ ★ ★ ½
P ★ ★

No dress restrictions
Street parking
All major credit cards
Full bar
Reservations not required

Lunch/
Dinner: Mon.-Thurs. 11:30AM-11:00PM
          Fri. & Sat. 11:30AM-1:00AM
          Sun. 3:30PM-11:00PM
Brunch: Sun. 10:00AM-3:00PM

A fun, informal, casual approach to dining is the secret of R. J. Grunts' success. A famous salad bar and creative menu, with steaks, shrimp, duck, homemade chili, and overstuffed sandwiches all highly touted customer favorites.

R. J. GRUNTS   7

1615 Milwaukee Avenue
Glenview, IL
(312) 635-7707

American

F ★ ★ ★
S ★ ★ ★
A ★ ★ ★ ½
P ★ ★

No dress restrictions
Lot parking
AE, DC, MC, V
Full bar
Reservations not required

Lunch/
Dinner: Mon.-Thurs. 11:30AM-11:00PM
          Fri. & Sat. 11:30AM-12:00AM
          Sun. 3:00PM-10:00PM
Brunch: Sun. 11:00AM-2:30PM

Warm, friendly, and informal, with a richly varied menu, this restaurant is as contemporary as the music that is featured. There's a great salad bar for starters, barbecued chicken and ribs, tacos, and omelettes, among other gustatory delights.

SAGE'S ON STATE   46

1255 North State Parkway
Chicago, IL
(312) 944-1557

American/Continental

F ★ ★ ★
S ★ ★ ★
A ★ ★ ★ ½
P ★ ★ ★

Jacket required, no denims
Valet parking
All major credit cards
Full bar
Reservations recommended

Dinner: Mon.-Thurs. 5:00PM-12:00AM
          Fri. & Sat. 5:00PM-1:00AM
          Closed Sunday

Dine in the midst of Victorian splendor in this handsome restaurant. Renowned for fresh seafoods and prime dry-aged beef; the wine, cognac, and cordial list is extensive — the dessert menu diverse. And, there is a friendly piano bar inviting you to linger.

SAGE'S SAGES   8

75 West Algonquin Road
Arlington Heights, IL
(312) 593-6200

American/Continental

F ★ ★ ★
S ★ ★ ★
A ★ ★ ★ ½
P ★ ★ ★

Jacket required
Valet and lot parking
All major credit cards
Full bar
Reservations recommended

Lunch/
Dinner: Mon.-Fri. 11:30AM-12:00AM
          Sat. 11:30AM-1:00AM
Brunch/
Dinner: Sun. 11:30AM-10:00PM

At Sage's Sages you can dine in your choice of a trio of rooms, each with its own distinctive ambiance. The menu accents prime beef and fresh seafood — with food preparation and service both highly satisfactory. There's a solid wine, cognac, and cordial list; and dancing in the piano bar.

SAGE'S WEST   79

2900 S. Highland Avenue
Downers Grove, IL
(312) 964-0550

American/Continental

F ★ ★ ★
S ★ ★ ★
A ★ ★ ★ ½
P ★ ★ ★

No dress restrictions
Valet and lot parking
All major credit cards
Full bar
Reservations recommended

Lunch/
Dinner: Mon.-Fri. 11:00AM-12:00AM
         Sat. 11:00AM-1:00AM
Brunch/
Dinner: Sun. 11:00AM-9:00PM

At Sage's West you will find the candlelit dining room decorated with World War I memorabilia, creating a casual though urbane atmosphere. Skillfully prepared and presented prime, dry-aged beef and fresh seafood are menu staples.

SALVATORE'S 26

525 West Arlington Place
Chicago, IL
(312) 528-1200

Italian

F ★ ★ ★
S ★ ★ ★
A ★ ★ ★
P ★ ★ ½

Good taste in dress required
Valet parking
All major credit cards
Full bar
Reservations required

Lunch: Mon.-Sat. 11:30AM-2:30PM
Dinner: Sun.-Thurs. 5:30PM-10:30PM
         Fri. & Sat. 5:30PM-12:00AM

A haven from the city bustle, Salvatore's offers you three quiet dining rooms, and dignified professional service. Unique pastas, seafood, and veal dishes are featured — with exquisite desserts and fine wines offered.

SINCLAIR'S 3

Forest at Westminster
Lake Forest, IL
(312) 295-8300

American

F ★ ★ ★
S ★ ★ ★
A ★ ★ ★
P ★ ★ ★

Jacket required on weekends
Lot and street parking
All major credit cards
Full bar
Reservations required

Dinner: Tues.-Thurs. 5:30PM-10:00PM
         Fri. & Sat. 5:30PM-11:00PM
         Sun. 5:00PM-9:00PM
         Closed Monday

Owner Gordon Sinclair offers you a choice of two dining rooms, each with its own personality — decorated with traditional materials used in contemporary ways. The à la carte menu is based on pasta dishes and simply prepared grilled meats and fish that reflect seasonal availability.

SU CASA 71

49 East Ontario Street
Chicago, IL
(312) 943-4041

Mexican

F ★ ★ ★
S ★ ★ ½
A ★ ★ ★
P ★ ★

No T-shirts, shorts, or sweat suits
Valet parking
All major credit cards
Full bar
Reservations not required

Lunch/
Dinner: Mon.-Fri. 11:30AM-12:30AM
          Sat. 5:00PM-12:30AM
          Closed Sunday

For two decades Su Casa has been attracting diners with their mildly spiced Mexican cuisine, served in an antique-enhanced Spanish hacienda setting. Dishes run the gamut from tacos to elaborate seafood entrées. Ask for salsa if you're a hot-chili aficionado.

SWEETWATER   44

1028 North Rush Street
Chicago, IL
(312) 787-5552

American/Continental

F ★ ★ ★ ½
S ★ ★ ★
A ★ ★ ★ ½
P ★ ★ ★

Good taste in dress required
Valet parking
AE, MC, V
Full bar
Reservations required

Lunch: Daily 11:30AM-3:00PM
Dinner: Nightly 5:00PM-11:30PM

A skylit bar, indoor sidewalk café, and three smart dining areas form a dazzling setting in which to enjoy excellent food. Sweetwater, a favorite Chicago celebrity haunt, serves seafood, prime rib, steaks, and Italian cuisine featuring homemade pastas.

SZECHWAN HOUSE   70

600 North Michigan Avenue
Chicago, IL
(312) 642-3900

Chinese

F ★ ★ ★ ½
S ★ ★ ★
A ★ ★ ★ ½
P ★ ★ ★

Good taste in dress required
Valet parking
All major credit cards
Full bar
Reservations required

Lunch/
Dinner: Sun.-Thurs. 11:30AM-10:30PM
          Fri. & Sat. 11:30AM-11:00PM

While the tangy foods of Szechwan and Hunan provinces are featured here, you will also find the milder Mandarin and Taiwanese cuisines included on the menu. The Peking Duck is much lauded; other chef's specialties include Squab in Bamboo Cup, Two Flavor Lamb, and Whole Steamed Fish in Rice Wine.

TANGO   23

Hotel Belmont
3172 North Sheridan Road
Chicago, IL
(312) 935-0350

French/Seafood

F ★ ★ ★
S ★ ★ ★ ½
A ★ ★ ★
P ★ ★ ★

Jacket preferred
Valet parking
AE, MC, V
Full bar
Reservations required

Lunch: Tues.-Sat. 11:30AM-2:30PM
Dinner: Nightly 5:00PM-11:00PM

Avant-garde décor and a handsome collection of prints and statuary set the stage for a surfeit of seafood. Twenty-five fresh ocean and lake fish are featured nightly in intriguing presentations ranging from mesquite-grilled to Creole-inspired entrées.

TOWER GARDEN 9

9925 Gross Point Road
Skokie, IL
(312) 673-4450

Continental

F ★ ★ ★
S ★ ★ ★
A ★ ★ ★
P ★ ★ ★

Jacket preferred
Lot parking
All major credit cards
Full bar
Reservations required

Lunch: Mon.-Fri. 11:30AM-3:00PM
Dinner: Mon.-Sat. 4:30PM-11:00PM
Closed Sunday

Dine in a verdant garden setting where skylights, tropical plants, and colorful flowers create a mini-Eden. Fresh fish, sautéed sweetbreads in caper sauce, medallions of veal, rack of lamb, and fowl roasted on a French rotisserie are among the menu highlights.

TRUFFLES 63

151 East Wacker Drive
Chicago, IL
(312) 565-4299

French/Continental

F ★ ★ ★ ½
S ★ ★ ★ ½
A ★ ★ ★ ½
P ★ ★ ★ ★

Good taste in dress required
Lot parking
All major credit cards

Full bar
Reservations required

Dinner: Mon.-Sat. 6:00PM-10:15PM
Closed Sunday

Truffles is distinguished by its subdued romantic setting, flawless service, finely prepared food, and menu-complementing wine list. Fresh seafoods and steaks augment the classic French menu. Dessert soufflés are a heavenly grand finale.

UN GRANDE CAFÉ 34

2300 Lincoln Park West
Chicago, IL
(312) 348-8886

French

F ★ ★ ★
S ★ ★ ★ ½
A ★ ★ ★
P ★ ★ ★

No dress restrictions
Valet parking
All major credit cards
Full bar
Reservations not required

Dinner: Mon.-Thurs. 6:00PM-11:00PM
Fri. & Sat. 6:00PM-12:00AM
Closed Sunday

This French bistro-style restaurant concentrates on preparing and serving French provincial dishes exceptionally well. An intriguing variety of daily specials are featured, as are pâtés, hearty soups, and grilled fresh fish.

THE WATERFRONT   61

1015 North Rush Street
Chicago, IL
(312) 943-7494

Seafood

F ★ ★ ★ ½
S ★ ★ ★ ½
A ★ ★ ★ ½
P ★ ★ ★

No shorts or T-shirts
Street parking
AE, MC, V
Full bar
Reservations not required

Lunch/
Dinner: Mon.-Thurs. 11:30AM-12:00AM
Fri. & Sat. 11:30AM-1:00AM
Sun. 11:30AM-11:00PM

A beautifully contrived Cape Cod setting surrounds you as you feast on such dishes as cioppini, whole dungeness crab, live lobster, red snapper, Dover sole, king crab legs, Mazatlan prawns, and rainbow trout at Marvin Corman's The Waterfront. Crusty sourdough bread and a gourmet salad bar are included with your dinner.

YOSHI'S CAFÉ   20

3257 North Halsted Street
Chicago, IL
(312) 248-6160

Continental

F ★ ★ ★ ½
S ★ ★ ★ ½
A ★ ★ ★ ½
P ★ ★ ★ ½

No dress restrictions
Street parking
AE, MC, V
Full bar
Reservations required

Lunch: Tues.-Sat. 11:30AM-2:00PM
Dinner: Tues.-Thurs. 5:30PM-10:00PM
Fri. & Sat. 5:30PM-10:30PM
Sun. 5:00PM-9:00PM
Brunch: Sun. 12:00PM-3:00PM
Closed Monday

A small storefront location has become a sophisticated setting where food to delight discriminating epicures is featured. Chef Yoshi Katsumura reigns in the kitchen where his consummate skill in continental cookery and his Japanese sense of aesthetics combine to produce beautifully prepared and presented cuisine.

ZAVEN'S   37

260 East Chestnut Street
Chicago, IL
(312) 787-8260

Continental

F ★ ★ ★ ½
S ★ ★ ★ ½
A ★ ★ ★
P ★ ★ ★ ½

Good taste in dress required
Garage parking
All major credit cards
Full bar
Reservations required

Lunch: Mon.-Fri. 11:30AM-2:30PM
Dinner: Nightly 5:30PM-11:00PM

Strolling into the world of Zaven's is like taking a quick gourmet tour of the Middle East and Continental Europe. The menu features dishes reflecting a diversity of ethnic backgrounds — all authentically prepared. The service is smooth and competent.

Cincinnati

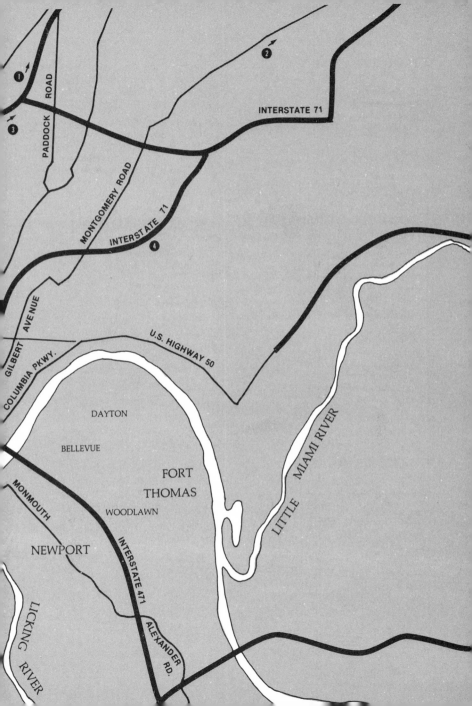

CHARLEY'S CRAB 2

9769 Montgomery Road
Montgomery, OH
(513) 891-7000

Seafood

F ★ ★ ★
S ★ ★ ★
A ★ ★ ★
P ★ ★ ★

Good taste in dress required
Valet and lot parking
All major credit cards
Full bar
Reservations recommended

Dinner: Mon.-Thurs. 5:00PM-10:00PM
          Fri. & Sat. 5:00PM-11:00PM
          Sun. 5:00PM-9:00PM

Charley's Crab is located in an historical
home built in 1849 and has a cozy Cape
Cod décor and a warm homelike atmosphere. Fresh seafood is flown in daily
(popular non-seafood dishes are also
available). Specialties include Charley's
Bucket (an East Coast clambake), and
Spanish Paella.

CHESTER'S ROAD HOUSE 2

9678 Montgomery Road
Cincinnati, OH
(513) 793-8700

American

F ★ ★ ★
S ★ ★ ★
A ★ ★ ★
P ★ ★ ½

No muscle shirts or shorts
Lot parking
All major credit cards
Full bar
Reservations recommended

Lunch: Mon.-Fri. 11:30AM-2:30PM
Dinner: Mon.-Fri. 5:30PM-10:30PM
          Sat. 5:30PM-11:00PM
          Sun. 4:00PM-9:30PM

A casual, plant-filled converted old home,
complete with a tree growing in one of the
dining rooms, is the inviting setting of Lee
and Michael Comisar's restaurant. Rack of
baby lamb, steaks, chops, fresh-daily seafood, and daily specials are highlights of
the bill of fare.

CHINA GOURMET 4

3340 Erie Avenue
Cincinnati, OH
(513) 871-6612

Chinese

F ★ ★ ★ ½
S ★ ★ ★
A ★ ★ ½
P ★ ★ ½

No dress restrictions
Lot parking
CB, DC, MC, V
Full bar
Reservations required

Lunch/
Dinner: Daily 11:00AM-11:00PM

Named the best Chinese restaurant for six
consecutive years by *Cincinnati Magazine,*
China Gourmet serves Cantonese and
Szechwan style cuisine, prepared to your
taste, and attractively presented. The
modern Oriental artwork used in the décor creates a quietly intimate atmosphere.

DOCKSIDE VI 2

Quality Inn Central
4747 Montgomery Road
Cincinnati, OH
(513) 351-7400

Seafood

F ★ ★ ★
S ★ ★ ★
A ★ ★ ★
P ★ ★ ½

Good taste in dress required
Lot parking
All major credit cards
Full bar
Reservations required

Dinner: Mon.-Fri. 5:30PM-10:30PM
Sat. 5:30PM-11:30PM
Sun. 4:30PM-9:30PM

As nautical as a seaman's chantey, Dockside VI specializes in fresh seafood prepared in a variety of ways, under the skilled supervision of Chef Dominic. A fish lover's paradise, complete with a rugged and attractive wharf-like décor.

THE EDWARDS   6

529 East 5th Street
Cincinnati, OH
(513) 381-2030

Italian

F ★ ★ ★
S ★ ★ ★
A ★ ★ ★
P ★ ★ ½

No dress restrictions
Lot and street parking
All major credit cards
Full bar
Reservations not required

Lunch: Tues.-Fri. 11:30AM-1:30PM
Dinner: Tues.-Thurs. 5:30PM-9:30PM
Fri. & Sat. 5:30PM-11:00PM
Sun. 5:00PM-9:00PM
Closed Monday

Edwards brings you the classic elegance of mahogany and marble as a sophisticated setting for presenting award-winning cuisine. Five kinds of pasta are made daily; only fresh fish, veal, and vegetables are served. Choice Italian vintages highlight a broad wine list.

EMPEROR'S WOK   5

11355 Chester Road
Cincinnati, OH
(513) 772-6200

American/Chinese

F ★ ★ ★
S ★ ★ ★
A ★ ★ ★ ½
P ★ ★

Good taste in dress required
Lot parking
All major credit cards
Full bar
Reservations required

Lunch: Mon.-Fri. 11:00AM-2:00PM
Sun. 11:30AM-3:00PM
Dinner: Mon.-Thurs. 5:00PM-10:00PM
Fri. & Sat. 5:00PM-11:00PM
Sun. 3:00PM-9:00PM

An exquisitely decorated restaurant featuring furnishings and objets d'art imported from mainland China. In addition to American entrées the cuisine introduces you to the styles of cooking found in the Szechwan and Hunan provinces of China, and traditional Cantonese dishes.

GOURMET   7

Terrace Hilton
15 West Sixth Street
Cincinnati, OH
(513) 381-4000

French

F ★ ★ ★ ½
S ★ ★ ★ ½
A ★ ★ ★ ★
P ★ ★ ★ ★

Jacket and tie required
Valet parking
All major credit cards
Full bar
Reservations required

Dinner: Mon.-Sat. 5:00PM-11:00PM
Closed Sunday

Four magnificent antique ornaments were carefully selected to enhance the staging for the superior culinary artistry and professional service you can expect at the Gourmet. Look for specialties such as Loin of Venison with Huckleberries on the menu, which features precisely prepared classic French cuisine.

GRAND FINALE   1

Sharon and Congress Avenues
(Historic Village of Glendale)
Cincinnati, OH
(513) 771-5925

American/Continental

F ★ ★ ★ ½
S ★ ★ ★ ½
A ★ ★ ★
P ★ ★ ★

Good taste in dress required
Lot parking
All major credit cards
Full bar
Reservations not required

Lunch/
Dinner: Tues.-Sat. 11:30AM-11:00PM
Sun. 5:00PM-10:00PM
Brunch: Sun. 10:30AM-3:00PM
Closed Monday `

Owners/chef Larry and Cindy Youse have turned an historic Victorian home with a charming outdoor courtyard, into an award-winning restaurant with a friendly, casual air. You'll find such enticements as fresh fish, rack of lamb, steak salad, homemade breads and pastries, and great desserts here.

LA NORMANDIE   10
TAVERNE & CHOP HOUSE

118 East Sixth Street
Cincinnati, OH
(513) 721-2761

American

F ★ ★ ★
S ★ ★ ★
A ★ ★ ★
P ★ ★ ½

No muscle shirts or shorts
Valet parking for dinner
All major credit cards
Full bar
Reservations not required

Lunch: Mon.-Fri. 11:00AM-2:30PM
Dinner: Mon.-Sat. 5:00PM-11:00PM
Closed Sunday

Enjoy the feeling of casual ease you will find in this rustic tavern atmosphere. Steaks, chops, fresh fish, and baby rack of lamb, menu staples, are always good; or try the daily "blackboard" specials. Located in the center of the city, La Normandie makes dining downtown a special occasion.

MAISONETTE   13

114 East Sixth Street
Cincinnati, OH
(513) 721-2260

French

F ★ ★ ★ ★
S ★ ★ ★ ★
A ★ ★ ★ ½
P ★ ★ ★ ★

Jacket and tie required, no denims
Valet parking for dinner
All major credit cards
Full bar
Reservations required

Lunch: Mon.-Fri. 11:30AM-2:30PM
Dinner: Mon.-Fri. 6:00PM-10:30PM
Sat. 5:15PM-11:00PM
Closed Sunday

For the last 20 years, the elegant, intimate atmosphere and fine food and service have earned prestigious awards and customer accolades for Maisonette. Specialties, selected for freshness and seasonal availability, augment the standard menu of classic French cuisine.

MONTGOMERY INN   2

9440 Montgomery Road
Cincinnati, OH
(513) 791-3482

American

F ★ ★ ★ ½
S ★ ★ ½
A ★ ★ ½
P ★ ★ ½

Good taste in dress required
Lot parking
MC, V
Full bar
Reservations recommended

Lunch/
Dinner: Mon.-Fri. 11:00AM-12:30AM
Sat. 4:00PM-12:30AM
Sun. 4:00PM-9:30PM

Owned by the Ted Gregory family since it opened 33 years ago, Montgomery Inn has grown to be a large friendly establishment attracting an illustrious clientele. Barbecued ribs, chicken, and duckling are mainstays of the menu which features classic American dishes.

PIGALL'S   13

127 West 4th Street
Cincinnati, OH
(513) 721-1345

French

F ★ ★ ★ ★
S ★ ★ ★ ½
A ★ ★ ★ ★
P ★ ★ ★ ★

Jacket and tie required
Street and garage parking
All major credit cards
Full bar
Reservations required

Lunch: Mon.-Fri. 11:30AM-2:30PM
Dinner: Mon.-Fri. 5:30PM-10:00PM
Sat. 5:30PM-10:30PM
Closed Sunday

Chic and fashionably intimate, Pigall's is like a breath of Paris, with crystal chandeliers, colorful bouquets, candles, and lovely table settings. Against this fitting backdrop, classic French cuisine is prepared and presented with continental mastery.

ROBERT'S   3

Carrousel Inn
8001 Reading Road
Cincinnati, OH
(513) 821-5110

American

F ★ ★ ★
S ★ ★ ★
A ★ ★ ★
P ★ ★ ½

Good taste in dress required
Lot parking
All major credit cards
Full bar
Reservations required

Dinner: Mon.-Thurs. 5:00PM-10:00PM
Fri. & Sat. 5:00PM-11:00PM
Brunch: Sun. 10:00AM-2:00PM

The refreshing, light airy ambiance you'll discover when you visit Robert's is reinforced by a bevy of lush green plants. The menu stresses freshness of ingredients and au naturel preparation, and features seafood, an array of salads, and an interesting variety of homemade pastas.

SAMURAI JAPANESE STEAK HOUSE   14

126 East 6th Street
Cincinnati, OH
(513) 421-1688

Japanese

F ★ ★ ★ ½
S ★ ★ ★
A ★ ★ ★
P ★ ★ ★

Jacket required
Lot parking
All major credit cards
Full bar
Reservations required

Lunch: Mon.-Fri. 11:30AM-2:00PM
Dinner: Mon.-Thurs. 5:30PM-10:00PM
         Fri. 5:30PM-11:00PM
         Sat. 5:00PM-11:30PM
         Sun. 4:00PM- 9:00PM

At Samurai, your private chef, a virtuoso at the grill and cutting board, cooks your food at the table. The restaurant is comfortable and well lit, and the preparation and presentation of your meal is a companionable activity, in which you are a fascinated participant.

SOVEREIGN   12

810 Matson Place
Cincinnati, OH
(513) 471-2250

Continental/American

F ★ ★ ★ ½
S ★ ★ ★
A ★ ★
P ★ ★ ★

No jeans
Lot parking
All major credit cards
Full bar
Reservations required

Dinner: Mon.-Fri. 5:00PM-10:30PM
          Sat. 5:30PM-11:00PM
          Sun. 4:00PM-9:00PM

Relax in a warm, romantic atmosphere and enjoy the panoramic view of the city and the nearby Kentucky hills, while dining on such superb house specialties as baby rack of lamb, chateaubriand for two, and dramatic flaming desserts served with gusto at tableside.

TOP OF THE CROWN   8

Clarion Hotel
141 West Sixth Street
Cincinnati, OH
(513) 352-2160

Nouveau Cuisine

F ★ ★ ★
S ★ ★ ★ ★
A ★ ★ ★
P ★ ★ ★

Jacket and tie required
Valet parking
All major credit cards
Full bar
Reservations required

Dinner: Mon.-Thurs. 6:00PM-10:00PM
          Fri. 5:30PM-9:30PM
          Sat. 5:30PM-10:00PM
Brunch: Sun. 10:00AM-2:30PM

This renowned revolving rooftop restaurant, 31 stories high, offers you a perfect spot to dine leisurely while viewing the city, the Ohio River, and the surrounding hills. Lobster Thermidor, rack of lamb, and chateaubriand are featured; and there are two chef's specialties available every evening.

Cleveland

AU PROVENCE 7

2195 Lee Road
Cleveland Heights, OH
(216) 321-9511

French/New Orleans Creole

F ★ ★ ★ ½
S ★ ★ ★ ½
A ★ ★ ★ ½
P ★ ★ ★ ½

No dress restrictions
Lot and street parking
All major credit cards
Full bar
Reservations recommended

Dinner: Mon.-Sat. 6:00PM-10:00PM
Closed Sunday

This small, intimate restaurant is a gastronome's delight and the winner of many awards. The well stocked wine cellar does double duty—the wines complement the French and New Orleans Creole menu—the room is used as a private party setting.

CHARLEY'S CRAB 20

25765 Chagrin Road
Beachwood, OH
(216) 831-8222

Seafood

F ★ ★ ★
S ★ ★ ★
A ★ ★ ★
P ★ ★ ★

Good taste in dress required
Valet parking
All major credit cards
Full bar
Reservations required

Lunch: Mon.-Fri. 11:30AM-2:30PM
Dinner: Mon.-Thurs. 5:00PM-11:00PM
Fri. & Sat. 5:00PM-12:00AM
Sun. 4:00PM-10:00PM

From three to five different fresh seafood entrées are offered each day at Charley's Crab, where the atmosphere is warm and friendly and "the finest seafood in Cleveland" is purported to be served. Charley's Bucket, a dinner favorite, gives you Maine lobster, dungeness crab, steamers, mussels, corn-on-the-cob, and red-skinned potatoes.

THE DOCK 11

11706 Clifton Boulevard
Cleveland, OH
(216) 221-4388

Seafood

F ★ ★ ★
S ★ ★ ★
A ★ ★ ★
P ★ ★ ½

Jacket required
Valet parking
AE, MC, V
Full bar
Reservations required

Lunch: Mon.-Fri. 11:30AM-2:00PM
Dinner: Mon.-Thurs. 5:00PM-10:00PM
Fri. & Sat. 5:00PM-12:00AM
Sun. 4:00PM-9:00PM

With handsome contemporary décor with dark oak, suede walls, and beveled glass adding distinctive touches, this restaurant is also enlivened with lavish use of plants and flowers. The atmosphere is friendly and congenial, and as the name suggests seafood entrées are the specialties of the house. Freshness and finest quality are stressed; therefore the menu varies with the seasons.

DON'S POMEROY HOUSE 23

13664 Pearl Road
Strongsville, OH
(216) 572-1111

American

F ★ ★ ★
S ★ ★ ★
A ★ ★ ★
P ★ ★ ½

Good taste in dress required, no jeans
Valet parking
All major credit cards
Full bar
Reservations required

Lunch: Mon.-Fri. 11:30AM-2:30PM
Dinner: Mon.-Thurs. 5:00PM-10:00PM
          Fri. & Sat. 5:00PM-12:00AM
          Sun. 4:00PM-9:00PM

This impressive restaurant occupies a lovely restored Victorian home built in 1847, which is listed in the National Registry of Historic Buildings. Fresh seafood, steaks, hearth-broiled rack of lamb, and strawberry duck are among the culinary treasures served in the four antique-furnished dining areas.

EARTH BY APRIL   8

2151 Lee Road at Cedar Road
Cleveland Heights, OH
(216) 371-1438

Seafood/Vegetarian

F ★ ★ ★
S ★ ★ ★
A ★ ★ ★
P ★ ★ ½

No dress restrictions
Lot parking
All major credit cards
Full bar
Reservations required

Lunch: Mon.-Sat. 11:00AM-3:00PM
          Sun. 11:00AM-2:30PM
Dinner: Mon.-Thurs. 5:00PM-11:00PM
          Fri. & Sat. 5:00PM-12:00AM
          Sun. 5:00PM-10:00PM

Earth by April exhibits a healthy respect for nature's bounty, serving imaginative chicken and veal entrées, fresh fish, seafood, seasonal vegetable dishes; and featuring an elaborate salad bar. The comfortable setting has quiet touches of elegance.

FRENCH CONNECTION   10

24 Public Square
Cleveland, OH
(216) 696-5600

French

F ★ ★ ★ ½
S ★ ★ ★ ½
A ★ ★ ★
P ★ ★ ★

Jacket and tie required
Lot parking
All major credit cards
Beer/Wine
Reservations required

Dinner: Mon.-Sat. 6:00PM-10:00PM
          Sun. 5:00PM-9:00PM

You'll find a formal atmosphere here, with antique furnishings, fresh flowers, soft music, and deft service to make you feel pampered. The menu is international in concept and features seasonal specialties; the food preparation is in the classic French tradition.

HOLLENDEN TAVERN   2

610 Superior Avenue
Cleveland, OH
(216) 621-0700

Continental

F ★ ★ ★
S ★ ★ ★
A ★ ★ ★
P ★ ★ ★

Jacket and tie required
Lot parking
All major credit cards

Full bar
Reservations required

Lunch: Mon.-Fri. 11:30AM-2:00PM
Dinner: Mon.-Fri. 5:00PM-10:00PM
          Closed Saturday and Sunday

For nearly two decades Hollenden Tavern has served a distinguished clientele in its handsome, clublike dining room. You'll find a varied award-winning menu, with emphasis on well-aged prime beef and other meats of highest quality.

JAMES TAVERN   19

28699 Chagrin Boulevard
Woodmere Village, OH
(216) 464-4660

American

F ★ ★ ★
S ★ ★ ★
A ★ ★ ★
P ★ ★ ★

No dress restrictions
Lot parking
All major credit cards
Full bar
Reservations recommended

Lunch: Mon.-Sat. 11:30AM-2:30PM
Dinner: Mon.-Thurs. 5:30PM-10:00PM
          Fri. & Sat. 5:30PM-11:00PM
          Sun. 5:00PM-9:00PM
Brunch: Sun. 10:30AM-3:00PM

Early American Colonial décor with wood burning fireplaces in the dining rooms creates an aura of warm hospitality at James Tavern. Prime Ribs of Beef, Savannah Pork Roast, Veal Madeira, Chicken Parmesan, pastas, and seafood specialties are featured.

JIM'S STEAK HOUSE   9

1800 Scranton Road
Cleveland, OH
(216) 241-6343

American

F ★ ★ ★
S ★ ★ ★
A ★ ★ ½
P ★ ★ ★

No dress restrictions
Lot parking
All major credit cards
Full bar
Reservations not required

Lunch/
Dinner: Sun.-Thurs. 11:00AM-10:00PM
          Fri. & Sat. 11:00AM-11:00PM

The perfect place to enjoy viewing Cleveland's skyline and watching the big ore freighters traverse the Cuyahoga River, is the glass-terrace dining room at Jim's Steak House. Prime aged steaks are the pièces de résistance here, and they are properly prepared and served.

J.J. GETTY'S   15

25651 Detroit Avenue
Westlake, OH
(216) 835-9332

American

F ★ ★ ★
S ★ ★ ★
A ★ ★ ★
P ★ ★ ½

No dress restrictions
Lot parking
AE, DC, MC, V
Full bar
Reservations not required

Lunch: Daily 11:00AM-2:30PM
Dinner: Nightly 5:00PM-11:00PM

You'll find friendly camaraderie reigns in this casually sophisticated restaurant featuring nightly entertainment in the lounge area. Prime rib, fresh seafood, steaks, and barbecued ribs are favorite highlights of the menu.

KEG & QUARTER   5

Swingo's Hotel
1800 Swingo's Court
Cleveland, OH
(216) 861-5501

Continental

F ★ ★ ★ ½
S ★ ★ ★ ½
A ★ ★ ★
P ★ ★ ★ ½

Jacket required
Valet parking
All major credit cards
Full bar
Reservations required

Lunch: Mon.-Fri. 11:00AM-3:00PM
Dinner: Mon.-Fri. 4:00PM-11:00PM
         Sat. 5:00PM-12:00AM
         Sun. 5:00PM-11:00PM

In a large, elegant room with stained glass windows and handsome chandeliers, Keg & Quarter maintains high standards of food preparation and service. The gourmet continental cuisine includes a fresh catch-of-the-day special, and a well rounded selection of entrées.

MR. KELLY'S   16

20412 Center Ridge
Rocky River, OH
(216) 333-1888

American/Italian

F ★ ★ ★
S ★ ★ ★
A ★ ★ ★
P ★ ★ ½

Jacket preferred
Valet parking
All major credit cards
Full bar
Reservations required

Lunch: Mon.-Fri. 11:30AM-2:30PM
Dinner: Mon.-Thurs. 5:00PM-11:00PM
         Fri. & Sat. 5:00PM-12:00AM
         Closed Sunday

Enjoy owner George Kelly's hospitality at this cosmopolitan tavern tucked in the woods. The ambiance is elegant, with fresh flowers, candles, crisp linens, and silver service. The menu offers a wide choice of American and Italian classic favorites smoothly served by a considerate staff.

PEARL OF THE ORIENT   14 & 18

19300 Detroit Road
Rocky River, OH
(216) 333-9902

20121 Van Aken Boulevard
Shaker Heights, OH
(216) 751-8181

Chinese

F ★ ★ ★
S ★ ★ ★
A ★ ★ ★ ½
P ★ ★ ★

No dress restrictions
Lot parking
All major credit cards
Full bar
Reservations required

Lunch: Mon.-Fri. 11:30AM-3:00PM
Dinner: Sun.-Thurs. 5:00PM-10:00PM
         Fri. & Sat. 5:00PM-11:30PM

The Pearl of The Orient combines a serenely elegant setting with award-winning Chinese haute cuisine. Northern and Szechwan specialties can be ordered spicy hot or mild. Wor Bar dishes, Mu Shu entrées, Peking Duck, and steamed whole sea bass are among the menu favorites.

PIER W 12

12700 Lake Avenue
Lakewood, OH
(216) 228-2250

Seafood

F ★ ★ ★ ½
S ★ ★ ★
A ★ ★ ★
P ★ ★ ★

Good taste in dress required
Valet parking on Fri. & Sat.
All major credit cards
Full bar
Reservations required

Lunch: Mon.-Fri. 11:30AM-3:00PM
Dinner: Mon.-Fri. 5:30PM-10:00PM
Sat. 5:30PM-12:00AM
Sun. 4:30PM-10:00PM
Brunch: Sun. 9:30AM-2:30PM

Enjoy the easy nautical ambiance of Pier W, located on the shore of Lake Erie, and offering you a great view of the lake and Cleveland. The bouillabaisse is highly touted, and the list of seafood entrées includes just-caught varieties of local freshwater fish.

RISTORANTE 22 GIOVANNI'S

25550 Chagrin Boulevard
Beachwood, OH
(216) 831-8625

Italian

F ★ ★ ★ ½
S ★ ★ ★ ½
A ★ ★ ★ ½
P ★ ★ ★ ★

Jacket and tie required
Valet parking
All major credit cards
Full bar
Reservations required

Lunch: Mon.-Fri. 11:30AM-2:30PM
Dinner: Mon.-Fri. 5:30PM-10:00PM
Sat. 5:30PM-10:30PM
Closed Sunday

An international staff provides gracious service in keeping with the opulent, formal atmosphere you will find here. Pastas and pastries are homemade; veal, beef, and fresh seafood dishes are complemented by delicate sauces.

SAMMY'S 3

1400 West 10th Street
Cleveland, OH
(216) 523-5560

Italian/Californian

F ★ ★ ★ ½
S ★ ★ ★
A ★ ★ ★
P ★ ★ ★ ★

Jacket required, no denims
Valet and street parking
All major credit cards
Full bar
Reservations required

Lunch: Mon.-Sat. 11:30AM-2:30PM
Dinner: Mon.-Thurs. 5:30PM-10:00PM
Fri. & Sat. 5:30PM-12:00AM
Closed Sunday

Bright and airy, this handsome eatery lets you view the Cuyahoga River through floor to ceiling glass walls. The cuisine tends to be eclectic with Italian dishes favored, and a fresh seafood specialty is offered daily. Nouvelle California entrées have a light, fresh touch. Boule de Neige, a triple chocolate dessert, makes a grand finale.

THE SAMURAI 21

23611 Chagrin Boulevard
Beachwood, OH
(216) 464-7575

Japanese

F ★ ★ ★
S ★ ★ ★
A ★ ★ ★
P ★ ★ ★

Jacket and tie required
Valet parking
All major credit cards
Full bar
Reservations required

Lunch: Mon.-Fri. 11:30AM-2:00PM
Dinner: Mon.-Thurs. 5:30PM-10:00PM
Fri. & Sat. 5:00PM-11:00PM
Sun. 4:30PM-9:00PM

Culinary magic is performed at your table at The Samurai, where the tradition of excellence inspired by the Samurai warriors of historic fame is manifest. Tempting specialties include Shrimp Flambé and tender Teppanyaki Filet Mignon.

THE TAVERNE OF   24
RICHFIELD

One Park Place
Richfield, OH
(216) 659-3155

American

F ★ ★ ★
S ★ ★ ★
A ★ ★ ★
P ★ ★ ★

Jacket required
Lot parking
All major credit cards
Full bar
Reservations required

Lunch/
Dinner: Daily 11:30AM-2:30AM

This antique-filled Victorian country inn, built in 1886, lets you return to the era of dignity, elegance, and chivalry. Quality prime beef is the specialty of the house; Duck à la Orange and rack of lamb are other fine entrées. An elaborate Sunday brunch is a popular attraction.

THAT PLACE ON   6
BELLFLOWER

11401 Bellflower Road
Cleveland, OH
(216) 231-4469

French

F ★ ★ ★
S ★ ★ ★
A ★ ★ ★ ½
P ★ ★ ★ ½

Jacket required after 6:00PM
Valet and lot parking
AE, MC, V
Full bar
Reservations required

Lunch: Mon.-Sat. 11:30AM-2:30PM
Dinner: Mon.-Sat. 5:30PM-10:00PM
Sun. 4:00PM-8:30PM

You'll find this intimate, romantic dining spot housed in a restored Tudor carriage house. The primarily French, though eclectic cuisine, may include such specialties as homemade pasta with sun-dried tomatoes, or smoked reindeer and Balsamic vinegar. Divine desserts are homemade.

THEATRICAL   4
RESTAURANT

711 Vincent Avenue
Cleveland, OH
(216) 241-6166

Continental

F ★ ★ ★
S ★ ★ ★
A ★ ★ ★
P ★ ★ ½

Good taste in dress required
Lot parking
AE, DC, MC, V
Full bar
Reservations not required

Lunch/
Dinner: Mon.-Sat. 11:00AM-1:30AM
Closed Sunday

A mecca for local and visiting sports and theatrical celebrities for nearly 50 years, this restaurant is a durable institution. Rolls, breads, and desserts are made on the premises. The menu features daily specials, and there is live entertainment in the evening.

TOP OF THE TOWN 1

100 Erie View Plaza
Cleveland, OH
(216) 771-1600

Continental

F ★ ★ ★
S ★ ★ ★
A ★ ★ ★
P ★ ★ ★

Good taste in dress required
Lot parking
All major credit cards
Full bar
Reservations required

Lunch: Mon.-Sat. 11:30AM-3:00PM
Dinner: Mon.-Thurs. 5:30PM-10:00PM
Fri. & Sat. 5:30PM-11:00PM
Closed Sunday

Enjoy an incomparable view of Cleveland and Lake Erie while dining at Top of The Town, located 39 stories high. The décor is smart and elegant with flickering candles and fresh flowers on snowy tablecloths. The cuisine is continental in character and the bill of fare offers a wide choice of well prepared entrées.

WAGON WHEEL 13

13114 Woodland Avenue
Cleveland, OH
(216) 561-6900

French

F ★ ★ ★
S ★ ★ ★
A ★ ★ ½
P ★ ★ ★

Jacket required
Lot parking
Credit cards not accepted
Full bar
Reservations required

Dinner: Mon.-Thurs. 5:30PM-10:30PM
Fri. & Sat. 5:30PM-12:00AM
Closed Sunday

Warm and intimate, Wagon Wheel reflects a proud Parisian heritage evidenced by owner Alfred Voisin's choice in décor, cuisine, and staff. Each meal is individually prepared to order, and your choice of entrées might include Duck à la Orange, Veal Parisienne, or Trout Amandine.

WINTERGARTEN 17

Marriott Inn-Airport
4277 West 150th Street
Cleveland, OH
(216) 252-5333

Continental

F ★ ★ ★
S ★ ★ ★
A ★ ★ ★
P ★ ★ ½

Jacket and tie required
Lot parking
All major credit cards
Full bar
Reservations required

Dinner: Mon.-Sat. 5:30PM-11:00PM
Brunch: Sun. 10:30AM-3:00PM

Wintergarten's second floor location lets you view the attractively planted ground level courtyard while dining. The décor is sleek and elegant, and perfectly in keeping with the epicurean quality of the continental cuisine.

Dallas/Ft.Worth

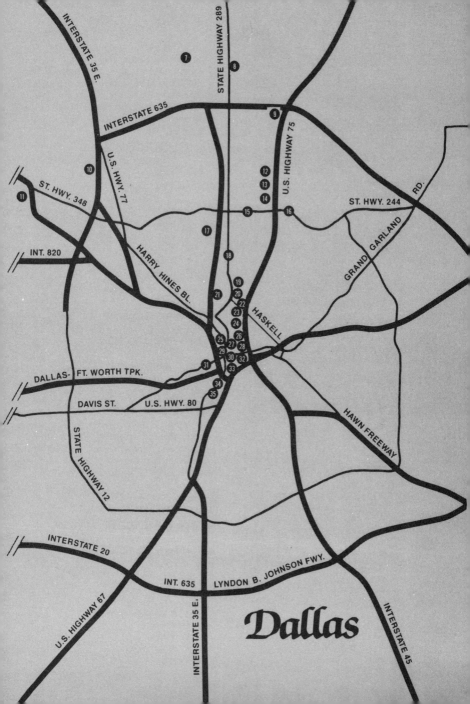

ANTARES 31

Hyatt Regency Hotel
300 Reunion Boulevard
Dallas, TX
(214) 651-1234

American/TexMex

F ★ ★ ★
S ★ ★ ★ ½
A ★ ★ ★ ½
P ★ ★ ★

Good taste in dress required
Lot parking
All major credit cards
Full bar
Reservations recommended

Lunch: Mon.-Sat. 11:00AM-2:00PM
Dinner: Nightly 6:00PM-11:00PM
Brunch: Sun. 10:30AM-2:30PM

Overlooking downtown Dallas, this revolving sky high restaurant gives you a fabulous view of the area and a setting that is chic and cosmopolitan. The service is smooth and the menu offers you classic American dishes or regional TexMex house specialties.

ARTHUR'S 16

1000 Campbell Center
Dallas, TX
(214) 361-8833

Continental

F ★ ★ ★ ½
S ★ ★ ★ ½
A ★ ★ ★ ★
P ★ ★ ★ ★

Jacket required
Valet parking
All major credit cards
Full bar
Reservations required

Lunch: Mon.-Fri. 11:30AM-2:30PM
Dinner: Sun.-Fri. 6:00PM-10:30PM
         Sat. 6:00PM-12:00AM

The hunting lodge feeling of this establishment reflects the handsome Old English décor. The service is polished, with tuxedoed waiters anticipating your needs. Here you can savor a wide range of well prepared continental dishes.

AUGUST MOON 8

15030 Preston Road
Dallas, TX
(214) 385-7227

Chinese

F ★ ★ ★
S ★ ★ ★
A ★ ★ ★
P ★ ★ ★

Good taste in dress required
Lot parking
All major credit cards
Full bar
Reservations not required

Lunch/
Dinner: Sun.-Thurs. 11:00AM-10:30PM
         Fri. & Sat. 11:00AM-11:00PM

Owner/host Sam Tsay and his courteous staff serve authentic dishes from different regions of China, prepared by five gourmet chefs, in your choice of four beautifully decorated dining rooms. Adventurous dishes such as frog legs with macadamia nuts augment traditional entrées.

BOBBI 14

Northpark East Center
8854 North Central Expressway
Dallas, TX
(214) 691-5833

American

F ★ ★ ★
S ★ ★ ★
A ★ ★ ½
P ★ ★

Good taste in dress required
Valet parking
All major credit cards
Full bar
Reservations not required

Lunch/
Dinner: Sun.-Thurs. 11:30AM-12:00AM
Fri. & Sat. 11:30AM-4:00AM

This is "eat, drink, and be merry" country, and you'll find an eclectic menu ranging from innovative salads to gourmet pizzas plus more robust entrées and an array of irresistible desserts. The atmosphere is casually elegant and there is dancing to add to the fun.

CAFÉ PACIFIC 18

24 Highland Park Village
(Preston & Mockingbird)
Dallas, TX
(214) 526-1170

Seafood

F ★ ★ ★ ★
S ★ ★ ★ ½
A ★ ★ ★ ★
P ★ ★ ★

No tennis shoes, faded jeans, or T-shirts
Lot and street parking
AE, MC, V
Full bar
Reservations recommended

Lunch: Daily 11:30AM-2:30PM
Dinner: Sun.-Thurs. 5:30PM-10:30PM
Fri. & Sat. 5:30PM-11:00PM

Italian marble floors, chandeliers, paneled walls, and flowering planters create an elegant ambiance at this much honored café. You'll be enticed by such specialties as fresh charcoaled salmon, crisp calamari, and Steak Oscar. The wine list is extensive and well priced.

CAFÉ ROYAL 32

Plaza of the Americas Hotel
650 North Pearl Street
Dallas, TX
(214) 747-7222

French

F ★ ★ ★ ★
S ★ ★ ★ ½
A ★ ★ ★ ★
P ★ ★ ★ ★

Jacket and tie required
Valet parking
All major credit cards
Full bar
Reservations required

Lunch: Mon.-Fri. 11:30AM-2:00PM
Dinner: Mon.-Sat. 6:30PM-10:30PM
Closed Sunday

A pastel peach and pink background against which paintings are displayed, creates a softly radiant atmosphere in this lively dining room. Here you will enjoy splendidly served exquisite French cuisine.

CALLUAUD'S RESTAURANT 24

2619 McKinney Avenue
Dallas, TX
(214) 823-5380

French

F ★ ★ ★ ★
S ★ ★ ★
A ★ ★ ★
P ★ ★ ★ ★

Jacket and tie required at dinner
Valet parking
AE, DC, MC, V
Full bar
Reservations required

Lunch: Mon.-Fri. 11:30AM-2:30PM
Dinner: Mon.-Sat. 6:00PM-10:30PM
Closed Sunday

Dining at Calluaud's is like entering a private and enchanted world created by the owners, Guy and Martine Calluaud. The décor is understated and elegant. It enhances the classic French cuisine that includes both traditional favorites and inspired innovative entrées.

CARRIAGE HOUSE 6

5136 Camp Bowie Boulevard
Fort Worth, TX
(817) 732-2873

Continental

F ★ ★ ★ ½
S ★ ★ ★
A ★ ★ ★
P ★ ★ ★

Good taste in dress required
Valet parking
All major credit cards
Full bar
Reservations required

Lunch: Mon.-Fri. 11:30AM-2:00PM
Dinner: Mon.-Sat. 6:00PM-11:00PM
Sun. 6:00PM-10:00PM
Brunch: Sun. 11:00AM-2:00PM

This posh establishment projects an intimate feeling, with colorful fresh flowers and glowing candles adding a touch of romance. The menu features classic continental fare, served by waiters in tuxedos. The wine list is of grand proportions.

CATTLEMEN'S 1

2456-58 North Main Street
Fort Worth, TX
(817) 624-3945

American

F ★ ★ ★ ½
S ★ ★ ½
A ★ ★ ½
P ★ ★ ★

Good taste in dress required
Lot and street parking
All major credit cards
Full bar
Reservations not required

Lunch/
Dinner: Mon.-Fri. 11:00AM-10:30PM
Sat. 4:30PM-10:30PM
Sun. 4:00PM-10:00PM

Since 1947, Cattlemen's, located near the stockyard, has been serving sizzling steaks, calf fries, chicken, and seafood to a large and loyal clientele who appreciate both the quality and abundance of the food and the hospitable, relaxed western atmosphere. Be prepared to wait (and well worth waiting for).

THE CHIMNEY 12

9739 North Central Expressway
Dallas, TX
(214) 369-6466

Swiss/Austrian

F ★ ★ ★
S ★ ★ ★
A ★ ★ ★
P ★ ★ ★

Jacket and tie preferred
Lot parking
All major credit cards
Full bar
Reservations required

Lunch: Mon.-Sat. 11:30AM-2:00PM
Dinner: Mon.-Sat. 6:00PM-10:30PM
Closed Sunday

The glowing fireplace, friendly waitresses, and gemütlich Old World air of this charming restaurant are conducive to comfortable relaxed dining. Select from a menu devised by chef/owner Heinz Prast to feature dishes with a Tyrolian flair, including several veal entrées and Rehsteak Chimney (venison from Montana).

CHIQUITA'S   21

3810 Congress
Dallas, TX
(214) 521-0721

TexMex/Mexican

F ★ ★ ★
S ★ ★ ★
A ★ ★ ★
P ★ ★

Good taste in dress required
Lot parking
AE, MC, V
Beer/Wine
Reservations not required

Lunch/
Dinner: Mon.-Thurs. 11:30AM-10:30PM
Fri. & Sat. 11:30AM-11:00PM
Closed Sunday

Bright paper flowers on the stark white walls, pre-Columbian artifacts, and paintings from Mexico add a fiesta flavor to the festive, fanciful décor of this popular eatery. You'll find TexMex dishes and Mexico City-style Mexican cuisine sharing billing on the menu.

THE ENCLAVE   13

8325 Walnut Hill
Dallas, TX
(214) 363-7487

Continental

F ★ ★ ★ ½
S ★ ★ ★ ½
A ★ ★ ★ ½
P ★ ★ ★ ★

Jacket required
Lot parking
All major credit cards
Full bar
Reservations required

Lunch: Mon.-Fri. 11:00AM-2:30PM
Dinner: Mon.-Sat. 6:00PM-11:00PM
Closed Sunday

Sparkling chandeliers, mirrors, carved antique furnishings, fresh flowers, and candles all contribute to the rich elegance of this Old World restaurant, where continental cuisine is featured. The menu is diverse, offering you lots of good options. Dinner service is formal.

ENJOLIE   11

Mandalay Four Seasons Hotel
221 South Las Colinas Boulevard
Irvine, TX
(214) 556-0800

French

F ★ ★ ★
S ★ ★ ★ ½
A ★ ★ ★ ½
P ★ ★ ★ ★

Jacket and tie required
Valet parking
All major credit cards
Full bar
Reservations required

Lunch: Mon.-Fri. 11:30AM-2:30PM
Dinner: Mon.-Sat. 6:30PM-10:30PM
Closed Sunday

This handsome, open dining room is lavished with foliage plants and brilliant flowers; antique furnishings add to the formal air. Classic French cuisine is featured, and it is authentically prepared. You'll find solicitous service and a pleasing ambiance to enhance your enjoyment of the excellent food.

FAUSTO'S   31

Hyatt Regency Hotel
300 Reunion Boulevard
Dallas, TX
(214) 651-1234

Italian

F ★ ★ ★ ½
S ★ ★ ★ ½
A ★ ★ ★ ★
P ★ ★ ★ ½

Good taste in dress required
Valet parking
All major credit cards
Full bar
Reservations required

Dinner: Mon.-Sat. 6:30PM-10:30PM
Brunch: Sun. 10:30AM-2:30PM

Sedate and intimate, with candlelight and colorful flowers, this restaurant projects an image of understated elegance. Seafood plays a stellar role on the menu, which is built around treasured classic Italian entrées. Expect polished and professional service.

FRENCH ROOM   33

Adolphus Hotel
1321 Commerce
Dallas, TX
(214) 742-8200

French

F ★ ★ ★
S ★ ★ ★ ½
A ★ ★ ★ ½
P ★ ★ ★ ★

Jacket and tie required
Valet parking
All major credit cards
Full bar
Reservations required

Dinner: Mon.-Sat. 6:30PM-10:30PM
          Closed Sunday

Dignified and elegant, the French Room is furnished à la Louis XV and XVI and features hand-crafted Italian chandeliers. Chef Jean Banchet is responsible for the award-winning cuisine that includes both classic French dishes and those prepared in the nouvelle manner.

IL SORRENTO   15

8616 Turtle Creek Boulevard
Dallas, TX
(214) 352-8759

Italian

F ★ ★ ★ ½
S ★ ★ ★ ½
A ★ ★ ★ ½
P ★ ★ ★ ★

Jacket and tie preferred
Valet parking
All major credit cards
Full bar
Reservations required

Dinner: Sun.-Fri. 5:30PM-11:00PM
          Sat. 5:30PM-12:00AM

Il Sorrento has charm and character. It is decorated in the manner of an old piazza, and has been pleasing discriminating customers for more than 30 years. House specialties include Veal Suprema, Pansotti, and a host of delicious seafood dishes.

JAVIER'S   20

4912 Cole
Dallas, TX
(214) 521-4211

Mexican/Continental

F ★ ★ ★
S ★ ★ ★
A ★ ★ ★
P ★ ★ ½

Good taste in dress required
Lot and street parking
All major credit cards
Full bar
Reservations required

Dinner: Sun.-Thurs. 5:30PM-10:30PM
          Fri. & Sat. 5:30PM-11:30PM

Javier's is decorated with stunning antiques from many regions of Mexico, and dining here has the flair and flavor of a south-of-the-border travel adventure. Continental cuisine features beef, chicken, shrimp, and red snapper prepared in a manner reminiscent of a fine Mexico City restaurant.

JEAN-CLAUDE   29

2404 Cedar Springs
Dallas, TX
(214) 748-6619/871-0818

French

F ★ ★ ★ ½
S ★ ★ ★
A ★ ★ ★
P ★ ★ ★ ★

Jacket and tie required
Lot parking
All major credit cards
Full bar
Reservations required

Dinner: Tues.-Sat. seatings at
         6:00PM and 9:00PM
         Closed Sunday and Monday

In a charming French provincial setting, owner Jean-Claude Prevot presents five-course, fixed-price dinners with a choice of eight entrées, prepared with all fresh ingredients, and served with aplomb by tuxedoed waiters.

JOE T. GARCIA'S   2

2210 North Commerce Street
Fort Worth, TX
(817) 624-0266

TexMex/Mexican

F ★ ★ ★
S ★ ★ ★
A ★ ★ ★
P ★ ★

No dress restrictions
Lot parking
Credit cards not accepted
Full bar
Reservations not required

Lunch: Mon.-Fri. 11:00AM-2:30PM
Dinner: Mon.-Fri. 5:00PM-10:30PM
         Sat. 11:00AM-11:00PM
         Sun. 2:00PM-10:00PM

This 50-year old establishment occupies a former home and is famous for comfortable indoor/outdoor dining. Filled with antiques, and a display of past governor's pictures, you feel like part of Ft. Worth history when you visit this family style restaurant. The menu couples TexMex specialties with authentic Mexican fare.

JOE T. GARCIA'S   7

4440 Beltline Road
North Dallas, TX
(214) 458-7373

TexMex/Mexican

F ★ ★ ★
S ★ ★ ★
A ★ ★ ★
P ★ ★

Good taste in dress required
Lot parking
AE, MC, V
Full bar
Reservations not required

Lunch: Mon.-Fri. 11:00AM-3:00PM
Dinner: Mon.-Fri. 5:00PM-11:00PM
         Sat. 11:00AM-11:00PM
         Sun. 2:00PM-10:00PM
Brunch: Sun. 11:00AM-2:30PM

A chip off the old Ft. Worth block, and owned by the same famous restaurant family, this Joe T. Garcia's establishment offers a gardenlike setting in which to enjoy great TexMex and traditional Mexican cooking. You'll find a regular gallery of celebrity photos adding to the décor.

JOZEF'S 26

2719 McKinney Avenue
Dallas, TX
(214) 826-5560

Seafood

F ★ ★ ★ ½
S ★ ★ ★
A ★ ★ ★
P ★ ★ ★

Good taste in dress required
Lot parking
All major credit cards
Full bar
Reservations required

Lunch: Mon.-Fri. 11:00AM-2:30PM
Dinner: Sun.-Thurs. 6:00PM-10:00PM
         Fri. & Sat. 6:00PM-11:00PM

At Jozef's you'll enjoy fresh seafood specialties served in a warm, elegant environment. Savor such delicacies as hand-picked lump crabmeat, live Maine lobster, fresh sea scallops, and seasonal fresh vegetables. Natural ingredients (whole grain flours, brown rice, and honey) are used.

L'ENTRECOTE 35

Lowe's Anatole Hotel
2201 Stemmons Freeway
Dallas, TX
(214) 748-1200

Continental

F ★ ★ ★ ½
S ★ ★ ★ ½
A ★ ★ ★ ★
P ★ ★ ★ ★

Jackets required
Valet parking
All major credit cards
Full bar
Reservations required

Dinner: Nightly 6:00PM-10:30PM

Impressive and elegant, you'll find this a romantic dining spot with soothing harp music, candlelight, and rosebuds on the tables. The many flambé items featured on the menu are served skillfully tableside. The cuisine and wine list will not disappoint you.

LES SAISONS 19

165 Turtle Creek Village
Dallas, TX
(214) 528-1102

French

F ★ ★ ★ ½
S ★ ★ ★ ½
A ★ ★ ★ ½
P ★ ★ ★

Jacket preferred, no blue jeans
Lot parking
All major credit cards
Full bar
Reservations required

Lunch: Daily 11:30AM-5:00PM
Dinner: Sun.-Fri. 5:00PM-11:00PM
         Sat. 5:00PM-12:00AM

A country French atmosphere complete with fabric-covered walls, and colorful plants, invites you to dine leisurely at this comfortable eatery. The cuisine is also country French, with a wide choice of succulent, hearty entrées, such as Dover sole and entrecôte steak.

THE MANSION ON 28
TURTLE CREEK

2821 Turtle Creek Boulevard
Dallas, TX
(214) 559-2100

American Southwest

F ★ ★ ★ ★
S ★ ★ ★ ★
A ★ ★ ★ ★
P ★ ★ ★ ★

Jacket and tie required
Valet parking
All major credit cards
Full bar
Reservations required

Lunch: Mon.-Fri. 12:00PM-2:00PM
Dinner: Mon.-Thurs. 6:00PM-10:30PM
         Fri. & Sat. 6:00PM-11:00PM
         Sun. 6:00PM-10:30PM
Late
Supper: Mon.-Thurs. 10:30PM-12:00AM
         Fri. & Sat. 11:00PM-12:00AM
Brunch: Sat. 12:00PM-2:00PM
         Sun. 11:00AM-2:00PM

Housed in the renovated Sheppard King mansion on Turtle Creek, this restaurant offers you resplendent décor, exceptionally smooth service, and a seasonally changing menu of superbly prepared American regional specialties, such as chicken with wild rice, and oysters in season.

MARIO'S   19

135 Turtle Creek Village
Dallas, TX
(214) 521-1135

Italian/Continental

F ★ ★ ★ ½
S ★ ★ ★ ½
A ★ ★ ★
P ★ ★ ★

Jacket and tie required, no jeans
Valet parking
All major credit cards
Full bar
Reservations required

Dinner: Sun.-Thurs. 6:00PM-10:30PM
         Fri. & Sat. 6:00PM-11:30PM

Your choice of three distinctively decorated dining rooms, exceptionally polished service, and a wide selection of Italian and continental dishes await you at Mario's. A variety of fish, veal, and pasta dishes are offered and the fettuccine has been highly acclaimed.

MICHEL   4

3851 Camp Bowie
Fort Worth, TX
(817) 732-1231

French

F ★ ★ ★
S ★ ★ ★
A ★ ★ ★
P ★ ★ ★ ★

Jacket and tie required
Valet parking
All major credit cards
Full bar
Reservations required

Dinner: Tues.-Thurs. 6:00PM-10:00PM
         Fri. & Sat. seatings at
         6:00PM and 9:00PM
         Closed Sunday and Monday

Owner Michel Baudouin strives to offer the best food, best of French and California wines, and the best service possible at Michel, which occupies a charming older home. The fixed-price, five-course menu varies daily, reflecting what is available fresh from the marketplace.

MOZART'S   9

Sheraton Park Central
12720 Merit Drive
Dallas, TX
(214) 385-3000

Continental

F ★ ★ ★ ½
S ★ ★ ★
A ★ ★ ½
P ★ ★

Jacket preferred
Lot parking
All major credit cards
Beer/Wine
Reservations required

Lunch: Mon.-Fri. 11:30AM-2:00PM

The chandelier is from Vienna, and there is a wealth of crystal, mirrors, and beveled glass to reflect its pristine beauty in this gracious establishment. The continental menu offers you a broad assortment of entrées, adapted from the classics to please contemporary tastes.

MR. PEPPE   17

5617 West Lovers Lane
Dallas, TX
(214) 352-5976

French

F ★ ★ ★
S ★ ★ ★
A ★ ★ ★
P ★ ★ ★

Jacket required, no blue jeans
Lot parking
All major credit cards
Full bar
Reservations recommended

Dinner: Mon.-Sat. 6:00PM-10:00PM
Closed Sunday

At Mr. Peppe's you'll find Maître d'/ owner Albert Schanfelberger has created a charming European-style café with a warm, inviting ambiance. Since 1958 this restaurant has been noted for consistently good cuisine, featuring such gustatory delights as duck prepared with kiwi, papaya, and berries.

NEWPORT'S   27

703 McKinney in the Brewery
Dallas, TX
(214) 954-0220

Seafood

F ★ ★ ★
S ★ ★ ★
A ★ ★ ★
P ★ ★ ★

No dress restrictions
Valet and lot parking
All major credit cards
Full bar
Reservations recommended

Lunch: Mon.-Fri. 11:30AM-2:30PM
Dinner: Mon.-Thurs. 5:30PM-10:30PM
Fri. & Sat. 5:30PM-11:00PM
Closed Sunday

Owner Jack Baum has turned an old brewery into one of the neatest rustic restaurants in town. There's a 60-foot-deep natural spring fed well as a center of attraction, and such culinary joys as mesquite-grilled swordfish. The individually baked cheesecake is too good to resist, and the wine list deserves your attention.

OLD SAN FRANCISCO   10
STEAK HOUSE

10965 Composite
Dallas, TX
(214) 357-0484

American

F ★ ★ ★
S ★ ★ ★
A ★ ★ ★
P ★ ★ ½

Good taste in dress required
Valet parking
All major credit cards
Full bar
Reservations required

Dinner: Mon.-Thurs. 5:00PM-11:00PM
Fri. & Sat. 5:00PM-12:00AM
Sun. 4:00PM-11:00PM

Expect the unexpected at this grand establishment, where the 30-foot-high ceiling allows plenty of room for the girl on the red velvet swing. The décor is early '20s and the menu favors fish, steak, and prime rib. Two grand pianos help make dining here an entertaining experience.

OLD SWISS HOUSE 5

5412 Camp Bowie Boulevard
Fort Worth, TX
(817) 877-1531

Continental

F ★ ★ ★ ½
S ★ ★ ★ ½
A ★ ★ ★ ½
P ★ ★ ★

Jacket required
Valet parking
All major credit cards
Full bar
Reservations required

Dinner: Mon-Thurs. 6:00PM-10:00PM
         Fri. & Sat. 6:00PM-10:30PM
         Closed Sunday

Owner/chef Walter Kaufmann has composed a near perfect collage using all the elements that make dining a superlative experience. The décor is formal and elegant, highlighted with works of art; the service is polite and urbane; and the cuisine includes exceptional specialties.

THE OLD WARSAW 22
(La Vieille Varsovie)

2610 Maple Avenue
Dallas, TX
(214) 528-0032

French

F ★ ★ ★ ½
S ★ ★ ★
A ★ ★ ★ ½
P ★ ★ ★ ★

Jacket required
Valet parking
All major credit cards
Full bar
Reservations required

Dinner: Sun.-Thurs. 6:00PM-11:00PM
         Fri. & Sat. 6:00PM-12:00AM

This often-honored restaurant has been setting standards for classic French cuisine in Dallas for more than three decades. The ambiance is intimate, the service suave, and chef Cherif Brahmi produces magic meals.

PLUM BLOSSOM 34

2201 Stemmons Freeway
Dallas, TX
(214) 748-1200

Chinese

F ★ ★ ★ ½
S ★ ★ ★
A ★ ★ ★
P ★ ★ ★ ½

Jacket required, tie preferred
Valet and lot parking
All major credit cards
Full bar
Reservations required

Dinner: Mon.-Sat. 6:00PM-10:30PM
         Closed Sunday

You'll find this room a marvel of elegant European decor, with the quiet Oriental mood achieved through the subtle use of Chinese antiques. This restaurant offers you a wonderful range of Mandarin Chinese dishes.

PYRAMID ROOM 30

Fairmont Hotel
1717 North Akard Street
Dallas, TX
(214) 720-2020

Continental

F ★ ★ ★ ½
S ★ ★ ★ ½
A ★ ★ ★ ½
P ★ ★ ★ ★

Jacket and tie required
Valet parking
All major credit cards
Full bar
Reservations required

Lunch: Mon.-Fri. 11:30AM-2:00PM
Dinner: Nightly 6:00PM-10:00PM

When you see the inverted pyramid chandelier of golden glass that dominates the décor, you will immediately realize where this room got its name. In the midst of all this splendor you'll find well prepared continental cuisine and adroit service.

RAPHAEL'S   23

3701 McKinney
Dallas, TX
(214) 521-9640

Mexican/TexMex

F ★ ★ ★
S ★ ★ ★
A ★ ★ ★
P ★ ★ ½

Good taste in dress required
Lot parking
AE
Full bar
Reservations required

Lunch: Mon.-Fri. 11:30AM-3:00PM
Dinner: Mon.-Fri. 5:30PM-10:30PM
Sat. 12:00PM-10:30PM
Closed Sunday

This bright and cheerful restaurant has an Aztec mural on the wall, and a homelike flower-filled, joyous atmosphere. A medley of Mexican favorites and TexMex specialties is featured. The salsa is piquante and the Margaritas potent.

ROUTH STREET CAFÉ   25

3005 Routh Street at Cedar Springs
Dallas, TX
(214) 871-7161

American

F ★ ★ ★ ½
S ★ ★ ★ ½
A ★ ★ ★
P ★ ★ ★ ★

Good taste in dress required
Valet parking
AE, DC, MC, V
Full bar
Reservations required

Dinner: Tues.-Sat. 6:00PM-10:30PM
Closed Sunday and Monday

Fresh native products of the Southwest are emphasized in the American cuisine prepared by chef Stephan Pyles for the daily changing, fixed-price, 5-course gourmet meals served here. The fare is innovative and exciting, the service attentive, and the all-American wine list well thought out.

TEQUILLO'S   3

Hilton Hotel
1701 Commerce Street
Fort Worth, TX
(817) 335-7000

Mexican

F ★ ★ ★
S ★ ★ ★
A ★ ★ ★
P ★ ★ ★

Good taste in dress required
Lot parking
All major credit cards
Full bar
Reservations required

Lunch: Mon.-Fri. 11:30AM-2:00PM
Dinner: Mon.-Thurs. 5:30PM-10:00PM
Fri. & Sat. 5:30PM-11:00PM
Closed Sunday

This delightful restaurant is built around a central fountain surrounded by lush greenery. In this garden/courtyard setting you can sip Margaritas (offered in 14 flavors), listen to the romantic music of strolling Mariachis, and select from a wide menu based on classic Mexican cuisine.

Denver

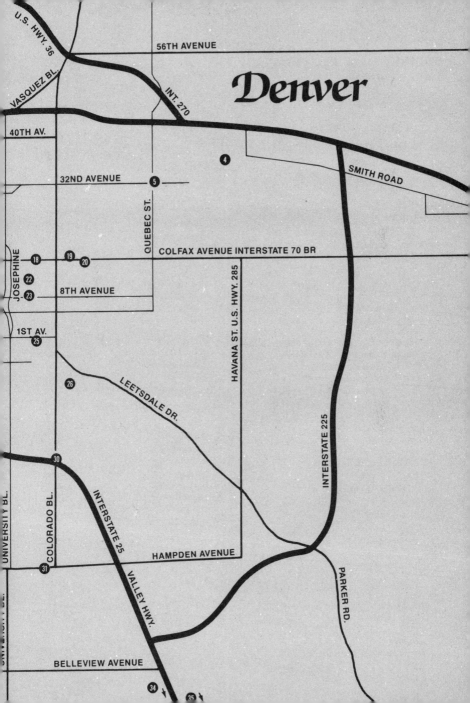

BABY DOE'S 7
MATCHLESS MINE

2520 West 23rd Avenue
Denver, CO
(303) 433-3386

American

F ★ ★ ★ ½
S ★ ★ ★ ½
A ★ ★ ★
P ★ ★ ★

No dress restrictions
Lot parking
All major credit cards
Full bar
Reservations not required

Lunch: Mon.-Sat. 11:00AM-2:30PM
Dinner: Mon.-Thurs. 5:00PM-11:00PM
Fri. & Sat. 5:00PM-12:00AM
Brunch: Sun. 9:00AM-2:30PM

Stake your claim on a table at this colorful restaurant that overlooks downtown Denver. The exterior resembles a mine, and there's dancing in the "Mineshaft Saloon." The dining room serves such entrées as choice steaks and prime rib, apple jack chicken, and fresh seafood.

BERARDI & SONS 8

1525 Blake Street
Denver, CO
(303) 623-7648

Italian

F ★ ★ ★
S ★ ★ ★
A ★ ★ ★
P ★ ★ ★

Good taste in dress required
Lot and street parking
All major credit cards
Full bar
Reservations recommended

Lunch: Mon.-Fri. 11:00AM-2:30PM
Dinner: Sun.-Thurs. 5:30PM-10:00PM
Fri. & Sat. 5:30PM-11:00PM

Enjoy romantic candlelight dining on hearty provincial Italian cuisine here, where house specialties include Beef Braciole, Veal Chops Milanese, Scampi Prosciutto, homemade pastas, and daily fresh seafood dishes. Italy's finest vintners are included on the wine list.

BRENDLES 12

1624 Market Street
Denver, CO
(303) 893-3588

American

F ★ ★ ★
S ★ ★ ★
A ★ ★ ★
P ★ ★ ½

No dress restrictions
Lot and street parking
All major credit cards
Full bar
Reservations recommended

Lunch: Mon.-Fri. 11:30AM-3:00PM
Dinner: Mon.-Sat. 5:30PM-10:30PM
Closed Sunday

A warm, rustic atmosphere created by brick walls, wood, and plants forms a pleasant setting for such gustatory delights as fettuccine with goat cheese, venison with current and cream sauce, and daily fresh seafood entrées.

BRITTANY HILL 7

9350 North Grant
Denver, CO
(303) 451-5151

American

F ★ ★ ★
S ★ ★ ★
A ★ ★ ★ ½
P ★ ★ ★ ½

Good taste in dress required
Valet parking
All major credit cards
Full bar
Reservations required

Lunch: Daily 11:00AM-2:30PM
Lite
Bite: Daily 2:30PM-4:00PM
Dinner: Mon.-Thurs. 5:00PM-11:00PM
Fri. & Sat. 5:00PM-12:00AM
Sun. 4:00PM-10:00PM

Wend your way to this unique establishment, sited in a castle on a hill, to enjoy dining in the grand manner, and a panoramic view of the dazzling Denver skyline. Steaks and fresh seafood are both popular highlights of the wide menu that focuses on well prepared American classic dishes.

BUCKHORN EXCHANGE 21

1000 Osage Street
Denver, CO
(303) 534-9505

American

F ★ ★ ★ ½
S ★ ★ ★
A ★ ★ ★
P ★ ★ ★

Good taste in dress required
Lot parking
All major credit cards
Full bar
Reservations required for dinner

Lunch: Mon.-Fri. 11:00AM-3:00PM
Dinner: Nightly 5:00PM-10:30PM

This 1893 historic landmark is Denver's oldest existing eating emporium, and museum of old west memorabilia including over 500 mounted game and fowl and a huge gun collection. Game meats including buffalo, elk, and quail are featured as are T-bone steaks and mountain trout.

CAFÉ GIOVANNI 6

1515 Market Street
Denver, CO
(303) 825-6555

Continental

F ★ ★ ★ ★
S ★ ★ ★ ★
A ★ ★ ★ ★
P ★ ★ ★ ½

Jacket preferred
Street parking
All major credit cards
Full bar
Reservations required

Lunch: Mon.-Fri. 11:30AM-3:00PM
Dinner: Mon.-Thurs. 5:30PM-10:00PM
Fri. & Sat. 5:30PM-11:00PM
Closed Sunday

Imagination and know-how have transformed a former warehouse into this warmly elegant and romantic café with real fireplaces, brick walls, gleaming brass, and polished oak detailing. The bill of fare is broad enough to content diners of every persuasion, with emphasis on French specialties and Northern Italian entrées.

CAFÉ PROMENADE 10

1430 Larimer Street
Denver, CO
(303) 893-2692

Classical European

F ★ ★ ★ ½
S ★ ★ ★ ½
A ★ ★ ★ ½
P ★ ★ ★

Good taste in dress required
Lot and street parking
All major credit cards
Full bar
Reservations recommended

Breakfast/
Lunch/
Dinner: Mon.-Sat. 9:00AM-11:30PM
  Closed Sunday

This classic European-style café, located in Larimer Square, a restored historical district, features two dining rooms and an outdoor patio. The cuisine emphasizes French and Northern Italian style cooking. A bountiful wine cellar and classical piano music nightly are beautiful bonuses.

CARRINGTON'S 5

Stouffer's Denver Inn
3203 Quebec Street
Denver, CO
(303) 321-3333

Continental

F ★ ★ ★ ½
S ★ ★ ★ ½
A ★ ★ ★ ½
P ★ ★ ★

Jacket required
Valet parking
All major credit cards
Full bar
Reservations required

Lunch: Daily 11:00AM-2:00PM
Dinner: Nightly 6:00PM-11:00PM

A portrait of perfection, this posh establishment is designed with all the elements imaginable combined to provide pleasurable dining. The setting is formal and opulent, the continental cuisine correctly prepared and served with precision.

CHATEAU PYRENEES 34

6538 South Yosemite Circle
Englewood, CO
(303) 770-6660

Continental/French

F ★ ★ ★ ½
S ★ ★ ★ ★
A ★ ★ ★ ½
P ★ ★ ★ ½

Jacket required
Valet parking
All major credit cards
Full bar
Reservations not required

Dinner: Mon.-Sat. 6:00PM-10:00PM
  Closed Sunday

Chateau Pyrenees occupies a lovely stone chateau with elegant appointments including original paintings, and an authentic Louis XVI grand piano. Fine continental and French cuisine is offered à la carte, and served graciously. Desserts are a specialty, and the wine list is superb.

THE CHRYSLER 25

2955 East First Avenue
Denver, CO
(303) 355-2955

American/Cajun

F ★ ★ ★ ½
S ★ ★ ★
A ★ ★ ★
P ★ ★

No dress restrictions
Valet and lot parking
All major credit cards
Full bar
Reservations required

Lunch: Mon.-Sat. 11:15AM-3:00PM
Dinner: Mon.-Sat. 5:00PM-11:30PM
  Sun. 5:00PM-12:00AM
Brunch: Sun. 10:00AM-3:00PM

You'll be captivated by the panoramic view of the Rocky Mountains that is yours to enjoy here. The ambiance is pure art déco, echoing the '30s and '40s. The cuisine includes succulent barbecue and Cajun specialties.

CHURCHILL'S   30

1730 South Colorado Boulevard
Denver, CO
(303) 756-8877

American

```
F  ★ ★ ★
S  ★ ★ ★
A  ★ ★ ★
P  ★ ★ ★
```

No dress restrictions
Lot parking
All major credit cards
Full bar
Reservations recommended

Lunch: Mon.-Fri. 11:30AM-2:00PM
Dinner: Mon.-Sat. 6:00PM-10:00PM
Brunch: Sun. 10:30AM-2:30PM

Handsome English Tudor décor and polished service make dining at Churchill's a special event. The extensive French nouvelle menu is augmented by prime quality steaks, prime rib, and fresh seasonal seafoods, all offered à la carte.

THE COLORADO MINE   26
COMPANY

4490 East Virginia Avenue
Denver, CO
(303) 321-6555

American

```
F  ★ ★ ★
S  ★ ★ ★  ½
A  ★ ★ ★
P  ★ ★ ★ ★
```

Good taste in dress required
Valet parking
All major credit cards
Full bar
Reservations recommended

Dinner: Mon.-Sat. 5:30PM-1:00AM
          Sun. 5:30PM-11:00PM

Dine in a lighter vein in the friendly, casual atmosphere of The Colorado Mine Company, designed to replicate an 1880s working mine. Prime rib, steaks, rainbow trout, and seafood are among the featured entrées favored by loyal Denverites.

DENIM BROKER   4

12100 East 39th Avenue
Denver, CO
(303) 371-6420

American

```
F  ★ ★ ★  ½
S  ★ ★ ★  ½
A  ★ ★ ★
P  ★ ★ ★
```

No dress restrictions
Lot parking
AE, MC, V
Full bar
Reservations not required

Lunch: Mon.-Fri. 11:00AM-2:00PM
Dinner: Mon.-Thurs. 5:00PM-10:00PM
          Fri. & Sat. 5:00PM-11:00PM
          Sun. 5:00PM-9:00PM

This casual and friendly spot has the flavor of the Old West with its 100-year-old St. Louis bar, and stained glass décor. Steaks, seafood, prime rib, and chicken are featured, and you'll enjoy a complimentary bowl of shrimp, served with all dinner entrées.

DUDLEY'S   24

1120 East 6th Avenue
Denver, CO
(303) 777-2790

French

```
F  ★ ★ ★  ½
S  ★ ★ ★  ½
A  ★ ★ ★
P  ★ ★ ★  ½
```

Good taste in dress required
Street parking
All major credit cards
Full bar
Reservations required

Lunch: Tues.-Sat. 11:30AM-2:00PM
Dinner: Tues.-Sat. 6:00PM-10:30PM
         Closed Sunday and Monday

This chic, intimate restaurant brings a touch of "Gay Paris" to the heart of downtown Denver. Jaunty, with bright bouquets of fresh flowers, and an inviting, friendly atmosphere, you'll find imaginative nouvelle cuisine emanating from the kitchen, remarkably good service, and a solid wine list.

DUGGAN'S   33

5151 South Federal Boulevard
Littleton, CO
(303) 795-1081

American/Mexican

F ★ ★ ★
S ★ ★ ★
A ★ ★ ★
P ★ ★ ½

Good taste in dress required
Lot parking
All major credit cards
Full bar
Reservations not required

Breakfast/
Lunch/
Dinner: Mon.-Fri. 6:45AM-2:00AM
         Sat. 8:00AM-2:00AM
         Sun. 8:00AM-12:00AM

A casual and relaxed atmosphere is a Duggan's specialty, together with their excellent barbecue, Mexican, and American cuisine. Prime rib, steaks, and fresh seafood are all featured on the somewhat eclectic menu. A piano-bar lounge adds congenial entertainment.

GASHO OF JAPAN   14

1627 Curtis Street
Denver, CO
(303) 892-5625

Japanese

F ★ ★ ★ ½
S ★ ★ ★
A ★ ★ ★ ½
P ★ ★ ½

Good taste in dress required
Valet parking for dinner
All major credit cards
Full bar
Reservations required

Lunch: Mon.-Sat. 11:30AM-2:30PM
Dinner: Mon.-Thurs. 5:00PM-10:00PM
         Fri. & Sat. 5:00PM-11:00PM
         Sun. 4:00PM-9:30PM

This unique restaurant was created inside a building, using pieces of a 300-400 year old Japanese farmhouse. The effect is marvelous. Teppanyaki grill cooking is featured with skilled chefs deftly chopping ingredients, then cooking teriyaki, sashimi, and sukiyaki at your table. The food preparation is dramatic—the results more than justify the effort.

H. BRINKER'S   35

7209 South Clinton
Englewood, CO
(303) 792-0285

American

F ★ ★ ★
S ★ ★ ★
A ★ ★ ★
P ★ ★ ★

Good taste in dress required
Lot parking
All major credit cards
Full bar
Reservations not required

Lunch/
Dinner: Mon.-Sat. 11:00AM-2:00AM
Brunch/
Lunch/
Dinner: Sun. 9:00AM-12:00AM

When you spot the huge windmill that's become a Denver landmark, you will have found H. Brinker's, with its breathtaking view of Denver and the Front Range. Fresh seafood and mesquite-broiled prime rib and steaks are house specialties.

JAKE'S   3

Regency Inn
3900 Elati Street
Denver, CO
(303) 458-0808

Continental

F ★ ★ ★
S ★ ★ ★
A ★ ★ ★
P ★ ★ ★

Jacket and tie required
Lot parking
All major credit cards
Full bar
Reservations required

Lunch: Mon.-Fri. 11:00AM-2:00PM
Dinner: Mon.-Sat. 6:00PM-10:00PM
           Closed Sunday

A rich mix of renaissance and baroque decorating styles creates a dramatic ambiance at this stylish establishment. The continental menu is well composed with a nice diversity of entrées offered, and the service is unobtrusive and smoothly rendered.

LE PROFIL   16

1560 Sherman Street
Denver, CO
(303) 861-1600

French

F ★ ★ ★ ½
S ★ ★ ★ ★
A ★ ★ ★ ½
P ★ ★ ★ ½

No dress restrictions
Valet and lot parking
All major credit cards
Full bar
Reservations recommended

Lunch: Mon.-Fri. 11:30AM-2:00PM
Dinner: Mon.-Sat. 6:00PM-10:00PM
           Closed Sunday

For 30 years, Le Profil has been serving classic French and continental cuisine in an atmosphere of relaxed elegance. Owner T. Michael Cook features such specialties as several exotic duckling dishes, veal prepared many ways and Beef Wellington; plus offering you a host of other gourmet entrées.

MANHATTAN CAFÉ   9

1620 Market Street
Denver, CO
(303) 893-0951

Continental

F ★ ★ ★
S ★ ★ ★
A ★ ★ ★
P ★ ★ ★

No dress restrictions
Lot and street parking
All major credit cards
Full bar
Reservations required

Lunch: Mon.-Fri. 11:00AM-2:30PM
Dinner: Mon.-Sat. 5:30PM-11:30PM
           Closed Sunday

A small, intimate replica of a New York café, decorated with original art of New York City scenes, Manhattan Café offers you a distinctive ambiance. Specialties of the house include veal and steaks, as well as fresh seafood which is flown in daily.

MARQUIS 15

The Fairmont Hotel
1750 Welton
Denver, CO
(303) 295-1200

French

F ★ ★ ★
S ★ ★ ★
A ★ ★ ★
P ★ ★ ★

Jacket required
Valet parking
All major credit cards
Full bar
Reservations required

Lunch: Mon.-Fri. 11:30AM-2:00PM
Dinner: Nightly 6:00PM-10:00PM

Resplendent in the French tradition for opulent décor, here you will find shimmering crystal chandeliers, spacious private booths, and elegent French furniture. The cuisine is carefully prepared in the classic manner and served with enough flair to make you feel as pampered as an honored guest.

MATAAM FEZ 19

4609 East Colfax Avenue
Denver, CO
(303) 399-9282

Moroccan

F ★ ★ ★ ½
S ★ ★ ★ ½
A ★ ★ ★ ½
P ★ ★ ★ ★

Good taste in dress required
Street parking
AE, DC, MC, V
Beer/Wine
Reservations required

Dinner: Sun.-Thurs. 6:00PM-9:30PM
Fri. & Sat. 6:00PM-10:30PM

Experience the exotic cuisine of North Africa while lounging on comfortable pillows at a low table under a draped tentlike ceiling. Your Moroccan meal begins with a hearty soup and traditional salads, moves leisurely to your choice of entrées such as lamb, couscous, game hen, or hare; and ends with delicate pastries and mint tea.

MON PETIT 2

7000 West 38th Avenue
Wheatridge, CO
(303) 424-4700

French

F ★ ★ ★ ★
S ★ ★ ★ ★
A ★ ★ ★ ½
P ★ ★ ★ ½

Good taste in dress required
Lot parking
All major credit cards
Full bar
Reservations required

Lunch: Mon.-Fri. 11:30AM-2:00PM
Dinner: Mon.-Sat. 6:00PM-10:00PM
Closed Sunday

Mon Petit occupies a refurbished 19th century home, with crystal chandelier-lit intimate dining areas, plus a popular patio. The menu is extensive, and your choice of 42 dinner entrees will be smoothly served by tuxedoed waiters. You'll also find a lavish dessert menu and many vintage wines.

NORMANDY FRENCH 18
RESTAURANT

1515 Madison Street
(at East Colfax Avenue)
Denver, CO
(303) 321-3311

French

F ★ ★ ★ ½
S ★ ★ ★ ½
A ★ ★ ★
P ★ ★ ★

Good taste in dress required
Valet and lot parking
All major credit cards
Full bar
Reservations recommended

Lunch: Tues.-Sat. 11:30AM-2:00PM
Dinner: Tues.-Sun. 5:00PM-10:30PM
          Closed Monday

You'll find red checkered tablecloths and fresh flowers adding to the rustic French Country Inn atmosphere at the Normandy. Hospitality, cuisine, service, and wines emulate fine European restaurants. Escalopes de Veaux "Marie Antoinette" is among the menu highlights.

PALACE ARMS   22

321 17th Street
Denver, CO
(303) 297-3111

Continental

F ★ ★ ★ ½
S ★ ★ ★ ½
A ★ ★ ★ ½
P ★ ★ ★ ½

Jacket and tie required
Lot parking
All major credit cards
Full bar
Reservations required

Lunch: Mon.-Fri. 11:30AM-2:00PM
Dinner: Nightly 6:00PM-10:00PM

The consistent quality of the gourmet cuisine served here has earned many awards for this renowned establishment. The historical décor is rich with 19th century antiques. The menu is graced with such specialties as Rocky Mountain rainbow trout and succulent prime rib.

PIERRE'S QUORUM   17

233 East Colfax (at Grant)
Denver, CO
(303) 861-8686

French

F ★ ★ ★
S ★ ★ ★ ★
A ★ ★ ★
P ★ ★ ★ ½

Jacket required
Valet and lot parking
All major credit cards
Full bar
Reservations recommended

Lunch: Mon.-Fri. 11:30AM-2:00PM
Dinner: Mon.-Sat. 5:30PM-10:30PM
          Closed Sunday

Owner and host, Pierre Wolfe, has offered diners warm hospitality in an intimate, elegant setting for the past 25 years. His efforts have garnered many awards. You'll find Veal St. Jacques, Monk fish, swordfish, rack of lamb, and Steak Diane among the specialties of the house.

THE SAGE RESTAURANT   11

Oxford Hotel
1600 17th Street
Denver, CO
(303) 628-5400/628-5533

American

F ★ ★ ★ ½
S ★ ★ ★ ½
A ★ ★ ★
P ★ ★ ★

No dress restrictions
Valet, lot, and street parking
All major credit cards
Full bar
Reservations recommended

Breakfast: Mon.-Fri. 6:30AM-10:30AM
Lunch: Daily 11:00AM-2:00PM
Dinner: Nightly 5:30PM-10:30PM

A resplendent Victorian setting and impeccable service make dining at The Sage reminiscent of the grandeur of a bygone era. The new American cuisine includes a daily pasta selection, veal, game hen, steaks, prime rib, and a bevy of interesting seafood dishes.

SAN MARCO ROOM 23

The Brown Palace Hotel
321 17th Street
Denver, CO
(303) 297-3111

Continental

F	★	★	★	½
S	★	★	★	½
A	★	★	★	½
P	★	★	★	½

Jacket and tie required
on Fri. & Sat. nights
Valet and lot parking
All major credit cards
Full bar
Reservations required

Breakfast: Daily 6:30AM-11:00AM
Lunch: Daily 11:30AM-2:00PM
Dinner: Mon.-Thurs. 6:00PM-10:00PM
Fri. & Sat. 6:30PM-10:30PM

This popular and prestigious Brown Palace Hotel dining room tempts patrons with a wide range of continental classics that are well prepared and adroitly served. Live big band music on Friday and Saturday nights makes the pleasant tradition of a dinner-dancing evening a memorable reality.

TANTE LOUISE 20

4900 East Colfax
Denver, CO
(303) 355-4488

French

F	★	★	★	★
S	★	★	★	½
A	★	★	★	½
P	★	★	★	

No dress restrictions
Street parking
All major credit cards
Full bar
Reservations required

Lunch: Mon.-Fri. 11:30AM-2:00PM
Dinner: Mon.-Sat. 5:30PM-10:30PM
Closed Sunday

Your choice of several intimate, well decorated dining rooms helps make dining here a special experience. Owner Corky Douglass and his staff use freshest ingredients and an innovative approach to food preparation.

WELLSHIRE INN 31

3333 South Colorado Boulevard
Denver, CO
(303) 759-3333

Continental

F	★	★	★	½
S	★	★	★	½
A	★	★	★	★
P	★	★	★	★

No dress restrictions
Lot parking
All major credit cards
Full bar
Reservations required

Lunch: Mon.-Sat. 11:30AM-2:30PM
Dinner: Mon.-Thurs. 5:30PM-10:00PM
Fri. & Sat. 5:30PM-11:00PM
Sun. 5:30PM-9:30PM
Brunch: Sun. 10:00AM-2:00PM

Housed in a Tudor mansion sited on a golf course, this spacious establishment offers you a verdant view and excellent continental cuisine. Owner Leo Goto maintains high standards, providing you with the luxury of formal dinner service, and such niceties as roses for the ladies.

Detroit

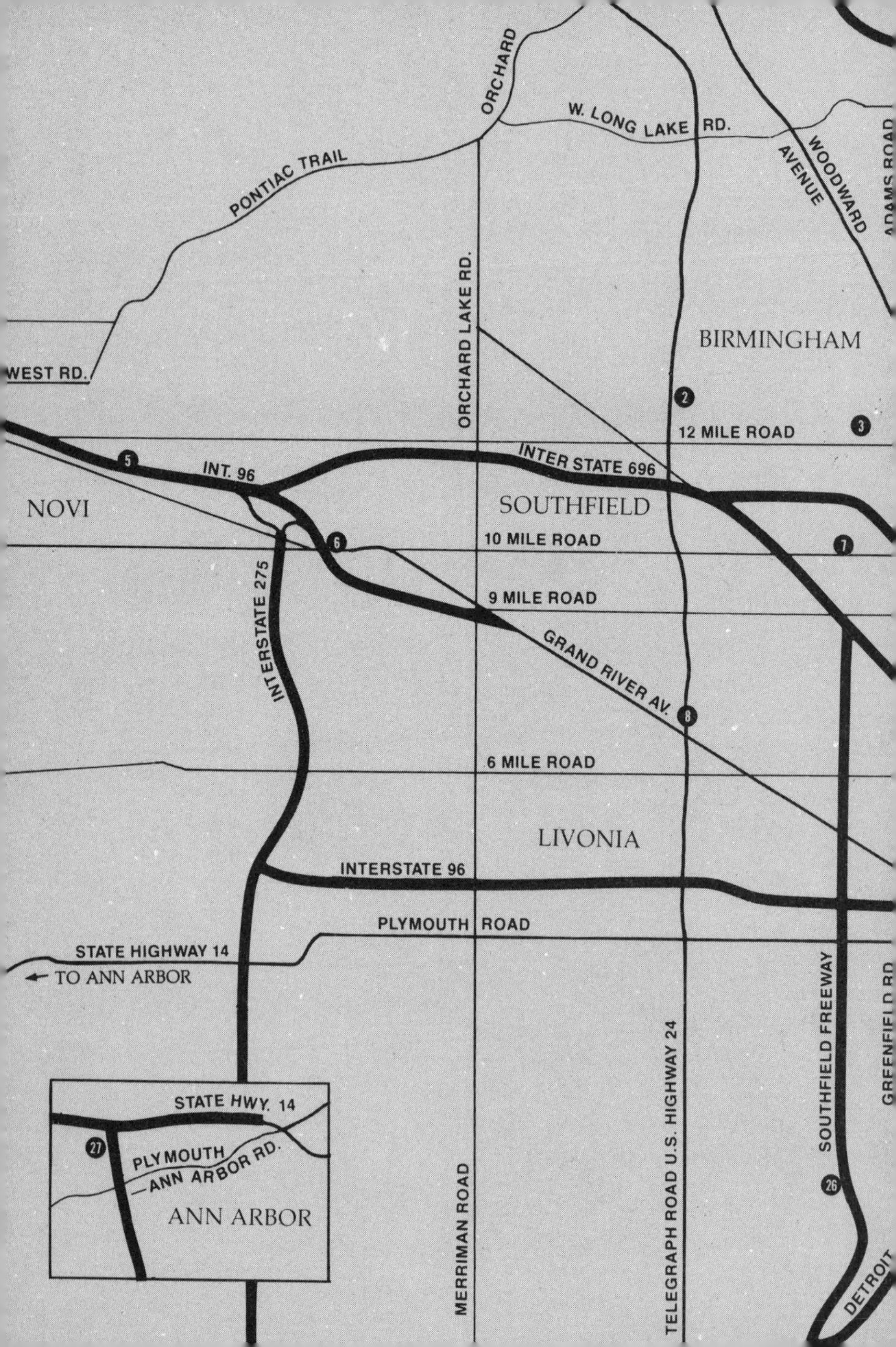

ORCHARD
W. LONG LAKE RD.
PONTIAC TRAIL
WOODWARD AVENUE
ADAMS ROAD
ORCHARD LAKE RD.
BIRMINGHAM
WEST RD.
2
3
12 MILE ROAD
5
INT. 96
INTER STATE 696
NOVI
SOUTHFIELD
6
10 MILE ROAD
7
9 MILE ROAD
INTERSTATE 275
GRAND RIVER AV.
8
6 MILE ROAD
LIVONIA
INTERSTATE 96
PLYMOUTH ROAD
STATE HIGHWAY 14
← TO ANN ARBOR
STATE HWY. 14
27
PLYMOUTH
—ANN ARBOR RD.
ANN ARBOR
MERRIMAN ROAD
TELEGRAPH ROAD U.S. HIGHWAY 24
SOUTHFIELD FREEWAY
GREENFIELD RD
26
DETROIT

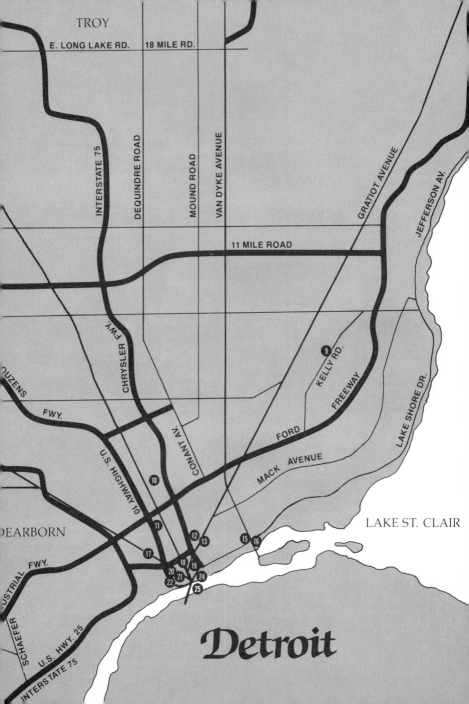

AH WOK   6

41563 West 10 Mile Road
Novi, MI
(313) 349-9260

Chinese

F ★ ★ ★ ½
S ★ ★ ★
A ★ ★ ½
P ★ ★ ½

Good taste in dress required
Lot parking
All major credit cards
Full bar
Reservations required

Lunch/
Dinner: Mon.-Thurs. 11:00AM-9:30PM
          Fri. & Sat. 11:00AM-11:30PM
          Sun. 12:00PM-9:30PM

The décor at Ah Wok is low-key with subtle Oriental touches. In this comfortable atmosphere gourmet Cantonese cuisine highlights the menu with specialties such as Singapore rice noodles, rainbow lobster, Mongolian beef, and Peking Duck. Mandarin and Szechwan dishes are also available.

ALDO'S   9

19143 Kelly Road
Detroit, MI
(313) 839-2150

Italian

F ★ ★ ★ ½
S ★ ★ ★ ½
A ★ ★ ½
P ★ ★ ★

Good taste in dress required
Lot and street parking
Credit cards not accepted
Full bar
Reservations required

Dinner: Tues.-Sat. 5:00PM-10:00PM
          Sun. 4:00PM-10:00PM

Chef/owner Aldo Ottaviani offers you traditional Northern Italian cuisine prepared with all fresh ingredients, in his spacious, homey restaurant. Meat is cut to order, pasta is homemade. Veal dishes are a specialty, steaks and chops are also featured.

CARL'S CHOP HOUSE   17

3020 Grand River
Detroit, MI
(313) 833-0700/831-9749

American

F ★ ★ ★ ½
S ★ ★ ★ ½
A ★ ★ ★ ½
P ★ ★ ★

Good taste in dress required
Valet parking
All major credit cards
Full bar
Reservations recommended

Lunch/
Dinner: Daily 11:30AM-1:00AM

For more than half a century, Carl Rosenfield's Chop House has been dispensing warm hospitality and Paul Bunyan-sized portions of hearty fare to a loyal clientele. Steaks, chops, prime rib, and seafood are the house specialties that earn rave reviews from customers.

CAUCUS CLUB   20

150 West Congress
Detroit, MI
(313) 965-4970

American/Continental

F ★ ★ ★ ½
S ★ ★ ★ ½
A ★ ★ ★ ½
P ★ ★ ★ ★

Jacket and tie required at dinner, no jeans
Valet parking for dinner
All major credit cards
Full bar
Reservations required

Lunch/
Dinner: Mon. 11:00AM-7:00PM
Tues.-Fri. 11:00AM-1:00AM
Sat. 5:00PM-1:00AM
Closed Sunday

A bastion of businessmen, with a relaxed, clublike atmosphere, the Caucus Club is decorated with a toby mug collection, fine paintings, and objets d'art. The menu features grilled fresh fish and meats; marinated baby back ribs and a heartwarming chili are noteworthy specialties of the house.

THE GANDY DANCER 27

401 Depot Street
Ann Arbor, MI
(313) 769-0592

Seafood

F ★ ★ ★ ½
S ★ ★ ★ ½
A ★ ★ ★
P ★ ★ ★

No dress restrictions
Lot and street parking
AE, DC, MC, V
Full bar
Reservations not required

Lunch: Mon.-Fri. 11:30AM-3:00PM
Dinner: Mon.-Thurs. 5:00PM-11:00PM
Fri. & Sat. 5:00PM-12:00AM
Sun. 3:00PM-10:00PM

A Michigan Central Railroad station, built in 1886, and renovated in 1971 to serve as a restaurant is the home of The Gandy Dancer. The menu may offer you a choice of as many as 16 different seafood dishes, prepared with fresh water and salt water fish, flown in daily.

THE GOLDEN MUSHROOM 7

18100 West Ten Mile Road
Southfield, MI
(313) 559-4230

Continental

F ★ ★ ★ ½
S ★ ★ ★ ½
A ★ ★ ★
P ★ ★ ★

Jacket and tie required
Valet and lot parking
All major credit cards
Full bar
Reservations required

Lunch/
Dinner: Mon.-Thurs. 11:30AM-11:00PM
Fri. & Sat. 11:30AM-12:00AM
Closed Sunday

An enchanted rendevous, set in a natural woodland, The Golden Mushroom is popular with the media as well as with romantic duos. Master Chef Milos Cihelka produces magic daily specials including fresh fish, wild game, and veal dishes. The wine list is excellent.

JACQUES SEAFOOD 2

30100 Telegraph Road
Bingham Farms, MI
(313) 642-1373

Continental

F ★ ★ ★ ½
S ★ ★ ★ ½
A ★ ★ ★
P ★ ★ ★

Jacket and tie required
Valet parking
AE, DC, MC, V
Full bar
Reservations recommended

Lunch/
Dinner: Mon.-Fri. 11:00AM-11:00PM
          Sat. 6:00PM-11:00PM
          Closed Sunday

Impressive and elegant, with French antique furnishings, a well planted spacious atrium, and a romantic ambiance, you can look forward to a rewarding experience when you visit here. Seafood dominates the menu, but there are also many well prepared continental entrées.

JOE MUER'S   12

2000 Gratiot Avenue
Detroit, MI
(313) 567-1088

Seafood

F ★ ★ ★ ½
S ★ ★ ★ ½
A ★ ★ ★
P ★ ★ ★

Jacket and tie required
Valet parking
AE, DC, MC, V
Full bar
Reservations not required

Lunch/
Dinner: Mon.-Thurs. 11:15AM-10:00PM
          Fri. 11:15AM-10:30PM
          Sat. 5:00PM-11:00PM
          Closed Sunday

Restaurateur Joe Muer proudly states that every item placed on a diner's plate is fresh at this popular 50-year-old Detroit dining institution. The atmosphere is clublike, and the assortment of seafood reflects seasonal availability from the markets of the world.

LA ROTISSERIE   26

Hyatt Regency Hotel
Fairlane Town Center
Dearborn, MI
(313) 593-1234

Continental

F ★ ★ ★ ½
S ★ ★ ★ ½
A ★ ★ ★ ½
P ★ ★ ★ ½

Jacket required, no blue jeans
Valet and lot parking
All major credit cards
Full bar
Reservations required

Dinner: Mon.-Sat. 6:00PM-10:30PM
          Closed Sunday

This elegant showplace restaurant specializes in roast duckling prepared six diffcrnt ways. You are also offered a selection of veal, lamb, beef, and Chinese dishes and two daily specials ranging from rack of veal, to venison, to swordfish.

LELLI'S   10

7618 Woodward Avenue
Detroit, MI
(313) 871-1590

Italian

F ★ ★ ★ ½
S ★ ★ ★ ½
A ★ ★ ★ ½
P ★ ★ ½

Good taste in dress required
Valet parking
All major credit cards
Full bar
Reservations required

Lunch/
Dinner: Mon.-Fri. 11:00AM-10:00PM
          Sat. 11:00AM-11:00PM
          Closed Sunday

A huge old home, given a charming Mediterranean flavor, has housed this family-owned restaurant since 1939. Mike Lelli continues this success story offering heaping plates of homemade pastas with tantalizing sauces, and generous portions of beautifully prepared prime meats.

LONDON CHOP HOUSE   22

155 West Congress
Detroit, MI
(313) 962-6735

American/Continental

F ★ ★ ★ ★
S ★ ★ ★ ★
A ★ ★ ★ ★
P ★ ★ ★ ★

Jacket and tie required
Valet parking for dinner
All major credit cards
Full bar
Reservations required

Lunch/
Dinner: Mon.-Sat. 11:00AM-2:00AM
           Closed Sunday

A favorite haunt of Detroit's epicures, the London Chop House has an aura of elegant informality and a clublike following of food devotees. Master chef Jimmy Schmidt adds contemporary touches to the distinguished cuisine with emphasis on seafood and aged prime meat dishes.

MARIO'S   11

4222 Second Avenue
Detroit, MI
(313) 833-9425

Italian

F ★ ★ ★ ½
S ★ ★ ★ ½
A ★ ★ ★
P ★ ★ ★ ½

Good taste in dress required
Valet parking
All major credit cards
Full bar
Reservations not required

Lunch/
Dinner: Mon.-Fri. 11:30AM-12:00AM
           Sat. & Sun. 4:00PM-12:00AM

Mario's has been purveying Italian cuisine in the same location for 35 years, where fireside dining is an integral part of the warm congenial atmosphere. Flaming drinks and desserts are spectacular.

THE MONEY TREE   25

333 West Fort Street
Detroit, MI
(313) 961-2445

French/Continental

F ★ ★ ★ ½
S ★ ★ ★ ½
A ★ ★ ★ ½
P ★ ★ ★ ½

Jacket and tie required
Lot parking
All major credit cards
Full bar
Reservations required

Lunch: Mon.-Fri. 11:30AM-2:30PM
Dinner: Tues.-Wed. 6:00PM-9:00PM
           Thurs. 5:30PM-9:00PM
           Fri. & Sat. 5:30PM-10:00PM
           Closed Sunday

In a Parisian mode, this gourmet favorite has an open, airy feeling, and offers a petite outdoor café for summer dining. The nouvelle cuisine offered here adds an exciting new dimension to innovative cookery. Luncheon salads, crêpes, and quiche are excellent—dinner entrées are diverse and dramatic.

NEW HELLAS CAFÉ   19

583 Monroe Street
Detroit, MI
(313) 961-5544

Greek

F ★ ★ ★ ½
S ★ ★ ★ ½
A ★ ★ ★
P ★ ★

Good taste in dress required
Lot parking
All major credit cards
Full bar
Reservations required

Lunch/
Dinner: Sun. Thurs. 11:00AM-2:00AM
         Fri. & Sat. 11:00AM-3:00AM

This family owned restaurant has been offering classic Greek cuisine to enthusiastic
customers since 1901. Owner Gus Anton
continues this tradition with undiminished zest and zeal. A warm, casual,
friendly place to enjoy rich moussaka,
lamb and rice entrées, spinach pie, or any
of a host of other savory specialties.

PONTCHARTRAIN 18
WINE CELLARS

234 West Larned
Detroit, MI
(313) 963-1785

Continental

F ★ ★ ★ ½
S ★ ★ ★ ½
A ★ ★ ★ ½
P ★ ★ ★ ½

Jacket required at dinner
Valet parking for dinner
AE, DC, MC, V
Beer/Wine
Reservations recommended

Lunch: Mon-Sat. 11:30AM-2:30PM
Dinner: Mon.-Sat. 5:30PM-9:30PM
         Closed Sunday

This dimly lit, romantic bistro, opened in
1935, has attracted a large and loyal following who appreciate the fine service,
good wine list, and award-winning food.
Specialties include Escargots de Bourgogne, Gazpacho, Gigot D'Agneau, Veal
Cordon Bleu, and Braised Sweetbreads.

RAPHAEL'S 5

Sheraton-Oaks Hotel
27000 Sheraton Drive
Novi, MI
(313) 348-5000/348-5555

French

F ★ ★ ★ ½
S ★ ★ ★ ½
A ★ ★ ★
P ★ ★ ★ ★

Jacket and tie required
Valet parking
All major credit cards
Full bar
Reservations required

Dinner: Tues.-Sat. 5:00PM-1:00AM
         Closed Sunday and Monday

Impressively plush, this intimate dining
spot concentrates on creative food preparation and presentation. Raphael's sets
high standards for quality, and emphasizes innovative entrées such as molasses-
marinated duck breasts prepared in game
stock with kiwi and Chambord.

RESTAURANT DUGLASS 3

29269 Southfield Road
Southfield, MI
(313) 424-9244

French

F ★ ★ ★ ½
S ★ ★ ★ ½
A ★ ★ ★ ½
P ★ ★ ★ ½

Jacket and tie required
Valet parking
AE, DC, MC, V
Full bar
Reservations required

Lunch: Tues.-Fri. 11:00AM-2:00PM
Dinner: Mon.-Sat. 6:00PM-10:00PM
         Closed Sunday

Owner/chef Duglass' ode to the good life includes crystal chandeliers, bronze sculptures, luxuriant plants, music, and such special touches as fresh violets on each table in spring. The daily changing menu is chef's choice and reflects innovative preparation of seasonal ingredients.

THE ROYAL EAGLE   16

1415 Parker
Detroit, MI
(313) 331-8088

Polish

F ★ ★ ★ ½
S ★ ★ ★ ½
A ★ ★ ★
P ★ ★ ★

Good taste in dress required
Lot parking
CB, DC, MC, V
Full bar
Reservations required

Dinner: Wed.-Sat. 5:00PM-10:00PM
           Sun. 4:00PM-8:00PM
           Closed Monday and Tuesday

The ambiance is European of the 1930s era, with antiques and memorabilia lending authenticity, at this romantic dining spot. The cuisine is Eastern European, with emphasis on Polish specialties such as Veal Paprikas, Beef Polonaise, and roast duck.

SHEIK RESTAURANT   13

316 East Lafayette Street
Detroit, MI
(313) 964-8441

Lebanese

F ★ ★ ★ ½
S ★ ★ ★ ½
A ★ ★ ★
P ★ ★

No dress restrictions
Lot and street parking
MC, V
Full bar
Reservations not required

Lunch/
Dinner: Tues.-Fri. 11:00AM-10:00PM
           Sat. 4:00PM-11:00PM
           Sun. 3:00PM-10:00PM
           Closed Monday

The Sheik is a family restaurant started by owner Esther Michael's father in 1923. It is warm, friendly, exhuberant, and the winner of international awards. Lamb, prepared some 20 different ways, highlights the menu which also includes an excellent assortment of other Lebanese foods.

THE SUMMIT   24

Westin Hotel
Renaissance Center
Detroit, MI
(313) 568-8600

American

F ★ ★ ★ ½
S ★ ★ ★ ½
A ★ ★ ★
P ★ ★ ★ ½

Good taste in dress required
Lot parking
All major credit cards
Full bar
Reservations required

Lunch: Mon.-Sat. 11:30AM-2:30PM
Dinner: Nightly 5:30PM-10:30PM
Brunch: Sun. 10:30AM-3:00PM

On top of the world's tallest hotel, this revolving restaurant lets you view the U.S., Canada, and the Detroit River from a new perspective, 71 stories high. The ambiance is expansive and elegant, and you'll find an ambitious menu featured here that runs the gamut from Bourbon Street Chicken to Veal Forestière.

TOP OF THE PONTCH 21

Pontchartrain Hotel
2 Washington Boulevard
Detroit, MI
(313) 965-0200

Continental

F ★ ★ ★
S ★ ★ ★
A ★ ★ ★
P ★ ★ ½

Jacket required
Valet parking
All major credit cards
Full bar
Reservations required

Breakfast: Daily 7:00AM-11:30AM
Lunch: Daily 11:30AM-2:30PM
Dinner: Nightly 5:00PM-11:00PM

Lofty ideals in restaurant elegance are exemplified in this large dining room that crowns the Pontchartrain Hotel. The view is fascinating, the décor smart and cosmopolitan, and the dulcet tones of harp music add a touch of romance at the dinner hour. The menu offers a medley of Mediterranean, French, and continental cuisine.

TOPINKA'S 8
COUNTRY HOUSE

24010 West 7 Mile Road
Detroit, MI
(313) 531-9000

American

F ★ ★ ★ ½
S ★ ★ ★ ½
A ★ ★ ★ ½
P ★ ★ ★

Good taste in dress required
Valet parking
All major credit cards
Full bar
Reservations required

Lunch: Daily 11:00AM-4:00PM
Dinner: Nightly from 4:00PM

Enter the magic land of luxurious comfort, with the country house theme enhanced by paintings, and a roaring evening fire. The décor is a rich montage of reds and blacks—casual but elegant in feeling. Traditional American foods are featured including prime rib, for which the house is renowned.

VAN DYKE PLACE 15

649 Van Dyke
Detroit, MI
(313) 821-2620

French

F ★ ★ ★ ½
S ★ ★ ★ ½
A ★ ★ ★ ½
P ★ ★ ★ ★

Jacket and tie required
Valet parking
AE, MC, V
Full bar
Reservations required

Lunch: Mon.-Fri. 11:30AM-2:00PM
Dinner: Mon.-Sat. 6:00PM-9:30PM
          Closed Sunday

Named the best restaurant in Detroit for three consecutive years, Van Dyke Place presents you with an American perspective of French cuisine—French in technique—American in ingenuity. The restored turn-of-the-century townhouse location has a splendid sense of grandeur.

Honolulu

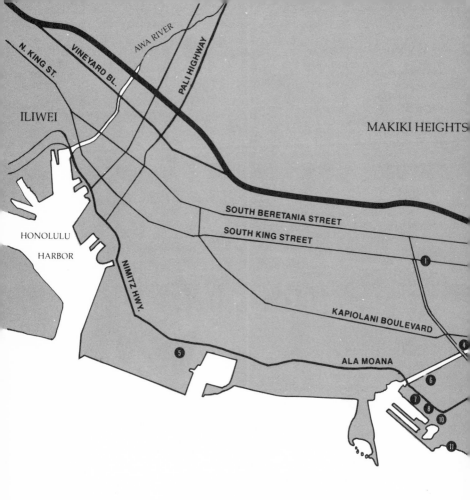

N. KING ST.

VINEYARD BL.

AWA RIVER

PALI HIGHWAY

ILIWEI

MAKIKI HEIGHTS

HONOLULU

HARBOR

SOUTH BERETANIA STREET

SOUTH KING STREET

NIMITZ HWY.

KAPIOLANI BOULEVARD

1

4

5

ALA MOANA

6

7

8

10

11

Honolulu

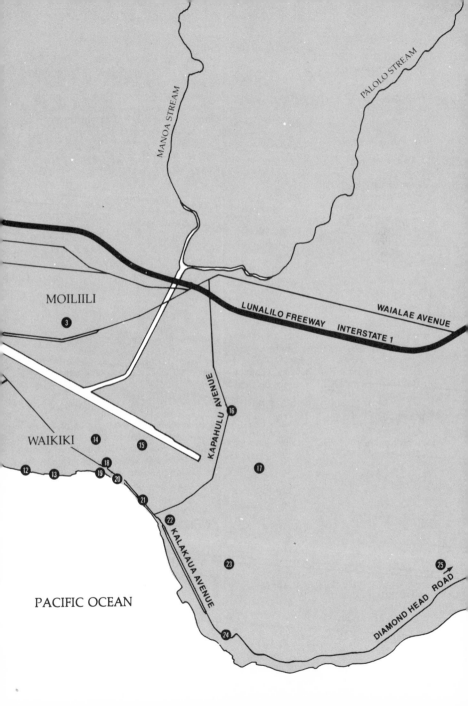

ALFRED'S AT THE 1
CENTURY CENTER

1750 Kalakaua Avenue
Honolulu, HI
(808) 955-5353

French/Continental

F ★ ★ ★ ½
S ★ ★ ★ ½
A ★ ★ ★
P ★ ★ ★ ½

Good taste in dress required
Valet parking
CB, DC, MC, V
Full bar
Reservations recommended

Lunch: Mon.-Fri. 11:00AM-2:00PM
Dinner: Tues.-Sat. 6:00PM-10:00PM
          Closed Sunday

Alfred Vollenweider, owner/chef, has
conjured up the perfect setting for intimate dining at his gourmet establishment.
The luncheon menu includes up to 30 different selections and dinner classics range
from fresh island fish to Emince de Veau
Zurichoise.

BAGWELLS 2424   18

Hyatt Regency Waikiki
2424 Kalakaua Avenue
Honolulu, HI
(808) 922-9292

French

F ★ ★ ★ ★
S ★ ★ ★ ★
A ★ ★ ★ ★
P ★ ★ ★ ★

Dress shirt and slacks for men
Valet, lot, and street parking
All major credit cards
Full bar
Reservations required

Dinner: Mon.-Thurs. 6:00PM-10:00PM
          Fri.-Sun. 6:30PM-10:30PM

In an atmosphere of bronze, velvets and
rosewood, chef Yves Menoret offers
award-winning French cuisine with deft
Polynesian touches. Tempting specialties
include the array of shellfish on ice, red
snapper soup baked in puff pastry, and
sautéed breast of Long Island duck.

THE BISTRO AT   17
DIAMOND HEAD

3058 Monsarrat Avenue
Honolulu, HI
(808) 735-4444

French

F ★ ★ ★ ½
S ★ ★ ★ ½
A ★ ★ ★ ½
P ★ ★ ★

Good taste in dress required
Valet parking
All major credit cards
Full bar
Reservations required

Dinner: Nightly 6:00PM-11:00PM
Late
Supper: Nightly 11:00PM-1:30AM

While the atmosphere is opulent, turn-of-
the-century Parisian, and the mood is private and romantic, The Bistro calls itself a
simple French kitchen with an unpretentious menu and cooking done with a light
hand.

BON APPETIT   11
RESTAURANT

1778 Ala Moana Boulevard
Honolulu, HI
(808) 942-3837

French

F ★ ★ ★ ½
S ★ ★ ★
A ★ ★ ★
P ★ ★ ★

No dress restrictions
Lot parking
All major credit cards
Full bar
Reservations recommended

Dinner: Mon.-Sat. from 5:30PM
Closed Sunday

Guy and Jacqueline Banal, chef/owner and welcoming hostess, have created this intimate gourmet rendezvous featuring "La cuisine du marche," based on what's best and freshest at the market.

CANLIS 7

2100 Kalakaua Avenue
Honolulu, HI
(808) 923-2324

American

F ★ ★ ★ ½
S ★ ★ ★
A ★ ★ ★ ½
P ★ ★ ★ ★

Dress shirt and slacks for men
Valet parking
All major credit cards
Full bar
Reservations recommended

Lunch: Mon.-Fri. 11:30AM-2:30PM
Dinner: Nightly 6:00PM-10:45PM
Late
Menu: Wed.-Sat. 10:45PM-1:30AM

Waterfalls, a koi pond, and lavish use of orchids create a lush tropical setting at Tony Canlis' lovely restaurant. An award winner for 30 years, Kimono-clad waitresses serve you a host of well prepared American specialties.

CHAMPEAUX'S 8

Ilikai Hotel
1777 Ala Moana Boulevard
Honolulu, HI
(808) 949-3811

Continental

F ★ ★ ★ ½
S ★ ★ ★ ★
A ★ ★ ★ ½
P ★ ★ ★ ½

No shorts, slippers, or tank top/T-shirts
Lot parking
All major credit cards
Full bar
Reservations required

Dinner: Nightly 6:00PM-10:00PM
Brunch: Sun. 10:00AM-2:00PM

Champeaux's is perched 30 stories high atop the Ilikai, giving you a sweeping view of Waikiki, Honolulu, and the Pacific Ocean. Daily seafood specials augment the full menu of continental specialties. The gourmet cuisine is well prepared and served with polished finesse.

CHEZ MICHEL 6

Eaton Square
444 Hobron Lane
Honolulu, HI
(808) 955-7866/955-7867

French

F ★ ★ ★ ½
S ★ ★ ★ ★
A ★ ★ ★ ½
P ★ ★ ★ ★

Good taste in dress required
Valet parking
All major credit cards
Full bar
Reservations recommended

Lunch: Mon.-Sat. 11:30AM-3:00PM
Dinner: Nightly 6:00PM-10:00PM

Tucked away in a cloistered garden, the setting at Chez Michel is cool, green, lush, and tropical. Your selections from the classic French menu are prepared to your order and the service is deft and attentive. A carefully selected wine list complements the gourmet cuisine.

HALA TERRACE   25

Kahala Hilton Hotel
5000 Kahala Avenue
Honolulu, HI
(808) 734-2211

Continental/American

F ★ ★ ★ ½
S ★ ★ ★
A ★ ★ ★ ½
P ★ ★ ★

Good taste in dress required
Valet parking
All major credit cards
Full bar
Reservations recommended

Breakfast: Daily 6:30AM-11:00AM
Lunch: Daily 11:30AM-2:45PM
Dinner: Mon.-Sat. 6:30PM-8:00PM
Buffet: Sun. 6:00PM-9:00PM

Opening to the ocean, this bit of tropical paradise adds Hawaiian/Oriental touches to its classic continental/American fare. Papaya is featured in several dishes, as are macadamia nuts and pineapple. The resulting cuisine is richly infused with regional flavors.

HANOHANO ROOM   13

Sheraton Waikiki Hotel
2255 Kalakana Avenue
Honolulu, HI
(808) 922-4422

American/French

F ★ ★ ★
S ★ ★ ★
A ★ ★ ★ ½
P ★ ★ ★ ★

Good taste in dress required
Valet parking
All major credit cards
Full bar
Reservations required

Dinner: Nightly 6:00PM-10:00PM

This imposing dining room sits like a tiara atop the hotel, giving you a brilliant view of the city and Diamond Head. The menu offers you such selections as chateaubriand, double New York lamb chops, catch of the day, and a special Caesar salad.

HY'S STEAK HOUSE   15

2440 Kuhio Avenue
Honolulu, HI
(808) 922-5555

Continental

F ★ ★ ★ ½
S ★ ★ ★ ★
A ★ ★ ★ ½
P ★ ★ ★ ★

No shorts, slippers, tank tops
Valet parking
AE, DC, MC, V
Full bar
Reservations required

Dinner: Nightly from 6:00PM

Tuxedoed waiters provide quiet unobtrusive service in keeping with the dignified, elegant old English decor found in Hy's main dining room. Steak is a specialty, as is rack of lamb cooked over the Keawe, with continental entrées rounding out the menu. Voted one of Hawaii's favorite restaurants in 1984.

JOHN DOMINIS   5

43 Ahui Street
Honolulu, HI
(808) 523-0958

Seafood

F ★ ★ ★ ½
S ★ ★ ★ ½
A ★ ★ ★ ½
P ★ ★ ★ ½

Good taste in dress required
Valet parking
All major credit cards

Full bar
Reservations recommended

Dinner: Nightly 5:30PM-10:30PM

Standing on a promontory overlooking the Ala Moana Harbor and the Pacific this restaurant gives you a parade of boats and seafood galore. Island fish—such as ono, hapuu, opelu are available in season; Maine lobster and Maryland crabs arrive fresh in a near constant stream. The cioppino (a savory seafood stew) is considered unbeatable.

KEO'S THAI CUISINE   16

625 Kapahulu Avenue
Honolulu, HI
(808) 737-8240/737-9250

Thai

F ★ ★ ★
S ★ ★ ★
A ★ ★ ½
P ★ ★

No dress restrictions
Lot parking
AE, MC, V
Full bar
Reservations required

Lunch: Mon.-Fri. 11:00AM-2:00PM
Dinner: Nightly 5:30PM-10:30PM

The restaurant Keo Sananikone has fashioned has a casually elegant garden setting glorified with fresh orchids. You can choose from more than 200 dishes, representing Thai cuisine at its finest, with a special vegetarian menu featuring locally grown produce included.

THE MAILE RESTAURANT   25

Kahala Hilton Hotel
5000 Kahala Avenue
Honolulu, HI
(808) 734-2211

Continental

F ★ ★ ★ ½
S ★ ★ ★ ★
A ★ ★ ★ ½
P ★ ★ ★ ★

Jacket required
Valet parking
All major credit cards
Full bar
Reservations recommended

Dinner: Nightly 6:30PM-9:30PM

A winding stairway lush with orchids leads you to this fairyland restaurant, where the kimona-clad staff makes every diner feel like an honored guest. While the cuisine is continental, the chef adds Oriental seasonings to create such delicacies as Mahi Mahi Caprice, and Roast Duckling Waialae. There is an excellent wine list, and table d'hôte or à la carte service.

MANDARIN PALACE   14

Hotel Miramar
2345 Kuhio Avenue
Honolulu, HI
(808) 926-1110

Chinese

F ★ ★ ★
S ★ ★ ★
A ★ ★ ★
P ★ ★

Good taste in dress required
Garage parking
All major credit cards
Full bar
Reservations recommended

Lunch: Daily 11:00AM-2:00PM
Dinner: Nightly 5:30PM-10:00PM

Dine here in Oriental opulence, surrounded by luxurious appointments and magnificent fresh flower arrangements. Peking Duck is a house specialty, vieing in popularity with Island Pineapple Chicken, Mongolian Lamb, and a succulent beef with sautéed bell pepper entrée.

MATTEO'S 23

364 Seaside Avenue
Honolulu, HI
(808) 922-5551

Italian

F ★ ★ ★ ½
S ★ ★ ★
A ★ ★ ★ ½
P ★ ★ ★

No dress restrictions
Valet parking
All major credit cards
Full bar
Reservations not required

Dinner: Nightly 6:00PM-2:00AM

The savory dishes of Southern Italy are
featured at this spacious, comfortable restaurant. Owner Wanda Fusco offers you
such specialties as shrimp scampi, chicken
à la Wanda, lasagna, and cannelloni. A full
complement of choice veal dishes are also
available.

MICHEL'S AT THE 24
COLONY SURF

2895 Kalakaua Avenue
Honolulu, HI
(808) 923-5751

French/Continental

F ★ ★ ★ ★
S ★ ★ ★ ★
A ★ ★ ★ ★
P ★ ★ ★ ★

Jacket required after 6:00PM
Valet parking
All major credit cards
Full bar
Reservations recommended

Breakfast: Daily 7:00AM-10:00AM
Lunch: Mon.-Fri. 11:30AM-2:30PM
Dinner: Nightly 6:00PM-11:00PM
Brunch: Sun. 11:00AM-2:30PM

Dine in luxurious ease at Michel's, where a
window wall the length of the restaurant
opens to the magnificent seascape. Savor
such specialties as Canard Rôti à
L'Orange, Opakapaka, Longe De Veau
Rôti, and Carré D'Agneau Provencale,
that have garnered illustrious dining
awards for 23 years.

NICK'S FISHMARKET 19

Waikiki Gateway Hotel
2070 Kalakaua Avenue
Honolulu, HI
(808) 955-6333

Seafood

F ★ ★ ★ ★
S ★ ★ ★ ½
A ★ ★ ★ ½
P ★ ★ ★ ½

Good taste in dress required
Valet parking
All major credit cards
Full bar
Reservations recommended

Dinner: Nightly 6:00PM-2:00AM

This plush establishment is decorated
with aquariums, and has a music room
with nightly entertainment. Fresh island
fish is featured, but you'll also find live
Maine lobsters, veal piccata, linguini with
clams, and terrific steaks. The combination Seafood Louis Salad, the wine list,
and the dessert menu all earn rave
reviews.

PROTEA 22

2500 Kuhio Avenue
Honolulu, HI
(808) 922-0811

French/Continental

F ★ ★ ★ ½
S ★ ★ ★
A ★ ★ ★ ½
P ★ ★ ★ ½

Good taste in dress required
Valet parking
All major credit cards
Full bar
Reservations required

Dinner: Nightly 6:00PM-10:00PM

The Protea specializes in cuisine that is expertly prepared tableside, and presented graciously, under the direction of Philip Kopiczko, Maître d'. The décor is lush and exotic; the wine cellar well thought out. Chef Guido Ulmann's baked Ono En Croûte Sauce Choron is one of the culinary masterpieces served here.

SHIP'S TAVERN   20

Surfrider Hotel
2363 Kalakaua Avenue
Honolulu, HI
(808) 922-3111

American

F ★ ★ ★ ½
S ★ ★ ★ ½
A ★ ★ ★ ½
P ★ ★ ★ ½

Good taste in dress required
Valet and lot parking
All major credit cards
Full bar
Reservations recommended

Dinner: Nightly 6:00PM-11:00PM

A sweeping view of Waikiki, and authentic nautical décor lure locals and tourists to this delightful dining spot. You'll find enticing daily specials, live Maine lobster, fresh island prawns, and excellent steaks on the bill of fare. Homemade Molokai bread is another special bonus.

SUMMIT   4

Ala Moana Americana Hotel
410 Atkinson Drive
Honolulu, HI
(808) 955-4811

Continental

F ★ ★ ★ ½
S ★ ★ ★
A ★ ★ ★ ½
P ★ ★ ★

Good taste in dress required, no shorts
Lot parking
All major credit cards
Full bar
Reservations required

Lunch: Mon.-Sat. 11:30AM-2:00PM
          Sun. 10:00AM-2:00PM
Dinner: Mon.-Sun. 6:00PM-10:00PM

Plan an unhurried visit to the Summit to enjoy dining on such specialties as escargot bisque, medallions of veal Oscar, fresh spinach salad, and Longshire lamb chops. The ambiance is pleasant and relaxing, the cuisine worthy of appreciating in a leisurely fashion.

TAHITIAN LANAI   10

1811 Ala Moana Boulevard
Honolulu, HI
(808) 946-6541

Continental/Polynesian

F ★ ★ ★ ½
S ★ ★ ★ ½
A ★ ★ ★ ½
P ★ ★ ★

Good taste in dress required
Valet and lot parking
All major credit cards
Full bar
Reservations recommended

Breakfast/
Lunch/
Dinner: Daily 7:00AM-10:00PM

This unique restaurant offers tropical out-door and thatched hut Hawaiian-style dining in a setting like a bit of "Eden." Breakfasts feature banana muffins, popovers, and Eggs Benedict. The lunch and dinner menu includes a wide range of continental favorites and a good choice of Polynesian specialties.

THE THIRD FLOOR   21

Hawaiian Regent Hotel
2552 Kalakaua Avenue
Honolulu, HI
(808) 922-6611

Continental

F ★ ★ ★ ★
S ★ ★ ★ ★
A ★ ★ ★ ★
P ★ ★ ★ ★

Jacket preferred
Valet parking
All major credit cards
Full bar
Reservations required

Dinner: Nightly 6:30PM-11:00PM

Sandwiched between the Regent's second and fourth floors is one of Hawaii's finest restaurants. Heraldic banners hang from the ceiling and a fountain and small fish pond add to the wonderful feeling. House specialties include medallion of veal Forêt Noire and a succulent rack of spring lamb. There is a groaning pastry cart, and real Irish coffee.

TRATTORIA   12

2168 Kalia Road
Honolulu, HI
(808) 923-8415

Italian

F ★ ★ ★ ½
S ★ ★ ★
A ★ ★ ★
P ★ ★ ★

Good taste in dress required
Valet parking
All major credit cards
Full bar
Reservations recommended

Dinner: Nightly 5:30PM-11:15PM

Frescoed ceilings and walls, an Italian troubadour who sings nightly, and a villa-like setting put you right in the mood for savoring authentic Northern Italian cuisine. You'll find such specialties as Veal Piccata, rack of lamb, Lobster Fra Diavolo, linguine, scampi, and cannelloni included on the menu.

WILLOWS   3

901 Hausten Street
Honolulu, HI
(808) 946-4808

Continental

F ★ ★ ★ ½
S ★ ★ ★
A ★ ★ ★ ½
P ★ ★ ★

No shorts, tank tops, or thongs
Valet parking
All major credit cards
Full bar
Reservations required

Lunch: Daily 11:30AM-1:30PM
Dinner: Nightly 6:00PM-9:00PM

For 40 years this enchanting island restaurant with its thatched pavilions, tropical plantings, waterfalls, pond, palms, and weeping willow trees has symbolized "Hawaii" to tourists. The Poi Dinner served here is a not-to-be-missed celebration of island bounty. Equally famed for chicken and shrimp curry and sky-high coconut cream or lemon meringue pie.

Houston

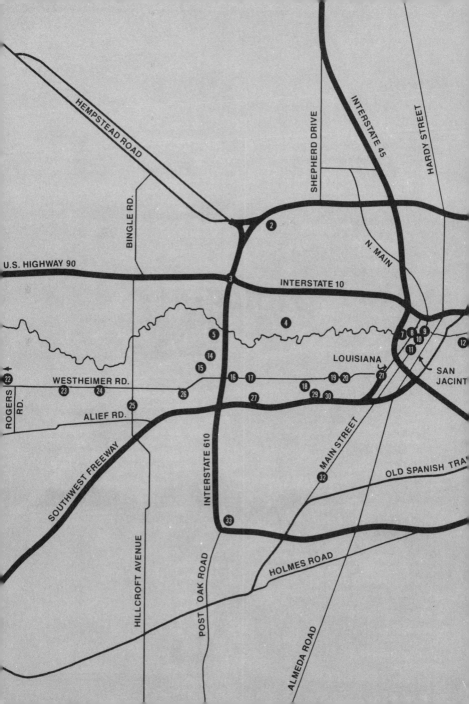

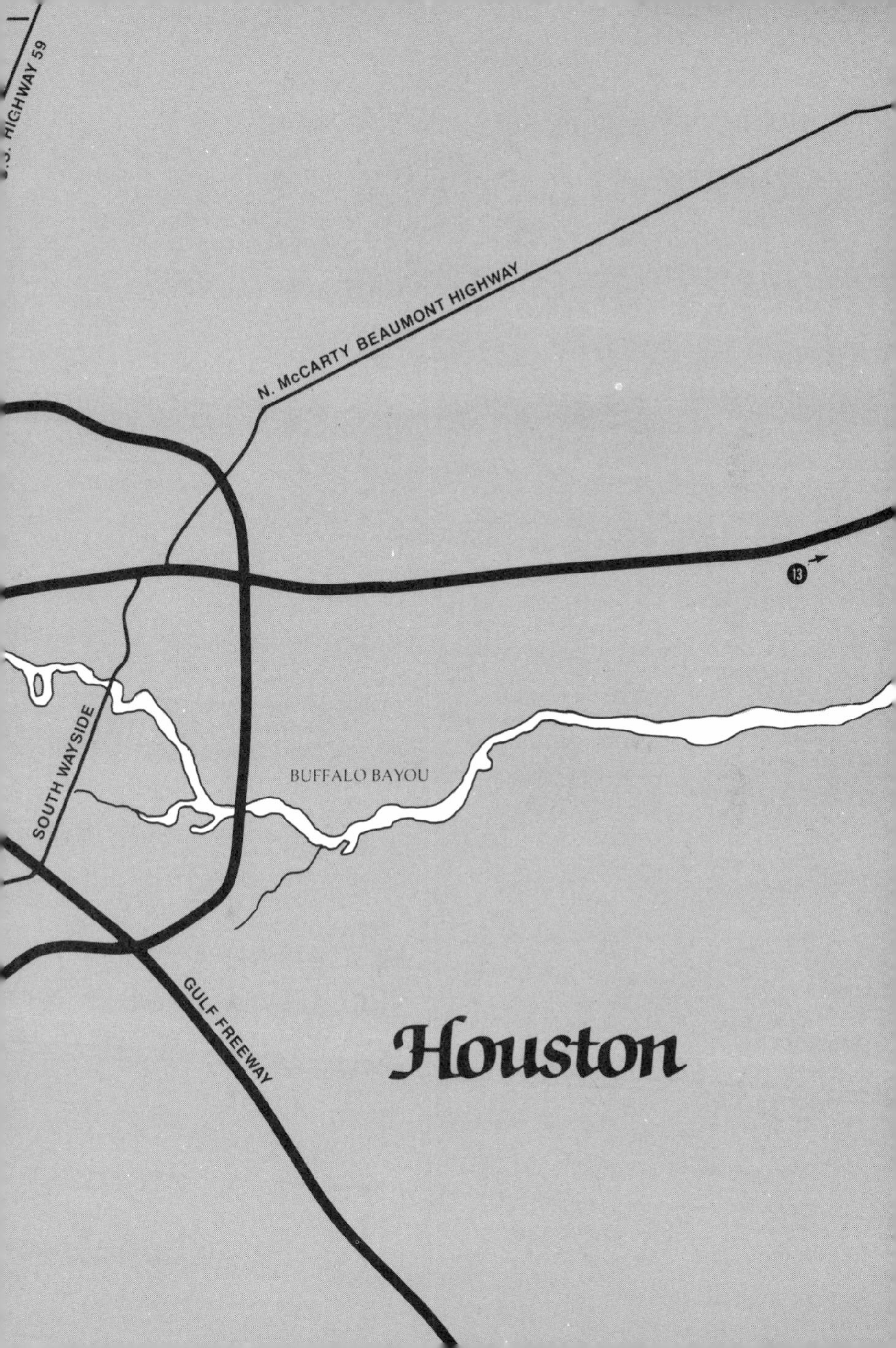

HIGHWAY 59
N. McCARTY BEAUMONT HIGHWAY
13
SOUTH WAYSIDE
BUFFALO BAYOU
GULF FREEWAY
Houston

BRENNAN'S   21

3300 Smith Street
Houston, TX
(713) 522-9711

Creole/Seafood

F ★ ★ ★ ½
S ★ ★ ★ ½
A ★ ★ ★
P ★ ★ ★

Jacket required
Valet parking
All major credit cards
Full bar
Reservations required

Lunch: Mon.-Fri. 11:30AM-2:30PM
Dinner: Nightly 6:00PM-10:00PM
Brunch: Sat. & Sun. 10:30AM-2:30PM

This august establishment occupies one of
Houston's oldest buildings and overlooks
a New Orleans style courtyard umbrellaed
in summer with green leafy trees. The
mood is casual elegance; the food based on
rich Creole traditions, but lightened with a
host of American entrées featuring fresh
regional ingredients.

BROWNSTONE   29

2736 Virginia
Houston, TX
(713) 528-2844

American

F ★ ★ ★
S ★ ★ ★
A ★ ★ ★
P ★ ★

Good taste in dress required
Lot and street parking
All major credit cards
Full bar
Reservations not required

Lunch: Mon.-Fri. 11:30AM-2:00PM
Dinner: Mon.-Sun. 6:00PM-12:00AM
Brunch: Sun. 11:00AM-3:00PM

A collection of antiques from around the
world lends a sense of eclectic elegance to
The Brownstone, which offers you dining
room, courtyard, and poolside seating.
The varied menu runs the gamut from
Beef Wellington to tasty gumbo.

CAFÉ MUSTACHE   16

4702 Westheimer
Houston, TX
(713) 621-6281

French/Continental

F ★ ★ ★
S ★ ★ ★
A ★ ★ ★
P ★ ★ ★

Good taste in dress required
Valet and lot parking
All major credit cards
Full bar
Reservations required

Lunch: Mon.-Sat. 11:00AM-2:30PM
Dinner: Mon.-Thurs. 6:00PM-10:30PM
         Fri. & Sat. 6:00PM-11:00PM
Brunch: Sun. 11:00AM-3:00PM

When you feel a need to unwind and take
life easy, pay a visit to this casual bistro
with its French café ambiance. There's
even a plant-filled deck for leisurely al
fresca summer dining. The menu is quite
diverse, including veal roulade with a
pine-nut stuffing, and red snapper in a
peppery sauce à la Vera Cruz.

THE CARLYLE   15
RESTAURANT

5430 Westheimer
Houston, TX
(713) 871-1534

Continental/French

F ★ ★ ★ ½
S ★ ★ ★ ½
A ★ ★ ★ ½
P ★ ★ ★ ½

Jacket and tie required
Valet parking
All major credit cards
Full bar
Reservations required

Lunch: Mon.-Fri. 11:30AM-2:00PM
Dinner: Mon.-Thurs. 6:00PM-11:00PM
Fri. & Sat. 6:00PM-12:00AM
Closed Sunday

Enter the world of contemporary splendor and dine surrounded by marble and mirrors — silk wall coverings and silver accents. Oysters Rockefeller, rack of lamb, seafood crêpes, roast duckling in ginger, veal filets with morels, and steamed salmon with chardonay sauce are highlights of the menu.

CHARLEY'S 517   7

517 Louisiana
Houston, TX
(713) 224-4438

Continental/American

F ★ ★ ★ ½
S ★ ★ ★ ½
A ★ ★ ★ ½
P ★ ★ ★ ½

Jacket required
Valet parking
All major credit cards
Full bar
Reservations required

Lunch: Mon.-Fri. 11:30AM-2:00PM
Dinner: Mon.-Sat. 6:00PM-11:00PM
Closed Sunday

You'll find Charley's 517 firmly entrenched in the heart of the theater district, and in the hearts of Houston connoisseurs. The epitome of understated elegance, where distinguished chef Amy Ferguson offers a seasonally changing menu of continental classics tempered with innovative American ingredients.

D'AMICO'S   18

2407 Westheimer
Houston, TX
(713) 524-5551

Italian

F ★ ★ ★ ½
S ★ ★ ★
A ★ ★ ★
P ★ ★ ★

Jacket preferred
Lot parking
All major credit cards
Full bar
Reservations required

Lunch: Mon.-Fri. 11:30AM-2:00PM
Dinner: Mon.-Sat. 6:00PM-11:15PM
Closed Sunday

Tony Rao's romantic restaurant continues to lure a loyal clientele of aficionados of fresh pastas and Northern Italian cuisine. A not-to-be-missed specialty is Trout Toto (fresh lump crabmeat over filet of trout, drizzled with lemon butter sauce).

DELMONICO'S   26

Westin Galleria
5060 West Alabama
Houston, TX
(713) 960-8100

Continental

F ★ ★ ★
S ★ ★ ★
A ★ ★ ★
P ★ ★ ★

Jacket required
Lot parking
All major credit cards
Full bar
Reservations required

Lunch: Mon.-Fri. 11:30AM-2:00PM
Dinner: Sun.-Thurs. 6:00PM-11:00PM
Fri.-Sat. 6:00PM-11:30PM

The setting here is suave and elegant with stained glass windows, brass chandeliers, European antiques, candlelight, and flowers. The cuisine is strictly continental and the service professional. There is piano music in the evening, and 18 vintage wines that may be ordered by the glass.

FOULARD'S   24

10001 Westheimer
Houston, TX
(713) 789-1661

French/Continental

F ★ ★ ★ ½
S ★ ★ ★
A ★ ★ ★
P ★ ★ ★ ½

Good taste in dress required
Lot parking
All major credit cards
Full bar
Reservations recommended

Lunch: Daily 11:00AM-2:30PM
Dinner: Nightly 6:00PM-12:00AM

Country side décor and a warm atmosphere endear Foulard's to the hearts of Houston diners. The house specializes in fresh seafood from the Gulf, steaks, veal, Duckling under Presse, and stuffed Cornish hen and quail. Try the flambé desserts — they're spectacular.

THE GREAT CARUSO   23

10001 Westheimer
In the Carillon Center
Houston, TX
(713) 780-4900

Continental

F ★ ★ ★
S ★ ★ ★
A ★ ★ ★ ½
P ★ ★ ½

Jacket and tie required
Valet parking
All major credit cards
Full bar
Reservations required

Dinner: Nightly 6:00PM-2:00AM

Savants of the opera and of fine food dote on Ernest & Spero Criezis' restaurant, with its spectacular opera-house décor and continuous Broadway and operatic musical entertainment. You'll quickly discern that prime beef and milk fed veal play an important role in the beautifully prepared cuisine.

HARRY'S KENYA   10

1160 Smith at Dallas (Downtown)
Houston, TX
(713) 650-1980

Continental

F ★ ★ ★ ½
S ★ ★ ★ ½
A ★ ★ ★ ½
P ★ ★ ★ ½

Jacket required
Valet parking at dinner
Garage parking at lunch
All major credit cards
Full bar
Reservations required

Lunch: Mon.-Fri. 11:00AM-2:00PM
Dinner: Mon.- Sat. 6:00PM-11:00PM
          Closed Sunday

Take a gourmet's safari to Harry's Kenya where hunting trophies displayed in a club-like atmosphere, distinguish the décor. The menu offers a comprehensive selection of continental dishes; wildlife specialties are a feature of the house.

HUGO'S WINDOW BOX 8

Hyatt Regency Hotel
1200 Louisiana Street
Houston, TX
(713) 654-1234

French

F ★ ★ ★ ½
S ★ ★ ★ ½
A ★ ★ ★ ½
P ★ ★ ★ ½

Jacket required
Valet parking
All major credit cards
Full bar
Reservations required

Lunch: Daily 11:30AM-1:30PM
Dinner: Nightly 6:00PM-10:00PM

This romantic, intimate supper club overlooks a plant-filled atrium, and provides you with live music and a dance floor, in addition to gourmet quality French cuisine. This establishment has won many awards for its food and its ambiance.

KAPHAN'S 32

7900 South Main at Kirby
Houston, TX
(713) 668-0491

American

F ★ ★ ★
S ★ ★ ★
A ★ ★ ½
P ★ ★ ½

No dress restrictions
Valet and lot parking
All major credit cards
Full bar
Reservations not required

Lunch/
Dinner: Thurs.-Tues. 11:30AM-11:30PM
          Closed Wednesday

Established in 1927, Kaphan's is a revered institution with Houston's seafood devotees. Here you can feast hearty on such choice viands as Louisiana crawfish, lobsters, oysters dichotomy, crabmeat, redfish, and Gulf shrimp and trout. Beef and charbroiled chicken are also available.

LA COLOMBE D'OR 20

3410 Montrose Boulevard
Houston, TX
(713) 524-7999

French

F ★ ★ ★ ½
S ★ ★ ★ ½
A ★ ★ ★ ½
P ★ ★ ★ ½

Jacket required
Valet and lot parking
All major credit cards
Full bar
Reservations required

Dinner: Mon.-Fri. 7:00PM-11:00PM
          Sat. 7:00PM-12:00AM
          Closed Sunday

You'll find La Colombe D'Or occupying the ground floor of a unique small hotel fashioned after a French chateau. The décor is European, elegant and prestigious. Here owner Steven Zimmerman offers exquisitely prepared French cuisine to the delight of Houston's most discerning diners.

LA RESERVE 5

Inn on the Park
Four Riverway
Houston, TX
(713) 871-8181

Continental

F ★ ★ ★ ½
S ★ ★ ★ ½
A ★ ★ ★
P ★ ★ ★ ½

Jacket required at lunch
Jacket and tie required at dinner
Valet parking
All major credit cards
Full bar
Reservations required

Lunch: Mon.-Fri. 11:00AM-2:00PM
Dinner: Mon.-Sat. 6:30PM-10:30PM
Closed Sunday

La Reserve is an elegantly appointed, award-winning restaurant featuring a daily changing menu and an extensive wine list. Specialties include Pheasant Mousse in Blueberry Vinegar Sauce and Tian of Lamb with Truffle Butter Sauce.

LA TOUR D'ARGENT 2

2011 Ella Boulevard
Houston, TX
(713) 864-9864

French

F ★ ★ ★ ½
S ★ ★ ★ ½
A ★ ★ ★ ½
P ★ ★ ★ ½

Jacket and tie required
Valet parking
All major credit cards
Full bar
Reservations required

Lunch: Mon.-Fri. 11:30AM-2:00PM
Dinner: Mon.-Sat. 6:30PM-11:00PM
Closed Sunday

A heritage log cabin with the ambiance of "old world" Europe is the home of La Tour d'Argent, winner of many prestigious awards. A harpist provides melodic accompaniment as you dine on such French specialties as chateaubriand, or Carré d'Agneau Persille.

LE RESTAURANT 9
DE FRANCE

Hotel Méridien
400 Dallas Street
Houston, TX
(713) 759-0202

French

F ★ ★ ★ ½
S ★ ★ ★
A ★ ★ ★ ½
P ★ ★ ★ ½

Jacket required
Valet parking
All major credit cards
Full bar
Reservations required

Lunch: Mon.-Fri. 11:00AM-2:00PM
Dinner: Mon.-Sat. 6:00PM-10:00PM
Closed Sunday

Reflecting the grand Gallic image of the hotel in which it is ensconced, this internationally acclaimed restaurant has built its reputation with impeccably prepared nouvelle French cuisine. Noted house specialties include an outstanding lobster salad, and Le Leuillete de Pomme Reinette (a heavenly apple tart).

MAGNOLIA BAR & GRILL 30

6000 Richmond Avenue
Houston, TX
(713) 781-6207

Cajun

F ★ ★ ★
S ★ ★ ★
A ★ ★ ½
P ★ ★ ½

Good taste in dress required
Lot parking
All major credit cards
Full bar
Reservations not required

Lunch/
Dinner: Mon.-Thurs 11:00AM-11:00PM
        Fri. & Sat. 11:00AM-12:00AM
        Sun. 10:30AM-10:00PM

Revel in the sumptuous atmosphere of old
New Orleans in this handsome dining
spot with its ceiling fans, Tiffany lamps,
and big 18th-century redwood bar. Here
you can feast on such taste treats as
shrimp Creole, and grilled flounder stuffed with crabmeat dressing.

MAISON DE VILLE   11

Four Seasons Hotel
1300 Lamar
Houston, TX
(713) 650-1300

French

F ★ ★ ★ ½
S ★ ★ ★
A ★ ★ ★
P ★ ★ ★ ½

Jacket required
Valet parking
All major credit cards
Full bar
Reservations required

Breakfast: Mon.-Sat. 6:00AM-11:00AM
Lunch: Mon.-Sat. 11:00AM-2:00PM
Dinner: Nightly 6:00PM-11:00PM
Brunch: Sun. 11:00AM-3:00PM

Great central clusters of jubilant flowers en-
liven the subdued elegance of this maroon
and mauve dining room that looks out on
the leafy verdancy of the hotel atrium. The
classic French cuisine would delight the
staunchest purist.

MAXIM'S   27

3755 Richmond
Houston, TX
(713) 877-8899

French/Continental   •

F ★ ★ ★ ½
S ★ ★ ★ ½
A ★ ★ ★ ½
P ★ ★ ★

Jacket and tie required
Valet parking
All major credit cards
Full bar
Reservations required

Lunch/
Dinner: Mon.-Fri. 11:00AM-11:00PM
        Sat. 5:00PM-12:00AM
        Closed Sunday

This regal grande dame of Houston's chic
eateries has been serving outstanding
haute cuisine to an elite clientele for nigh
on to four decades. Owners Camille and
Ronnie Bermann place emphasis on Gulf
seafoods, but present a diverse menu including rack of lamb and prime beef
entrées. The wine cellar is considered
among the best in the Southwest.

NINFA'S   12

2704 Navigation
Houston, TX
(713) 228-1175

Mexican

F ★ ★ ★
S ★ ★ ★
A ★ ★ ½
P ★ ★

No dress restriction
Lot parking
All major credit cards
Beer/Wine
Reservations required

Lunch/
Dinner: Sun.-Thurs. 11:00AM-10:00PM
        Fri. 11:00AM-11:00PM
        Sat. 12:00PM-11:00PM

The line forms to the right at Ninfa Lorenzo's informal eatery, with its pleasant back garden and spicy ethnic food. The menu that blends classic Mexican cookery with regional TexMex specialties, lures a hungry crowd. The tacos al carbon (barbecued beef or pork in a tortilla) win rave reviews.

PAPPASITO'S CANTINA   25

6445 Richmond Avenue
Houston, TX
(713) 784-5253

Mexican

F ★ ★ ★
S ★ ★ ★
A ★ ★
P ★ ★

Good taste in dress required
Lot parking
AE, MC, V
Full bar
Reservations not required

Lunch: Mon.-Fri. 11:00AM-3:00PM
Dinner: Mon.-Thurs. 5:30PM-11:00PM
          Fri. 5:00PM-12:00AM
Lunch/
Dinner: Sat. 11:00AM-12:00AM
          Sun. 11:00AM-11:00PM

With its patio, cactus plants, and comfortable casalike air, this newest brainchild of the successful restaurateur Pappas brothers offers enticing options to standard South-of-the-Border fare. You'll find the charbroiled swordfish, boned quail, jumbo shrimp, and baked red snapper on a quality par equal to the traditional Mexican cuisine.

RAINBOW LODGE   4

1 Birdsall
Houston, TX
(713) 861-8666

Continental

F ★ ★ ★ ½
S ★ ★ ★
A ★ ★ ★ ½
P ★ ★ ★

No dress restrictions
Valet parking
All major credit cards
Beer/Wine
Reservations required

Lunch: Tues.-Fri. 11:30AM-2:00PM
Dinner: Tue.-Fri. 6:30PM-10:00PM
          Sat. 6:00PM-10:30PM
          Sun. 6:30PM-9:30PM
Brunch: Sun. 10:30AM-2:00PM
          Closed Monday

This rustic retreat, resembling an old hunting lodge, is surrounded by lush gardens and overlooks Buffalo Bayou. The interior sports a handsome collection of antiques, antlers, and hunting trophies. The somewhat eclectic menu is augmented by daily specials, such as Beef Wellington, pheasant, and scampi.

RIVOLI   19

5636 Richmond
Houston, TX
(713) 789-1900

Continental/French

F ★ ★ ★ ½
S ★ ★ ★ ½
A ★ ★ ★
P ★ ★ ★ ½

Jacket required
Valet and lot parking
AE, DC, MC, V
Full bar
Reservations required

Lunch: Mon.-Fri. 11:30AM-2:00PM
Dinner: Mon.-Thurs. 6:00PM-10:30PM
          Fri. & Sat. 6:00PM-11:00PM
          Closed Sunday

Urbane and sophisticated, Ed Zielinsky's restaurant offers you the option of garden room seating in addition to the main dining room, where the aura is chic and romantic. The cuisine is continental with French overtones.

ROMERO'S   17

2400 Mid Lane
Houston, TX
(713) 961-1161

Italian

F ★ ★ ★
S ★ ★ ★
A ★ ★ ★
P ★ ★ ½

Jacket required
Lot parking
All major credit cards
Full bar
Reservations required

Lunch: Mon.-Fri. 11:00AM-2:30PM
Dinner: Mon.-Thurs. 5:30PM-10:00PM
Fri. & Sat. 5:30PM-11:00PM
Closed Sunday

The restored home, circa 1903, used by Tomas Romero to create his charming restaurant offers you a beautiful view of the Westheimer Village courtyard. In this charming setting you will enjoy traditional Italian cuisine, a wine list featuring American and European vintners, exquisite desserts, and espresso and cappuccino.

ROTISSERIE   22
FOR BEEF & BIRD

2200 Wilcrest
Houston, TX
(713) 977-9524

American

F ★ ★ ★ ½
S ★ ★ ★
A ★ ★ ★
P ★ ★ ★ ½

Jacket required
Valet parking
AE, MC, V
Full bar
Reservations required

Lunch: Mon.-Fri. 11:30AM-2:30PM
Dinner: Mon.-Sat. 6:00PM-10:30PM
Closed Sunday

This restaurant recaptures the spirit of America's heritage, as you dine in a Colonial setting with an open hearth and a rotisserie where steaks, ducks, pheasants and geese roast slowly. The fare is hearty and satisfying — the décor delightfully nostalgic.

SAN JACINTO INN   13

3915 Battleground Road
Houston, TX
(713) 479-2828

Seafood/American

F ★ ★ ★
S ★ ★ ★
A ★ ★
P ★ ★ ★

No dress restrictions
Lot parking
All major credit cards
Full bar
Reservations not required

Dinner: Tues.-Sat. 6:00PM-10:00PM
Lunch/
Dinner: Sun. 1:00PM—9:00PM

This quaint old roadhouse sited in the San Jacinto Battleground has been serving home-style cooking, family style, for more than 60 years. All-you-can-eat of such fare as fried catfish and chicken, oysters on the half shell, broiled shrimp and crab, and oven-hot homemade biscuits.

SWISS CHALET 3

511 South Post Oak Lane
Houston, TX
(713) 621-3333

Continental

F ★ ★ ★
S ★ ★ ★
A ★ ★ ½
P ★ ★ ★ ★

Good taste in dress required
Valet parking
All major credit cards
Full bar
Reservations recomended

Lunch: Mon.-Fri. 11:00AM-2:30PM
Dinner: Mon.-Fri. 5:00PM-1:00AM
          Sat. 5:00PM-2:00AM
          Closed Sunday

Renowned for its warmth, hospitality, and consistently fine food, Albert Martin's Swiss Chalet has been a favorite of Houstonians for more than 20 years. House specialties include Beef Bourguignonne, Veal Cordon Bleu, Rack of Lamb Provencale, plus choice rib eye steaks and filets.

TONY'S 33

1801 Post Oak Boulevard
Houston, TX
(713) 622-6778

Continental

F ★ ★ ★ ★
S ★ ★ ★ ★
A ★ ★ ★ ½
P ★ ★ ★ ★

Jacket and tie required
Valet parking
AE, DC, MC, V
Full bar
Reservations required

Lunch: Mon.-Fri. 11:30AM-2:00PM
Dinner: Mon.-Sat. 6:00PM-11:00PM
          Closed Sunday

Tony's offers you a choice of three dining rooms, each a serene flower-banked retreat from urban anxiety. Tony Vallone, owner, stresses quality and freshness of ingredients for preparation of the varied dishes that blend classic haute cuisine with contemporary nouvelle touches.

UNCLE TAI'S 14
RESTAURANT

1980 Post Oak Boulevard
Houston, TX
(713) 960-8000

Chinese

F ★ ★ ★ ½
S ★ ★ ★
A ★ ★ ★
P ★ ★ ★ ½

Jacket required for dinner
Lot parking
All major credit cards
Full bar
Reservations required

Lunch/
Dinner: Mon.-Thurs. 11:00AM-10:00PM
          Fri. 11:00AM-10:30PM
          Sat. 12:00PM-10:30PM
          Sun. 12:00PM-10:00PM

Owner/chef Tai Wen-Dah moved to Houston from New York City in 1979, bringing with him a new dimension in award-winning Chinese cuisine. You'll find spicy specials in the Hunan tradition among the 90-plus menu offerings which include Uncle Tai's Beef, smoked duck, and shredded pork.

Kansas City

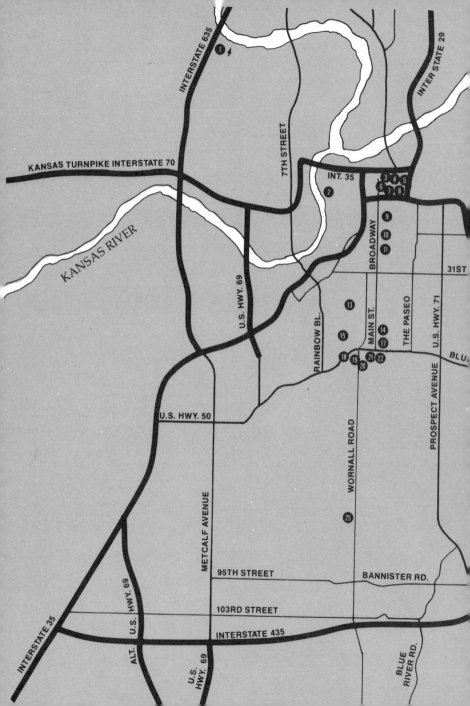

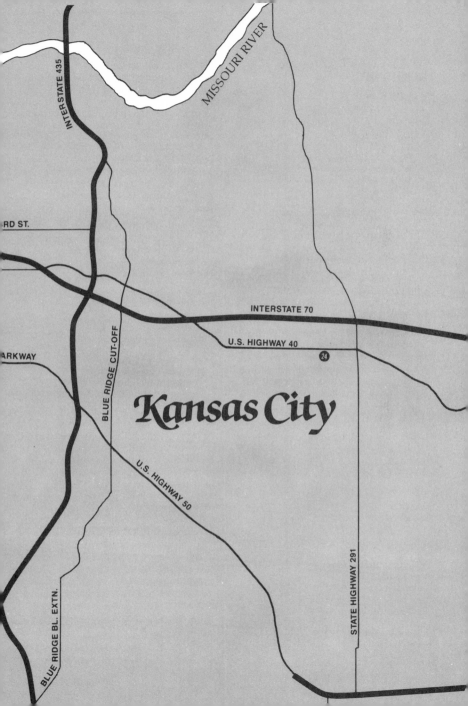

ALAMEDA PLAZA 20
ROOFTOP

Wornall Road at Ward Parkway
Kansas City, MO
(816) 756-1500

Continental

F ★ ★ ★
S ★ ★ ★
A ★ ★ ★ ½
P ★ ★ ★

Jacket and tie required at dinner
Lot parking
All major credit cards
Full bar
Reservations recommended

Lunch: Mon.-Sat. 11:30AM-2:00PM
Dinner: Mon.-Sat. 5:30PM-11:00PM
          Sun. 5:30PM-10:00PM
Brunch: Sun. 10:30AM-2:00PM

A consistent award-winner, this handsome restaurant gives you an inspiring
view of the famed Country Club Plaza,
while catering to your taste for fine continental cuisine. Chef Barbosa reigns in the
kitchen, and plans stellar nightly specials.

THE AMERICAN 11

Hall's Crown Center
Grand & 25th Street
Kansas City, MO
(816) 471-8050

American

F ★ ★ ★ ½
S ★ ★ ★ ½
A ★ ★ ★ ½
P ★ ★ ★

Jacket required
Valet parking
All major credit cards
Full bar
Reservations required

Dinner: Mon.-Thurs. 6:00PM-10:00PM
          Fri. & Sat. 6:00PM-11:00PM
          Closed Sunday

Three tiers of tables gives everyone dining
in this grandiose room a clear view of the
glittering Kansas City skyline. Regional
American foods are featured here, and
your choices might include Montana elk,
Nova Scotia salmon, South Dakota pheasant, or K.C. strip steaks.

ANNIE'S SANTA FE 21

100 Ward Parkway
Kansas City, MO
(816) 753-1621

Mexican

F ★ ★ ★ ½
S ★ ★ ★ ½
A ★ ★ ★ ½
P ★ ★

No dress restrictions
Lot parking
AE, DC, MC, V
Full bar
Reservations not required

Lunch/
Dinner: Mon.-Thurs. 11:00AM-11:00PM
          Fri. & Sat. 11:00AM-1:00AM
          Sun. 12:00PM-10:00PM

Annie's cheerful ambiance is created by a
collage of colorful artifacts and verdant
greenery. You'll feel at home in this
family-like restaurant that offers an eight-
page menu running the gamut of Mexican
taste treats from tacos to tortilla pizza. The
salsa may be mild or fiery hot, but the
Margaritas are always good and frosty.

BRISTOL BAR & GRILL 19

4740 Jefferson
Kansas City, MO
(816) 756-0606

Seafood

F ★ ★ ★ ½
S ★ ★ ★
A ★ ★ ★
P ★ ★ ★

Good taste in dress required
Lot and street parking
All major credit cards
Full bar
Reservations not required

Lunch: Mon.-Fri. 11:00AM-2:30PM
        Sat. 11:30AM-2:30PM
Dinner: Mon.-Thurs. 5:30PM-11:00PM
        Fri. 5:30PM-12:00AM
        Sat. 5:00PM-12:00AM
        Sun. 5:00PM-10:00PM

Considered one of the best seafood restaurants in the Midwest, you can feast here on fresh seafood flown in from the coasts and then mesquite-broiled to perfection. The menu changes daily but the ambiance remains staid, elegant, and pleasantly Victorian.

CARNEGIE'S   7

Embassy on the Park Hotel
1215 Wyandotte
Kansas City, MO
(816) 471-1333

Continental

F ★ ★ ★
S ★ ★ ★
A ★ ★ ★
P ★ ★ ★

Jacket and tie required on weekends
Valet parking
All major credit cards
Beer/Wine
Reservations recommended

Dinner: Tues.-Thurs. 5:30PM-10:00PM
        Fri. & Sat. 5:30PM-11:00PM
        Closed Sunday and Monday

This intimate dining spot is a charming candle-lit mecca for gourmets who like their dining intermingled with musical entertainment. Singing waiters and waitresses, backed by a grand piano accompaniment, serve opera and show tunes in tandem with your continental cuisine.

CRYSTAL PAVILION   11

2450 Grand Avenue
Kansas City, MO
(816) 471-2003

Eclectic

F ★ ★ ★
S ★ ★ ★
A ★ ★ ★
P ★ ★ ★

Good taste in dress required
Valet and lot parking
All major credit cards
Full bar
Reservations required

Lunch: Mon.-Fri. 11:30AM-2:30PM
Dinner: Mon.-Thurs. 6:00PM-10:00PM
        Fri. & Sat. 6:00PM-11:00PM
        Closed Sunday

This is a fun place with all glass walls, tile floors, and an exuberance of plants and flowers. Imaginative food preparation is stressed, and the kitchen dotes on developing innovative combinations of ingredients.

GAETANO'S   4

600 East 8th Street
Kansas City, MO
(816) 221-3685

Italian/American

F ★ ★ ★
S ★ ★ ★
A ★ ★ ★
P ★ ★

Good taste in dress required
Lot and street parking
All major credit cards
Full bar
Reservations not required

Lunch/
Dinner: Mon.-Thurs. 11:00AM-10:00PM
        Fri. & Sat. 11:00AM-11:00PM
        Closed Sunday

Milk fed veal specialties and homemade pasta dishes have been luring diners to Gaetano's for three decades. The refreshing new décor features lush hanging plants and a "forest" of greenery; with expanses of windows giving you a wide open view. The menu is diverse with something to please everyone.

GOLDEN OX   2

1600 Genesee Street
Kansas City, MO
(816) 842-2866

American

F ★ ★ ★ ½
S ★ ★ ★
A ★ ★ ½
P ★ ★

Good taste in dress required
Lot parking
AE, DC, MC, V
Full bar
Reservations required

Lunch: Mon.-Fri. 11:30AM-4:00PM
Dinner: Mon.-Fri. 4:00PM-10:00PM
          Sat. 5:00PM-10:30PM
          Sun. 4:00PM-9:00PM

This unpretentious steak house is located where the stockyards are, and is decorated with a Western motif. The food is good and plentiful with great steaks, seafood, and chicken—grilled and broiled—served with potato, salad, and garlic toast. Hearty fare for robust appetites.

HARRY STARKER'S   14

4708 Wyandotte
Kansas City, MO
(816) 753-3565

Continental

F ★ ★ ★ ½
S ★ ★ ★
A ★ ★ ★ ½
P ★ ★ ½

No dress restrictions
Street parking
All major credit cards
Full bar
Reservations not required

Lunch/
Dinner: Mon.-Thurs. 11:00AM-11:00PM
          Fri. & Sat. 11:00AM-12:00AM
          Sun. 4:00PM-10:00PM

As elegant as an Old English pub, with contemporary touches, this establishment has a warm, welcoming atmosphere. The continental cuisine offers a wide range of choices from rack of lamb, to Chicken Kiev, to a tempting prime rib. At Starker's you'll enjoy excellent food and service with a smile.

HEREFORD HOUSE   9

2 East 20th
Kansas City, MO
(816) 842-1080

American

F ★ ★ ★
S ★ ★ ★
A ★ ★ ★
P ★ ★ ½

Good taste in dress required
Valet parking
All major credit cards
Full bar
Reservations not required

Lunch/
Dinner: Mon. 11:00AM-10:00PM
          Tues.-Sat. 11:00AM-11:00PM
          Closed Sunday

A haven for steak-lovers, this dining spot succeeds admirably with its menu featuring prime rib, chicken, ribs, and a wide selection of steaks. The cooking style is charcoal broiled—the ambiance open and airy—and the décor as Western as a Stetson beaver hat.

HOULIHAN'S OLD PLACE 22

4743 Pennsylvania
Kansas City, MO
(816) 561-3141

American

F ★ ★ ★
S ★ ★ ★
A ★ ★ ★
P ★ ★

No dress restrictions
Lot and street parking
AE, DC, MC, V
Full bar
Reservations required on weekends

Lunch/
Dinner: Mon.-Sat. 11:00AM-12:00AM
Brunch: Sun. 11:00AM-3:00PM

Quaint and charming, this eatery, with its plant-brightened Irish décor, is a casual spot where you can enjoy crab Newburg, eggs Benedict, omelettes, roast duck, and good old K.C. steaks. Just the place for dining when you're not sure what you want, or where you really want to go.

ITALIAN GARDENS 5

1110 Baltimore
Kansas City, MO
(816) 221-9311

Italian/American

F ★ ★ ★ ½
S ★ ★ ★
A ★ ★ ½
P ★ ★

Good taste in dress required
Valet parking
All major credit cards
Full bar
Reservations not required

Lunch/
Dinner: Daily 11:00AM-11:00PM

For 55 years Italian Gardens has stood for fellowship and fine Italian food in the Kansas City community. A family owned institution that dispenses warm hospitality and a wide array of traditional entrées, carefully prepared by Italian women chefs.

JASPER'S 25

405 West 75th Street
Kansas City, MO
(816) 363-3003

Italian/Continental

F ★ ★ ★ ★
S ★ ★ ★ ★
A ★ ★ ★ ½
P ★ ★ ★ ★

Jacket required
Lot parking
All major credit cards
Full bar
Reservations required

Lunch: Mon.-Fri. 11:30AM-2:00PM
Dinner: Mon.-Sat. 6:00PM-10:00PM
          Closed Sunday

Jasper and Leonard Mirabile strive to make dining in their restaurant a memorable experience orchestrated for the total enjoyment of every diner. The wine cellar and superlative food continue to garner awards. You'll find each of their three dining rooms is elegant and inviting.

KING'S WHARF 1

Marriott Hotel
775 Brasilia
Kansas City, MO
(816) 464-2200

American

F ★ ★ ★
S ★ ★ ★
A ★ ★ ★
P ★ ★ ½

Good taste in dress required
Lot parking
All major credit cards
Full bar
Reservations not required

Breakfast/
Lunch/
Dinner: Daily 6:00AM-11:00PM

A travelers delight, and a favorite haunt of Kansas City residents, King's Wharf is a busy, bustling restaurant sited at the International Airport. Among the specialties of the house are the famous Kansas City Strip, and a succulent prime rib served in generous portions.

KONA KAI 17

Hilton Plaza Inn
45th & Main Street
Kansas City, MO
(816) 753-7400

Oriental/Polynesian/American

F ★ ★ ★
S ★ ★ ★
A ★ ★ ★
P ★ ★

Good taste in dress required
Valet and lot parking
All major credit cards
Full bar
Reservations required

Dinner: Nightly 5:00PM-10:30PM

Decorated with wicker furnishings and a display of colorful aquariums, this restaurant exudes Polynesian charm, and has a fun, relaxed, tropical atmosphere. Oriental, Polynesian, and American entrées are all available, and are authentically prepared.

LA BONNE AUBERGE 3

725 Main Street
Kansas City, MO
(816) 474-7025

French/American

F ★ ★ ★ ½
S ★ ★ ★ ½
A ★ ★ ★
P ★ ★ ★

Jacket required
Lot parking
AE, DC, MC, V
Full bar
Reservations required

Lunch: Mon.-Fri. 11:30AM-2:00PM
Dinner: Tues.-Sat. 5:30PM-10:30PM
Closed Sunday

An interesting selection of nouvelle French entrées plus a good range of classic American favorites are featured on the menu at this friendly establishment. The cafélike wine cellar atmosphere is a natural for this restaurant which features over 250 labels on the wine list.

LA MEDITERRANEE 18

4742 Pennsylvania
Kansas City, MO
(816) 561-2916

French

F ★ ★ ★ ½
S ★ ★ ★ ½
A ★ ★ ★ ½
P ★ ★ ★ ½

Good taste in dress required
Lot and street parking
All major credit cards
Full bar
Reservations required

Lunch: Mon.-Sat. 11:30AM-2:00PM
Dinner: Mon.-Sat. 6:00PM-10:00PM
Closed Sunday

Owner Gilbert Jahier has devised a cozy, elegant setting in which to present classic and nouvelle French cuisine, with specialties such as Raviole de Homard, Salmon Pistache, and Tournedos Gilbert.

THE PEPPERCORN DUCK CLUB 10

2345 McGee Street
Kansas City, MO
(816) 421-1234

Continental

F ★ ★ ★ ½
S ★ ★ ★ ½
A ★ ★ ★ ½
P ★ ★ ★ ½

Jacket required for dinner
Valet and lot parking
All major credit cards
Full bar
Reservations recommended

Lunch: Mon.-Fri. 11:30AM-2:00PM
Dinner: Sun.-Thurs. 5:30PM-10:00PM
          Fri. & Sat. 5:30PM-10:30PM
Brunch: Sun. 10:00AM-2:00PM

Shiny brass, polished wood, and colorful fresh flowers form a rich décor at the Duck Club, with a Market Island salad bar, and chocolate dessert display serving as a focal point. The cuisine includes a rotisserie duckling special, plus beef, steaks, barbecue, and seafood.

PLAZA III 15

4749 Pennsylvania Avenue
Kansas City, MO
(816) 753-0000

Continental

F ★ ★ ★ ½
S ★ ★ ★
A ★ ★ ★ ½
P ★ ★ ★

No dress restrictions
Lot parking
All major credit cards
Full bar
Reservations not required

Lunch: Mon.-Fri. 11:30AM-2:30PM
          Sat. 11:30AM-3:00PM
Dinner: Mon.-Thurs. 5:30PM-11:00PM
          Fri. & Sat. 5:30PM-12:00AM
          Sun. 5:00PM-10:00PM

You'll be greeted here by an atmosphere of Victorian splendor, enhanced with stained glass and a plethora of green plants. In this lovely setting a broad range of continental favorites are offered, including fresh fish, prime rib, rack of lamb, and those locally ubiquitous Kansas City steaks.

SAVOY GRILL 8

9th & Central Streets
Kansas City, MO
(816) 842-3890

American

F ★ ★ ★ ½
S ★ ★ ★ ½
A ★ ★ ★ ½
P ★ ★ ★ ½

No dress restrictions
Lot and street parking
All major credit cards
Full bar
Reservations not required

Lunch/
Dinner: Mon.-Sat. 11:00AM-11:00PM
          Sun. 4:00PM-10:00PM

The oldest restaurant in Kansas City, and a national landmark, the Savoy has been a haunt of leading citizens since 1903, when Kansas City was still a western outpost. The lobster and other seafoods are longtime menu highlights. Their place of honor is shared with world-famous Kansas City steaks.

STANFORD & SONS 13

504 Westport Road
Kansas City, MO
(816) 756-1450

American

F ★ ★ ★
S ★ ★ ★
A ★ ★ ★
P ★ ★

Good taste in dress required
Lot parking
All major credit cards
Full bar
Reservations recommended

Lunch/
Dinner: Sun.-Thurs. 11:00AM-11:00PM
        Fri. & Sat. 11:00AM-1:00AM
Brunch: Sun. 10:00AM-3:00PM

Located in the oldest building in Kansas City, Stanford & Sons surrounds you with turn-of-the-century, San Francisco style décor. The 60-item menu includes burgers, pasta, Mexican dishes, fish, steaks, and a host of other enticements. Try the quiche and cheesecake—both judged tops in Kansas City.

STEPHENSON'S FARM 24

16401 East 40 Hiway
Kansas City, MO
(816) 373-5400

American

F ★ ★ ★
S ★ ★ ★
A ★ ★ ★ ½
P ★ ★ ½

No dress restrictions
Lot parking
All major credit cards
Full bar
Reservations recommended

Lunch/
Dinner: Mon.-Thurs. 11:30AM-10:00PM
        Fri. & Sat. 11:30AM-11:00PM
        Sun. 10:00AM-9:00PM

Nestled in the woods, in a placid country setting, this home-style restaurant lures contented patrons with hickory-smoked meats; homemade pastries, relishes, and apple butter; and fabulous apple fritters. This wholesome, hearty fare, the relaxed rural atmosphere, and the warm friendly service make dining here a memorable event.

TOP OF THE CROWN 6

Westin Crown Center Hotel
One Pershing Road
Kansas City, MO
(816) 474-4400

Continental

F ★ ★ ★ ½
S ★ ★ ★ ½
A ★ ★ ★ ★
P ★ ★ ★ ½

Jacket required
Valet parking
All major credit cards
Full bar
Reservations required

Dinner: Nightly 6:00PM-11:00PM
Brunch: Sun. 10:00AM-2:30PM

A dramatic view of Kansas City, elegant décor, proficient tableside service, and nightly dancing make Top of the Crown a thoroughly enjoyable dining spot. Fresh seafood, lamb, and beef are featured on the menu, with unique house specialties offered nightly.

Las Vegas

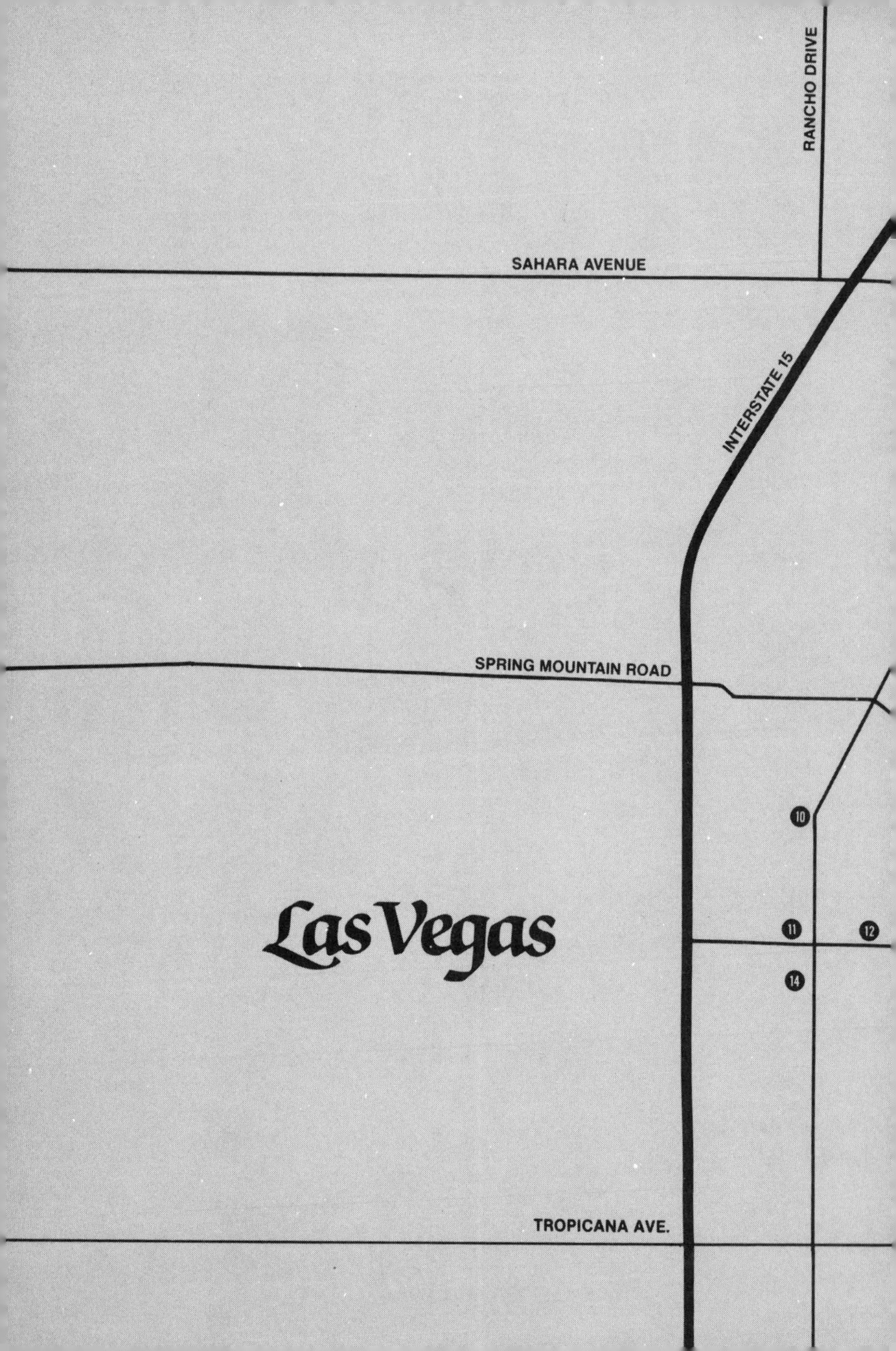
RANCHO DRIVE
SAHARA AVENUE
INTERSTATE 15
SPRING MOUNTAIN ROAD
10
Las Vegas
11
12
14
TROPICANA AVE.

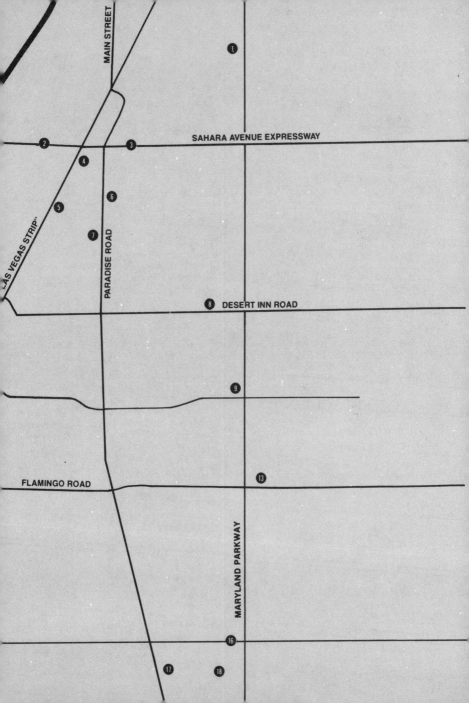

AH-SO JAPANESE 11
STEAK GARDEN

Caesar's Palace
3570 Las Vegas Boulevard South
Las Vegas, NV
(702) 731-7110

Japanese

F ★ ★ ★ ½
S ★ ★ ★
A ★ ★ ★
P ★ ★ ★ ★

Good taste in dress required
Valet parking
All major credit cards
Full bar
Reservations required

Dinner: Nightly 6:00PM-11:30PM

Escape the neon razzle-dazzle to dine in Ah-So's peaceful garden setting with its soothing splashing waterfall and gently flowing stream. In this special "world apart" you'll enjoy a fixed-price dinner that offers you a good choice of the finest Japanese cuisine.

ALPINE VILLAGE INN 7

3003 South Paradise Road
Las Vegas, NV
(702) 734-6888

German/Swiss/American

F ★ ★ ★ ½
S ★ ★ ★ ½
A ★ ★ ★ ½
P ★ ★ ★

No dress restrictions
Valet and lot parking
All major credit cards
Full bar
Reservations required

Dinner: Nightly 5:00PM-12:00AM

This charming replica of a Swiss chalet has been dispensing delicious, hearty Swiss and German fare and warm hospitality to residents and tourists since 1950. The homemade soups and breads, sauerbraten, Weiner Schnitzel, and fondue are long-time favorites.

ANDRE'S 1

401 South 6th Street
Las Vegas, NV
(702) 385-5016

French

F ★ ★ ★
S ★ ★ ★
A ★ ★ ★
P ★ ★ ★

Jacket required, no jeans, thongs, or T-shirts
Valet and street parking
All major credit cards
Full bar
Reservations required

Lunch: Mon.-Fri. 11:00AM-2:00PM
Dinner: Nightly 6:00PM-11:00PM

One of the oldest houses in downtown Las Vegas has been converted into the Southern French Provincial setting for this charming dining spot. The classic French cuisine is augmented by dishes prepared with fresh fish flown in from France and the east and west coasts.

BACCHANAL 11

Caesar's Palace
3570 Las Vegas Boulevard South
Las Vegas, NV
(702) 734-7110

Continental

F ★ ★ ★ ½
S ★ ★ ★ ★
A ★ ★ ★ ★
P ★ ★ ★ ★

Jacket preferred
Valet parking
All major credit cards

Full bar
Reservations required

Dinner: Nightly 6:00PM-11:30PM

Luxuriate in a setting that has all the trappings of an ancient Roman villa's private court and garden. A seven-course Roman feast, accompanied by three wines, is the Bacchanal's fixed-price specialty.

BATTISTA'S 12
HOLE IN THE WALL

4041 Audrie at Flamingo
Las Vegas, NV
(702) 732-1424

Italian

F ★ ★ ★ ½
S ★ ★ ★
A ★ ★ ★
P ★ ★ ½

Good taste in dress required
Lot parking
All major credit cards
Full bar
Reservations required

Dinner: Nightly 4:30PM-11:00PM

Battista Locatelli's personal congeniality has produced a restaurant with a warm, friendly atmosphere, where well prepared full-course Italian dinners are served with complimentary house wine. Opera-oriented décor and exuberant bursts of arias will add to your evening's pleasure.

BENIHANA VILLAGE 6

Las Vegas Hilton
3000 Paradise Road
Las Vegas, NV
(702) 732-5111

Japanese

F ★ ★ ★ ½
S ★ ★ ★ ½
A ★ ★ ★ ½
P ★ ★ ★ ½

Good taste in dress required
Valet and lot parking
All major credit cards
Full bar
Reservations required

Dinner: Nightly 6:00PM-11:00PM

Benihana's is a magnificent reproduction of a Japanese village complete with rock formations and streams. Different types of Japanese cuisine are featured in the four restaurant sections—hibachi, robata, tempura, and traditional dishes.

CHIN'S 8

2300 East Desert Inn Road
Las Vegas, NV
(702) 733-7764

Cantonese

F ★ ★ ★ ½
S ★ ★ ★ ½
A ★ ★ ★
P ★ ★

No dress restrictions
Lot and street parking
All major credit cards
Full bar
Reservations recommended

Dinner: Nightly 5:00PM-11:00PM

Dine in an aura of restrained oriental elegance at Chin's, where you will enjoy cooked-to-order Cantonese cuisine of the highest caliber, prepared with the freshest ingredients, and nicely presented. Chin's Beef and Strawberry Chicken, are two of many original recipes that are featured.

FERDINAND'S 17
RESTAURANT

5006 Maryland Parkway
Las Vegas, NV
(702) 798-6962

American

F ★ ★ ★ ½
S ★ ★ ★ ½
A ★ ★ ★ ½
P ★ ★ ★

No dress restrictions
Lot parking
All major credit cards
Full bar
Reservations not required

Dinner: Nightly 5:00PM-11:30PM

Ferdinand's gives you a rich mélange of casual elegance, a sense of intimacy, great jazz music, and well served fine cuisine. You'll find extraordinarily good fresh seafood, midwestern beef, chicken, and veal—accented by a distinctive California wine list.

GARCIA'S OF SCOTTSDALE   13

1030 East Flamingo Road
Las Vegas, NV
(702) 731-0628

Mexican

F ★ ★ ★
S ★ ★ ★
A ★ ★ ★
P ★ ½

Good taste in dress required
Lot parking
AE
Full bar
Reservations not required

Lunch/
Dinner: Fri. & Sat. 11:30AM-11:00PM
         Sun. 12:00PM-10:00PM
         Winter
         Mon.-Thurs. 11:30AM-10:00PM
         Spring, Summer, Fall
         Mon.-Thurs. 11:30AM-10:30PM

Large and spacious, Garcia's authentic Mexican décor, with fiesta-bright colors and lush hanging plants, creates a festive outdoor garden feeling. You'll find all your favorite Mexican dishes on the menu, including chimichangas and deep-fried ice cream.

GOLDEN STEER   2
STEAKHOUSE

308 West Sahara Avenue
Las Vegas, NV
(702) 384-4470

American/Italian

F ★ ★ ★
S ★ ★ ★ ½
A ★ ★ ★ ½
P ★ ★ ★

Good taste in dress required
Valet and lot parking
All major credit cards
Full bar
Reservations required

Dinner: Nightly 5:00PM-12:00AM

Old-time western décor creates a congenial environment for enjoying the fine prime rib, steaks, seafood, and Italian specialties that are featured at the Golden Steer. The quick, proficient service is deserving of the highest praise.

HOUSE OF LORDS   4

Sahara Hotel
2535 Las Vegas Boulevard South
Las Vegas, NV
(702) 737-2111

French

F ★ ★ ★ ½
S ★ ★ ★ ½
A ★ ★ ★ ½
P ★ ★ ★ ½

Jacket required
Valet parking
All major credit cards
Full bar
Reservations required

Dinner: Nightly 6:00PM-11:00PM

Sedate and formal, the House of Lords features handsome Old English décor and precise, courteous service. The menu offers you a wide selection of gourmet quality French cuisine.

LIBERACE'S 18
TIVOLI GARDENS

1775 East Tropicana Avenue
Las Vegas, NV
(702) 739-8762

Continental

F ★ ★ ★
S ★ ★ ★
A ★ ★ ★
P ★ ★ ★

Jacket required at dinner
Valet, lot, and street parking
All major credit cards
Full bar
Reservations required for dinner

Lunch/
Dinner: Daily 11:30AM-1:00AM

An inspired interpretation of the Tivoli Gardens in Copenhagen, where you'll enjoy foods of many countries served with theatrical flair in an international atmosphere. Several original recipes from *Liberace Cooks* are included in the continental cuisine.

PALACE COURT 11

Caesar's Palace
3570 Las Vegas Boulevard South
Las Vegas, NV
(702) 734-7110

French

F ★ ★ ★ ½
S ★ ★ ★ ½
A ★ ★ ★ ½
P ★ ★ ★ ★

Jacket required
Valet parking
All major credit cards
Full bar
Reservations required

Dinner: Nightly 6:30PM-11:00PM

When you feel you deserve to be treated like royalty (or if you are), dine at the Palace Court, with its gorgeous stained glass windows and large indoor evergreen tree. The à la carte menu features classic French haute cuisine.

PAMPLEMOUSSE 3

400 East Sahara Avenue
Las Vegas, NV
(702) 733-2066

French

F ★ ★ ★ ½
S ★ ★ ★
A ★ ★ ★ ½
P ★ ★ ★

No dress restrictions
Lot parking
All major credit cards
Beer/Wine
Reservations required

Dinner: Nightly 6:00PM-11:00PM

Escape the glitter of the strip and discover the quiet charm of Pamplemousse, in a romantic cottage that's just a two minute drive away. Memorable French cuisine including soufflés and delectable desserts will delight you, as will the diligent service.

RISTORANTE 5
DELMONICO

Riviera Hotel
2901 Las Vegas Boulevard South
Las Vegas, NV
(702) 734-5110, Ext. 363

Italian/French

F ★ ★ ★ ½
S ★ ★ ★
A ★ ★ ★ ½
P ★ ★ ★

Good taste in dress required
Valet parking
All major credit cards
Full bar
Reservations required

Dinner: Nightly 6:00PM-11:00PM

A gorgeous replica of a roof top café in Venice, complete with classic Italian décor is the setting you will find at Delmonico's. Dishes influenced by both Northern and Southern Italian cuisine are served. Vermicelli Bella Vista is a renowned house specialty.

SPANISH STEPS   11

Caesar's Palace
3570 Las Vegas Boulevard South
Las Vegas, NV
(702) 731-7560

American/Spanish

F ★ ★ ★ ½
S ★ ★ ★ ½
A ★ ★ ★ ½
P ★ ★ ★ ½

Good taste in dress required
Valet parking
All major credit cards
Full bar
Reservations required

Dinner: Nightly 6:00PM-12:30AM

Dine at a leisurely pace in the richly decorated, elegant Spanish Steps restaurant, to the pleasant accompaniment of live background music. Both classic American and Spanish style cuisine are featured on the bill of fare, providing you a wide selection of entrées from which to choose.

SULTAN'S TABLE   14

Dunes Hotel
3650 Las Vegas Boulevard South
Las Vegas, NV
(702) 737-4110

Continental

F ★ ★ ★ ½
S ★ ★ ★ ½
A ★ ★ ★ ½
P ★ ★ ★ ½

Jacket required
Valet parking
All major credit cards
Full bar
Reservations required

Dinner: Nightly 6:00PM-12:00AM

Sultan's Table transports you to the land where potentates reign. Violin and piano music beguiles your senses as you dine on beautifully prepared and served international dishes including French cuisine.

THE VINEYARD   9

3630 South Maryland Parkway
Las Vegas, NV
(702) 731-1606

Italian

F ★ ★ ★
S ★ ★ ★
A ★ ★ ½
P ★ ★

Good taste in dress required
Lot parking
AE, MC, V
Full bar
Reservations not required

Lunch/
Dinner: Sun.-Thurs. 11:00AM-11:00PM
          Fri. & Sat. 11:00AM-12:00AM

You'll find a fresh, colorful, casual ambiance at The Vineyard, where Italian favorites such as lasagna, cannelloni, mannicotti, scampi, Veal Parmigiana, and Fettuccine Alfredo are featured.

Los Angeles

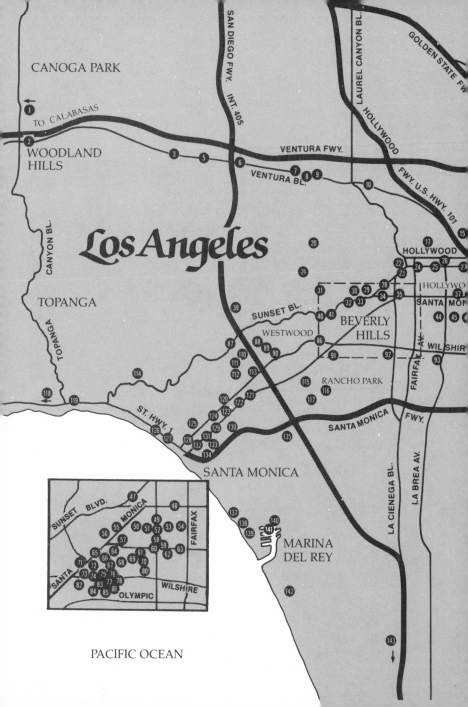

ADRIANO'S RISTORANTE   20

2930 Beverly Glen Circle
Los Angeles, CA
(213) 475-9807

Italian

F ★ ★ ★ ½
S ★ ★ ★
A ★ ★ ★
P ★ ★ ★

No dress restrictions
Lot parking
AE, MC, V
Full bar
Reservations required

Lunch:	Tues.-Sat. 11:30AM-2:30PM
Dinner:	Tues.-Sat. 6:00PM-10:30PM
	Sun. 6:00PM-11:00PM
Brunch:	Sun. 11:00AM-3:00PM
	Closed Monday

Adriano's brings all the charm of a small, elegant Italian country inn to a fashionable Bel Air address. Owner-host Adriano Rebora greets guests personally and offers them well prepared and exciting cuisine.

ALBERTO'S   52

8826 Melrose Avenue
Los Angeles, CA
(213) 278-2770

Italian

F ★ ★ ★ ½
S ★ ★ ★ ½
A ★ ★ ★ ½
P ★ ★ ★

No dress restrictions
Valet parking
All major credit cards
Full bar
Reservations required

Dinner: Nightly 5:00PM-1:00AM

When you are in the mood for wonderful Italian gourmet food served in a warm, elegant, yet comfortable atmosphere, Alberto's is a perfect choice. Only fresh fish, meats, and vegetables are used in food preparation.

ALBION'S   7

13422 Ventura Boulevard
Sherman Oaks, CA
(818) 981-6650

French

F ★ ★ ★ ½
S ★ ★ ★ ½
A ★ ★ ★ ★
P ★ ★ ★

No shorts
Valet parking
All major credit cards
Full bar
Reservations not required

Lunch:	Mon.-Sat. 11:30AM-2:00PM
Dinner:	Mon.-Sat. 6:00PM-10:00PM
	Closed Sunday

Experience the essence of France when dining at Albion's, where the elegant décor combines crystal chandeliers, antiques, and French paintings. A wide selection of dishes, prepared in the nouvelle manner, epitomize fine French cuisine.

AMBROSIA   143

695 Town Center
Costa Mesa, CA
(714) 751-6100

French/Continental

F ★ ★ ★ ★
S ★ ★ ★ ★
A ★ ★ ★ ½
P ★ ★ ★ ★

Jacket and tie required
Valet parking
All major credit cards
Full bar
Reservations required

Dinner: Nightly 4:00PM-1:00AM

Dine like royalty in the midst of Ambrosia's opulent Louie XV décor, with tuxedoed captains and waiters to cater to your every whim. A varied and well-fulfilled menu and vintage and domestic wines dating from 1865 make dining here an evening of grandeur.

ANTONIO'S   44

7472 Melrose Avenue
Los Angeles, CA
(213) 655-0480 or 655-3784

Mexican

F ★ ★ ★ ½
S ★ ★ ★
A ★ ★ ★
P ★ ★ ★

Good taste in dress required
Valet and street parking
AE,MC, V
Full bar
Reservations required

Lunch: Tues.-Sun. 12:00PM-3:00PM
Dinner: Tues.-Sun. 5:00PM-11:00PM
         Closed Monday

Antonio Gutierrez has extended the menu of his fine restaurant to encompass both traditional Mexican fare and less well known Mexican specialties that tempt and reward the adventuresome diner. Sauces and spices are unexcelled.

THE ARCHES   143

3334 West Coast Highway
Newport Beach, CA
(714) 645-7077

Continental

F ★ ★ ★ ½
S ★ ★ ★ ½
A ★ ★ ★
P ★ ★ ★

Good taste in dress required
Lot parking
All major credit cards
Full bar
Reservations recommended

Lunch: Mon.-Sat. 11:30AM-3:00PM
Dinner: Mon.-Sun. 5:00PM-1:00AM
Brunch: Sun. 10:30AM-3:00PM

The Arches has been luring Southern California's discerning diners for decades with their warm, friendly atmosphere, extensive menu, and award-winning wine list. House specialties include fresh abalone, bouillabaisse, Duck à la Orange, and Steak Diane.

AT MARTY'S   92

8657 West Pico Boulevard
Los Angeles, CA
(213) 272-1048

Continental

F ★ ★ ★
S ★ ★ ★
A ★ ★ ★
P ★ ★ ★

Good taste in dress required
Valet parking Friday and Saturday
Street parking weekdays
All major credit cards
Full bar
Reservations required

Dinner: Mon.-Thurs. 6:00PM-11:00PM
         Fri. 6:00PM-12:00AM
         Sat. 5:00PM-1:00AM
         Sun. 5:00PM-10:00PM

Step into the fun, colorful setting here and feel as if you're in an Eastside New York Supper Club of the '30s era. The ever-changing bill of fare features favorites from around the world.

AU CHAMBERTIN   134

708 Pico Boulevard
Santa Monica, CA
(213) 392-8738

French

F ★ ★ ★ ½
S ★ ★ ★
A ★ ★ ★
P ★ ★ ★

Jacket required
Valet and street parking
MC, V
Full bar
Reservations required

Dinner: Sun.-Thurs. 5:30PM-9:30PM
          Fri. & Sat. 5:30PM-10:00PM

The feeling here is one of crisp correctness, with jaunty fresh flowers on snowy tablecloths, and pleasant attentive service. The menu leans toward nouvelle French, and is spiced with daily changing specialties. Especially noteworthy are the variety of sea bass dishes and the lemon tart and chocolate mousse.

BEAUDRY'S   105

The Westin Bonaventure Hotel
404 South Figueroa Street
Los Angeles, CA
(213) 624-2664

Continental/American

F ★ ★ ★ ½
S ★ ★ ★ ½
A ★ ★ ★ ½
P ★ ★ ★

Jacket required
Valet and underground lot parking
All major credit cards
Full bar
Reservations recommended

Lunch: Mon.-Fri. 11:30AM-2:00PM
Dinner: Nightly 6:00PM-11:00PM

Beaudry's offers you intimate gourmet dining in an inviting, elegant ambiance. The menu offers a wide choice of entrées prepared with only the freshest ingredients, and presented attractively. A good selection of vintage wines is featured.

BEAURIVAGE   118

26052 Pacific Coast Highway
Malibu, CA
(213) 456-5733

Mediterranean

F ★ ★ ★ ½
S ★ ★ ★ ½
A ★ ★ ★ ½
P ★ ★ ★

Good taste in dress required
Lot parking
All major credit cards
Full bar
Reservations recommended

Dinner: Nightly 5:00PM-11:00PM
Brunch: Sun. 11:00AM-4:00PM

This romantic dining spot sparkles with Mediterranean élan. Owner Daniel Forge slants the bill of fare that is a medley of French, Italian, and Mediterranean cooking styles toward seasonally available fresh seafood and game, such as partridges and wild boar.

BEL-AIR HOTEL   31

701 Stone Canyon Road
Los Angeles, CA
(213) 472-1211

American

F ★ ★ ★ ½
S ★ ★ ★ ★
A ★ ★ ★ ★
P ★ ★ ★ ½

Jacket required after 6:00PM
Valet parking
All major credit cards
Full bar
Reservations recommended

Breakfast:Daily 7:00AM-10:30AM
Lunch: Mon.-Fri. 11:30AM-2:30PM
Dinner: Nightly 6:00PM-10:30PM
Brunch: Sat.-Sun. 11:30AM-2:30PM

Tucked away in the hills above Los Angeles, the Bel-Air is a picturesque and serene retreat where dining is a leisurely, special event. California-influenced cuisine, with such gustatory delights as fresh squab cured in honey and garlic, is offered.

BEL AIR SANDS HOTEL   113
THE CARIBBEAN TERRACE

11461 Sunset Boulevard
Los Angeles, CA 90049
(213) 476-6571

Continental

F ★ ★ ★ ½
S ★ ★ ★
A ★ ★ ★
P ★ ★ ★

No dress restrictions
Valet and lot parking
All major credit cards
Full bar
Reservations not required

Breakfast/
Lunch/
Dinner: Daily 7:00AM-10:30PM
Brunch: Sun. 10:00AM-2:30PM

Enjoy the tropical atmosphere found here, with poolside dining offered during the summer months. The menu tempts you with such exotic dishes as medallions of veal, lightly sautéed and finished with a rum, cream, and toasted coconut sauce, then garnished with baked papaya and bay shrimp.

BENIHANA   26,6

38 North La Cienega Boulevard
Beverly Hills, CA
(213) 659-1511

16226 Ventura Boulevard
Encino, CA
(818) 788-7121

Japanese

F ★ ★ ★
S ★ ★ ★
A ★ ★ ★ ½
P ★ ★ ★

Good taste in dress required
Valet parking
All major credit cards
Full bar
Reservations required

Lunch: Mon-Fri. 11:30AM-2:30PM
Dinner: Sun.-Thurs. 5:30PM-10:00PM
          Fri. & Sat. 5:30PM-11:00PM

Dining here is quite a delightful experience, as you watch in amazement while your Teppan-trained chef slivers meats and chops vegetables into tempting morsels to be quickly cooked and served sizzling from your tableside hibachi.

BERNARD'S   98

The Biltmore Hotel
515 South Olive Street
Los Angeles, CA
(213) 612-1580

French

F ★ ★ ★ ★
S ★ ★ ★ ★
A ★ ★ ★ ★
P ★ ★ ★ ½

Jacket required
Valet parking
All major credit cards
Full bar
Reservations required

Lunch: Mon.-Fri. 11:30AM-2:00PM
Dinner: Mon.-Thurs. 6:00PM-10:00PM
          Fri. & Sat. 6:00PM-10:30PM
          Closed Sunday

Here the mellow oak-paneled walls backdrop dramatic trees and lush green plants, setting the stage for an extraordinary dining experience. The impeccably prepared cuisine reflects carefully selected, fresh ingredients. The wine cellar is prestigious.

THE BISTRO   76

246 North Canon Drive
Beverly Hills, CA
(213) 273-5633

Continental

F ★ ★ ★ ½
S ★ ★ ★ ★
A ★ ★ ★ ½
P ★ ★ ★

Jacket required
Valet parking
All major credit cards
Full bar
Reservations required

Lunch: Mon.-Fri. 12:00PM-3:00PM
Dinner: Mon.-Sat. 6:00PM-11:00PM
    Closed Sunday

The Bistro, like a breath of Paris, attracts people from around the world who are magnetized by the Beverly Hills/Hollywood café glamour scene. A favorite spot for fabled parties or special-occasion evenings. The food is superb, the clientele intriguing.

BISTRO GARDEN   78

176 North Canon Drive
Beverly Hills, CA
(213) 550-3900

French/Continental

F ★ ★ ★ ½
S ★ ★ ★ ½
A ★ ★ ★ ★
P ★ ★ ★ ½

No dress restrictions
Lot parking

All major credit cards
Full bar
Reservations recommended

Lunch/
Dinner: Mon.-Sat. 11:30AM-12:00AM
    Closed Sunday

This lush and lovely garden patio setting lures a celebrity crowd with its fine cuisine and air of relaxed sophistication. The house specializes in seafood, but the menu abounds with delicacies including superb soufflés and heavenly desserts.

BOH!   125

1323 Montana Avenue
Santa Monica, CA
(213) 451-2504

Italian

F ★ ★ ★ ★
S ★ ★ ★ ½
A ★ ★ ★ ½
P ★ ★ ★ ½

Good taste in dress required
Valet parking
All major credit cards
Full bar
Reservations required

Lunch: Mon.-Fri. 11:30AM-2:30PM
Dinner: Mon.-Sat. 6:00PM-10:30PM
    Closed Sunday

You'll be served beautifully prepared Northern Italian cuisine by a formally attired staff in this suave Florentine villa setting. The pastas are homemade and fresh fish dishes are plentiful.

BOTTLE INN   143
RISTORANTE

26 22nd Street
Hermosa Beach, CA
(213) 376-9595

Italian

F ★ ★ ★
S ★ ★ ★
A ★ ★ ★
P ★ ★ ★

Good taste in dress required
Street parking
All major credit cards
Beer/Wine
Reservations recommended

Dinner: Nightly 5:30PM-11:30PM

This warm, cheery dinner house makes you feel as if you were visiting a close friend. Owner Joe Cantisani has wedded extraordinary Italian cuisine with a wine list judged one of 10 best in America. (Alfredo Sedo was named California Restaurant Writers Sommelier of the year.) House specialties include Tortellini alla Panne, and Scampi Genovese.

BOUILLABAISSE 3

16820 Ventura Boulevard
Encino, CA
(818) 990-4850

Continental

F ★ ★ ★ ½
S ★ ★ ★
A ★ ★ ★
P ★ ★ ★ ★

Good taste in dress required
Valet parking
All major credit cards
Beer/Wine
Reservations required

Lunch: Mon.-Fri. 11:30AM-2:30PM
Dinner: Tues.-Sat. 7:00PM-8:30PM
         Closed Sunday

Specializing in Bouillabaisse à la Marseillaise, this restaurant succeeds admirably by supplementing their specialty with a limited dinner menu of veal dishes, chateaubriand, and fresh fish. The food is fabulous, the French-country décor charming, and the service exemplary.

CAFÉ FOUR OAKS 21

2181 North Beverly Glen
Los Angeles, CA
(213) 474-9317

American

F ★ ★ ★ ½
S ★ ★ ★ ½
A ★ ★ ★
P ★ ★ ★

No dress restrictions
Lot parking
MC, V
Full bar
Reservations required

Dinner: Wed.-Sun. 6:00PM-9:30PM
Brunch: Sun. 10:30AM-2:30PM
         Closed Monday and Tuesday

The setting for this country inn is a converted two-story Victorian home surrounded by the sylvan beauty of a rustic canyon. Fresh, original American dishes are featured. They are served with panache at this intimate dining spot.

CHANTECLAIR 143

18912 MacArthur Boulevard
Irvine, CA
(714) 752-8001

French/Continental

F ★ ★ ★ ½
A ★ ★ ★ ½
A ★ ★ ★ ½
P ★ ★ ★ ★

Jacket required for dinner
Valet parking
All major credit cards
Full bar
Reservations recommended

Lunch: Mon.-Fri. 11:00AM-2:30PM
Dinner: Mon.-Sun. 6:00PM-10:00PM
Brunch: Sun. 10:30AM-2:30PM

Designed like an English Tudor home, the many beautifully decorated dining rooms include The Conservatory, The Veranda, and The Grande Salon. The à la carte menu features beef, veal, chicken, and fish dishes and there are daily specials for both lunch and dinner.

THE CHARTHOUSE   119, 88

1097 Glendon
Los Angeles, CA
(213) 208-8034

18412 West Pacific Coast Highway
Malibu, CA
(213) 454-9321

American

F ★ ★ ★
S ★ ★ ★
A ★ ★ ★
P ★ ★ ½

Good taste in dress required
Valet-Malibu, lot and street parking Los Angeles
All major credit cards
Full bar
Reservations not required

Dinner: Sun.-Thurs. 5:00PM- 10:00PM
          Fri.& Sat. 5:00PM-11:00PM

This pair of restaurants is part of a trendy chain featuring architecture and décor tailored to fit each specific location. Primarily beef and seafood houses, the menu includes dishes to appeal to every taste, as well as nightly fresh fish specials.

CHASEN'S   57

9039 Beverly Boulevard
Los Angeles, CA
(213) 271-2168

Continental

F ★ ★ ★ ½
S ★ ★ ★
A ★ ★ ★ ½
P ★ ★ ★ ★

Jacket and tie required
Valet parking
Credit cards not accepted
Full bar
Reservations required

Dinner: Tues.-Sun. 6:00PM-12:00AM
          Closed Monday

The Hollywood elite and world famous have flocked to this legendary establishment for five decades. The atmosphere is posh and clubby, and the menu features entrées from around the world. "Gourmet chili" is a house specialty that is eternally popular.

CHAYA BRASSERIE   68

8741 Alden Drive
Los Angeles, CA
(213) 859-8833

Contemporary International

F ★ ★ ★ ½
S ★ ★ ★
A ★ ★ ★
P ★ ★ ½

Good taste in dress required
Valet and street parking
MC, V
Full bar
Reservations not required

Lunch: Mon.-Fri. 11:30AM-2:30PM
Tea: Mon.-Fri. 2:30PM-6:00PM
Dinner: Sun.-Thurs. 6:00PM-10:30PM
          Fri. & Sat. 6:00PM-11:00PM
Late
Supper: Mon.-Sat. 10:30PM-12:00AM

Chaya Brasserie is a refreshing change-of-pace restaurant built around a central atrium planted with bamboo reaching toward the skylight. The menu is an interesting melding of California, Milanese, and Oriental cooking techniques and ingredients that results in tantalizing specialties.

CHEZ CARY   143

571 South Main Street
Orange, CA
(714) 542-3595

Continental

F ★ ★ ★ ★
S ★ ★ ★ ★
A ★ ★ ★ ½
P ★ ★ ★ ★

Jacket and tie required
Valet parking
All major credit cards
Full bar
Reservations required

Dinner: Sun.-Fri. 6:30PM-10:30PM
          Sat. 5:30PM-10:30PM

Easy elegance with touches of grandeur make dining here a special experience. The décor is plush red velvet with crystal chandeliers and the service is inspired. Fresh fish, prime steaks, and fowl are included in the daily specials that highlight a wide menu.

CHIANTI   44

7383 Melrose Avenue
Los Angeles, CA
(213) 653-8333

Italian

F ★ ★ ★ ½
S ★ ★ ★ ½
A ★ ★ ★ ½
P ★ ★ ★ ½

No dress restrictions
Valet parking
All major credit cards
Full bar
Reservations required

Dinner: Nightly 5:30PM-11:30PM

This venerable establishment, with its refreshing art nouveau atmosphere features the Alta Cucina of Northern Italy. Here you will find such savory specialties as osso buco, saltimbocca, and veal piccata, prepared and served with effortless ease.

CHINOIS ON MAIN   138

2709 Main Street
Santa Monica, CA
(213) 392-9025

French/Chinese

F ★ ★ ★ ½
S ★ ★ ★ ½
A ★ ★ ★
P ★ ★ ★

Jacket preferred
Valet parking
AE, MC, V
Full bar
Reservations required for dinner

Lunch: Wed.-Fri. 11:30AM-2:00PM
Dinner: Nightly 6:00PM-11:00PM

Owner Wolfgang Puck has created a dramatic setting here in which to present his creative cuisine. The menu is a rich mélange of such items as Mandarin pancakes, specialty salads with duck and scallops, sizzling catfish, Peking duck served in four courses, lobster, and salmon with black and gold noodles.

THE CHRONICLE   14

897 Granite Drive
Pasadena, CA
(818) 792-1179

Continental/American

F ★ ★ ★
S ★ ★ ★ ½
A ★ ★ ★ ½
P ★ ★ ★

Good taste in dress required
Valet parking
All major credit cards
Full bar
Reservations recommended

Lunch: Mon.-Sat. 11:30AM-2:30PM
Dinner: Mon.-Sat. 5:30PM-10:30PM
          Sun. 5:00PM-10:00PM

If you enjoy the warm intimacy of a clublike atmosphere, you will delight in The Chronicle's authentic turn-of-the-century bar/grill décor. Fresh seafood specialties, veal and beef entrées, and outstanding salads are complemented by an impressive wine list.

THE CHRONICLE   137

2640 Main Street
Santa Monica, CA
(213) 392-4956

French

F ★ ★ ★ ½
S ★ ★ ★ ½
A ★ ★ ★ ½
P ★ ★ ★

Good taste in dress required, no shorts or sandals
Valet parking
All major credit cards
Full bar
Reservations required

Lunch: Mon.-Fri. 11:30AM-2:30PM
Dinner: Mon.-Thurs. 6:00PM-10:00PM
          Fri.-Sat. 6:00PM-11:30PM
          Sun. 5:00PM-10:00PM

A meticulously restored grand old house, circa 1902, and Victorian décor form the dramatic staging for such enticing dishes as saddle of lamb with fresh berries and Fresh Mussels aux Merlot. The wine list is well thought out.

COCK 'N BULL   32

9170 Sunset Boulevard
West Hollywood, CA
(213) 273-0081 or 276-7814

English/American

F ★ ★ ★
S ★ ★ ★
A ★ ★ ★
P ★ ★ ★

Good taste in dress required
Valet parking
All major credit cards
Full bar
Reservations required

Lunch/
Dinner: Daily 11:15AM-1:00AM

Since 1937 the Cock 'n Bull has been a Sunset Boulevard institution with a clublike clientele of sports, entertainment, and political personalities. The drinks are generous, the oyster bar exceptional, and the fare hearty. Renowned for their sumptuous buffet.

COLETTE   83

Beverly Pavilion Hotel
9360 Wilshire Boulevard
Beverly Hills, CA
(213) 273-1151

French

F ★ ★ ★ ½
S ★ ★ ★
A ★ ★ ★
P ★ ★ ½

No dress restrictions
Valet parking
All major credit cards
Full bar
Reservations required

Breakfast: Daily 7:00AM-11:00AM
Lunch: Daily 11:30AM-2:30PM
Dinner: Nightly 6:00PM-10:30PM

International travelers and local gastronomes pay their compliments to the chef by making frequent return visits to this fashionable dining spot. In the kitchen, Patrick Healy, conjures up a seasonally changing menu featuring such unique viands as a "Salade Rustique" of smoked duck and roasted quail.

THE CORKSCREW   112

11647 San Vicente Boulevard
Los Angeles, CA
(213) 826-5501

English Beef House

F ★ ★ ★
S ★ ★ ★
A ★ ★ ★
P ★ ★ ½

Good taste in dress required
Valet parking
All major credit cards
Full bar
Reservations required

Lunch: Mon.-Fri. 11:30AM-3:00PM
Dinner: Mon.-Fri. 5:00PM-10:00PM
            Sat. & Sun. 5:00PM-10:30PM

The Corkscrew, in the tradition of great English Beef Houses, focuses its bill of fare on choice steaks and prime rib roast. The food is well prepared, the service is attentive, and the atmosphere as British as the "changing of the guard."

THE COTERIE   30

Beverly Hills Hotel
9641 Sunset Boulevard
Beverly Hills, CA
(213) 276-2251

Continental

F ★ ★ ★ ½
S ★ ★ ★ ½
A ★ ★ ★ ½
P ★ ★ ★ ★

Jacket required
Valet parking
All major credit cards
Full bar
Reservations required

Dinner: Nightly 6:30PM-10:00PM

The Coterie is the hotel's gourmet dining room, and it provides you with a neat art déco setting for intimate dining. The cuisine is classically prepared and carefully presented. The wine list reflects thoughtful selections.

THE COVE   96

3191 West 7th Street
Los Angeles, CA
(213) 388-0361

Continental

F ★ ★ ★ ½
S ★ ★ ★ ½
A ★ ★ ★
P ★ ★ ★

Jacket required
Valet parking
All major credit cards
Full bar
Reservations recommended

Lunch: Mon.-Fri. 11:30AM-5:00PM
Dinner: Mon.-Sat. 5:00PM-11:00PM
            Closed Sunday

The Cove remains the same resplendent and popular mid-Wilshire restaurant it was when it made its debut in 1951. The old-world atmosphere is pleasantly relaxing and the food and service eminently satisfactory. Noted for its Rhineland-inspired entrées.

CUTTERS   130

2425 Colorado Avenue
Santa Monica, CA
(213) 453-3588

Continental

F ★ ★ ★
S ★ ★ ★ ½
A ★ ★ ½
P ★ ★

No dress restrictions
Valet and lot parking
AE, MC, V
Full bar
Reservations not required

Lunch/
Dinner: Daily 11:00AM-2:00AM

Cutters' menu changes with the seasons and encompasses a wide range of types of food, giving you a wonderful freedom of choice. This trendy concept encourages "unstructured" dining for every mood and taste. A sleek, "spur of the moment" restaurant.

DA VINCI   71

9737 Santa Monica Boulevard
Beverly Hills, CA
(213) 273-0960

Italian

F ★ ★ ★ ½
S ★ ★ ★ ½
A ★ ★ ★ ½
P ★ ★ ★

Good taste in dress required
Valet and street parking
All major credit cards
Full bar
Reservations recommended

Lunch: Mon.-Fri. 11:30AM-2:30PM
Dinner: Mon.-Sat. 5:30PM-11:00PM
         Closed Sunday

Tastefully decorated with a soft peach and pale green color scheme, Dominique De-Nichilo's restaurant blends elegance with a warm, welcoming feeling. Homemade pastas, fresh fish as available, and imported wild Italian mushrooms (Porcini) are featured on the bill of fare.

DAN TANA'S   35

9071 Santa Monica Boulevard
Los Angeles, CA
(213) 275-9444

Italian

F ★ ★ ★ ½
S ★ ★ ★ ½
A ★ ★ ½
P ★ ★ ½

Good taste in dress required
Valet parking
All major credit cards
Full bar
Reservations recommended

Dinner: Mon.-Sat. 5:00PM-1:00AM
         Sun. 5:00PM-12:00AM

Head for Dan Tana's when you want to peek at celebrities and enjoy a candlelit, flower-bedecked, intimate atmosphere. The cuisine reflect's owner Dan Tana's Trieste heritage. The wine list includes French, Italian, and California vintners.

DANTE PALISADES   114

1032 Swarthmore Avenue
Pacific Palisades, CA
(213) 459-7561

DANTE WILSHIRE   120

11917 Wilshire Boulevard
Los Angeles, CA
(213) 479-3991

Italian

F ★ ★ ★
S ★ ★ ★
A ★ ★ ★
P ★ ★ ½

No dress restrictions
Lot parking
AE, MC, V
Beer/Wine
Reservations required

Lunch: Tues.-Fri. 11:30AM-2:30PM
Dinner: Tues.-Sun. 5:30PM-10:30PM
         Closed Monday

At Dante's the focus is on fine cuisine, served and prepared with immaculate attention to detail. The setting is attractive, but understated, dramatizing the food. Homemade pastas, nicely sauced fresh seafoods, and a variety of veal dishes are among the house specialties.

DAR MAGHREB   25

7651 Sunset Boulevard
Los Angeles, CA
(213) 876-7651

Moroccan

F ★ ★ ★ ½
S ★ ★ ★
A ★ ★ ★ ★
P ★ ★ ★

Good taste in dress required
Valet parking
MC, V
Full bar
Reservations required on weekends

Dinner: Mon.-Fri. 6:00PM-11:00PM
               Sat. 5:30PM-11:00PM
               Sun. 5:30PM-10:30PM

Dine in regal splendor in a replica of a 15th century sultan's palace. You'll recline on luxurious low sofas to savor the lavish six-course feast of rich Moroccan food served by costumed waiters. A dining event as exotic as the featured belly dancer.

DONATELLO'S   111

11712 San Vicente Boulevard
Los Angeles, CA
(213) 820-9719

Italian

F ★ ★ ★
S ★ ★ ★
A ★ ★ ★
P ★ ★ ½

Jacket preferred
Valet, lot, and street parking
All major credit cards
Full bar
Reservations required

Lunch: Mon.-Fri. 11:30AM-2:00PM
Dinner: Mon.-Sat. 5:30PM-10:30PM
               Closed Sunday

This restaurant is owner Stephen Kastelan's tribute to the glory of Rome, from the elegant décor, to the formally attired waiters, and the Roman-style cooking. Here you'll savor such dishes as fettuccine pescatora, osso buco, and veal chops with light caper sauce. Pastas, desserts, and bread are made on the premises.

EL CHOLO   109

1121 South Western Avenue
Los Angeles, CA
(213) 734-2773

Mexican

F ★ ★ ★
S ★ ★ ★
A ★ ★ ½
P ★ ½

No dress restrictions
Valet and lot parking
AE, MC, V
Full bar
Reservations recommended

Lunch/
Dinner: Mon.-Thurs. 11:00AM-10:00PM
               Fri. & Sat. 11:00AM-11:00PM
               Sun. 11:00AM-9:00PM

This venerable L.A. landmark, with its hacienda ambiance, has been dispensing warm hospitality and spicy food since 1927. The same chef has reigned in the kitchen for more than 50 years, offering well prepared traditional Mexican dishes, and specialties such as green corn tamales, featured in the summer.

EL PADRINO   73

Beverly Wilshire Hotel
9500 Wilshire Boulevard
Beverly Hills, CA
(213) 275-4282

Continental

F ★ ★ ★ ½
S ★ ★ ★ ½
A ★ ★ ★ ½
P ★ ★ ★

Jacket preferred
Valet parking
All major credit cards
Full bar
Reservations recommended

Lunch: Mon.-Sat. 11:30AM-5:00PM
Dinner: Mon.-Sun. 5:00PM-11:00PM
Late
Supper: Mon.-Sun. 11:00PM-1:00AM
Brunch: Sun. 10:00AM, 12:00PM,
         and 2:00PM seatings

The saddle in the entry and the leather and dark wood walls create a California ranchero setting in which to relax and leisurely enjoy the wide range of creative continental dishes offered here. The late supper menu is intriguing, and the Sunday brunch very popular.

EMILIO'S   45

6602 Melrose Avenue
Los Angeles, CA
(213) 935-4922

Italian

F ★ ★ ★ ½
S ★ ★ ★ ½
A ★ ★ ★ ½
P ★ ★ ★

Jacket and tie preferred
Valet parking
All major credit cards
Full bar
Reservations recommended

Lunch: Thurs. & Fri. 11:30AM-3:00PM
Dinner: Sun.-Thurs. 5:00PM-12:00AM
         Fri.& Sat. 5:00PM-12:30AM

Cuisine from all regions of Italy is offered by owner Emilio Baglioni in this cozy restaurant with its six differently decorated dining areas. The bread, pastas, and ice cream are homemade and the menu offers a multitude of choices, including tempting daily specials.

EN BROCHETTE   85

9018 Burton Way
Beverly Hills, CA
(213) 276-9990

International

F ★ ★ ★
S ★ ★ ★
A ★ ★ ★ ½
P ★ ★ ½

No dress restrictions
Valet parking
All major credit cards
Beer/Wine
Reservations required

Lunch: Daily 11:30 AM-3:00PM
Dinner: Nightly 6:00PM-10:00PM

A gracious old Spanish-style home with lushly planted outdoor dining areas forms a lovely setting for relaxed California-style dining. The varied menu features dishes from many nations, prepared with the freshest and finest of native ingredients.

THE EXCELSIOR   69

Rodeo Collection Penthouse Level
421 North Rodeo Drive
Beverly Hills, CA
(213) 275-5100

French/Italian/Continental

F ★ ★ ★ ½
S ★ ★ ★ ½
A ★ ★ ★ ½
P ★ ★ ★ ½

Jacket required at dinner
Valet, lot, and street parking
All major credit cards
Full bar
Reservations recommended

Lunch: Tues.-Fri. 12:00PM-3:00PM
          Sat. 11:30AM-3:00PM
          Sun. 11:00AM-3:00PM
Dinner: Tues.-Sat. 7:00PM-10:30PM
          Closed Monday

A posh, art-déco penthouse setting creates an elegant aura at The Excelsior. Homemade pastas, pastries, and ice creams, plus unique veal and fresh fish dishes are house specialties. An elaborate Champagne buffet is a luncheon menu feature.

FIASCO   140

4451 Admiralty Way
Marina del Rey, CA
(213) 823-6395

Californian

F ★ ★ ★
S ★ ★ ★
A ★ ★ ★
P ★ ★ ½

No dress restrictions
Lot parking
All major credit cards
Full bar
Reservations not required

Lunch/
Dinner: Mon.-Fri. 11:30AM-2:00AM
         Sat. & Sun. 10:00AM-2:00AM

Set like a jewel on the Marina's main channel, Fiasco gives you a fascinating view whether you dine inside, or on the glassed-in outdoor deck. The cuisine is based on the freshest of seafoods and meats, and good pastas. A fine selection of California wines is available.

THE FINE AFFAIR   39

666 North Sepulveda Boulevard
Los Angeles, CA
(213) 476-2848/472-5555

French/Continental

F ★ ★ ★ ½
S ★ ★ ★ ½
A ★ ★ ★
P ★ ★ ★ ★

Jacket preferred
Valet, lot, and street parking
AE, MC, V
Full bar
Reservations recommended

Lunch: Tues.-Fri. 11:00AM-2:30PM
Dinner: Tues.-Sun. 6:00PM-11:00PM
Brunch: Sun. seatings at
         11:00AM & 1:00PM
         Closed Monday

An alluring country-French setting with green and white lattice work, plants, colorful flowers, and handpainted China on crisp pink linen add to the enjoyment of continental and French cuisine served here. Specialties include rack of lamb and a variety of fresh fish entrées. Among the homemade desserts you'll find a special Napoleon and fresh fruit tarts.

THE FISHMARKET   41

9229 Sunset Boulevard
Los Angeles, CA
(213) 550-1544

Continental/Seafood

F ★ ★ ★
S ★ ★ ★
A ★ ★ ★
P ★ ★ ★ ½

Jacket required in the disco lounge
Valet parking
All major credit cards
Full bar
Reservations required

Lunch: Daily 11:30AM-3:00PM
Dinner: Nightly 6:00PM-12:00AM

Anticipate a joyous outing when you head for The Fishmarket. Nick's special salad, Abalone Ricci, Hawaiian fish, and steak and veal dishes all win accolades. The service is consistently good. Enjoy dancing or nightcaps in the adjacent disco lounge.

FIVE CROWNS   143

3801 East Pacific Coast Highway
Corona del Mar, CA
(714) 760-0331

Continental

F ★ ★ ★ ½
S ★ ★ ★ ½
A ★ ★ ★ ½
P ★ ★ ★ ½

Jacket preferred, no beach wear or shorts
Valet parking
All major credit cards
Full bar
Reservations recommended

Dinner: Nightly from 5:00PM
Brunch: Sun. 10:30AM-3:00PM

A replica of Ye Old Bell, the oldest inn in England, this picturesque restaurant with timbered walls and ceilings and a fireplace in every room, serves prime rib with Yorkshire pudding prepared the British way, and features roast duckling and rack of lamb. The wine list contains 1400 choice labels.

FRANÇOIS   100

555 South Flower Street
Los Angeles, CA
(213) 680-2727

French

F ★ ★ ★
S ★ ★ ★ ½
A ★ ★ ★ ½
P ★ ★ ★ ★

Jacket required
Lot and street parking
All major credit cards
Full bar
Reservations recommended

Lunch: Mon.-Fri. 11:00AM-2:00PM
Dinner: Mon.-Sat. 6:30PM-10:30PM
          Closed Sunday

A setting of dignified elegance, attentive personal service, and a menu featuring internationally acclaimed, innovative European dishes have earned an enviable reputation for François. A restaurant of charm and character with a wine list including rare vintages.

GAETANO'S   1

23536 Calabasas Road
Calabasas, CA
(818) 716-6100

Italian

F ★ ★ ★ ½
S ★ ★ ★ ½
A ★ ★ ★
P ★ ★ ★

Good taste in dress required
Lot and street parking
AE, MC, V
Beer/Wine
Reservations required

Lunch: Tues.-Fri. 11:30AM-3:00PM
Dinner: Tues.-Sun. 5:00PM-10:30PM
          Closed Monday

Owner/host Gaetno Palmeri greets you personally in his delightful restaurant with its indoor/outdoor dining options and Roman garden atmosphere. Many of the dishes offered here are unusual; and there are often up to seven specialties ranging from veal to fish to homemade pasta offered nightly. For a refreshing finish, try the cantaloupe ice cream served in a cantaloupe shell—it is absolutely blissful.

GATSBY'S 110

11500 San Vicente Boulevard
Los Angeles, CA
(213) 820-1476

Italian

F ★ ★ ★
S ★ ★ ★
A ★ ★ ★
P ★ ★ ½

Jacket required
Valet parking
All major credit cards
Full bar
Reservations recommended

Lunch: Mon.-Fri. 11:30AM-2:30PM
Dinner: Mon.-Sat. 5:30PM-11:00PM
Closed Sunday

As the name suggests, the authentic '20s decor here salutes F. Scott Fitzgerald's novel *The Great Gatsby*. The emphasis is on fine service and excellent food, with such specialties as Cannelloni Florentine and Veal Valdastana.

THE GINGER MAN 82

369 North Bedford Drive
Beverly Hills, CA
(213) 273-7585

American/Continental

F ★ ★ ★
S ★ ★ ★
A ★ ★ ★
P ★ ★ ★

No dress restrictions
Valet parking after 6:00PM
AE, MC, V
Full bar
Reservations recommended

Lunch: Daily 11:30AM-4:00PM
Dinner: Nightly 5:30PM-10:30PM
Late
Supper: Nightly 10:30PM-1:00AM

Rub elbows with your favorite stars in this New York-style restaurant-bar. Owners Carroll O'Connor and Patrick O'Neal offer lunch and dinner specialties ranging from huge burgers, omelettes, and salads, to Beef Wellington and veal chops or salmon en croûte.

GIUSEPPE! 63

8256 Beverly Boulevard
Los Angeles, CA
(213) 653-8025

Italian

F ★ ★ ★ ½
S ★ ★ ★ ½
A ★ ★ ★ ½
P ★ ★ ★ ½

Good taste in dress required
Valet parking
AE, MC, V
Full bar
Reservations required

Lunch: Mon.-Fri. 11:30AM-3:00PM
Dinner: Mon.-Thurs. 6:00PM-11:00PM
Fri. & Sat. 6:00PM-12:00AM
Closed Sunday

You'll be greeted by your host, Giuseppe Bellisario, in a warm indoor garden environment, created with fresh flowers and tastefully displayed plants and hanging baskets, and offered such enticing entrées as traditional fettuccine, veal dishes, and pastas created to order. The wine list and desserts are both notable.

GLADSTONE'S 4 FISH 127

17300 Pacific Coast Highway
Pacific Palisades, CA
(213) GL 4-FISH

Seafood

F ★ ★ ★ ½
S ★ ★ ½
A ★ ★ ★
P ★ ★ ★

No dress restrictions
Valet parking
All major credit cards
Full bar
Reservations recommended

Breakfast/
Lunch/
Dinner: Daily 7:00AM-11:00PM

Owner Bob Morris attracts patient crowds to this restaurant with the nautical decor, ocean view, and friendly ambiance. You'll feast on Maine lobster to order, scallops, and shrimp charcoaled over mesquite wood, or have "All you can eat" of shrimp on Monday, clams and oysters on Tuesday, trout on Wednesday, or scallops on Thursday.

THE GRILL   75

9560 Dayton Way
Beverly Hills, CA
(213) 276-0615

American

F ★ ★ ★ ½
S ★ ★ ★
A ★ ★ ★
P ★ ★ ★

Good taste in dress required
Valet parking
AE, MC, V
Full bar
Reservations required

Lunch/
Dinner: Mon.-Sat. 11:30AM-12:30AM
          Closed Sunday

When you have a hankering for prime steaks, chops, and fresh seafood, served in a very traditional grill setting, stroll up the alley behind Giorgios to the corner of Rodeo Drive and Dayton Way, and discover this off-the-alley charmer of a restaurant devoted to cooking the good old American way.

GUIDO'S   121

11980 Santa Monica Boulevard
West Los Angeles, CA
(213) 820-6649

Italian/Continental

F ★ ★ ★ ½
S ★ ★ ★ ½
A ★ ★ ★
P ★ ★ ½

No dress restrictions
Valet parking
All major credit cards
Full bar
Reservations required

Lunch: Mon.-Fri. 11:30AM-3:00PM
Dinner: Nightly 5:00PM-12:00AM

The patina of polished wood, a blazing hearth, and soft lighting create a warm, relaxing atmosphere at Guido's. The bricked patio, filled with colorful flowers is an inviting spot for outdoor dining. The food is outstanding, as is the wine list.

GULLIVER'S   141

13181 Mindanao Way
Marina del Rey, CA
(213) 821-8866

American

F ★ ★ ★ ½
S ★ ★ ★
A ★ ★ ★
P ★ ★ ★

Good taste in dress required
Lot parking
MC, V
Full bar
Reservations required

Lunch: Mon.-Fri. 11:30AM-2:30PM
Dinner: Mon.-Thurs. 5:30PM-10:00PM
Fri. & Sat. 5:00PM-11:00PM
Sun. 4:00PM-10:00PM

Enter the world of 18th Century England when you travel here, and enjoy hearty fare served by costumed wenches and squires. You can feast on prime rib (cut to your order), or a choice of steaks, veal, fish, duck, and chicken entrées.

HARRY'S BAR AND AMERICAN GRILL 81

2020 Avenue of the Stars
Los Angeles, CA
(213) 277-2333

Italian/American

F ★ ★ ★
S ★ ★ ★
A ★ ★ ★
P ★ ★ ★

No dress restrictions
Valet parking
AE, MC, V
Full bar
Reservations required

Lunch: Mon.-Sat. 11:30AM-3:00PM
Dinner: Nightly 5:30PM-11:30PM

Created in the image of Harry's Bar in Florence, Italy, this sister-restaurant is a Century City institution. The menu is varied featuring fresh pastas, fresh fish, veal specialties, prime steaks and chops, and classic Northern Italian dishes.

THE HOBBIT 143

2932 East Chapman Avenue
Orange, CA
(714) 997-1972 Reservations
(714) 997-3181 Cancellations

Continental

F ★ ★ ★ ½
S ★ ★ ★ ½
A ★ ★ ★ ½
P ★ ★ ★ ★

Good taste in dress required
Lot parking
All major credit cards
Beer/Wine
Reservations required

Dinner: One seating per night,
Tues.-Sat. 7:30PM
Sun.-7:00PM
Closed Monday

Chef Michael Philippi and Maître d' John Balesky, co-owners, orchestrate a unique dining experience at The Hobbit, where a nine-course dinner is prepared for one seating per night. The menu changes weekly and the food and service are consistently excellent.

IL GIARDINO 80

9235 West Third Street
Beverly Hills, CA
(213) 275-5444

Italian

F ★ ★ ★
S ★ ★ ★
A ★ ★ ★
P ★ ★ ★

No dress restrictions
Valet, lot, and street parking
All major credit cards
Beer/Wine
Reservations recommended

Lunch: Mon.-Sat. 11:30AM-2:00PM
Dinner: Mon.-Sat. 6:30PM-10:00PM
Closed Sunday

This authentic Italian restaurant with its refreshingly verdant garden setting is devoted to serving Tuscan-style cuisine. Critically acclaimed entrées include ravioli filled with spinach, risotto with seafood, gnocchi with a Gorgonzola cheese sauce, and a piquant seafood salad.

INDIA GITANJALI   43

414 North LaCienega Boulevard
Los Angeles, CA
(213) 657-2117

Indian

F ★ ★ ★ ½
S ★ ★ ★
A ★ ★ ★
P ★ ★ ½

Good taste in dress required
Valet and lot parking
All major credit cards
Beer/Wine
Reservations recommended

Dinner: Sun.-Thurs. 6:00PM-10:30PM
          Fri.& Sat. 6:00PM-11:00PM

Restaurant writers and critics have heaped
praise on this exotic restaurant, which is
devoted to serving the gourmet cuisine of
North India. You can savor succulent lamb
curries and fresh made-to-order breads,
or try the many seafood or vegetarian
specialties. An award-winning wine list is
also offered by owner P.K. Chadda.

THE IVY   70

113 North Robertson Boulevard
Los Angeles, CA
(213) 274-8303

American

F ★ ★ ★
S ★ ★ ★
A ★ ★ ★
P ★ ★ ★ ½

No dress restrictions
Valet parking
All major credit cards
Full bar
Reservations recommended

Lunch: Mon.-Fri. 11:30AM-3:00PM
          Sat. 11:30AM-3:30PM
Dinner: Mon.-Fri. 6:00PM-11:00PM
          Sat. 6:00PM-11:30PM
          Closed Sunday

Early American artifacts and antiques
form the backdrop in this comfortable dining spot with its eclectic bill of fare. You'll
find baby back ribs, rack of lamb and veal,
crabcakes, fish grilled over mesquite, and
baked chicken chardonnay sharing honors on the menu. There are daily specials
and yummy desserts that include a lemon
cake lavished with white chocolate.

JACK'S AT THE BEACH   129

2700 Wilshire Boulevard
Santa Monica, CA
(213) 396-1831

Seafood/Nouvelle Cuisine

F ★ ★ ★
S ★ ★ ★
A ★ ★ ★
P ★ ★ ★

Jacket required
Valet parking
All major credit cards
Full bar
Reservations required

Lunch: Daily 11:30AM-2:30PM
Dinner: Nightly 5:30PM-10:30PM

The convivial atmosphere and genial host,
Tilo, have lured celebrities from around
the world to this Southern California
"landmark" restaurant for 38 years. You'll
find the nouvelle cuisine emphasizes fresh
seafood, but also includes interesting
meat entrées.

JADE WEST   91

2040 Avenue of the Stars
Los Angeles, CA
(213) 556-3388

Chinese

F ★ ★ ★ ½
S ★ ★ ★
A ★ ★ ★
P ★ ★ ½

Good taste in dress required
Valet parking
All major credit cards
Full bar
Reservations required

Lunch: Mon.-Fri. 11:30AM-3:00PM
Dinner: Mon. 3:00PM-9:00PM
          Tues.-Fri. 3:00PM-11:00PM
          Sat. & Sun. 4:30PM-11:00PM

Luxuriate in the Oriental ambiance created by hand-crafted works of art that beautify this gracious Century City restaurant. Szechwan, Cantonese, Peking, and Shanghai dishes are included on the menu. The service is unobtrusive, and the Polynesian drinks potent and inventive.

JIMMY'S   33

201 Moreno Drive
Beverly Hills, CA
(213) 879-2394

French/Continental

F ★ ★ ★ ★
S ★ ★ ★ ★
A ★ ★ ★ ★
P ★ ★ ★ ★

Jacket required at lunch
Jacket and tie required at dinner
Valet parking
All major credit cards
Full bar
Reservations required

Lunch: Mon.-Fri. 11:30AM-3:00PM
Dinner: Mon.-Sat. 6:00PM-12:00AM
          Closed Sunday

Luxe and lovely, Jimmy's air of understated elegance is exemplified by the Baccarat chandeliers and Limoges china. A chic place to see and be seen, while enjoying your selections from an ambitious menu. Host and owner, Jimmy Murphy, sets a gracious standard for service.

KNOLL'S BLACK   123
FOREST INN

2454 Wilshire Boulevard
Santa Monica, CA
(213) 395-2212

German

F ★ ★ ★ ½
S ★ ★ ★ ½
A ★ ★ ★
P ★ ★ ★ ½

Good taste in dress required
Valet parking
All major credit cards
Full bar
Reservations required

Lunch: Tues.-Fri. 11:30AM-3:00PM
Dinner: Tues.-Sun. 5:30PM-10:30PM
          Closed Monday

Offering you a choice of two dining rooms and an outdoor garden, this popular restaurant has all the charm of a Swiss chalet. Famous for Kalbshaxe (veal shank), roast goose, venison, and for their outstanding selection of authentically prepared European pastries.

LA BELLA FONTANA   23

Beverly Wilshire Hotel
9500 Wilshire Boulevard
Beverly Hills, CA
(213) 275-4282

French

F ★ ★ ★ ½
S ★ ★ ★ ½
A ★ ★ ★ ½
P ★ ★ ★ ★

Jacket and tie required
Valet parking
All major credit cards
Full bar
Reservations required

Lunch: Mon.-Fri. 12:00PM-3:00PM
Dinner: Mon.-Sat. 6:00PM-11:00PM
  Closed Sunday

Ornate and lovely with a splashing three-tiered fountain as a focal point, this restaurant has an air of formal elegance that harmonizes with the character of the food. Hors d'oeuvres, appetizers, salads, and entrées such as veal with truffles, pheasant, salmon, and tournedos St. Michel are flawlessly prepared and served graciously.

LA BRUSCHETTA 89

1621 Westwood Boulevard
Los Angeles, CA
(213) 477-1052

Italian

F ★ ★ ★
S ★ ★ ★
A ★ ★ ★
P ★ ★ ★

Jacket required
Valet parking
All major credit cards
Beer/Wine
Reservations required

Dinner: Mon.-Fri. 5:30PM-10:30PM
  Sat. 5:30PM-11:00PM
  Closed Sunday

Floral displays, lush plants, and a gallery of contemporary paintings invite you to enter this spacious dining room. The formal feeling is modified by the presence of wine racks, indicative of the vintages

available. The culinary presentations tend to be lightly sauced, in the Northern Italian manner.

LA COURONNE 12

142 South Lake Avenue
Pasadena, CA
(818) 793-3151

French

F ★ ★ ★ ½
S ★ ★ ★
A ★ ★ ★
P ★ ★ ★

Good taste in dress required
Valet and street parking
All major credit cards
Full bar
Reservations recommended

Lunch: Tues.-Fri. 11:30AM-2:00PM
Dinner: Tues.-Thurs. 6:00PM-9:00PM
  Fri. & Sat. 6:00PM-11:00PM
  Closed Sunday

A rare combination of all the amenities requisite to "civilized" dining have been assembled here by owner Lud Renick. The décor is chic and elegant; you'll use fine crystal, china, and silver service. The wine list includes over 750 labels, and the classic French cuisine is properly prepared and well presented.

LA DOLCE VITA 65

9785 Santa Monica Boulevard
Beverly Hills, CA
(213) 278-1845

Italian

F ★ ★ ★ ½
S ★ ★ ★ ½
A ★ ★ ★ ½
P ★ ★ ★ ½

Jacket required
Valet parking
All major credit cards

Full bar
Reservations required

Dinner: Mon.-Sat. 5:00PM-11:00PM
Closed Sunday

An entertainment industry favorite for 19 years, La Dolce Vita serves carefully prepared cuisine made with fresh ingredients. The atmosphere is warm and intimate, and the service is impeccable. The dessert menu and wine list both praiseworthy.

LA FAMIGLIA   67

453 North Canon Drive
Beverly Hills, CA
(213) 276-6208

Italian

F ★ ★ ★ ★
S ★ ★ ★ ½
A ★ ★ ★ ½
P ★ ★ ★ ½

No dress restrictions
Valet parking
All major credit cards
Full bar
Reservations required

Lunch: Mon.-Fri. 11:30AM-2:30PM
Dinner: Mon.-Thurs. 5:00PM-11:00PM
Fri. & Sat. 5:00PM-1:00AM
Closed Sunday

When you have a penchant for savory Northern Italian food, visit Joe Patti's comfortable, inviting restaurant. Calamari in a red sauce served in a crock or a cauldron is a house specialty. Fresh fish, veal chops and veal piccata, and scampi are also featured and there is a light menu for calorie counters.

LA PETITE CHAYA   18

1930 Hillhurst Avenue
Los Angeles, CA
(213) 665-5991

French/Japanese

F ★ ★ ★
S ★ ★ ★
A ★ ★ ★
P ★ ★ ★

Good taste in dress required
Valet and street parking
AE, MC, V
Full bar
Reservations required

Dinner: Mon.-Thurs. 6:00PM-10:30PM
Fri. & Sat. 6:00PM-11:00PM
Closed Sunday

You'll find contemporary Japanese art displayed on off-white walls and a skylit garden room here, that create a clean, modernist Japanese aura. The innovative cuisine is based on fresh and seasonal California, French, and Oriental ingredients and cooking techniques.

LA SCALA   56

9455 Santa Monica Boulevard
Beverly Hills, CA
(213) 275-0579

Italian

F ★ ★ ★ ½
S ★ ★ ★ ½
A ★ ★ ★ ½
P ★ ★ ★ ★

Jacket and tie preferred
Valet parking
AE, MC, V
Full bar
Reservations required

Lunch: Mon.-Fri. 11:30 AM-2:30PM
Dinner: Mon.-Sat. 5:00PM-12:00AM
Closed Sunday

Jean Leon's Florentine-style restaurant is a time-honored Los Angeles landmark with a series of romantic and intimate dining banquettes. Chef Emilio Nunez offers an excellent selection of dishes including Linguine Genovese and Fettuccine Leon. The wine cellar is exceptionally diverse.

LA SERRE   9

12969 Ventura Boulevard
Studio City, CA
(818) 990-0500

French

F ★ ★ ★ ½
S ★ ★ ★ ½
A ★ ★ ★ ½
P ★ ★ ★ ★

Jacket required
Valet parking
AE, MC, V
Full bar
Reservations required

Lunch: Mon.-Fri. 12:00PM-2:30PM
Dinner: Mon.-Sat. 6:00PM-10:30PM
         Closed Sunday

You'll find visiting La Serre like stepping into an enchanted garden that has elegance and great chic. Daily gourmet specialties include a wide variety of fresh fish, Maine lobster, and prime meats. The food presentation is beautifully contrived.

LA TOQUE   24

8171 Sunset Boulevard
Los Angeles, CA
(213) 656-7515

Contemporary French

F ★ ★ ★ ½
S ★ ★ ★
A ★ ★ ★
P ★ ★ ★ ★

Jacket preferred
Valet parking
All major credit cards
Full bar
Reservations required

Lunch: Mon.-Fri. 11:45AM-2:15PM
Dinner: Mon.-Thurs. 6:30PM-10:30PM
         Fri. & Sat. 6:00PM-10:30PM
         Closed Sunday

Owner-chef Ken Frank devises a new menu daily, reflecting the finest available foods in the market and the method of preparation they inspire. This creative cuisine is served with élan in a small restaurant reminiscent of a romantic French country auberge.

LAUTREC   2

22160 Ventura Boulevard
Woodland Hills, CA
(818) 704-1185

Continental

F ★ ★ ★
S ★ ★ ★
A ★ ★ ★
P ★ ★ ★

Good taste in dress required
Valet parking
All major credit cards
Full bar
Reservations recommended

Lunch/
Dinner: Mon.-Sat. 11:00AM-12:00AM
Brunch: Sun. 11:00AM-4:00PM

You'll find a warm, glowing aura in this portrait pretty restaurant with its natural oak, shiny brass, cut glass, fresh flowers, and flattering burgundy and pink color scheme. The continental menu has French flair, and lamb and seafood are house specialties.

LAWRY'S THE PRIME RIB   59

55 North LaCienega Boulevard
Beverly Hills, CA
(213) 652-2827

American

F ★ ★ ★ ½
S ★ ★ ★ ½
A ★ ★ ★
P ★ ★ ★ ½

Good taste in dress required
Valet parking
All major credit cards
Full bar
Reservations recommended

Dinner: Mon.-Thurs. 5:00PM-11:00PM
         Fri. & Sat. 5:00PM-12:00AM
         Sun. 3:00PM-11:00PM

Prime rib is the only entrée served in this legendary old English-style restaurant. It is cut to your specifications, tableside, and served with Yorkshire pudding and a crisp salad. The service is smooth and pleasant, and the desserts, made on the premises, are superb.

LAWRY'S WESTSIDE   60
BROILER

116 North LaCienega Boulevard
Beverly Hills, CA
(213) 655-8686

American

F ★ ★ ★ ½
S ★ ★ ★ ½
A ★ ★ ★
P ★ ★ ★

Good taste in dress required
Valet and street parking
AE, MC, V
Full bar
Reservations recommended

Lunch: Mon.-Fri. 11:30AM-2:30PM
Dinner: Nightly 5:00PM-11:00PM

Contemporary décor with wicker and upholstered pieces and well displayed modern art form an inviting ambiance here. You can prelude your dinner with a variety of unusual appetizers and salads, then enjoy fresh fish or a fine steak broiled to order over mesquite charcoal. Other sumptuous entrées are also available.

LE CHARDONNAY   48

8284 Melrose Avenue
Los Angeles, CA
(213) 655-8880

French

F ★ ★ ★ ½
S ★ ★ ★ ½
A ★ ★ ★ ½
P ★ ★ ★

Good taste in dress required
Valet parking
All major credit cards
Full bar
Reservations required

Lunch: Mon.-Fri. 12:00PM-2:00PM
Dinner: Mon.-Sat. 6:00PM-11:00PM
         Closed Sunday

This art nouveau, turn-of-the-century bistro has handsome carved wood moldings, and mirrors, tiles, and gleaming brass enhancing the décor. A wood-burning rotisserie and mesquite grill add distinguishing subtle flavors to the innovative French cuisine.

LE DOME   29

8720 Sunset Boulevard
Los Angeles, CA
(213) 659-6919

French

F ★ ★ ★ ½
S ★ ★ ★
A ★ ★ ★ ★
P ★ ★ ★

Jacket preferred
Valet parking
AE, DC, MC, V
Full bar
Reservations required

Lunch: Mon.-Fri. 12:00PM-6:00PM
Dinner: Mon.-Thurs. 6:00PM-12:00AM
         Fri. & Sat. 6:00PM-1:00AM
         Closed Sunday

A large circular bar dominates the décor of Le Dome, and elegantly appointed rooms branch out from it. Hearty soups, unusual salads, and homemade desserts round out the menu that features five daily fresh fish specials, prime beef, fresh rabbit and veal shank.

L'ERMITAGE   53

730 North LaCienega Boulevard
Los Angeles, CA
(213) 652-5840

French

F ★ ★ ★ ★
S ★ ★ ★ ★
A ★ ★ ★ ★
P ★ ★ ★ ★

Jacket preferred
Valet parking
All major credit cards
Full bar
Reservations required

Dinner: Mon.-Sat. 6:30PM-12:00AM
Closed Sunday

An inner patio, cozy fireplace, and air of warm elegance will make you feel as if you are dining in a luxurious private home. Fresh Atlantic ocean fish, duck, veal, French-style breast of chicken, and souf- flés typify the menu offerings. Homemade pastries, sorbet, and ice cream are featured finales.

L'ESCOFFIER   86

Beverly Hilton Hotel
9876 Wilshire Boulevard
Beverly Hills, CA
(213) 274-7777

French

F ★ ★ ★ ★
S ★ ★ ★ ★
A ★ ★ ★ ★
P ★ ★ ★ ★

Jacket and tie required
Valet and lot parking
All major credit cards
Full bar
Reservations required

Dinner: Mon.-Sat. 6:30PM-10:30PM
Closed Sunday

L'Escoffier gives you an enchanting view from its penthouse setting, and it has been recently refurbished, adding a rosy glow to its elegant atmosphere. Its legendary reputation for fine service and classic French cuisine continues. Danceable music and an excellent wine list will add to your dining pleasure.

LE ST.GERMAIN   46

5955 Melrose Avenue
Los Angeles, CA
(213) 467-1108

French

F ★ ★ ★ ★
S ★ ★ ★ ★
A ★ ★ ★ ★
P ★ ★ ★ ½

No dress restrictions
Valet parking
All major credit cards
Full bar
Reservations required

Lunch: Mon.-Fri. 12:00PM-2:30PM
Dinner: Mon.-Sat. 6:00PM-10:30PM
Closed Sunday

Feel pampered and luxurious while dining in the sumptuous setting created by opu- lent velvet walls, with mirrors reflecting lavish fresh flower arrangements. The tra- ditional French cuisine is of epicurean qu- ality, and it is served with deserving flourish.

LE SAINT MICHEL   131

3218 Santa Monica Boulevard
Santa Monica, CA
(213) 829-3173

French

F ★ ★ ★ ½
S ★ ★ ★ ½
A ★ ★ ★
P ★ ★ ★

Good taste in dress required
Lot and street parking
AE, CB, DC
Beer/Wine
Reservations required

Dinner: Tues.-Sun. 6:00PM-10:30PM
           Closed Monday

Small, quiet, and dignified, here you will find specialized food in a pleasing French country atmosphere. The cuisine focuses on seafood and duck, prepared with imaginative accents that produce dishes of extraordinary quality. The bouillabaisse is consistently good and very popular.

LES ANGES   126

14809 Pacific Coast Highway
Santa Monica, CA
(213) 454-1331

French

F ★ ★ ★ ½
S ★ ★ ★ ½
A ★ ★ ★ ½
P ★ ★ ★ ★

Jacket preferred
Valet parking
All major credit cards
Full bar
Reservations recommended

Dinner: Tues.-Sat. from 6:30PM
           Sun. from 6:00PM
           Closed Monday

Experience the taste delights of modern haute cuisine in a gray and white setting made resplendent with marble and mirrors. The menu changes nightly featuring such entrées as lobster infused with herbs, roast squab en salmis, and oysters with champagne sauce and caviar.

LES PYRENEES   132

2455 Santa Monica Boulevard
Santa Monica, CA
(213) 828-7503

French

F ★ ★ ★ ½
S ★ ★ ★ ½
A ★ ★ ★
P ★ ★ ★

Good taste in dress required
Lot and street parking
AE, MC, V
Full bar
Reservations recommended

Lunch: Tues.-Fri. 11:30AM-2:00PM
Dinner: Tues.-Sun. 5:30PM-10:00PM
          Closed Monday

The quiet charm of a petite Parisian café is echoed in Jacques Toulet's intimate eatery, where you can savor such gustatory delights as Veal Normande or Florentine, quail, mini-duck with fresh pear, fresh fish, or roast veal with fresh spinach and bearnaise sauce.

LEW MITCHELL'S   93
ORIENT EXPRESS

5400 Wilshire Boulevard
Los Angeles, CA
(213) 935-6000

Chinese

F ★ ★ ★ ½
S ★ ★ ★ ½
A ★ ★ ★ ½
P ★ ★ ★ ½

Good taste in dress required
Valet and lot parking
AE, DC, MC, V
Full bar
Reservations recommended

Lunch: Mon.-Fri. 11:30AM-2:30PM
Dinner: Nightly from 6:00PM

Indulge in your choice of Mandarin or Szechwan style Chinese dishes, meticulously prepared and served in an atmosphere of understated sophistication. A limited offering of continental favorites supplements the large selection of Oriental entrées.

L'ORANGERIE   49

903 North La Cienega Boulevard
Los Angeles, CA
(213) 652-9770

French

F ★ ★ ★ ★
S ★ ★ ★ ★
A ★ ★ ★ ★
P ★ ★ ★ ★

Jacket required
Valet parking
All major credit cards
Full bar
Reservations required

Dinner: Nightly 6:30PM-10:45PM

This regal restaurant with its high arched windows, open spacious feeling, and elegant atmosphere is perfect for festive occasions. Veal dishes, prepared with three different mustard sauces, and fresh fish flown from France are noteworthy.

MA MAISON   54

8368 Melrose Avenue
Los Angeles, CA
(213) 655-1991

French

F ★ ★ ★ ★
S ★ ★ ★ ★
A ★ ★ ★ ½
P ★ ★ ★ ★

Jacket preferred
Valet parking
All major credit cards
Full bar
Reservations required

Lunch: Mon.-Sat. 12:00PM-2:30PM
Dinner: Mon.-Sat. 6:30PM-10:30PM
         Closed Sunday

This restaurant, housed in a converted bungalow with inviting garden and patio areas, has become a mecca for discerning diners since it opened in 1972. Owner Patrick Terrail stresses customer comfort, deft service, and an imaginative menu based on the freshest and best available ingredients.

MADAME WU'S   122
GARDEN

2201 Wilshire Boulevard
Santa Monica, CA
(213) 828-5656

Chinese

F ★ ★ ★ ½
S ★ ★ ★ ½
A ★ ★ ★ ½
P ★ ★ ★ ½

Good taste in dress required
Jacket and tie required in Imperial Room
Valet, lot, and street parking
All major credit cards
Full bar
Reservations recommended

Lunch/
Dinner: Sun.-Fri. 11:30AM-10:00PM
         Sat. 5:00PM-10:30PM

Madame Sylvia Wu's personal charisma is reflected in this tasteful restaurant that has attracted a loyal clientele since its opening more than two decades ago. Cantonese and Szechwan dishes are featured in the extensive menu; the food is prepared and served with great skill.

MALDONADO'S 13

1202 East Green Street
Pasadena, CA
(818) 796-1126 or (213) 681-9462

Continental

F ★ ★ ★ ½
S ★ ★ ★ ½
A ★ ★ ★ ½
P ★ ★ ★ ★

Jacket required
Valet parking
AE, MC, V
Full bar
Reservations required

Lunch: Mon.-Fri. 11:00AM-2:00PM
Dinner: Tues.-Sun. Seatings at 6:00PM
              and 9:00PM

Enjoy the best of two worlds at Maldonado's: good food and musical entertainment. The menu changes seasonally and includes fresh fish, veal, and fowl specialties. Light opera and musical comedy performed by professional artists provides a grand finale.

MANDARETTE 62

8386 Beverly Boulevard
Los Angeles, CA
(213) 655-6115

Chinese

F ★ ★ ★
S ★ ★ ★
A ★ ★ ½
P ★ ½

Good taste in dress required
Street parking
MC, V
Beer/Wine
Reservations not required

Lunch/
Dinner: Sun.-Thurs. 11:30AM-12:00AM
              Fri. & Sat. 11:30AM-1:00AM

Philip Chiang's Chinese café serves a wonderful assortment of sophisticated dishes from all over China, cooked without cornstarch or oil. Green onion pancakes, delicately spiced won-tons in paper-thin wrappers doused in fiery Hunanese sauce, and the original hamburger Mandarette—pork and chili sauce in small crisp homemade buns typify the cuisine you will find here.

THE MANDARIN 64

430 North Camden Drive
Beverly Hills, CA
(213) 272-0267

Chinese

F ★ ★ ★ ½
S ★ ★ ★ ½
A ★ ★ ★ ½
P ★ ★ ½

Good taste in dress required
Valet parking
All major credit cards
Full bar
Reservations required

Lunch: Mon.-Fri. 11:30AM-3:30PM
Dinner: Mon.-Sat. 5:00PM-11:00PM
              Sun. 5:00PM-10:30PM

Luxuriant and spacious with Chinese antiques integrated into the décor, The Mandarin mirrors its San Francisco sister's success. Northern Chinese specialties such as Peking Duck, Beggar's Chicken, and 5-Spiced Shrimp are flawlessly prepared and graciously served.

THE MARQUIS WEST   133

3110 Santa Monica Boulevard
Santa Monica, CA
(213) 828-4567

Continental

F ★ ★ ★ ½
S ★ ★ ★ ½
A ★ ★ ★
P ★ ★ ★

Jacket required, tie preferred
Valet parking
All major credit cards
Full bar
Reservations required

Lunch: Mon.-Fri. 11:30AM-2:30PM
Dinner: Nightly 5:30PM-10:30PM

A consistent winner of awards, this restaurant has a large and loyal clientele of gastronomes who appreciate the excellent continental and Northern Italian cuisine, the thoughtful service, and the plush atmosphere. The menu is extensive and your choice of entrées is immense.

MARRAKESH   143 & 8

1100 West Coast Highway
Newport Beach, CA
(714) 645-8384

13003 Ventura Boulevard
Studio City, CA
(818) 788-6354

Moroccan

F ★ ★ ★ ½
S ★ ★ ★ ½
A ★ ★ ★ ½
P ★ ★ ★

Good taste in dress required
Valet and street parking
All major credit cards
Full bar
Reservations recommended

Dinner: Mon.-Thurs. 5:30PM-10:00PM
           Fri.-Sun. 5:30PM-11:00PM

Enter the fabled world of Arabian nights and sink into the cushioned comfort of a richly appointed tent, where waiters wearing djellabahs serve your lavish seven-course dinner. Your feast might include chicken, fish, rabbit, quail, and squab prepared in traditional Moroccan manner.

MATTEO'S   115

2321 Westwood Boulevard
Los Angeles, CA
(213) 475-4521

Italian

F ★ ★ ★
S ★ ★ ★
A ★ ★ ★
P ★ ★ ★

Good taste in dress required
Valet parking
All major credit cards
Full bar
Reservations required

Dinner: Tues.-Sun. 5:00PM-2:00AM
           Closed Monday

In this warmly intimate celebrity haunt you can join the stars watching the Lionel train chug along its track just below the ceiling! You'll find all your favorite Italian specialties on the menu, including Chicken Kastner, made with parsley, garlic, and butter.

MAURO'S   19

514 South Brand Boulevard
Glendale, CA
(818) 247-5541

Italian

F ★ ★ ★ ½
S ★ ★ ★
A ★ ★ ★
P ★ ★ ★

Good taste in dress required
Valet parking
AE, MC, V
Full bar
Reservations required at dinner

Lunch: Mon.-Fri. 11:30AM-2:30PM
Dinner: Mon.-Sat. 5:30PM-10:30PM
         Closed Sunday

When you've a yen for southern Italian cooking, served in an elegant Roman restaurant atmosphere, this establishment is a perfect choice. Entrées include beef, veal, chicken, and fish dishes plus a wide selection of freshly made pastas.

MAX AU TRIANGLE   72

233 North Beverly Drive
Beverly Hills, CA
(213) 550-8486

French

F ★ ★ ★ ½
S ★ ★ ★ ½
A ★ ★ ★
P ★ ★ ★ ★

Jacket required, tie preferred
Valet parking
AE, DC, MC, V
Full bar
Reservations required

Lunch: Mon.-Fri. 12:00PM-2:30PM
Dinner: Mon.-Sat. 7:00PM-10:30PM
         Closed Sunday

This restaurant attests to the legendary artistry of chef/owner Joachim B. Splichal. The setting is spacious and contemporary, the wine list well contrived, the service exemplary, and the food exceptional. The prix fixe, multi-course lunch and dinner menus are supplemented by à la carte choices. The dessert list is lengthy and luring.

MICHAEL'S   128

1147 Third Street
Santa Monica, CA
(213) 451-0843

French

F ★ ★ ★ ★
S ★ ★ ★ ★
A ★ ★ ★ ★
P ★ ★ ★ ★

Jacket required
Lot and street parking
All major credit cards
Full bar
Reservations required

Lunch: Mon.-Fri. 12:00PM-2:00PM
Dinner: Nightly 6:30PM-9:45PM

Owner Michael McCarty has transformed a '30s residence into a mecca for devotees of modern American and contemporary French cuisine. Everything served is a creative production from the crisp salads to the homemade pastas, to the daily specials such as fresh fish from New Zealand, or squab with raspberry vinegar sauce.

MON GRENIER   5

18040 Ventura Boulevard
Encino, CA
(818) 344-8060

French

F ★ ★ ★ ½
S ★ ★ ★ ½
A ★ ★ ★ ½
P ★ ★ ★ ½

Good taste in dress required
Lot and street parking
AE, MC, V
Full bar
Reservations required

Dinner: Mon.-Sat. 6:00PM-10:00PM
         Closed Sunday

A simulated attic setting, complete with antique furnishings, creates a delightfully different ambiance at Andre Lion's treasure trove of a restaurant. Daily specialties may include entrées such as Salmon en Croûte, quail, and fresh fish dishes. Desserts are daily creations planned as an integral part of the cuisine.

MONIQUE 143

31727 Coast Highway
South Laguna, CA
(714) 499-5359

French

F ★ ★ ★
S ★ ★ ★
A ★ ★ ★
P ★ ★ ½

No dress restrictions
Street parking
MC, V
Beer/Wine
Reservations recommended

Lunch: Tues.-Sat. 12:00PM-2:30PM
Dinner: Tues.-Sun. 6:30PM-10:30PM
        Closed Monday

Arriving at this change-of-pace Gallic bistro is like strolling into the French country side. You can opt to dine indoors or on the flower-decked patio where the Pacific Ocean provides its restful background sound. The cuisine is based on pure, fresh ingredients prepared in the classic French manner.

MOONSHADOWS 118

20356 Pacific Coast Highway
Malibu, CA
(213) 456-3010

American

F ★ ★ ★ ½
S ★ ★ ½
A ★ ★ ★
P ★ ★ ½

No dress restrictions
Valet and street parking
All major credit cards
Full bar
Reservations not required

Dinner: Mon.-Sat. from 5:00PM
         Sun. from 4:00PM

Spend a romantic evening in a splendidly appointed dining room that offers a superb ocean view. (The heated patio might even tempt you to dine under the stars.) There's a jumbo salad bar to whet your appetite before selecting from fresh fish, steak, and lobster entrées.

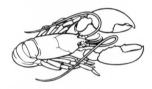

MORTON'S 50

8800 Melrose Avenue
Los Angeles, CA
(213) 276-5205

American

F ★ ★ ★
S ★ ★ ★ ½
A ★ ★ ★
P ★ ★ ★

Jacket preferred
Valet parking
AE, MC, V
Full bar
Reservations required

Dinner: Mon.-Sat. 6:00PM-11:30PM
         Closed Sunday

A sophisticated celeb oasis, as busy as central casting, with a daily-changing menu as fascinating as the clientele. Among the enticing entrées you may find chicken marinated in lime, grilled swordfish, tenderloin of lamb, and smoked chicken salad. The chocolate truffle cake has an enviable reputation!

MR. CHOW   66

344 North Camden Drive
Beverly Hills, CA
(213) 278-9911

Chinese

F ★ ★ ★ ½
S ★ ★ ★
A ★ ★ ★
P ★ ★ ★ ½

No dress restrictions
Valet parking
AE, DC, MC, V
Full bar
Reservations required

Lunch: Daily 12:00PM-2:30PM
Dinner: Nightly 6:30PM-12:00AM

Sleek and contemporary, this establishment features classic Peking cuisine, with all food prepared to order, presented in a setting that is sophisticated art nouveau. One of the strengths of this refreshing, change-of-pace restaurant is its Peking pasta department.

MR. STOX   143

1105 East Katella Avenue
Anaheim, CA
(714) 634-2994

Californian/Continental

F ★ ★ ★ ½
S ★ ★ ★
A ★ ★ ★
P ★ ★ ½

Good taste in dress required
Valet parking
All major credit cards
Full bar
Reservations required

Lunch: Mon.-Fri. 11:00AM-3:00PM
Dinner: Mon.-Thurs. 5:00PM-10:00PM
         Fri. & Sat. 5:00PM-11:00PM
         Sun. 4:00PM-9:00PM

A rambling California mission-style structure houses Mr. Stox, now owned and managed by the Marshall family, whose restaurant expertise is much in evidence. Mesquite-broiled fresh seafood, lamb, veal, duck, and prime rib are featured.

MUSSO & FRANK GRILL   27

6667 Hollywood Boulevard
Hollywood, CA
(213) 467-7788 / 467-5123

Continental

F ★ ★ ★
S ★ ★ ★
A ★ ★ ★
P ★ ★ ★

Good taste in dress required
Valet and lot parking
All major credit cards
Full bar
Reservations recommended

Lunch/
Dinner: Mon.-Sat. 11:00AM-11:00PM
         Closed Sunday

Musso & Frank Grill has played a starring role in the Hollywood scene since 1919; in fact, the movie industry grew up dining here. Try their hearty daily specials such as homemade chicken pot pie, sauerbraten and potato pancakes, corned beef and cabbage, and bouillabaisse.

ODORIKO RESTAURANT   61

8500 Beverly Boulevard
Los Angeles, CA
(213) 659-5744

Japanese

F ★ ★ ★
S ★ ★ ★
A ★ ★ ★
P ★ ★

No dress restrictions
Garage parking
MC, V
Full bar
Reservations required

Lunch/
Dinner: Mon.-Fri. 11:30AM-10:30PM
         Sat. & Sun. 11:30AM-11:00PM

There is something new 'neath the culinary sun, and owner Barbara Lee has found it. Here Kanto (northern) and Kansai (southern) Japanese style cuisine is served in a serene, enclosed Japanese garden setting. You might try Kaiseki, a three-course traditional dinner; or the Shogun Combination, an unusual array of every kind of sushi and sashimi, with equally gratifying results.

ORLANDO-ORSINI 117

9575 West Pico Boulevard
Los Angeles, CA
(213) 277-6050

Italian

F ★ ★ ★ ½
S ★ ★ ★ ½
A ★ ★ ★
P ★ ★ ★ ★

Jacket required
Valet parking
All major credit cards
Full bar
Reservations recommended

Lunch: Mon.-Fri. 12:00PM-2:30PM
Dinner: Mon.-Sat. 6:00PM-11:00PM
         Closed Sunday

This clubby spot projects a self-assured, warm and intimate aura. Here owners Gianni and Gigi Orlando and Stefano Orsini present their interpretation of Northern Italian cooking, as well as traditional favorites. The pastas and pastries are both homemade.

OSCAR'S 15

Premier Sheraton
555 Universal Terrace Parkway
Universal City, CA
(818) 506-2500

American

F ★ ★ ★ ½
S ★ ★ ★ ½
A ★ ★ ★ ½
P ★ ★ ★ ★

Jacket required
Valet and lot parking
All major credit cards
Full bar
Reservations recommended

Dinner: Mon.-Sat. 6:00PM-10:00PM
         Closed Sunday

This regal establishment is a triumph of turn-of-the-century décor. Among the enticing entrées you will find blackened New Orleans style tenderloin and red snapper seared with crabmeat and shrimp in a coconut sauce. For dessert, the lemon soufflé with vanilla sauce is perfect.

PACIFIC DINING CAR 97

1310 West Sixth Street
Los Angeles, CA
(213) 483-6000

American

F ★ ★ ★ ½
S ★ ★ ★
A ★ ★ ½
P ★ ★ ★ ½

Good taste in dress required
Valet parking
MC, V
Full bar
Reservations recommended

Breakfast/
Lunch/
Dinner: Open 24 hours every day

Since 1921 this family owned restaurant has been purveying Eastern prime beef, aged and cut in the house cooling box and cooked to order over a charcoal broiler, to a devoted clientele. Wesley Idol carries on the familiar tradition for highest quality meat, fresh seafoods, and veal specialties.

PALESAI 47

9043 Sunset Boulevard
Los Angeles, CA
(213) 275-9724

Thai

F ★ ★ ★
S ★ ★ ★
A ★ ★ ★
P ★ ★ ★

Good taste in dress required
Valet parking
AE, DC, MC, V
Beer/Wine
Reservations required

Lunch: Mon.-Fri. 11:30AM-2:30PM
Dinner: Mon.-Sat. 6:00PM-10:30PM
Closed Sunday

Uncluttered and contemporary, the designer décor you will find here counterplays the stark white high ceiling with vivid accents of red and yellow. The service is formal, and the cuisine exciting. Palesai Duckling and the seafood special are popular entrée choices. Banana flambé is a spectacular finish to your meal.

PALETTE 36

8290 Santa Monica Boulevard
West Hollywood, CA
(213) 654-7045

French/Chinese

F ★ ★ ★
S ★ ★ ★
A ★ ★ ★
P ★ ★ ★

Good taste in dress required
Valet parking
All major credit cards
Full bar
Reservations required

Dinner: Sun.-Thurs. 6:00PM-11:00PM
Fri. & Sat. 6:00PM-12:00AM

A glorified revival of the glamorous Hollywood ambiance of the '40s and '50s is evidenced here. Your gastronomical whims will be catered to by six chefs from Shanghai—a sextet of food artists dedicated to achieving culinary excellence with many types of food.

THE PALM 34

9001 Santa Monica Boulevard
Los Angeles, CA
(213) 550-8811

American

F ★ ★ ★ ½
S ★ ★ ★
A ★ ★ ★
P ★ ★ ★ ★

Good taste in dress required
Valet parking
All major credit cards
Full bar
Reservations recommended

Lunch/
Dinner: Mon.-Fri. 12:00PM-10:30PM
Sat. & Sun. 5:00PM-10:30PM

It is only fitting that this offspring of the New York Palm have sawdust on the floor, caricatures of the famous on the walls, and serve huge portions of what is widely acclaimed as the best steak and lobster in town. You'll also find daily specials, great bread, and yummy New York cheesecake.

PAPADAKIS TAVERNA 144

301 West 6th Street
San Pedro, CA
(213) 548-1186

Greek

F ★ ★ ★
S ★ ★ ★
A ★ ★ ★
P ★ ★ ★

No dress restrictions
Lot parking
MC, V
Beer/Wine
Reservations required

Lunch: Tues.-Fri. 11:30AM-2:00PM
Dinner: Tues.-Sun. 5:00PM-10:00PM
Closed Monday

A visit to this tavern is a joyful event. The ambiance is happy, festive, warm and friendly; the service efficient. Quality ingredients translate into carefully prepared dishes in the best Greek tradition, such as moussaka, roast lamb, and shish kabob.

PASTEL 69

421 North Rodeo Drive
Beverly Hills, CA
(213) 274-9775/6/7

French/Continental

F ★ ★ ★
S ★ ★ ★
A ★ ★ ★
P ★ ★ ★

Good taste in dress required
Valet and underground garage parking
AE, MC, V
Full bar
Reservations recommended

Lunch: Daily 11:30AM-3:00PM
Dinner: Nightly 6:30PM-11:00PM

Fresh, fashionable, informal and fun, Pastel is a French rotisserie where spit-broasted chickens are featured. The menu also includes a variety of fish, steak, and lobster dishes; a good salad selection, homemade pastries, and an ample wine list.

PAVAN 107

Hyatt Regency
711 South Hope Street
Los Angeles, CA
(213) 629-3220

California Nouvelle

F ★ ★ ★ ½
S ★ ★ ★ ½
A ★ ★ ★
P ★ ★ ★

No shorts or levis
Valet parking
All major credit cards
Full bar
Reservations required

Lunch: Mon.-Fri. 11:30AM-2:00PM
Dinner: Mon.-Fri. 6:00PM-10:00PM
Closed Saturday and Sunday

Pavan's reputation for excellence has been firmly established in just three years. Peach-toned glass, marble floors, and comfortable velvet seating handsomely backdrop the innovative cuisine. Chef Carl Heinz augments the menu with two gourmet lunch and dinner specials daily.

PEPPONE 87

11628 Barrington Court
Los Angeles, CA
(213) 476-7379

Italian

F ★ ★ ★ ½
S ★ ★ ★
A ★ ★ ★
P ★ ★ ★ ½

No dress restrictions
Lot and street parking
AE, DC, MC, V
Full bar
Reservations required

Lunch: Tues.-Fri. 11:30AM-2:30PM
Dinner: Tues.-Sun. 5:30PM-11:30PM
      Closed Monday

Your wish is Gianni Paoletti's command when it comes to food preparation at this romantic hideaway. So, if the wonderful variety of homemade traditional pasta dishes, the veal, chicken, and fresh fish entrées don't tempt you, your special request will be graciously honored. And, there's a blue-ribbon wine list.

PERINO'S 94

4101 Wilshire Boulevard
Los Angeles, CA
(213) 383-1222

Continental

F ★ ★ ★ ½
S ★ ★ ★ ½
A ★ ★ ★ ½
P ★ ★ ★ ★

Jacket required at lunch, jacket and tie required at dinner
Valet parking
All major credit cards
Full bar
Reservations required

Lunch: Mon.-Fri. 11:30AM-2:30PM
Dinner: Mon.-Sat. 5:00PM-10:00PM
      Closed Sunday

For five decades this fine restaurant has been a respected and avant leader in the fine art of elegant dining in Southern California. The tradition is undimmed. Continental favorites are featured on the 170 item menu, including veal, fresh fish, steak, and homemade pasta entrées.

POLO LOUNGE 40

Beverly Hills Hotel
9641 Sunset Boulevard
Beverly Hills, CA
(213) 276-2251

Continental

F ★ ★ ★ ½
S ★ ★ ★ ½
A ★ ★ ★ ½
P ★ ★ ★ ½

Jacket required after 6:00PM, no shorts
Valet parking
All major credit cards
Full bar
Reservations required

Breakfast/
Lunch/
Dinner: Daily 7:00AM-1:00AM

A rendevous for show business celebrities since 1912, the Polo Lounge lets you "star-track" at breakfast, lunch, or dinner. The setting is sumptuous, service discreet, and the food delicious. A loggia and patio offer enticing options to lounge dining.

PONTEVECCHIO 124

2518 Wilshire Boulevard
Santa Monica, CA
(213) 829-1112

Italian

F ★ ★ ★
S ★ ★ ★
A ★ ★ ★
P ★ ★ ★

Good taste in dress required
Lot and street parking
All major credit cards
Full bar
Reservations recommended

Dinner: Nightly 5:30PM-11:00PM

In an atmosphere of romantic elegance, you'll savor choices from the menu owner

Giancarlo Zaretti developed using favorite recipes from his native Rome. Linguine Pescatora and Vitello Valdastona are typical of the classic entrées. The pastas and desserts, including ice cream, are made on the premises.

PREGO 77

362 North Camden Drive
Beverly Hills, CA
(213) 277-7346

Italian

F ★ ★ ★
S ★ ★ ★
A ★ ★ ★
P ★ ★ ½

Good taste in dress required
Valet parking
AE, MC, V
Full bar
Reservations recommended

Lunch/
Dinner: Mon.-Sat. 11:30AM-12:00AM
         Sun. 5:00PM-12:00AM

This popular Italian trattoria mirrors modern Milanese surroundings, in the heart of Beverly Hills. You'll find homemade pasta, pizza baked in an oak-burning oven, and mesquite-grilled fresh fish and meats featured on the menu.

THE PRINCESS 101

10131 Constellation Boulevard
Los Angeles, CA
(213) 553-1011

Continental

F ★ ★ ★ ½
S ★ ★ ★ ½
A ★ ★ ★ ½
P ★ ★ ★ ½

Jacket required
Valet parking
All major credit cards

Full bar
Reservations recommended

Lunch: Mon.-Fri. 11:30AM-2:30PM
Dinner: Mon.-Sat. 6:00PM-10:30PM
         Closed Sunday

Designed with palatial proportions, the setting here is elegant, on a grand scale. The menu offers a wide choice of creative entrées such as veal chop with morel sauce, bass with red pepper sauce, and John Dory with tarragon.

RANGOON 55
RACQUET CLUB

9474 Santa Monica Boulevard
Beverly Hills, CA
(213) 274-8926

Continental

F ★ ★ ★
S ★ ★ ★
A ★ ★ ★
P ★ ★ ★

Jacket required at dinner
Valet and lot parking
All major credit cards
Full bar
Reservations recommended

Lunch: Mon.-Fri. 11:00AM-3:00PM
Dinner: Mon.-Sat. 6:00PM-12:30AM
         Closed Sunday

Host/owner Manny Zwaaf's "club" invites everyone to share the warm sense of camaraderie one finds here. The cuisine features the finest ingredients transformed into a potpourri of award-winning French, English, American, and South Asian gustatory delights.

RAVEL 102

Sheraton Grande Hotel
333 South Figueroa Street
Los Angeles, CA
(213) 617-1133

Californian

F ★ ★ ★ ½
S ★ ★ ★ ½
A ★ ★ ★ ½
P ★ ★ ★ ½

Jacket required
Valet parking
All major credit cards
Full bar
Reservations required

Lunch: Mon.-Fri. 11:30AM-2:00PM
Dinner: Mon.-Fri. 6:00PM-10:00PM
Closed Saturday and Sunday

Bringing you a new dimension in pleasurable dining in downtown Los Angeles, this lovely dining room offers outstanding California cuisine complemented by a noteworthy wine list. Dainty roses etched in leaded glass create an aura of charming intimacy for enjoying the innovative food.

REX II RISTORANTE   104

617 South Olive Street
Los Angeles, CA
(213) 627-2300

Italian

F ★ ★ ★ ★
S ★ ★ ★
A ★ ★ ★
P ★ ★ ★ ★

Jacket required
Valet parking
All major credit cards
Full bar
Reservations required

Lunch: Mon.-Fri. 12:00PM-1:30PM
Dinner: Mon.-Sat. 7:00PM-9:30PM
Closed Sunday

Discover the enchantment of Rex II, sited in downtown L.A.'s historic Oviatt Building. The Lalique glass entry, and carved oak columns are impressive; the dining room spacious. Dishes such as Tagliatelle with dried Porcini Mushrooms and Turbot with Tarragon Sauce are menu highlights.

THE RITZ   143

880 Newport Center Drive
Newport Beach, CA
(714) 720-1800

Continental

F ★ ★ ★ ½
S ★ ★ ★ ½
A ★ ★ ★ ½
P ★ ★ ★ ★

Jacket required after 6:00PM
Valet parking
AE, DC, MC, V
Full bar
Reservations required

Lunch: Mon.-Fri. 11:30AM-3:00PM
Dinner: Mon.-Sat. 6:00PM-11:00PM
Closed Sunday

Here, restaurateur Hans Prager has created an Orange County showplace with a warm and comfortable atmosphere. The menu reflects his long career as an innovator of culinary art. The extensive wine list is carefully planned to complement the cuisine.

R. J.'s THE RIB JOINT   72

252 North Beverly Drive
Beverly Hills, CA
(213) 274-7427

American

F ★ ★ ★
S ★ ★ ★
A ★ ★
P ★ ★ ½

No dress restrictions
Valet and lot parking
All major credit cards
Full bar
Reservations recommended

Lunch/
Dinner: Mon.-Thurs. 11:30AM-10:00PM
           Fri. & Sat. 11:30AM-11:00PM
Brunch/
Dinner: Sun. 11:00AM-10:00PM

This is a great spot to share with friends and family who like relaxed dining and sawdust scuffling. Pork ribs, beef ribs, and special chicken and fish dishes are among the 55 items on the menu. The "Green Grocer" salad bar is a veritable extravaganza of fresh produce and tasty tidbits.

ROMEO & JULIET   74

435 North Beverly Drive
Beverly Hills, CA
(213) 273-2292

Continental/Italian

F ★ ★ ★
S ★ ★ ★
A ★ ★ ★
P ★ ★ ★

Jacket preferred
Valet and street parking
AE, MC, V
Full bar
Reservations recommended

Lunch: Mon.-Fri. 11:30AM-2:30PM
Dinner: Mon.-Sat. 5:30PM-11:00PM
        Closed Sunday

You'll find this a warm, intimate dining spot with a mauve color scheme and abundant fresh flowers. Owner Vito Sasso, an attentive host, offers homemade pastas, and such dishes as medallions of veal with mozzerella and tomatoes, plus unusual daily specials.

RUTH'S CHRIS   84
STEAK HOUSE

224 South Beverly Drive
Beverly Hills, CA
(213) 859-8744

American

F ★ ★ ★
S ★ ★ ★
A ★ ★ ½
P ★ ★ ★

Good taste in dress required
Valet parking
AE, MC, V
Full bar
Reservations required

Lunch/ Dinner: Daily 11:30AM-11:30PM

Patterned after the first Ruth's Chris, established 20 years ago in New Orleans, this restaurant is dedicated to "serving the best steaks you ever tasted." Broiling is done in a specially designed oven which is a closely guarded restaurant secret. The results are great.

ST. ESTEPHE   143

2640 Sepulveda Boulevard
Manhattan Beach, CA
(213) 545-1334

Southwestern American

F ★ ★ ★ ½
S ★ ★ ★ ½
A ★ ★ ★ ½
P ★ ★ ★

Good taste in dress required
Lot parking
AE, MC, V
Beer/Wine
Reservations required on weekends

Lunch: Mon.-Fri. 11:00AM-2:00PM
Dinner: Tues.-Sat. 6:00PM-10:00PM
        Closed Sunday

This unique Santa Fe-style restaurant with its pueblo décor and serene desert ambiance entices you with contemporary cuisine featuring unusual food combinations. The menu is highlighted with weekly and daily specials such as ravioli prepared with New Mexican-style carne adoboda with a chevré cream sauce.

ST. MORITZ   10

11720 Ventura Boulevard
Studio City, CA
(818) 980-1122

Continental

F ★ ★ ★ ½
S ★ ★ ★ ½
A ★ ★ ★
P ★ ★ ★

No dress restrictions
Valet parking
AE, MC, V
Full bar
Reservations recommended

Lunch: Tues.-Fri. 11:00AM-2:00PM
Dinner: Tues.-Sun. 5:00PM-10:00PM
          Closed Monday

Owners Irwin Hoffberg, manager, and
Wolfgang Braun, chef, blend alpine charm
and continental cuisine for your enjoyment here. You may dine al fresca in a
garden setting when the weather is warm,
and select from an à la carte menu or blackboard specials. Fresh fish, veal, and beef,
served with garden-fresh vegetables are
the house mainstays.

SAN DIMAS MANSION   106

121 North San Dimas Avenue
San Dimas, CA
(714) 599-9391

French/Continental/American

F ★ ★ ★
S ★ ★ ★
A ★ ★ ★ ½
P ★ ★ ★

Jacket required
Lot parking
All major credit cards
Full bar
Reservations recommended

Dinner: Nightly from 5:00PM
Brunch: Sun. 10:30AM-2:30PM

When you visit this restored 1897 Victorian mansion, you return to an era of
gentility. A butler ushers you into the
world of tapestry-covered walls, velvet
and lace, and ornate antique mirrors. The
cuisine exemplifies high standards, the
wine list is varied, and the desserts are
homemade.

SCANDIA   28

9040 Sunset Boulevard
West Hollywood, CA
(213) 278-3555 or 272-9521

Scandinavian/Continental

F ★ ★ ★ ½
S ★ ★ ★
A ★ ★ ★
P ★ ★ ★

Jacket required
Valet parking
All major credit cards
Full bar
Reservations recommended

Lunch/
Dinner: Tues.-Sat. 11:30AM-2:00AM
Brunch/
Dinner: Sun. 11:00AM-1:00AM
          Closed Monday

Scandia has been showered with awards
for 31 years, and you will find they are
justly deserved. Renowned for fresh fish
and seafood, milk-fed veal, Scandinavian
dishes, and a superb wine list. The spacious dining rooms have the luxurious continental aura that invites lingering.

SEVENTH STREET   99
BISTRO

815 West Seventh Street
Los Angeles, CA
(213) 627-1242

French

F ★ ★ ★ ½
S ★ ★ ★
A ★ ★ ★
P ★ ★ ★

Good taste in dress required
Valet parking
All major credit cards
Full bar
Reservations recommended

Lunch: Mon.-Fri. 11:30AM-2:00PM
Dinner: Mon.-Sat. 6:00PM-10:00PM
         Closed Sunday

The Italian Romanesque Fine Arts Building, circa 1927, now houses this tranquil dining spot. Chef Laurent Quenioux (formally at Maxim's of Paris) transforms fresh California viands into unique specialties prepared in the French manner. All dishes can be ordered à la carte.

72 MARKET STREET   139

72 Market Street
Venice, CA
(213) 392-8720

American

F ★ ★ ★
S ★ ★ ★
A ★ ★ ½
P ★ ★ ★

Good taste in dress required
Valet parking
AE, MC, V
Full bar
Reservations required

Lunch: Tues.-Sat. 11:30AM-2:30PM
Dinner: Sun.-Thurs. 6:00PM-11:00PM
         Fri. & Sat. 6:00PM-11:30PM
Brunch: Sun. 11:00AM-2:30PM

Skylights, wood, copper, and concrete create a dramatic architectural statement at this friendly restaurant. You'll find crayfish, oysters, and clams at the popular oyster bar, and a menu that features such diverse entrées as Cajun-style meatloaf and steak tartar.

SPAGO   22

1114 Horn Avenue
Los Angeles, CA
(213) 652-4025

Californian

F ★ ★ ★ ★
S ★ ★ ★ ★
A ★ ★ ★ ★
P ★ ★ ★ ★

No shorts
Valet parking
AE, MC, V
Full bar
Reservations required

Dinner: Nightly 6:00PM-11:30PM

You'll find trend-setting entrées such as Lobster Ravioli with Fresh Sorrel, Duck Sausage Pizza (served sizzling from oak-burning ovens), grilled tuna, and Sonoma County lamb included in owner-chef Wolfgang Puck's creative cuisine.

STUDIO GRILL   38

7321 Santa Monica Boulevard
Los Angeles, CA
(213) 874-9202

Continental

F ★ ★ ★
S ★ ★ ★ ★
A ★ ★ ★ ½
P ★ ★ ★

Good taste in dress required
Valet parking
All major credit cards
Full bar
Reservations recommended

Lunch: Mon.-Fri. 12:00PM-2:30PM
Dinner: Mon.-Sat. 6:00PM-11:30PM
         Closed Sunday

Here owner Ardison Phillips has created an atmosphere that transcends the vagaries of changing fashion. You'll find his paintings on display, lavish fresh flower bouquets, and an eclectic menu including calamari, steaks, rack of lamb, homemade pastas, and daily specialties.

TEA ROOM 37
ST. PETERSBURG

8500 Beverly Boulevard
Top Floor Beverly Center
Los Angeles, CA
(213) 657-8830

Russian

F ★ ★ ★
S ★ ★ ★
A ★ ★ ★
P ★ ★ ★

No dress restrictions
Valet and lot parking
AE, MC, V
Full bar
Reservations required

Lunch: Daily 11:30AM-3:00PM
Dinner: Mon.-Thurs. 6:00PM-10:00PM
         Fri.-Sun. 6:00PM-12:00AM

Here you can overlook the Hollywood Hills while dining on an interesting assortment of Russian delicacies that were favored during the era of the Czars. The setting is romantic, and the cuisine from the Blini to the Trout Muscovite, authentically prepared. The service is stately and the ambiance as Russian as a samovar.

THEME ROOM 142
RESTAURANT

201 World Way
Los Angeles, CA
(213) 646-5471

American

F ★ ★ ★ ★ ½
S ★ ★ ★
A ★ ★ ★
P ★ ★ ★ ★

Jacket preferred
Valet parking
AE, MC, V
Full bar
Reservations recommended

Lunch: Mon.-Sat. 11:00AM-2:30PM
Midday: Daily 2:30PM-5:00PM
Dinner: Mon.-Sat. 5:30PM-10:30PM
         Sun. 5:00PM-10:00PM
Brunch: Sun. 10:00AM-2:30PM

California's regional bounty is much in evidence in the cuisine featured in this sophisticated restaurant with its panoramic airport view. Chef Michel Blanche devises imaginative entrées to complement the menu mainstays: fresh seafoods, rack of lamb, and prime rib.

A THOUSAND CRANES 103

New Otani Hotel
120 South Los Angeles Street
Los Angeles, CA
(213) 629-1200

Japanese

F ★ ★ ★
S ★ ★ ★
A ★ ★ ★
P ★ ★ ★

No dress restrictions
Valet and garage parking
All major credit cards
Full bar
Reservations recommended

Lunch: Daily 11:30AM-2:00PM
Dinner: Nightly 6:00PM-10:00PM

Here you may enjoy a variety of Japanese dining experiences, while viewing a traditional Japanese garden built on a rooftop in downtown L.A. There are tempura and sushi bars, private tatami rooms, and a dining room featuring traditional cuisine, with shabu-shabu and sukiyaki prepared tableside.

385 NORTH   58

385 North LaCienega Boulevard
Los Angeles, CA
(213) 657-3850

French/Japanese

```
F  ★ ★ ★ ½
S  ★ ★ ★
A  ★ ★ ★
P  ★ ★ ★
```

Good taste in dress required, no shorts
Valet parking
All major credit cards
Full bar
Reservations required

Lunch: Tues.-Fri. 11:30AM-2:30PM
Dinner: Mon.-Sat. 6:00PM-11:00PM
          Sun. 5:30PM-10:00PM
Late
Supper: Mon.-Sat. 10:30PM-12:30AM

Inside the art déco facade of this sleekly contemporary restaurant you will find a high-tech dining area with a central display kitchen where you can watch chef/owner Roy Yamaguchi perform his culinary sleight of hand with magical dishes.

THE TOWER   108

Transamerica Center
1150 South Olive Street
Los Angeles, CA
(213) 746-1554

French

```
F  ★ ★ ★ ½
S  ★ ★ ★ ½
A  ★ ★ ★ ½
P  ★ ★ ★ ½
```

Jacket and tie required
Valet parking
All major credit cards
Full bar
Reservations required

Lunch: Mon.-Fri. 11:30AM-2:30PM
Dinner: Mon.-Sat. 6:00PM-10:00PM
          Closed Sunday

Topping one of L.A.'s tallest buildings, The Tower affords you a panoramic view of the sprawling city. The classical French cuisine includes daily specials that may include fresh seafood flown in from the Eastern seaboard, choice cuts of beef, veal, lamb, and pork. The wine list is excellent, the setting a joy.

TRADER VIC'S   86

Beverly Hilton Hotel
9876 Wilshire Boulevard
Beverly Hills, CA
(213) 274-7777

International

```
F  ★ ★ ★ ½
S  ★ ★ ★ ½
A  ★ ★ ★ ½
P  ★ ★ ★ ½
```

Jacket required
Valet and lot parking
All major credit cards
Full bar
Reservations required

Dinner: Sun.-Thurs. 4:30PM-12:30AM
          Fri.& Sat. 4:30PM-1:30AM

You can almost hear the tradewinds blow when you venture into this award-winning South Sea's paradise with its tiki gods and tropical gardens. The food is as exotic as the drinks and décor, with Polynesian specialties and dishes such as Indonesian rack of lamb, cooked to perfection in the round Chinese clay ovens.

TRUMPS   51

8764 Melrose Avenue
Los Angeles, CA
(213) 855-1480

Californian/American

```
F  ★ ★ ★ ★
S  ★ ★ ★ ½
A  ★ ★ ★ ★
P  ★ ★ ★ ½
```

Good taste in dress, jacket preferred in the evening
Valet parking
AE, MC, V
Full bar
Reservations recommended

Lunch: Mon.-Sat. 11:45AM-3:00PM
Tea: Mon.-Sat. 3:30PM-5:30PM
Dinner: Mon.-Wed. 6:00PM-11:30PM
         Thurs.-Sat. 6:00PM-12:00AM
         Closed Sunday

Bright, light, open, and airy with white walls displaying changing artwork, this restaurant is a triumph in contemporary décor. The menu is exciting and eclectic offering you choices such as salmon tartar, plantains and caviar, or sautéed chicken with roasted garlic and candied lemon rind.

VALENTINO 135

3115 Pico Boulevard
Santa Monica, CA
(213) 829-4313

Italian

F ★ ★ ★ ½
S ★ ★ ★ ½
A ★ ★ ★ ½
P ★ ★ ★ ½

Good taste in dress required
Valet parking
All major credit cards
Full bar
Reservations required

Dinner: Mon.-Sat. 5:00PM-12:00AM
         Closed Sunday

Visiting chefs who exchange ideas keep the cuisine served here fresh and contemporary. The staff is poised and self confident and the atmosphere most conducive to relaxed dining. The wine list is also remarkably good.

WESTWOOD MARQUIS HOTEL
THE DYNASTY ROOM 90

930 Hilgard Avenue
Los Angeles, CA
(213) 208-8765

Continental

F ★ ★ ★ ½
S ★ ★ ★ ½
A ★ ★ ★ ½
P ★ ★ ★ ½

Jacket required
Valet parking
All major credit cards
Full bar
Reservations required

Dinner: Nightly 6:00PM-11:00PM

Glorified with T'ang Dynasty porcelains and Erté prints, this restaurant entices you with excellent cuisine and elegant surroundings. The service is precise and polished, and the bill of fare offers you a wide range of classic continental favorites. And, for a final touch of luxury, a harpist plays soothing background music nightly.

THE WINDSOR 95

3198 West Seventh Street
Los Angeles, CA
(213) 382-1261

Continental

F ★ ★ ★ ½
S ★ ★ ★ ★
A ★ ★ ★ ½
P ★ ★ ★ ½

Jacket required
Valet parking
All major credit cards
Full bar
Reservations recommended

Lunch: Mon.-Fri. 11:30AM-2:30PM
Dinner: Nightly 5:00PM-11:30PM

Ben Dimsdale's secluded sanctuary has been luring discriminating diners to the mid-Wilshire area since the '40s. The French table service is superlative, the food invariably good. Freshest produce and choicest meats are used in the preparation of a wide range of entrées including Tournedoes of Beef, a house specialty.

YAMASHIRO   17

1999 North Sycamore Avenue
Los Angeles, CA
(213) 466-5125

Japanese/Continental

F ★ ★ ★ ½
S ★ ★ ★
A ★ ★ ★ ½
P ★ ★ ★

Good taste in dress required
Valet and lot parking
MC, V
Full bar
Reservations required for dinner

Lunch/
Dinner: Daily 11:30AM-2:00AM

Yamishiro occupies an Oriental palace that is a Southern California landmark built 75 years ago. There are heated outdoor terraces and beautiful garden courts that afford spectacular views. The award-winning menu offers sushi, full Japanese feasts, and continental entrées.

YAMATO   116 & 143

Century Plaza Hotel
2025 Avenue of the Stars
Los Angeles, CA
(213) 277-1840

60 Fashion Island
Newport Beach, CA
(714) 644-4811

Japanese

F ★ ★ ★ ½
S ★ ★ ★ ½
A ★ ★ ★
P ★ ★ ½

Good taste in dress required
Valet and lot parking
All major credit cards
Full bar
Reservations required

Lunch: Mon.-Fri. 11:30AM-2:30PM
Dinner: Mon.-Sat. 5:00PM-11:30PM
          Sun. 4:30PM-11:00PM

Japanese cuisine takes on new stature at the Yamato locations. You'll find a sushi bar, your choice of tatami rooms or classic seating, and chicken and steaks skillfully cooked on teppans by deft knife wielders with an innate understanding and respect for the food they are preparing.

Palm Springs

DAR MAGHREB

42-300 Bob Hope Drive
Rancho Mirage, CA
(619) 568-9486

Moroccan

F ★ ★ ★ ½
S ★ ★ ★
A ★ ★ ★ ★
P ★ ★ ★

Good taste in dress required
Valet parking
MC, V
Full bar

Reservations required on weekends and recommended on weekdays
Dinner: Mon.-Fri. 6:00PM-11:00PM
          Sat. 5:30PM-11:00PM
          Sun. 5:30PM-10:30PM

No mirage or desert fantasy, Dar Maghreb is an exact replica of a 15th century Moroccan palace where you are invited to recline on comfortable sofas and feast on a princely meal.

GASTON'S

777 Tahquitz-McCallum
Palm Springs, CA
(619) 320-7750

French

F ★ ★ ★ ★
S ★ ★ ★ ★
A ★ ★ ★ ★
P ★ ★ ★ ½

Jacket preferred
Valet parking
All major credit cards
Full bar
Reservations recommended

Lunch: Mon.-Fri. 11:30AM-2:15PM
Dinner: Mon.-Sat. 6:00PM-11:00PM
        Closed Sunday

Winner of every major restaurant award in the Southwest, this celebrity-favored eatery is dedicated to excellence. The famed executive chef produces legendary cuisine, such as green mussels with poivrondous sauce.

LA CAVE

70-064 Highway 111
Rancho Mirage, CA
(619) 324-4673

French

F ★ ★ ★ ½
S ★ ★ ★ ½
A ★ ★ ★ ★
P ★ ★ ★ ★

Jacket required
Valet parking
All major credit cards
Full bar
Reservations required

Dinner: Tues.-Sun. from 6:00PM
        Closed Monday

Enjoy impeccably prepared classic French cuisine in a romantic subterranean setting replete with fresh flowers, crystal, sterling, and linen napery. The availability of fresh ingredients establishes each day's menu.

LE VALLAURIS

385 West Tahquitz-McCallum
Palm Springs, CA
(619) 325-5059

French

F ★ ★ ★ ½
S ★ ★ ★ ½
A ★ ★ ★ ★
P ★ ★ ★ ★

Jacket preferred
Valet parking
All major credit cards
Full bar
Reservations required

Lunch: Tues.-Sat. 12:00PM-2:30PM
Dinner: Tues.-Sun. 6:00PM-10:30PM
Brunch: Sun. 11:30AM-2:30PM
        Closed Monday

Fresh seafood including Maine lobster, is the specialty of this illustrious establishment that lures a sports and entertainment clientele. You'll find a lovely patio for casual dining, nightly music, and a well rounded menu of gourmet French cuisine.

LORD FLETCHER INN

70-385 Highway 111
Rancho Mirage, CA
(619) 328-1161

English

F ★ ★ ★ ½
S ★ ★ ★ ½
A ★ ★ ★ ½
P ★ ★ ★

Good taste in dress required
Valet parking
MC, V
Full bar
Reservations recommended

Dinner: Mon.-Sat. 5:00PM-11:00PM
         Closed Sunday

Posh and very British, Ron Fletcher's inn is filled with antiques that create a sedate, genteel atmosphere. The menu features traditional British fare such as whole braised lamb shanks and veal shanks, short ribs, and fresh fish.

MEDIUM RARE

70-064 Highway 111
Rancho Mirage, CA
(619) 328-6563

Continental

F ★ ★ ★ ½
S ★ ★ ★ ½
A ★ ★ ★
P ★ ★ ★

No dress restrictions
Valet parking
AE, DC, MC, V
Full bar
Reservations recommended

Lunch: Mon.-Fri. from 11:30 AM
Dinner: Nightly from 5:00PM

There's an air of casual elegance in this warm and inviting modern English pub setting, that offers a choice of four theme dining rooms. The menu is varied offering prime rib, fresh seafoods, rack of lamb, and other house specialties.

THE TAPESTRY ROOM

Sheraton Plaza
400 East Tahquitz-McCallum
Palm Springs, CA
(619) 320-6868

Continental

F ★ ★ ★ ½
S ★ ★ ★ ★
A ★ ★ ★ ½
P ★ ★ ★ ★

Jacket preferred
Valet parking
All major credit cards
Full bar
Reservations recommended

Dinner: Wed.-Thurs. & Sun.
         6:00PM-10:00PM
         Fri. & Sat. 6:00PM-10:30PM
         Closed Monday & Tuesday

Pink on pink décor with deep purple and black accents forms a flattering background for the presentation of a marvelous array of continental cuisine, complemented by a well thought-out wine list. Winner of the coveted Palm Springs' "Restaurant of the Year" award.

WALLY'S DESERT TURTLE

71-775 Highway 111
Rancho Mirage, CA
(619) 568-9321

French/Continental

F ★ ★ ★ ½
S ★ ★ ★ ½
A ★ ★ ★ ★
P ★ ★ ★ ★

Jacket required
Valet parking
AE, MC, V
Full bar
Reservations required

Dinner: Mon.-Sat. 6:00PM-10:30PM
         Closed Sunday

When nothing but a touch of ultra-elegance will do, head for Wally's Desert Turtle. The entry is lavished with flowers, and mirrored columns reflect the opulent appointments. The cuisine is prepared and served with classic grace; the menu offering you French/Continental dishes.

Miami

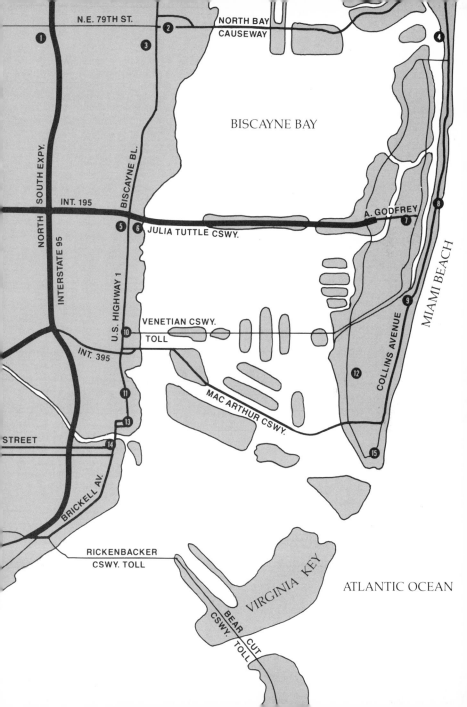

ARTHUR'S EATING HOUSE 10

1444 Biscayne Boulevard
Miami, FL
(305) 371-1444

American/Continental

F ★ ★ ★ ½
S ★ ★ ★
A ★ ★ ★ ½
P ★ ★ ★

Good taste in dress required
Valet parking
All major credit cards
Full bar
Reservations not required

Lunch/
Dinner: Daily 11:30AM-12:00AM

Arthur Horowitz is a restaurateur with impeccable taste for wines, cuisine, and fine art. His Eating House reflects these qualities. The menu is an ambitious blend of continental and American dishes, with imaginative specials featured daily. You'll also find exceptional desserts and a solid list of premier wines.

CAFÉ CHAUVERON 4

9561 East Bay Harbor Drive
Bay Harbor Islands, FL
(305) 866-8779

French

F ★ ★ ★ ★
S ★ ★ ★ ★
A ★ ★ ★ ★
P ★ ★ ★ ★

Jacket required
Valet parking
All major credit cards
Full bar
Reservations required

Dinner: Nightly 6:00PM-11:00PM
          Closed June 1 to September 30

A consistent award winner, Café Chauveron is considered one of the world's finest dining places. Owner André R. Chauveron presents French haute cuisine, served with the respect it deserves, in a waterfront setting that epitomizes old world charm and elegance.

CASA VECCHIA 1

209 North Birch Road
Fort Lauderdale, FL
(305) 463-7575

Italian

F ★ ★ ★ ★
S ★ ★ ★ ★
A ★ ★ ★ ★
P ★ ★ ★ ½

Jacket preferred
Valet parking
All major credit cards
Full bar
Reservations required

Dinner: Nightly
          Winter 6:00PM-10:30PM
          Summer 6:30PM-10:00PM

Dine surrounded by gardens overlooking the intracoastal waterway, in the graceful historic home that is now Casa Vecchia. Exquisite furnishings, paintings, and objets d'art create a luxurious ambiance. "Fresh" and "homemade" are key characteristics of the Northern Italian house specialties you will find here.

CENTRO VASCO 17

2235 S.W. 8th Street
Miami, FL
(305) 643-9606

Spanish/Basque

F ★ ★ ★
S ★ ★ ★
A ★ ★ ★
P ★ ★ ½

No dress restrictions
Valet parking
All major credit cards
Full bar
Reservations not required

Lunch/
Dinner: Daily 12:00PM-11:30PM

Compliments to the owner/chef, Juan Saizarbitoria, for creating this rustic haven dedicated to exemplary Spanish-Basque cuisine. Renowned for filet Madrilene du Centro Vasco, broiled tournedo of beef, Zarzuela (a seafood medley), ox tail Bordalesa, and superb paella.

CHEZ VENDÔME   20

700 Biltmore Way
Coral Gables, FL
(305) 443-4646

French/Continental

F   ★ ★ ★ ½
S   ★ ★ ★
A   ★ ★ ★ ½
P   ★ ★ ★ ½

Jacket required
Valet parking
All major credit cards
Full bar
Reservations required

Lunch: Mon.-Sat. 11:30AM-3:00PM
Dinner: Mon.-Sat. 5:30PM-11:00PM
          Closed Sunday

This opulent replica of Maxim's in Paris is decorated with historical portraits and lithographs, and plush red velvet seats and banquettes. A guitar player and pianist provide an impressive accompaniment to the classic French and continental cuisine, which includes such entrées as rack of lamb and Sole Véronique.

CHRISTINE LEE'S   4
GASLIGHT

18401 Collins Avenue
Miami Beach, FL
(305) 931-7700

Chinese/Continental

F   ★ ★ ★
S   ★ ★ ★
A   ★ ★ ★
P   ★ ★ ★

Jacket required
Valet parking
All major credit cards
Full bar
Reservations required

Dinner: Nightly 5:00PM-12:00AM

Oriental décor and an intimate, friendly atmosphere have made Christine Lee's Gaslight a perpetual crowd-pleaser. Cantonese and Szechwan-style Chinese cuisine are featured, as well as prime American sirloin.

CHRISTINE LEE'S   1
NORTHGATE

6191 Rock Island Road
Fort Lauderdale, FL
(305) 726-0430

Chinese/Continental

F   ★ ★ ★
S   ★ ★ ★
A   ★ ★ ★
P   ★ ★ ★

Jacket required
Valet parking
All major credit cards
Full bar
Reservations required

Dinner: Nightly 5:00PM-12:00AM

You'll find a California-casual ambiance at Christine Lee's Northgate, decorated with luxuriant lush green plants. The Chinese dishes feature specialties in the Szechwan style, as well as Cantonese cuisine. A choice array of prime steaks is also available.

CHRISTY'S 22

3101 Ponce de Leon Boulevard
Coral Gables, FL
(305) 446-1400

American

F ★ ★ ★ ½
S ★ ★ ★
A ★ ★ ★
P ★ ★ ★ ½

Good taste in dress required
Lot parking
All major credit cards
Full bar
Reservations required

Lunch/
Dinner: Mon.-Fri. 11:30AM-11:00PM
Sat. 5:00PM-12:00AM
Sun. 4:00PM-11:00PM

Brass sconces on red walls, and crisp white tablecloths give Christy's the air of a venerable men's club. Prime aged beef is the specialty of the house, with duck, veal, fresh fish, shrimp, chicken and lobster included in the wide menu offerings.

CYE'S RIVERGATE 14

444 Brickell Avenue
Miami, FL
(305) 358-9100

American/Continental

F ★ ★ ★
S ★ ★ ★
A ★ ★ ★
P ★ ★ ★

Good taste in dress required
Valet parking
All major credit cards
Full bar
Reservations required for dinner

Lunch: Mon.-Fri. 11:30AM-4:00PM
Dinner: Mon.-Sat. 5:30PM-12:00AM
Closed Sunday

Cye's Rivergate offers you a choice of over 30 entrées including classic favorites of American and continental cuisine such as Maine lobster, prime steaks, fresh fish, and uniquely prepared duck and chicken.

THE DEPOT 25

5830 South Dixie Highway
Miami, FL
(305) 665-6261

American/Continental

F ★ ★ ★ ½
S ★ ★ ★
A ★ ★ ★ ½
P ★ ★ ★

Jacket required
Valet and lot parking
All major credit cards
Full bar
Reservations required

Dinner: Nightly 5:00PM-2:00AM

All aboard for a visit to the recreated Larkin Train Station, where you will dine in an 85-year old Presidential dining car, or at glass topped tables that display operating model trains. Choo-choo specials include Maine lobster, prime beef and veal, jumbo prawns, and stone crab.

THE DOWN UNDER 1 RESTAURANT

3000 East Oakland Park Boulevard
Fort Lauderdale, FL
(305) 563-4123

French

F ★ ★ ★
S ★ ★ ★
A ★ ★ ★ ½
P ★ ★ ★ ½

Good taste in dress required
Valet parking
All major credit cards
Full bar
Reservations not required

Lunch: Wed.-Fri. 11:30-AM-2:00PM
Dinner: Nightly 6:00PM-10:30PM

Here you will discover an elegant waterfront restaurant decorated with Victorian and Belle Epoque objets d'art. The French menu under the direction of chef Christian Blanchon blends classic and eclectic offerings into award-winning cuisine. The wine list has also won national recognition.

EL BODEGON CASTILLA 16

2499 S.W. 8th Street
Miami, FL
(305) 649-0863

Spanish

F ★ ★ ★
S ★ ★ ★
A ★ ★ ★
P ★ ★ ★

Good taste in dress required
Lot parking
AE, MC, V
Full bar
Reservations required

Lunch/
Dinner: Mon.-Thurs. 12:00PM-11:00PM
         Fri.-Sun. 12:00PM-12:00AM

One strolls into this cozy Spanish inn through a colorful garden entry, to be greeted by the cheerful Spanish flag red and yellow color scheme. The traditional cuisine is carefully prepared to emphasize the interesting and subtle differences found in the cooking methods and ingredients of the various regions of Spain.

EMBERS 9

245 22nd Street
Miami Beach, FL
(305) 538-4345

American

F ★ ★ ★
S ★ ★ ★
A ★ ★ ★
P ★ ★ ★ ½

Good taste in dress required
Valet parking
All major credit cards
Full bar
Reservations required

Dinner: Nightly 4:00PM-11:30PM

This vintage establishment has been producing exemplary American cuisine for nearly 40 years. The atmosphere is comfortable with touches of elegance. One catches the aroma of hickory smoke as chicken, ribs, duck, and other meats turn on spits in the open brick ovens.

FONTAINEBLEAU HILTON 8
DINING GALLERIES

4441 Collins Avenue
Miami Beach, FL
(305) 538-2000

Continental/American

F ★ ★ ★ ★
S ★ ★ ★ ★
A ★ ★ ★ ★
P ★ ★ ★ ★

Jacket required
Valet parking
All major credit cards
Full bar
Reservations required

Lunch: Mon.-Fri. 11:30AM-2:30PM
Dinner: Nightly 6:00PM-12:00PM

Showered with illustrious awards, this restaurant successfully combines European elegance with graceful tropical touches. Expect to find flawless service and beautifully prepared cuisine featuring entrées such as Veal Romanoff, crown roast of lamb, chateaubriand, and tournedoes d'Longeville.

FOOD AMONG THE FLOWERS   5

21 N.E. 36th Street
Miami, FL
(305) 576-0000

Continental/Italian

F ★ ★ ★ ½
S ★ ★ ★ ½
A ★ ★ ★ ½
P ★ ★ ★

Jacket required
Lot parking
AE, MC, V
Full bar
Reservations required

Lunch/
Dinner: Mon.-Sat. 11:00AM-11:30PM
          Closed Sunday

This floral fantasy land with its fountains and statues and luxuriance of plants has the aura of a tropical paradise created just for your pleasure. The service is attentive, there is restful live music, and the continental cuisine and Italian specialties are of the highest caliber.

THE FORGE   7

432 Arthur Godfrey Road
Miami Beach, FL
(305) 538-8533

American

F ★ ★ ★
S ★ ★ ★ ½
A ★ ★ ★ ½
P ★ ★ ★ ★

Jacket required
Valet parking
All major credit cards

Full bar
Reservations required

Dinner: Nightly 6:00PM-2:30AM

You'll find this striking art nouveau restaurant lavished with paintings, sculptures, and murals. Choice beef and fresh seafood are mainstays of the broad menu. The wine list is comprised of more than 1,000 labels.

FRENCH CONNECTION   21

219 Palermo Avenue
Coral Gables, FL
(305) 442-8587

French

F ★ ★ ★ ½
S ★ ★ ★
A ★ ★ ★
P ★ ★ ★

Good taste in dress required,
Jacket preferred
Street parking
All major credit cards
Full bar
Reservations required

Lunch: Daily 11:30AM-2:30PM
Dinner: Sun.-Thurs. 6:00PM-11:00PM
         Fri. & Sat. 6:00PM-11:30PM

This tres chic establishment, furnished with French antiques, offers you an elegant ambiance, romanced with roses and candlelight. Fresh ingredients are emphasized in menu offerings and the cuisine is creatively prepared. Grilled foods are cooked on heated lava stones, imported from France.

GATTI'S   12

1427 West Avenue
Miami Beach, FL
(305) 673-1717

Continental/Italian

F ★ ★ ★ ½
S ★ ★ ★
A ★ ★ ★
P ★ ★ ★

Jacket required
Valet parking
All major credit cards
Full bar
Reservations required

Dinner: Tues.-Sun. 5:30PM-10:30PM
Closed Monday

This family owned restaurant, now under the direction of Michael Gatti, has occupied the same modest house since 1924, where drinks are served in the garden patio entry. Crisp white linen, tuxedoed waiters, and roses on the tables add an air of formal elegance. Local seafood, steaks, chops, and stone crabs are mainstays of the menu.

JOE'S STONE CRAB   15

227 Biscayne Street
Miami Beach, FL
(305) 673-0365

Seafood

F ★ ★ ★ ½
S ★ ★ ★
A ★ ★ ½
P ★ ★ ½

Good taste in dress required,
no shorts
Valet and lot parking
All major credit cards
Full bar
Reservations not required

Lunch: Tues.-Sat. 11:30AM-2:00PM
Dinner: Nightly 5:00PM-10:00PM

This Miami tradition has been going strong since 1913, and is the area's oldest eatery. Seafood, steaks, stone crab (brought in by Joe's fishing fleet), and Key lime pie are the house specialties, and they are devoured in great quantities by the loyal fans who flock here.

KALEIDOSCOPE   24

3112 Commodore Plaza
Coconut Grove, FL
(305) 446-5010

Swiss/Continental

F ★ ★ ★
S ★ ★ ★
A ★ ★ ★
P ★ ★ ½

No dress restrictions
Lot and street parking
AE, MC, V
Beer/Wine
Reservations recommended

Lunch: Daily 11:30AM-3:00PM
Dinner: Nightly 6:00PM-11:00PM

Enjoy dining indoors or on the terrace at this unique restaurant with its sophisticated tropical setting. The bill of fare is varied and the food prepared creatively. You'll also discover a range of house specialties with Swiss accents interesting enough to tempt the most discerning diner.

LA BELLE ÉPOQUE   4

1045 95th Street
Bay Harbor Island, FL
(305) 865-6011

French

F ★ ★ ★ ½
S ★ ★ ½
A ★ ★ ★
P ★ ★ ★

Jacket required
Valet parking
All major credit cards
Full bar
Reservations required

Dinner: Nightly 6:00PM-10:30PM

Countrified but elegant, here you'll find a water wheel and gurgling fountain and the option of dining in the verdant patio. There is an extensive, well thought out wine list, and an interesting array of entrées.

LA VIEILLE MAISON   3

770 East Palmetto Park Road
Boca Raton, FL
(305) 391-6701

French

F ★ ★ ★ ★
S ★ ★ ★ ★
A ★ ★ ★ ★
P ★ ★ ★ ★

Jacket required
Valet parking
All major credit cards
Full bar
Reservations required

Dinner: Nightly seatings at
          6:00PM and 9:00PM

La Vieille Maison, repeatedly honored with illustrious awards, is a triumph of good taste and perfectionism. Co-owners Leonce Picot and Al Kocab have transformed a grand old house into a gastronomic haven where costly edibles, flown in from round the world, surface in superlative prix-fixe, five-course dinners.

LE DOME   1

333 Sunset Drive
Fort Lauderdale, FL
(305) 463-3303

Continental

F ★ ★ ★ ½
S ★ ★ ★
A ★ ★ ★ ★
P ★ ★ ★

Jacket required
Valet parking
AE, DC, MC, V

Full bar
Reservations required

Dinner: Nightly 5:00PM-10:00PM

Occupying a penthouse aerie atop the Four Seasons condominium, Le Dome lets you gaze out over the twinkling lights of Fort Lauderdale while savoring your food. Formally attired waiters provide dignified service; continental cuisine is well prepared.

LE FESTIVAL   19

2120 Salzedo Street
Coral Gables, FL
(305) 442-8545

French

F ★ ★ ★ ½
S ★ ★ ★
A ★ ★ ★ ½
P ★ ★ ★

Good taste in dress required
Lot and street parking
AE, MC, V
Full bar
Reservations required

Lunch: Mon.-Fri. 11:45AM-2:30PM
Dinner: Mon.-Thurs. 6:00PM-10:30PM
          Fri. & Sat. 6:00PM-11:00PM

Much honored Le Festival is a gustatory salute to dining in the French manner. Owner Jacques Baudean presents brilliantly prepared French cuisine with house specialties including innovative red snapper and rack of lamb dishes and Chicken Normande. Homemade desserts provide a grand finale.

LES TROIS   1
MOUSQUETAIRES

International Building
2447 East Sunrise Boulevard
Fort Lauderdale, FL
(305) 564-7513

French

F ★ ★ ★ ½
S ★ ★ ★
A ★ ★ ★
P ★ ★ ½

Good taste in dress required
Lot parking
All major credit cards
Beer/Wine
Reservations required

Lunch: Mon.-Fri. 12:00PM-2:30PM
Dinner: Mon.-Sat. 6:00PM-10:00PM
         Closed Sunday

As French as the Champs Élysées, this petite restaurant offers you highly personalized service in a relaxed sidewalk café atmosphere. The emphasis is on gourmet cuisine prepared with fresh ingredients and attractively presented.

PAVILLON GRILL 13

The Pavillon Hotel
100 Chopin Plaza
Miami, FL
(305) 372-4494

French

F ★ ★ ★ ½
S ★ ★ ★ ½
A ★ ★ ★ ½
P ★ ★ ★ ★

Jacket and tie required
Valet and lot parking
All major credit cards
Full bar
Reservations required

Lunch: Mon.-Fri. 12:00PM-2:30PM
Dinner: Mon.-Sat. 6:30PM-10:30PM
         Closed Sunday

Green Brazilian marble columns, polished mahogany panelling, and English leather banquettes form the rich background against which Maître de Cuisine Guy Gateau presents his nouvelle haute cuisine. Such specialties as medallions of lamb marinated in buttermilk, served with

fresh pasta, and ragoût of lobster with Chantrelle mushrooms are featured in this award-winning restaurant.

THE PLUM ROOM 1
OF YESTERDAY'S

3001 East Oakland Park Boulevard
Fort Lauderdale, FL
(305) 561-4400

French/Continental

F ★ ★ ★ ½
S ★ ★ ★ ½
A ★ ★ ★ ★
P ★ ★ ★ ★

Jacket preferred
Valet and lot parking
AE, MC, V
Full bar
Reservations required

Dinner: Nightly 7:00PM-11:00PM

All the elements that make dining a memorable experience blend harmoniously at Peter Goldhahn's The Plum Room. The setting is urbane, the service polished, the wine list extensive, and the cuisine exemplary. Wild game and fowl entrées are house specialties.

RAIMONDO'S 23

4612 Le Jeune Road
Coral Gables, FL
(305) 666-9919

Italian/Continental

F ★ ★ ★ ½
S ★ ★ ★ ½
A ★ ★ ★
P ★ ★ ★ ★

No dress restrictions
Valet parking
AE, CB, DC
Full bar
Reservations required

Dinner: Nightly 6:00PM-11:00PM

Raimondo's offers you a relaxed atmosphere, a display of modern paintings, attentive European service, and innovative cuisine. Northern Italian dishes are creatively prepared.

REFLECTIONS   11

301 Miamarina Parkway Drive
Miami, FL
(305) 371-6433

American

F ★ ★ ★ ½
S ★ ★ ★
A ★ ★ ★
P ★ ★ ★ ½

Jacket required
Valet and lot parking
All major credit cards
Full bar
Reservations required

Lunch: Daily 12:00PM-3:00PM
Dinner: Nightly 6:00PM-11:00PM

This terraced restaurant with its floor to ceiling windows gives you a beautiful view of downtown Miami and the busy Marina. The setting is elegant and romantic and the service gracious and courtly. The gourmet American cuisine is inventive and satisfying; seafood specialties are a feature of the house.

TUTTLE'S AT THE   6
CHARTER CLUB

600 N.E. 36th Street
Miami, FL
(305) 576-7676

Continental

F ★ ★ ★ ½
S ★ ★ ★
A ★ ★ ★ ½
P ★ ★ ★ ½

Jacket preferred
Valet parking
All major credit cards
Full bar
Reservations recommended

Lunch: Mon.-Fri. 11:30AM-3:00PM
Dinner: Nightly from 6:00PM
Brunch: Sun. 11:00AM-2:30PM

Plush and fashionable, Tuttle's is an elitist restaurant acclaimed as an architectural masterpiece. Chef/owner Peter Whitcup presents fine continental cuisine, including such specialties as Duckling Melba, individual rack of lamb, with a veal and fresh fish entrée offered nightly.

VINTON'S   18

La Palma Hotel
116 Alhambra Circle
Coral Gables, FL
(305) 445-2511

French/Swiss

F ★ ★ ★ ½
S ★ ★ ★ ½
A ★ ★ ★ ½
P ★ ★ ★

Jacket required
Street parking
All major credit cards
Beer/Wine
Reservations required

Lunch: Mon.-Fri. 11:45AM-2:30PM
Dinner: Mon.-Sat. 6:30PM-10:30PM
            Closed Sunday

Expect to enjoy award-winning food in this elegant eatery that is sited on the ground floor of a posh old hotel. Owners Hans and Susan Eichmann provide such niceties as foot pillows and fresh flowers for the ladies, and sherbet served mid-meal to refresh the palate. You'll find a hearty bouillabaisse, and Swiss-accented French cuisine featured here.

Minneapolis/St. Paul

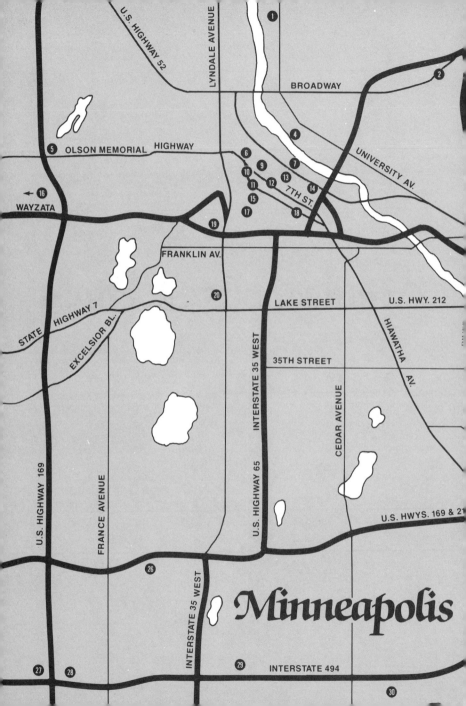

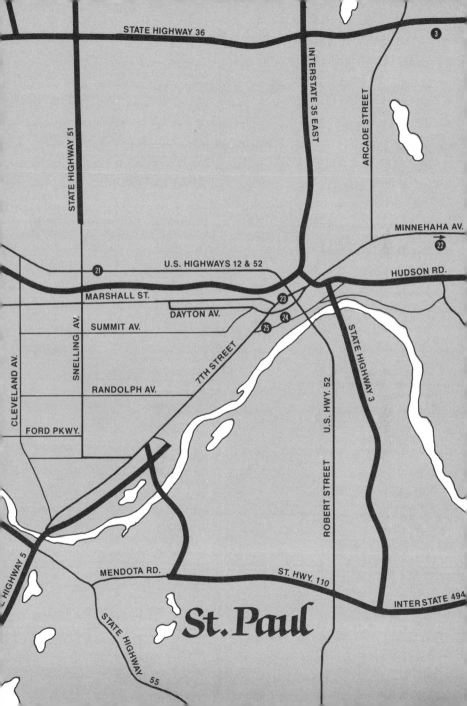

THE ANCHORAGE   2

1330 Industrial Boulevard
Minneapolis, MN
(612) 379-4444

Seafood

F ★ ★ ★
S ★ ★ ★
A ★ ★ ★ ½
P ★ ★ ★ ½

Jacket and tie preferred
Lot parking
All major credit cards
Full bar
Reservations required

Breakfast/
Lunch/
Dinner: Daily 6:30AM-10:30PM

A five-tiered restaurant projecting a nautical flavor and agleam with polished brass, The Anchorage offers you a choice of over 60 seafood dinner entrées plus daily specials at lunch and dinner. Fresh regional seafoods such as California abalone and Maine lobsters are flown in daily.

BLACK FOREST INN   20

1 East 26th Street
Minneapolis, MN
(612) 872-0812

German/Continental

F ★ ★ ★
S ★ ★ ★
A ★ ★ ★
P ★ ★ ½

No dress restrictions
Lot parking
AE, DC, MC, V
Full bar
Reservations not required

Lunch/
Dinner: Mon.-Sat. 11:00AM-1:00AM
          Sun. 12:00PM-12:00AM

This friendly, bohemian beer tavern turned inn has been dispensing warm hospitality and hearty food for the past two decades. Owners Erich and Joanne Christ present such dishes as bratwurst and sauerkraut, wiener schnitzel, and apple strudel, among the German specialties plus other continental fare.

THE BLUE HORSE   21

1355 University Avenue
St. Paul, MN
(612) 645-8101

Continental

F ★ ★ ★
S ★ ★ ★ ½
A ★ ★ ★
P ★ ★ ★

Jacket required
Valet parking
All major credit cards
Full bar
Reservations recommended

Lunch/
Dinner: Mon.-Fri. 11:00AM-1:00AM
          Sat. 4:00PM-1:00AM
          Closed Sunday

This sterling establishment has been an award-winning champion for nearly 25 years. While the bill of fare is varied the house specializes in fresh fish selections, all flown in daily, such as red king salmon, bay scallops, mussels, and regional varieties. The wine list is excellent with many of California's finest boutique wineries represented.

BOSTON SEA PARTY   26

7801 Xerxes Avenue South
Bloomington, MN
(612) 884-3355

Seafood

F ★ ★ ★ ½
S ★ ★ ★ ½
A ★ ★ ★ ½
P ★ ★ ★

Good taste in dress required
Lot parking
All major credit cards
Beer/Wine
Reservations recommended

Lunch: Mon.-Fri. 11:30AM-2:00PM
Dinner: Mon.-Thurs. 5:00PM-10:00PM
Fri. & Sat. 5:00PM-10:30PM
Sun. 4:30PM-9:00PM

Dine hearty here, in an atmosphere that echoes a New England wharfside inn. Buffet-style presentation entices you with cold shrimp, caviar, seafood creole, crab, herring, and scallops; then lets you choose a small lobster, broiled filet, swordfish, or salmon steak for your entrée.

CAMELOT 28

5300 West 78th Street
Bloomington, MN
(612) 835-2455

Continental

F ★ ★ ★
S ★ ★ ★
A ★ ★ ★
P ★ ★ ★ ½

Jacket and tie required
Valet parking
All major credit cards
Full bar
Reservations recommended

Lunch/
Dinner: Daily 10:00AM-1:00AM

Recapture the days of gallantry and knighthood at Camelot, a contemporary restaurant in a medieval stone castle, complete with drawbridge, moat, turrets, armor, and a great round table. Prime rib, Steak Diane, fresh seafood, and duckling are among the favored entrées.

CHEZ COLETTE 27

Hotel Sofitel
5601 West 78th Street
Bloomington, MN
(612) 835-1900

French

F ★ ★ ★ ½
S ★ ★ ★
A ★ ★ ★
P ★ ★ ★

No dress restrictions
Valet and lot parking
All major credit cards
Full bar
Reservations recommended

Breakfast: Daily 6:30AM-11:00AM
Lunch: Daily 11:30AM-3:00PM
Dinner: Nightly 5:30PM-11:00PM

Classic French cuisine with well handled regional touches is the order of the day at this delightful brasserie, which captures the mood of Paris emerging into the 20th century. Hearty house specialties include a rich bouillabaisse and French onion soup. Freshly made croissants make breakfast here a special treat.

CHI-CHI'S 29

7717 Nicollett
Minneapolis, MN
(612) 866-3433

Mexican

F ★ ★ ★
S ★ ★ ★
A ★ ★ ½
P ★ ★

Good taste in dress required
Lot parking
All major credit cards
Full bar
Reservations required

Lunch/
Dinner: Mon.-Thurs. 11:00AM-11:00PM
          Fri. & Sat. 11:00AM-12:00AM
          Sun. 11:00AM-10:00PM

The place to enjoy jumbo Margaritas and your favorite Mexican dishes in a casual, relaxed, fiesta atmosphere. Chi-Chi's offers you a choice of more than 60 items, including enchiladas, flautas, and deep-fried crispy chimichangas, a house specialty.

510 RESTAURANT   19

510 Groveland Avenue
Minneapolis, MN
(612) 874-6440

French

F ★ ★ ★ ½
S ★ ★ ★ ½
A ★ ★ ★ ★
P ★ ★ ★ ½

No dress restrictions
Valet and street parking
All major credit cards
Beer/Wine
Reservations required

Lunch: Mon.-Fri. 11:30AM-2:00PM
Dinner: Mon.-Sat. 6:00PM-10:00PM
          Closed Sunday

Located in the oldest cooperative apartment building in Minneapolis, circa 1920, 510's décor projects an aura of old world elegance. Classic and nouvelle French cuisine varies seasonally, and includes daily specials at both lunch and dinner. The extensive wine list emphasizes premium California varieties.

FOREPAUGH'S   25

276 South Exchange Street
St. Paul, MN
(612) 224-5606

French

F ★ ★ ★
S ★ ★ ★ ½
A ★ ★ ★ ½
P ★ ★ ★

Jacket and tie preferred
Lot parking
AE, MC, V
Full bar
Reservations recommended

Lunch: Mon.-Fri. 11:30AM-2:00PM
Dinner: Mon.-Sat. 5:30PM-9:30PM
          Sun. 4:00PM-8:00PM
Brunch: Sun. 11:30AM-2:00PM

The restored 1870 Forepaugh mansion creates a marvelous 9-room Victorian setting for the splendid presentation of French cuisine. Forepaugh's owner Martin E. Decker, and chef-owner Bernard Lagarde feature fresh seafood, veal, beef, an enticing array of desserts, and a fine selection of wines.

FUJI-YA   7

420 South 1st Street
Minneapolis, MN
(612) 339-2226

Japanese

F ★ ★ ★ ½
S ★ ★ ★ ½
A ★ ★ ★ ½
P ★ ★ ★

Good taste in dress required
Lot parking
AE, MC, V
Full bar
Reservations recommended

Lunch: Mon.-Fri. 11:30AM-2:30PM
Dinner: Mon.-Thurs. 5:00PM-9:00PM
          Fri. & Sat. 5:00PM-10:00PM
          Closed Sunday

This authentically created Japanese restaurant was designed by architect Shinichi Okada to serve as a serene dining retreat. Owner Reiko Weston offers her guests a menu and type of service perfectly attuned to the setting. The sushi bar is popular; tempura, shabu-shabu, sukiyaki, and teriyaki among the specialties.

JAX CAFÉ 1

1928 University Avenue, N.E.
Minneapolis, MN
(612) 789-7297

American/Continental

```
F  ★ ★ ★ ½
S  ★ ★ ★ ½
A  ★ ★ ½
P  ★ ★ ★
```

Good taste in dress required
Lot and street parking
All major credit cards
Full bar
Reservations recommended

Lunch: Mon.-Sat. 11:00AM-3:00PM
Dinner: Mon.-Sat. 4:00PM-11:00PM
         Sun. 3:00PM-9:00PM
Brunch: Sun. 10:00AM-3:00PM

Family owned and operated, Jax has been a Minneapolis landmark for five decades. Picture windows let you view the Old World garden setting, complete with its own trout stream. You'll find fresh lobster and fish, year-round; seasonal rainbow trout; plus sizzling steaks, and prime rib featured on the wide menu.

LA TERRASSE 27

Hotel Sofitel
5601 West 78th Street
Bloomington, MN
(612) 835-1900

French

```
F  ★ ★ ★
S  ★ ★ ★
A  ★ ★ ★
P  ★ ★
```

No dress restrictions
Valet and lot parking
All major credit cards
Full bar
Reservations not required

Lunch/
Dinner: Daily 11:00AM-3:00AM

With its casual sidewalk café atmosphere, and open, airy gardenlike feeling achieved through the judicious use of foliage plants, this eatery offers you a fine option for spur-of-the-moment dining. Drop in for a light French meal, quiche, innovative sandwiches, French onion soup, or simply to sample the great chocolate mousse.

LA TORTUE 11

100 North 6th Street
Minneapolis, MN
(612) 332-3195

Continental

```
F  ★ ★ ★ ½
S  ★ ★ ★
A  ★ ★ ★
P  ★ ★ ★ ★
```

Jacket preferred
Street parking
All major credit cards
Full bar
Reservations not required

Lunch: Mon.-Fri. 11:30AM-2:30PM
         Sat. 12:00PM-2:30PM
Dinner: Mon.-Sat. 5:30PM-10:00PM
         Closed Sunday

You'll find La Tortue, with its provincial French inn atmosphere, in historic Butler Square. Daily and monthly specials add zest and seasonal interest to the classic continental menu that includes such entrées as duck with mustard sauce, tenderloin of lamb, and sweetbreads with spinach.

LATOUR   30

The Registry Hotel
7901 24th Avenue South
Bloomington, MN
(612) 854-2244

French

F ★ ★ ★ ½
S ★ ★ ★ ½
A ★ ★ ★ ½
P ★ ★ ★ ½

Jacket preferred
Valet and lot parking
All major credit cards
Full bar
Reservations recommended

Lunch: Mon.-Fri. 11:00AM-2:00PM
Dinner: Mon.-Sat. 6:00PM-11:00PM
Brunch: Sun. 11:00AM-2:30PM

At Latour you'll find the continental, French nouvelle, and American cuisine enhanced by the elegant country French ambiance. Owner Charles W. Lanphere offers you fresh pâtés; such specialties as bouillabaisse à la Marseillaise, chateaubriand, duckling with blueberry sauce; and a choice of more than 200 labels on the wine list.

LE CAFÉ ROYAL   27

Hotel Sofitel
5601 West 78th Street
Minneapolis, MN
(612) 835-1900

French

F ★ ★ ★ ½
S ★ ★ ★
A ★ ★ ★ ½
P ★ ★ ★ ★

No dress restrictions
Valet and lot parking
All major credit cards
Full bar
Reservations recommended

Lunch: Mon.-Fri. 11:30AM-3:00PM
Dinner: Mon.-Sat. 5:30PM-11:00PM
          Closed Sunday

Richly appointed, with a regal color scheme, this restaurant is a glittering tribute to "the good life." Classic French cuisine is attentively presented with formal French service. You may select from entrées such as Dover sole, shrimp, and Chinese peapods in champagne sauce.

LE CARROUSEL   30

11 East Kellogg Boulevard
St. Paul, MN
(612) 292-1900

Continental

F ★ ★ ★ ½
S ★ ★ ★
A ★ ★ ★ ½
P ★ ★ ★

Good taste in dress required,
no jeans or T-shirts
Lot and street parking
AE, DC, MC, V
Full bar
Reservations recommended

Lunch: Mon.-Fri. 11:30AM-2:30PM
Dinner: Sun.-Thurs. 5:30PM-10:30PM
          Fri. & Sat. 5:30PM-11:30PM

You can watch the Mississippi rolling by, 22 floors below, or enjoy a panoramic view in the revolving portion of Le Carrousel, while savoring duckling, walleyed pike, Chicken Oskar, or flambé items done tableside. The cuisine is well prepared and the atmosphere is pleasantly romantic.

L'ETOILE   24

St. Paul Hotel
350 Market Street
St. Paul, MN
(612) 292-9292

French

F ★ ★ ★ ½
S ★ ★ ★
A ★ ★ ★
P ★ ★ ★ ★

Jacket and tie preferred
Valet and street parking
AE, MC, V
Full bar
Reservations required

Lunch: Mon.-Fri. 11:30AM-2:30PM
Dinner: Mon.-Sat. 6:00PM-10:00PM
          Closed Sunday

Shimmering crystal and an emerald green color scheme form a resplendent background for the presentation of classic French cuisine at L'Etoile. The menu features fresh fish, lamb "Paul Bocuse" (in pastry shell with spinach), rack of lamb, and native Minnesota produce.

LORD FLETCHER'S OF THE LAKE   16

3746 Sunset Drive
Spring Park, MN
(612) 471-8513

American

F ★ ★ ★
S ★ ★ ★
A ★ ★ ★ ½
P ★ ★ ½

Good taste in dress required
Valet and lot parking
All major credit cards
Full bar
Reservations recommended

Dinner: Winter hours
          Mon.-Thurs. 5:30PM-9:30PM
          Fri. & Sat. 5:30PM-10:00PM
          Sun. 4:30PM-9:00PM
          (Open later during the
          summer months.)

This gourmand's lakeside retreat lures a faithful clientele who bask in the English setting with its warming hearth and Lake Minnetonka view. Here you can enjoy substantial portions of fresh fish, homemade pastas, prime rib, and steaks.

LOWELL INN   22

102 North 2nd Street
Stillwater, MN
(612) 439-1100

American

F ★ ★ ★ ½
S ★ ★ ★ ½
A ★ ★ ★ ½
P ★ ★ ★ ★

Good taste in dress required,
Jacket and tie required on Fri. & Sat.
Lot parking
All major credit cards
Full bar
Reservations required

Lunch: Mon.-Sat. 12:00PM-2:00PM
          Sun. 12:30PM-2:30PM
Dinner: Mon.-Thurs. 6:00PM-8:00PM
          Fri. & Sat. 6:00PM-9:30PM
          Sun. 5:00PM-7:30PM

In this resplendent Colonial/Victorian setting four-course gourmet meals are offered, which may include fondue, a choice of beef or shrimp, and a light and lovely English green grape dessert.

THE MARQUIS   10

Marquette Hotel
710 Marquette Avenue
Minneapolis, MN
(612) 332-7200

American

F ★ ★ ★
S ★ ★ ★
A ★ ★ ★
P ★ ★ ★ ½

Good taste in dress required
Lot parking

All major credit cards
Full bar
Reservations recommended

Lunch: Mon.-Fri. 11:30AM-2:00PM
Dinner: Mon.-Thurs. 6:00PM-10:00PM
          Fri. & Sat. 6:00PM-10:30PM
          Closed Sunday

Dignified service and a stately ambiance create the perfect atmosphere for enjoying the gourmet cuisine at Marquis. Select from entrées such as Beef Tenderloin with Bordelaise Sauce, or Sauté Salmon with Cranberry Crème Fraîche Mint Sauce.

MURRAY'S   6

24 South 6th Street
Minneapolis, MN
(612) 339-0909

American

F ★ ★ ★
S ★ ★ ★
A ★ ★ ★
P ★ ★ ★ ½

No dress restrictions
Lot parking
All major credit cards
Full bar
Reservations required

Lunch/
Dinner: Mon.-Sat. 11:00AM-11:00PM
          Sun. 4:00PM-10:00PM

Although newly refurbished, Murray's retains its mood of comfortable elegance, and continues to feature live, soft, dinner music. Butter-knife-tender succulent steaks, fresh fish, and breads baked on the premises are house specialties.

THE NANKIN   9

2 South 7th Street
Minneapolis, MN
(612) 333-3303

Chinese/American

F ★ ★ ★
S ★ ★ ★
A ★ ★
P ★ ★

No dress restrictions
Public ramp parking
All major credit cards
Full bar
Reservations not required

Lunch/
Dinner: Mon.-Thurs. 11:00AM-11:00PM
          Fri. & Sat. 11:00AM-12:00AM
          Sun. 12:00PM-8:00PM

Nankin has been dispensing Chinese cuisine in the Twin Cities area since 1919. It is a venerated local institution. The menu offers over 100 items including chow mein and chop suey, with many Szechwan and Cantonese-style specialties featured. A full range of traditional American food is also available.

THE NEW FRENCH CAFÉ   14

128 North 4th Street
Minneapolis, MN
(612) 338-3790

French

F ★ ★ ★ ½
S ★ ★ ★
A ★ ★ ★
P ★ ★ ★ ½

No dress restrictions
Street parking
AE, DC, MC, V
Full bar
Reservations recommended

Breakfast: Mon.-Fri. 8:00AM-11:00AM
Lunch: Mon.-Fri. 11:30AM-2:00PM
Dinner: Mon.-Sat. 5:30PM-9:30PM
           Sun. 5:30PM-9:00PM
Late
Supper: Fri. & Sat. 9:30PM-12:00AM
Brunch: Sat. & Sun. 8:00AM-2:00PM

Even though The New French Café occupies a renovated warehouse, it manages to project the feeling of a small, comfortable, intimate restaurant. The menu changes with the seasons, and every item offered, including the bread, is made fresh daily from scratch. The wine list echoes the excellence of the food.

ORION ROOM   18

5000 IDS Center
80 South 8th Street
Minneapolis, MN
(612) 349-6250

American

F ★ ★ ★ ½
S ★ ★ ★ ½
A ★ ★ ★ ½
P ★ ★ ★

Jacket and tie preferred
Lot parking
All major credit cards
Full bar
Reservations recommended

Dinner: Sun.-Fri. 5:30PM-10:00PM
         Sat. 6:00PM-10:00PM

Survey the dazzling city, 50 floors below, while dining in the sophisticated seclusion of the beautiful Orion Room. The broad menu of classic American dishes is highlighted with such specialties as Minnesota wild rice soup, and innovative fresh fish entrées.

PRONTO RISTORANTE   17

Hyatt Regency Hotel
1300 Nicollet Avenue South
Minneapolis, MN
(612) 333-4414

Italian

F ★ ★ ★ ½
S ★ ★ ★
A ★ ★ ★ ½
P ★ ★ ★

Good taste in dress required
Lot and public ramp parking
All major credit cards
Full bar
Reservations recommended

Lunch: Mon.-Fri. 11:30AM-2:00PM
Dinner: Mon.-Fri. 5:00PM-11:30PM
         Sat. 12:00PM-11:00PM
         Sun. 5:30PM-10:00PM
Brunch: Sun. 11:00AM-2:00PM

Pronto Ristorante offers you a choice of two types of dining rooms: a contemporary, open-kitchen room where you can watch fresh pasta being made, or a more traditional setting with elegant décor. Both rooms serve a wide variety of Northern Italian specialties and feature the wines of Italian vintners.

ROSEWOOD ROOM   13

Northstar Hotel
618 Second Avenue South
Minneapolis, MN
(612) 338-2288

American

F ★ ★ ★ ½
S ★ ★ ★
A ★ ★ ★ ½
P ★ ★ ★ ½

Jacket and tie preferred, no jeans
Valet and lot parking
All major credit cards
Full bar
Reservations recommended

Lunch: Mon.-Sat. 11:30AM-2:00PM
Dinner: Nightly 6:00PM-10:00PM
Brunch: Sun. 10:00AM-2:00PM

For two decades the Rosewood Room has been garnering awards for dining excellence. You'll find out why when you visit this distinctive dining room and sample the cuisine that features an unequaled harvest of "the best and freshest meat, fish, and fowl" from America's heartland.

TAIGA   4

201 Main Street, S.E.
Minneapolis, MN
(612) 331-1138

Chinese

F ★ ★ ★ ½
S ★ ★ ★
A ★ ★ ★
P ★ ★ ½

Good taste in dress required
Lot and street parking
AE, DC, MC, V
Full bar
Reservations recommended

Lunch: Tues.-Sat. 11:30AM-2:30PM
Dinner: Tues.-Thurs. 5:00PM-9:00PM
          Fri. & Sat. 5:00PM-10:00PM
Brunch/
Dinner: Sun. 11:30AM-7:00PM
          Closed Monday

Restaurateur Reiko Weston has created a beautiful haven for relaxed dining, on the banks of the Mississippi. The Chinese cuisine includes Mandarin, Cantonese, Peking, and Szechwan specialties, offering you a wide range of choices. The food is well prepared and attractively presented; the service quiet and unobtrusive.

VENETIAN INN   3

2814 Rice Street
St. Paul, MN
(612) 484-7215

Italian/American

F ★ ★ ★ ½
S ★ ★ ★ ½
A ★ ★ ½
P ★ ★

Good taste in dress required
Lot parking
All major credit cards
Full bar
Reservations required

Lunch: Mon.-Sat. 11:00AM-3:00PM
Dinner: Mon.-Sat. 3:00PM-10:00PM
          Closed Sunday

A Twin Cities' treasure, the Venetian Room has been serving premier Italian food to an appreciative clientele for the last 55 years. Under the direction of the Vitale family, authentic Northern and Southern Italian dishes are correctly prepared and courteously presented.

WINE CELLAR INN   12

Northstar Inn
618 2nd Avenue South
Minneapolis, MN
(612) 338-2288

American/Continental

F ★ ★ ★ ½
S ★ ★ ★ ½
A ★ ★ ★
P ★ ★ ★ ½

Jacket required, tie preferred
Lot parking
All major credit cards
Full bar
Reservations recommended

Dinner: Nightly 6:00PM-10:00PM

The rustic simplicity of this wine cellar setting is a study in contrast with the sparkling presentation accorded the excellent cuisine. You'll find classical baroque background music and choices such as Northern Sky Venison, rack of lamb, baby Michigan Coho salmon, and grilled swordfish among the nine daily entrées.

New Orleans

New Orleans

LAKE PONTCHARTRAIN CAUSEWAY (TOLL)

ST. HWY. 3046

PONTCHARTRAIN BL.

LA

2

INTERSTATE 10

VETERANS MEMORIAL BOULEVARD

INTERSTATE 610

WILLIAMS BOULEVARD

ST. HWY. 49

CLEARVIEW PKWY.

GREATER NEW ORLEANS EXPWY.

PONTCHARTRAIN

AIRLINE HWY.

JEFFERSON HIGHWAY

S. CARROLLTON AV.

BROADWAY

JEFFERSON AV.

STATE HIGHWAY 18

RIVER RD.

ST. HWY. 541

MAGAZINE

BRIDGE CITY AV.

33

OLD SPANISH TRAIL

34

LOUISIANA ST.

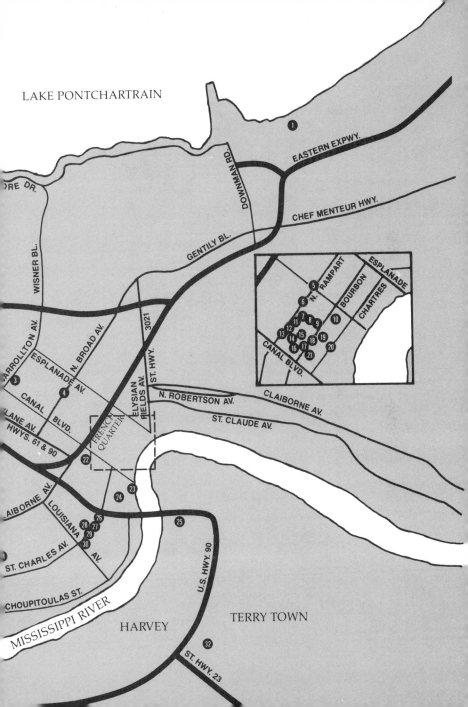

LAKE PONTCHARTRAIN

EASTERN EXPWY.

CHEF MENTEUR HWY.

DOWNMAN RD.

GENTILY BL.

WISNER BL.

RE DR.

N. BROAD AV.

CARROLLTON AV.

ESPLANADE AV.

3021

ST. HWY.

ELYSIAN FIELDS AV.

N. ROBERTSON AV.

CLAIBORNE AV.

ST. CLAUDE AV.

CANAL BLVD.

N. RAMPART
BOURBON
CHARTRES
ESPLANADE

CANAL BLVD.

FRENCH QUARTER

LANE AV.

HWYS. 61 & 90

CLAIBORNE AV.

LOUISIANA

ST. CHARLES AV.

AV.

CHOUPITOULAS ST.

MISSISSIPPI RIVER

HARVEY

TERRY TOWN

U.S. HWY. 90

ST. HWY. 23

ANTOINE'S 7

713 Saint Louis Street
New Orleans, LA
(504) 581-4422/581-4044

Creole

F ★ ★ ★ ½
S ★ ★ ★ ½
A ★ ★ ★
P ★ ★ ★ ½

Jacket required at dinner
Street parking
All major credit cards
Full bar
Reservations recommended

Lunch: Mon.-Sat. 12:00PM-2:30PM
Dinner: Mon.-Sat. 5:30PM-9:30PM
Closed Sunday

Operated since 1840 by the same family, Antoine's is a 15-dining room historic landmark and gourmet shrine now directed by Bernard Guste, a fifth-generation family member. Oysters Rockefeller made their debut here; you'll find them on the à la carte menu along with Pompano en Papillote, and Cotelettes d'Agneau Grilles.

ARNAUD'S 12

813 Bienville Street
New Orleans, LA
(504) 523-5433

Creole

F ★ ★ ★
S ★ ★ ★ ½
A ★ ★ ★ ½
P ★ ★ ★

Jacket and tie preferred
Street parking
AE, CB, MC, V
Full bar
Reservations not required

Lunch: Mon.-Fri. 11:30AM-2:30PM
Dinner: Nightly 6:00PM-10:00PM
Brunch: Sun. 10:00AM-2:30PM

The largest restaurant in the French Quarter, Arnaud's, founded in 1918 by Count Arnaud Cazenave, has been restored to its former glory by proprietor Archie Casbarian. Specialties such as Oysters Bienville and Shrimp Arnaud—with its spicy red sauce—are served, as is fine traditional New Orleans cuisine.

BEGUE'S 18

Royal Sonesta Hotel
300 Bourbon Street
New Orleans, LA
(504) 586-0300

French/Creole

F ★ ★ ★ ½
S ★ ★ ★ ½
A ★ ★ ★ ½
P ★ ★ ★

Jacket and tie preferred at dinner
Garage parking
All major credit cards
Full bar
Reservations recommended

Lunch: Mon.-Fri. 11:30AM-2:30PM
Dinner: Nightly 6:00PM-11:00PM
Brunch: Sun. 10:30AM-2:30PM

At Begue's, Executive Chef Michel Marcais, a Master Chef, combines his classic French training with Creole tradition to create an award-winning menu that features Louisiana seafood, and includes such dishes as Cream of Crawfish Soup, Veal with Morels, and Chateaubriand.

BON TON CAFÉ

401 Magazine Street
New Orleans, LA
(504) 524-3386

Cajun

F ★ ★ ★ ½
S ★ ★ ★ ½
A ★ ★ ★
P ★ ★ ★ ½

Good taste in dress required
Street parking
AE, MC, V
Full bar
Reservations required

Lunch: Mon.-Fri. 11:00AM-2:00PM
Dinner: Mon.-Fri. 5:00PM-9:30PM
           Closed Saturday and Sunday

Located in an old historic building, the Bon Ton with its red checkered tablecloths and warm, friendly atmosphere has been serving Louisiana seafood prepared from Cajun family recipes for the last 20 years.

BRENNAN'S 19

417 Royal Street
New Orleans, LA
(504) 525-9713

Creole

F ★ ★ ★ ½
S ★ ★ ★
A ★ ★ ★ ½
P ★ ★ ★ ½

Good taste in dress required
Lot parking
AE, MC, V
Full bar
Reservations recommended

Breakfast/
Lunch: Daily 8:00AM-2:30PM
Dinner: Nightly 6:00PM-10:00PM

At Brennan's you'll find twelve unique separate rooms and a lush tropical courtyard to entice you. Famed for breakfast, and the winner of countless awards, the dinner menu stresses beef, fowl, and veal dishes plus a wide selection of local seafood entrées. The wine list has been judged one of the 10 best in America.

BROUSSARD'S 11

819 Conti Street
New Orleans, LA
(504) 581-3866

Creole

F ★ ★ ★ ½
S ★ ★ ★ ½
A ★ ★ ★ ½
P ★ ★ ★ ½

Jacket required
Valet parking
All major credit cards
Full bar
Reservations required

Dinner: Nightly 5:30PM-12:00AM

Considered one of the cities most beautiful restaurants, Broussard's exudes intimate, European charm. Owners Joseph P. and Joseph C. Marcello stress freshness and quality in the French/Creole cuisine.

THE CARIBBEAN ROOM 29

Pontchartrain Hotel
2031 St. Charles Avenue
New Orleans, LA
(504) 524-0581

Creole

F ★ ★ ★ ½
S ★ ★ ★ ½
A ★ ★ ★ ½
P ★ ★ ★ ½

Jacket and tie required
Valet parking
All major credit cards
Full bar
Reservations recommended

Lunch: Sun.-Fri. 11:45AM-2:00PM
Dinner: Nightly 5:45PM-10:00PM

Located in the historic Garden District, this restaurant has been garnering awards since 1958. The décor reflects the splendor of old New Orleans, and the food is a revelation of fine traditional Creole cuisine. Trout Veronique, Shrimp Saki, and Red Snapper Pontchartrain highlight the menu.

CHRISTIAN'S 3

3835 Iberville Street
New Orleans, LA
(504) 482-4924

Creole

F ★ ★ ★ ½
S ★ ★ ★ ½
A ★ ★ ★ ½
P ★ ★ ★

Jacket and tie required
Lot and street parking
All major credit cards
Full bar
Reservations required

Lunch: Tues.-Sat. 11:30AM-2:00PM
Dinner: Tues.-Sat. 5:30PM-10:00PM
         Closed Sunday and Monday

Owner Christian Ansel has transformed a quaint old mid-city church into a beautiful setting for the presentation of French/Creole cuisine. Among the savory entrées are Oysters Roland (baked in a sauce of mushrooms, butter, and garlic), and Red Fish au Poivre Vert (sauced with fresh cream and green pepper corns).

COMMANDER'S PALACE 26

1403 Washington Avenue
New Orleans, LA
(504) 899-8221

Creole

F ★ ★ ★ ★
S ★ ★ ★ ★
A ★ ★ ★ ½
P ★ ★ ★ ★

Good taste in dress required
Valet parking
All major credit cards

Full bar
Reservations required

Lunch: Mon.-Fri. 11:30AM-2:00PM
Dinner: Nightly 6:30PM-10:00PM
Brunch: Sat. 11:00AM & 1:00PM
         Sun. 10:30AM, 11:00AM
         & 1:00PM

Housed in a splendid Victorian building in the Garden District, Commander's offers you a serene setting for enjoying exceptional cuisine. Freshness is the key—and everything used is as fresh as it can possibly be.

CORINNE DUNBAR'S 27

1617 St. Charles Avenue
New Orleans, LA
(504) 525-0689/525-2957

Creole

F ★ ★ ★
S ★ ★ ★ ½
A ★ ★ ★ ½
P ★ ★ ★ ★

Jacket and tie preferred
Street parking
Credit cards not accepted
Full bar
Reservations required

Dinner: Tues.-Sat. 6:00PM-9:30PM
         Closed Sunday and Monday

Corinne Dunbar's offers you distinctive Creole food in an elegant, circa 1840, Victorian home setting. Owner James J. Plauché, Jr. presents family-recipe specialties such as Oysters Dunbar, banana puffs, gumbos, and jambalaya, beautifully served on home-quality china, with handsome silver service.

COURT OF TWO SISTERS 10

613 Royal Street
New Orleans, LA
(504) 522-7261

Creole

F ★ ★ ★
S ★ ★ ★
A ★ ★ ★ ½
P ★ ★ ★ ½

Good taste in dress required
Lot parking
All major credit cards
Full bar
Reservations recommended

Breakfast/
Lunch: Daily 9:00AM-3:00PM
Dinner: Nightly 5:30PM-11:00PM

This delightful French Quarter institution occupies a French colonial home designed by an early territorial governor. There's a huge, lushly planted entry patio for balmy weather dining, and three gorgeous dining rooms. Here you'll find a friendly atmosphere, fabulous gumbo and such delicacies as shrimp Toulouse, sirloin tips à la Creole, and bananas Foster.

CROZIER'S RESTAURANT   1

7033 Read Lane
New Orleans, LA
(504) 241-8220

French

F ★ ★ ★ ½
S ★ ★ ★ ½
A ★ ★ ★ ½
P ★ ★ ★

Jacket preferred
Lot parking
AE, MC, V
Full bar
Reservations required for dinner

Lunch: Tues.-Fri. 11:30AM-2:00PM
Dinner: Tues.-Sat. 6:00PM-10:00PM
          Closed Sunday and Monday

Crozier's is cosily ensconced in a trim 2-story home, lavished with French décor. Chef-owner Gérard G. Crozier offers regional French cuisine including such specialties as Duck Pâté, Tournedos Gérard,

Steak au Poivre, Sweetbreads Meunière, Coq au Vin, salmon, and daily features.

FELIX'S   14

739 Iberville
New Orleans, LA
(504) 522-4440

American

F ★ ★ ★ ½
S ★ ★ ★
A ★ ★ ½
P ★ ★

Good taste in dress required
Garage parking
AE, MC, V
Full bar
Reservations not required

Lunch/
Dinner: Mon.-Thurs. 11:00AM-12:00AM
          Fri. & Sat. 11:00AM-1:30AM
          Closed Sunday

This French Quarter mecca for seafood buffs has an oyster bar along one side, and a dining room on the other. Filled with plants and paintings, this is a pleasant place to indulge in a wide choice of seafoods, and/or well prepared steaks.

GALATOIRE'S   17

209 Bourbon Street
New Orleans, LA
(504) 525-2021

Creole

F ★ ★ ★ ½
S ★ ★ ★
A ★ ★ ★
P ★ ★ ½

Jacket and tie required at dinner,
no blue jeans or shorts
Street parking
Credit cards not accepted

Full bar
Reservations not required

Lunch/
Dinner: Tues.-Sat. 11:30AM-9:00PM
Sun. 12:00PM-9:00PM
Closed Monday

Founded in 1905, this resplendent establishment features turn-of-the-century décor with mirrors on two walls, and antique brass ceiling fans. Menu highlights include Trout Amandine, Crab Meat Ravigotte, and fresh fish in season.

K-PAUL'S LOUISIANA KITCHEN 20

416 Chartres Street
New Orleans, LA
(504) 524-7394

Cajun/Creole

F ★ ★ ★ ★
S ★ ★ ★ ½
A ★ ★ ★
P ★ ★ ★

No dress restrictions
Lot and street parking
AE
Beer/Wine
Reservations not required

Dinner: Mon.-Fri. 5:30PM-10:00PM
Closed Saturday & Sunday

Owners Kay Henrichs and Paul Prudhomme, award-winning chef, have taken a straight forward approach in this New Orleanian-favored eatery, The décor is informal — the foods's the thing here. The menu changes daily and is always full of wonderful surprises.

LA LOUISIANE 16

725 Iberville Street
New Orleans, LA
(504) 523-4664

Creole/French

F ★ ★ ½
S ★ ★ ★ ½
A ★ ★ ★ ½
P ★ ★ ★

Jacket required
Lot parking
All major credit cards
Full bar
Reservations recommended

Dinner: Sun.-Thurs. 5:30PM-10:30PM
Fri. & Sat. 5:30PM-11:00PM

This is a "Rolls-Royce" among restaurants with an elegant romantic setting, formal table service, charming garden room, and aura of lush opulence. Here owners Joe Marcello and Nick Mosca present classic French and Creole dishes·

LE RUTH'S 25

636 Franklin Street
Gretna, LA
(504) 362-4914

Creole

F ★ ★ ★ ★
S ★ ★ ★ ½
A ★ ★ ★
P ★ ★ ★ ★

Jacket and tie required
Lot parking
MC, V
Beer/Wine
Reservations required

Dinner: Tues.-Sat. 5:45PM-10:00PM
Closed Sunday and Monday

Modern décor in a 125-year-old Victorian building merge triumphantly in chef/owners Laurence F. and Lee R. Le Ruth's tasteful, award-honored establishment. You'll find crab meat St. Francis, artichoke soup, lamb, and prime steaks all served with daily baked French bread. And, says Lee "We make the richest ice cream in the world!"

L'ESCALE 15

730 Bienville Street
New Orleans, LA
(504) 524-3022

French

F ★ ★ ★ ½
S ★ ★ ★ ½
A ★ ★ ★ ★
P ★ ★ ★ ½

Jacket required
Valet parking
All major credit cards
Full bar
Reservations recommended

Dinner: Mon.-Sat. 6:30PM-10:00PM
                 Closed Sunday

This romantic restaurant with its charming Parisian air has dim lighting that casts a golden glow, and soft piano mood music. The menu focuses on nouvelle French cookery, and features such superb entrées as sole soufflé Lafayette and filet of lamb wrapped with veal mousse and served with a Madeira sauce. The service is formal and faultless.

LOUIS XVI 6

829 Toulouse Street
New Orleans, LA
(504) 581-7000

French

F ★ ★ ★ ½
S ★ ★ ★ ½
A ★ ★ ★ ½
P ★ ★ ★ ★

Jacket and tie required
Valet parking
All major credit cards
Full bar
Reservations required

Breakfast: Daily 7:00AM-11:00AM
Dinner: Nightly 6:30PM-10:00PM

In this luxe multi-roomed restaurant you have a choice of several rooms with different views and distinctive décor. The mood is one of relaxed formality. Renowned for Beef Wellington, Trout Louis XVI, and fresh vegetable creams soups that vary with the seasons.

MAISON PIERRE 9

430 Rue Dauphine
New Orleans, LA
(504) 529-5521

French/Creole

F ★ ★ ★ ½
S ★ ★ ★
A ★ ★ ★ ½
P ★ ★ ★ ★

Good taste in dress required
Street parking
All major credit cards
Full bar
Reservations recommended

Dinner: Nightly 6:00PM-12:00AM

The Pierre Lacoste family, fourth generation restaurateurs, have composed a dining experience for you here that reflects the grandeur of an historic era. Stroll up the carriage way for cocktails in the 200-year-old patio before entering the picturesque 1786 Bordeaux Cottage, the home of this restaurant. Then savor a gala seven-course dinner of haute French/Creole cuisine that changes with the seasons.

MOSCA'S 34

4137 U.S. Highway 90 West
Jefferson Parish, LA
(504) 436-9942

Italian

F ★ ★ ★ ½
S ★ ★ ★ ½
A ★ ★ ★
P ★ ★ ★

No dress restrictions
Lot parking
Credit cards not accepted
Full bar
Reservations required

Dinner: Tues.-Sat. 5:30PM-9:30PM
          Closed Sunday and Monday

This family owned restaurant has been serving shrimp, oysters, and chicken, homemade spaghetti, ravioli, and sausage, and fresh crab salad, done "Mosca's own style" to appreciative diners for decades. John P. Mosca continues the tradition established by his father and mother of serving a short menu of well prepared food.

PASCAL'S MANALE   31

1838 Napolean Avenue
New Orleans, LA
(504) 895-4877

Italian

F   ★ ★ ★ ½
S   ★ ★ ★ ½
A   ★ ★ ★
P   ★ ★ ★

Good taste in dress required, no shorts
Lot parking
All major credit cards
Full bar
Reservations not required

Lunch/
Dinner: Mon.-Fri. 11:45AM-10:00PM
          Sat. 4:00PM-10:30PM
          Sun. 4:00PM-10:00PM

Family owned and operated since 1913, this grand old dining establishment, with its informal, intimate air, is the home of the famed original barbecued shrimp. Daily specials, steaks, veal, seafood, and Italian dishes created with heritage recipes are featured. Pastas and desserts are homemade.

RESTAURANT JONATHAN   5

714 North Rampart
New Orleans, LA
(504) 586-1930

Continental

F   ★ ★ ★ ½
S   ★ ★ ★ ½
A   ★ ★ ★ ½
P   ★ ★ ★ ★

Jacket and tie required, no jeans
Valet, lot, and street parking
All major credit cards
Full bar
Reservations required

Dinner: Nightly from 6:00PM

Housed in an historic French Quarter building restored in art déco design, this renowned dining spot offers you three floors of distinctive décor, and sublime cuisine. Chef Tom Cowman offers seasonal specialties and such entrées as roast Long Island duckling with a ginger and peach sauce and sautéed redfish with lump crabmeat topped with Bernaisse sauce.

RIB ROOM   8

Royal Orleans Hotel
621 St. Louis
New Orleans, LA
(504) 529-5333

Continental

F   ★ ★ ★ ½
S   ★ ★ ★ ½
A   ★ ★ ★ ½
P   ★ ★ ★ ★

Good taste in dress required,
no shorts or T-shirts
Lot parking
AE, MC, V
Full bar
Reservations required

Lunch: Mon.-Sat. 11:30AM-3:00PM
Dinner: Nightly 6:00PM-11:30PM
Brunch: Sun. 10:00AM-3:00PM

As you might expect, roast prime rib is the featured entrée of this woodsy, rustic restaurant with its high ceilings and plethora of plants and jaunty flowers. The menu offers other choices, equally well prepared, including a broad selection of New Orleans seafood.

RUTH'S CHRIS 4
STEAK HOUSE

711 North Broad Avenue
New Orleans, LA
(504) 821-4853

American

F ★ ★ ★ ½
S ★ ★ ★
A ★ ★
P ★ ★ ★

Good taste in dress required
Lot parking
All major credit cards
Beer/Wine
Reservations not required

Lunch/
Dinner: Daily 11:30AM-11:30PM

When you're in the mood for a great steak, visit Ruth Fertel's renowned establishment where only U.S. prime, Midwest, corn-fed beef is slowly aged to perfection. Each steak is cut by hand, broiled to your exact specifications, and served sizzling in butter sauce, with all your favorite accoutrements.

SAZERAC 22

Fairmont Hotel
University Place
New Orleans, LA
(504) 529-7111

French/Creole

F ★ ★ ★ ½
S ★ ★ ★ ½
A ★ ★ ★ ★
P ★ ★ ★ ★

Jacket and tie required
Lot parking
All major credit cards
Full bar
Reservations recommended

Lunch: Mon.-Fri. 11:30AM-2:00PM
Dinner: Nightly 6:30PM-11:00PM

Regal red velvet, black wood, high backed chairs, fresh flowers, glittering chandeliers, and formal service create a feeling of cosmopolitan elegance in this romantic room. Then there are the niceties like sculptured sorbet served before your entrée, and strolling musicians playing for your pleasure.

TCHOUPITOULAS 33
PLANTATION

6535 River Road
Waggaman, LA
(504) 436-1277

Creole

F ★ ★ ★
S ★ ★ ★
A ★ ★ ★
P ★ ★ ½

Good taste in dress required, no shorts
Lot parking
All major credit cards
Full bar
Reservations not required

Lunch: Mon.-Fri. 11:30AM-3:00PM
Dinner: Mon.-Sat. 5:30PM-10:00PM
         Sun. 12:00PM-9:00PM

The quintessence of Southern hospitality, this restaurant occupies a plantation cottage built in 1812, in a 12 acre wooded, rural garden. The atmosphere is friendly and informal, every dish is treated like a specialty, and the service is gracious and genteel. This serene dining spot is just a few minutes drive from the bustling city.

VERSAILLES   30

2100 Saint Charles Avenue
New Orleans, LA
(504) 524-2535

Creole/French

F ★ ★ ★ ½
S ★ ★ ★ ½
A ★ ★ ★ ½
P ★ ★ ★ ½

Jacket required
Valet parking
All major credit cards
Full bar
Reservations required

Dinner: Mon.-Sat. 6:00PM-10:30PM
         Closed Sunday

At the Versailles, Günter Preuss, European-trained owner/chef, and a highly honored restaurateur, orchestrates a superb dining experience. The décor echoes the splendor of the Palace of Versailles; the cuisine is memorable with such specialties as veal and crab meat, bouillabaisse, escargots, and chocolate pava.

WILLY COLN'S CHALET   32

2505 Whitney Avenue
Gretna, LA
(504) 361-3860

Continental

F ★ ★ ★ ½
S ★ ★ ★ ½
A ★ ★ ★
P ★ ★ ★

Good taste in dress required
Lot parking
All major credit cards
Full bar
Reservations required

Lunch: Thurs. & Fri. 11:30AM-2:00PM
Dinner: Tues-Sat. 6:00PM-10:00PM
         Closed Sunday and Monday

Owner/chef Willy Coln offers you a choice of four dining areas, each with its own unique Alpine atmosphere, at his Chalet. He prepares such specialties as roasted veal shank, Bahamian seafood chowder, ceviche, and Black Forest cake. And you'll be exposed to some delightful Creole touches in the masterful continental cuisine.

WINSTON'S   23

New Orleans Hilton
2 Poydras Street
New Orleans, LA
(504) 561-0500

French

F ★ ★ ★ ½
S ★ ★ ★ ★
A ★ ★ ★ ½
P ★ ★ ★ ★

Jacket and tie required
Valet, lot, and street parking
All major credit cards
Full bar
Reservations recommended

Dinner: Tues.-Sat. 6:00PM-11:00PM
Brunch: Sun. 9:00AM-3:00PM
         Closed Monday

Traditional New Orleans cooking, under the direction of chef Robert Williams, adds lustre to the French cuisine featured here. A "maid and butler" team review the verbal menu which might include soft shell crab with praline butter, redfish piquante, or braised rabbit au vin rouge. The décor is sumptuous with rare woods, fine antiques, and original artwork.

New York

AN AMERICAN PLACE 21

969 Lexington Avenue
New York, NY
(212) 517-7660

American

F ★ ★ ★ ½
S ★ ★ ★ ½
A ★ ★ ★ ½
P ★ ★ ★ ★

Jacket and tie required
Street parking
All major credit cards
Full bar
Reservations required

Dinner: Mon.-Sat. 6:00PM-11:00PM
         Closed Sunday

Owner/chef Larry Forgione has carved his niche as a front runner in the renaissance of gourmet American cuisine. In this small, beautifully detailed restaurant, he offers fixed price dinners created with native products. The menu is influenced by the seasons and the ingredients used are always at their peak.

ANDRÉE'S 19
MEDITERRANEAN

354 East 74th Street
New York, NY
(212) 249-6619

Mediterranean

F ★ ★ ★
S ★ ★ ★ ½
A ★ ★ ★
P ★ ★ ★ ★

Jacket preferred
Street or public garage parking
Credit cards not accepted
Bring your own spirits
Reservations required

Dinner: Tues.-Sat. 6:00PM-10:00PM
         Closed Sunday & Monday

The exquisite cuisine you will find here reflects the heritage and experience of owner/chef Andrée Abramoff. It is her enthusiasm and skill in producing the eclectic menu (with touches of French, Greek, Moroccan, and Spanish cooking all evidenced) that has won her international acclaim. Specialties include roast duck with green peppercorns and rack of lamb.

AUNTIE YUAN 32

1191-A 1st Avenue
New York, NY
(212) 744-4040

Taiwanese

F ★ ★ ★
S ★ ★ ★
A ★ ★ ★
P ★ ★ ★ ★

Jacket required
Lot parking
AE, DC
Full bar
Reservations required

Lunch/
Dinner: Mon.-Sat. 12:00PM-12:00AM
         Sun. 12:00PM-11:00PM

Designed for optimum dramatic impact, here you will find theatrically lighted flowers and jet black décor. The type of cooking featured is home style Taiwanese — and discriminating diners savor the subtle differences that distinguish the dishes served here from more commonly available types of Oriental cuisine.

BENIHANA THE 67
JAPANESE STEAKHOUSE

120 East 56th Street
New York, NY
(212) 593-1627

Japanese

F ★ ★ ★
S ★ ★ ★
A ★ ★ ★
P ★ ★ ½

No dress restrictions
Street parking
All major credit cards
Full bar
Reservations recommended

Lunch: Mon.-Sat. 12:00PM-2:30PM
Dinner: Mon.-Thurs. 5:30PM-11:00PM
          Fri. & Sat. 5:30PM-12:00AM
          Closed Sunday

If you like your food prepared with dramatic flair, head for this Oriental steakhouse, and watch a master actor/chef perform feats of culinary legerdemain right before your very eyes. Steak, shrimp, lobster, and chicken, together with their vegetable comrades, are transformed into succulent edibles cooked on your table hibachi or teppan grill.

BENIHANA THE   41
JAPANESE STEAKHOUSE

47 West 56th Street
New York, NY
(212) 581-0930

Japanese

F ★ ★ ★
S ★ ★ ★
A ★ ★ ★
P ★ ★ ½

No dress restrictions
Street parking
All major credit cards
Full bar
Reservations recommended

Lunch: Mon.-Sat. 12:00PM-2:30PM
Dinner: Mon.-Thurs. 5:30PM-11:00PM
          Fri. & Sat. 5:30PM-12:00AM
          Closed Sunday

Peaceful Samisen music accompanies the deft performance of your personal chef as he prepares your meal on a hibachi tableside at this Oriental eatery. Your choice of steak, shrimp, lobster, and chicken, with appropriate vegetables, are prepared with masterful precision and consummate showmanship.

BIANCHI &   117
MARGHERITA

186 West 4th Street
New York, NY
(212) 242-2756

Italian/American

F ★ ★ ★ ½
S ★ ★ ★ ½
A ★ ★ ★ ½
P ★ ★ ★

Good taste in dress required
Street parking
All major credit cards
Full bar
Reservations required

Dinner: Mon.-Sat. 5:00PM-1:00AM
          Closed Sunday

Casual and intimate, diners here are treated to exceptionally fine Northern Italian and American cuisine, served cheerfully by a staff selected for their congeniality and musical abilities. The atmosphere is fun and relaxed with extemporaneous singing of operatic arias and show tunes adding to the pleasant cacophony.

THE BLACK SHEEP CAFÉ   106

342 West 11th Street
New York, NY
(212) 242-1010

French

F ★ ★ ★
S ★ ★ ★
A ★ ★ ★
P ★ ★ ★

Good taste in dress required
Street parking
All major credit cards
Full bar
Reservations required

Dinner: Sun.-Fri. 6:00PM-11:30PM
          Sat. 6:00PM-12:00AM
Brunch: Sun. 12:00PM-4:00PM

The Black Sheep surrounds you with brick walls, candlelight, and drying herbs — the essence of "Village" charm, setting the scene for country French cooking featuring hearty dishes of Burgundy and Provence. Six-course dinners vary with the season.

BOMBAY PALACE   56

30 West 52nd Street
New York, NY
(212) 541-7777

Indian

F   ★ ★ ★
S   ★ ★ ★ ½
A   ★ ★ ★
P   ★ ★

Good taste in dress required
Free dinner parking
All major credit cards
Full bar
Reservations required

Lunch: Daily 12:00PM-3:00PM
Dinner: Nightly 5:30PM-11:30PM

Beautifully decorated and centrally located, Bombay Palace entices you with a "Palace Dinner" that introduces a good sampling of the exotic cuisine including such dishes as Tandoori Chicken with Prawns, Chicken Tikka, and Minced Lamb Kabob. A luncheon buffet is featured daily.

BON TEMPS ROULER   123

59 Reade Street
New York, NY
(212) 513-1333/1334

Cajun/Creole

F   ★ ★ ★
S   ★ ★ ★
A   ★ ★ ½
P   ★ ★ ★

No dress restrictions
Street parking
AE
Full bar
Reservations not required

Dinner: Mon.-Sat. 5:00PM-2:00AM
          Closed Sunday

This convivial restaurant introduces you to such bayou specialties as Voodoo stew, blackened shell steak, grilled redfish, barbecued shrimp, crawfish Yvonne, and alligator sausages, in an atmosphere that typifies a mellow New Orleans saloon. Owner Susan Trilling's apt name for her establishment is Cajun for "let the good times roll."

THE BOXTREE   86

250 East 49th Street
New York, NY
(212) 758-8320

Continental

F   ★ ★ ★
S   ★ ★ ★ ½
A   ★ ★ ★ ½
P   ★ ★ ★ ★

Jacket and tie required
Street parking
Credit cards not accepted
Full bar
Reservations required

Dinner: Nightly Seatings at
          6:30PM & 9:30PM

Prix fixe dinners featuring fresh ingredients prepared à la nouvelle, attract a clientele of serious diners to this petite, town house restaurant. With only eight tables, the atmosphere is intimate and clubby, and the service most attentive.

CAFÉ ARGENTEUIL 79

253 East 52nd Street
New York, NY
(212) 753-9273

French

F ★ ★ ★
S ★ ★ ★ ½
A ★ ★ ★
P ★ ★ ★ ★

Jacket and tie required
Lot and street parking
All major credit cards
Full bar
Reservations required

Lunch: Mon.-Fri. 12:00PM-3:00PM
Dinner: Mon.-Fri. 6:00PM-10:30PM
Sat. 6:00PM-11:00PM
Closed Sunday

Among New York's myriad French restaurants, this establishment continues to shine. The art nouveau décor, glowing candles, correct service, and house specialties earn a deserved reputation for food with finesse and a sense of éclat for this small café.

CAFÉ CARLYLE 12

76th Street at Madison Avenue
New York, NY
(212) 744-1600 or 570-7108

French

F ★ ★ ★
S ★ ★ ★ ★
A ★ ★ ★ ½
P ★ ★ ★ ★

Jacket and tie required at dinner
Lot and street parking

All major credit cards
Full bar
Reservations required

Lunch: Daily 12:00PM-3:00PM
Dinner: Nightly 6:00PM-1:00AM

A smart and intimate rendevous for epicures who fancy French cuisine, Café Carlyle provides you with a bountiful luncheon buffet, excellent gourmet dinners, and an ambiance established by Vertes' murals of smiling happy creatures.

CAFÉ DE BRUXELLES 105

118 Greenwich Avenue
New York, NY
(212) 206-1830

Belgian

F ★ ★ ★
S ★ ★ ★
A ★ ★ ½
P ★ ★

Good taste in dress required
Street parking
AE, MC, V
Full bar
Reservations recommended

Dinner: Mon.-Thurs. 5:00PM-11:00PM
Fri. & Sat. 6:00PM-12:00AM
Brunch: Sat. & Sun. 12:00PM-3:30PM

Picture perfect, this intimate bistro flaunts Belgian lace curtains, and a zinc-topped bar in its pleasant dark green and peach decorating scheme. Patrons flock here to enjoy the authentic Belgian cuisine with its Alsatian overtones, presented by owner Mike Sheber.

CAFÉ DE LA GARE 110

143 Perry Street
New York, NY
(212) 242-3553

French

F ★ ★ ★
S ★ ★ ★
A ★ ★ ★
P ★ ★ ★

Good taste in dress required
Street parking
Credit cards not accepted
Bring your own spirits
Reservations required

Dinner: Tues.-Sat. 6:00PM-10:30PM
         Closed Sunday & Monday

This dear-to-the-heart little Village bistro
has won instant critical acclaim by simply
presenting down-to-earth French home
cooking. Co-owners Christian Dalmas
and Jean Monceau, chef, offer cheerful,
friendly service and fare such as rabbit
sautéed with cabbage, pot au feu, blan-
quette de veau, succulent cassoulet, and
delectable fruit tarts.

CAFÉ DES ARTISTES   3

One West 67th Street
New York, NY
(212) 877-3500

Continental/American

F ★ ★ ★
S ★ ★ ★ ½
A ★ ★ ★ ½
P ★ ★ ★

Jacket required after 5:00PM
Street parking
All major credit cards
Full bar
Reservations required

Lunch: Mon.-Sat. 12:00PM-3:00PM
Dinner: Mon.-Sat. 5:30PM-12:30AM
         Sun. 5:00PM-11:00PM
Brunch: Sun. 10:00AM-4:00PM

A recently revitalized New York institution, Café des Artistes, with its risque
sylvan murals, lures a loyal clientele of
celebrities and discriminating diners. The

wine list is exemplary, the service professional, and the menu diverse and ever-
changing.

CAFÉ LUXEMBOURG   2

200 West 70th Street
New York, NY
(212) 873-7411

French

F ★ ★ ★
S ★ ★ ★
A ★ ★ ★
P ★ ★ ★

Good taste in dress required
Street parking
AE, MC, V
Full bar
Reservations required

Dinner: Mon.-Thurs. 5:30PM-12:30AM
         Fri. 5:30PM-1:30AM
         Sat. & Sun. 6:00PM-1:30AM

Busy, energetic, and sophisticated, this
fashionable café is decorated with old fixtures, and blessed with a kitchen that un-
derstands contemporary French cuisine.
The cassoulet, seafood sausage, and chicory salad are considered outstanding.
You'll find many entrées grilled over mesquite charcoal, and desserts that should
not be passed by.

CAFÉ UN DEUX TROIS   60

123 West 44th Street
New York, NY
(212) 354-4148

French

F ★ ★ ★
S ★ ★ ★ ★
A ★ ★ ★
P ★ ★

No dress restrictions
Lot parking
AE

Full bar
Reservations not required

Lunch/
Dinner: Mon.-Fri. 12:00PM-12:00AM
           Sat. & Sun. 4:00PM-12:00AM

A turn-of-the-century hotel lobby, magically restored to its former grandeur houses Café Un Deux Trois. Simple French café dishes are featured with daily changing specials. The atmosphere is friendly and convivial, inviting leisurely, relaxed dining.

CAMELBACK & CENTRAL   16

1403 Second Avenue
New York, NY
(212) 249-8380

Continental/American

F ★ ★ ★
S ★ ★ ★ ½
A ★ ★ ★ ½
P ★ ★

Good taste in dress required
Street parking
All major credit cards
Full bar
Reservations recommended

Lunch: Mon.-Fri. 11:30AM-3:00PM
Dinner: Nightly 5:00PM-11:00PM
Brunch: Sat. & Sun. 11:30AM-4:00PM

The art déco ambiance of Camelback & Central lures a lively clientele. Specialties include Roast Duck with Black Currants, grilled seafoods and meats, and Vegetable Tempura with Sherry Soy Sauce. The wine list includes both American and French vintners.

CAPRICCIO   44

33 East 61st Street
New York, NY
(212) 759-6684/757-7795

Italian

F ★ ★ ★
S ★ ★ ★ ½
A ★ ★ ★
P ★ ★ ★ ★

Jacket required
Lot and street parking
All major credit cards
Full bar
Reservations required

Lunch: Mon.-Fri. 12:00PM-3:00PM
Dinner: Mon.-Sat. 5:00PM-11:00PM
          Closed Sunday

Remo and Remegio Raicovich have catered to a discerning clientele for the past 13 years, at their flower-bedecked, garden-room restaurant. Emphasis is on northern-style Italian dishes, including gnocchi, Costoletta Valdostana, and a robust fish soup offered as a Friday special.

CARLYLE   12

76th Street at Madison Avenue
New York, NY
(212) 744-1600/570-7108

French

F ★ ★ ★
S ★ ★ ★ ★
A ★ ★ ★ ★
P ★ ★ ★ ★

Jacket and tie required
Lot and street parking
All major credit cards
Full bar
Reservations required

Lunch: Daily 12:00PM-2:30PM
Dinner: Nightly 6:00PM-10:45PM

Dining at the Carlyle will restore your faith in the quality concept and whet your appetite for return visits. Luxurious, comfortable surroundings set the scene for gracious service of superbly prepared French cuisine.

CAROLINA   57

355 West 46th Street
New York, NY
(212) 245-0058

American

F ★ ★ ★
S ★ ★ ★
A ★ ★ ½
P ★ ★ ★

No dress restrictions
Lot parking
MC, V
Full bar
Reservations required

Lunch: Mon.-Fri. 12:00PM-3:00PM
Dinner: Mon.-Sat. 6:00PM-12:00AM
          Sun. 12:00PM-8:00PM
Brunch: Sun. 11:30AM-3:30PM

This stellar addition to theater district dining combines tasteful décor, and genuine American-style cooking. Owners Martin Yerdon and Eileen Weinberg offer such enticements as house chili, green chili pepper soufflé, barbecued ribs and brisket, ham with cherry sauce; and biscuits, jalapeño corn bread, and desserts.

CELLAR IN THE SKY   122

One World Trade Center
New York, NY
(212) 938-1111

International/American

F ★ ★ ★
S ★ ★ ★ ½
A ★ ★ ★ ½
P ★ ★ ★ ★

Jacket and tie required, no denims
Free lot parking
All major credit cards
Full bar
Reservations required

Dinner: Mon.-Sat. 7:30PM seating
          Closed Sunday

Promptly at 7:30PM, three dozen diners begin the ritual of a seven-course prix fixe dinner, accompanied by five wines, in a unique working wine-cellar, 107 stories high. If you are among these fortunate few, you will find it a heady experience, well worth repeating.

CHANTERELLE   126

89 Grand Street
New York, NY
(212) 966-6960

French

F ★ ★ ★
S ★ ★ ★ ½
A ★ ★ ★ ½
P ★ ★ ★ ★

Jacket and tie preferred
Street parking
AE, MC, V
Full bar
Reservations required

Dinner: Tues.-Sat. 6:30PM-10:30PM
          Closed Sunday and Monday

Dine in an intimate, authentically restored petite 19th century room with a warm sense of old-world charm. Prix fixe dinners and a tasting menu feature specialties such as grilled seafood sausage, lobster in sauternes sauce, and homemade ice creams and sherbets.

CHATFIELD'S   48

208 East 60th Street
New York, NY
(212) 753-5070

American

F ★ ★ ★
S ★ ★ ★
A ★ ★ ★
P ★ ★ ★

No dress restrictions
Street parking
All major credit cards
Full bar
Reservations required

Lunch:	Mon.-Fri. 12:00PM-3:00PM
	Sat. 12:00PM-4:00PM
Dinner:	Mon.-Sat. 6:00PM-11:30PM
	Sun. 5:30PM-11:00PM
Brunch:	Sun. 12:00PM-4:00PM

With a toasty wood-burning fireplace to add to the homey warmth, this establishment presents a bevy of pasta dishes and innovative seafood and chicken entrées that lean heavily toward American cuisine prepared in the nouvelle manner.

CHELSEA PLACE 101

147 Eighth Avenue
New York, NY.
(212) 924-8413

Italian

F ★ ★ ★
S ★ ★ ★
A ★ ★ ★ ½
P ★ ★ ★

Good taste in dress required
Street parking
All major credit cards
Full bar
Reservations required

| Lunch: | Mon.-Fri. 12:00PM-2:30PM |
| Dinner: | Mon.-Sun. 5:30PM-11:30PM |

A lively inner sanctum overlooking outdoor gardens, Chelsea Place nestles behind an antique store that opens into a piano bar and provides access to the restaurant. Your reward for completing this treasure hunt is exceedingly good Northern Italian cuisine.

CHEZ PASCAL 5

151 East 82nd Street
New York, NY
(212) 249-1334

French

F ★ ★ ★
S ★ ★ ★ ½
A ★ ★ ★ ½
P ★ ★ ★ ★

Jacket required
Street parking
All major credit cards
Full bar
Reservations required

| Dinner: | Mon.-Sat. 6:00PM-11:30PM |
| | Closed Sunday |

Fresh flowers, flickering candles, pink brick walls, and handsome grey ultrasuede banquettes create a romantic aura at Chez Pascal. You'll find the portions are generous, and the service unobtrusive. House specialties include bouillabaisse, and duck in raspberries.

CHRIST CELLA 85

160 East 46th Street
New York, NY
(212) 697-2479

American

F ★ ★ ★
S ★ ★ ★ ★
A ★ ★ ★
P ★ ★ ★ ★

Jacket and tie required
Street parking
All major credit cards
Full bar
Reservations required

Lunch:	Mon.-Fri. 12:00PM-3:00PM
Dinner:	Mon.-Sat. 5:00PM-10:30PM
	Closed Sunday

Since 1926, Christ Cella has maintained a roster of loyal clients who are devotees of quality food. Rarely are they disappointed. Steaks, chops, and seafood are the menu mainstays. They are prepared and served with a sure hand.

CINCO DE MAYO　125

349 West Broadway
New York, NY
(212) 226-5255

Mexican

```
F  ★ ★ ★
S  ★ ★ ★
A  ★ ★ ½
P  ★ ★
```

No dress restrictions
Street parking
All major credit cards
Full bar
Reservations required

Lunch/
Dinner:　Tues.-Sun. 12:00PM-12:00AM
　　　　　Closed Monday

The haute cuisine of a top Mexico City restaurant is the style of cooking featured in this friendly, congenial, barlike dining spot. Here owner Jerry Stein creates a menu that blends peppery salsas, traditional mole, and more esoteric entrées that reflect the cosmopolitan tastes found in Mexico's largest city.

CLAIRE　100

156 Seventh Avenue
New York, NY
(212) 255-1955

Seafood

```
F  ★ ★ ★
S  ★ ★ ★
A  ★ ★ ★ ½
P  ★ ★
```

Good taste in dress required
Lot and street parking
AE, MC, V
Full bar
Reservations required

Lunch/
Dinner:　Daily 12:00PM-1:00AM

An upbeat rendition of owners Marvin and Claire Paige's Key West, Florida eatery, the décor here suggests the langorous tropics. A variety of seasonally available fresh seafood is featured—prepared with imaginative touches.

THE COACH HOUSE　115

110 Waverly Place
New York, NY
(212) 777-0303--0349

American

```
F  ★ ★ ★
S  ★ ★ ★
A  ★ ★ ★
P  ★ ★ ★ ★
```

Jacket and tie required
Street parking
AE
Full bar
Reservations required

Dinner:　Tues.-Sun. 6:00PM-11:00PM
　　　　　Closed Monday

This remodeled carriage house in Greenwich Village exudes the well-mannered genteel atmosphere of an old English inn. For 30 years, owner Leon Lianides has maintained the highest standard in food preparation and service. The baby rack of lamb is a perennial favorite.

CONTRAPUNTO　47

200 East 60th Street
New York, NY
(212) 751-8616

Pasta

F ★ ★ ★
S ★ ★ ★
A ★ ★ ½
P ★ ★ ½

Good taste in dress required
Street parking
AE, CB, MC, V
Full bar
Reservations not required

Lunch/
Dinner: Mon.-Sat. 12:00PM-11:00PM
         Sun. 5:00PM-10:00PM

Dedicated to creating unusual pasta dishes, not found elsewhere, this bright, cheerful eatery offers you a chic retreat near Bloomingdale's and movie theaters. You can choose from more than 20 well executed pastas presented nightly, or from the limited menu of alternate entrées.

DE MARCO 5

1422 3rd Avenue
New York, NY
(212) 744-2819

Italian

F ★ ★ ★
S ★ ★ ★
A ★ ★ ★
P ★ ★ ★ ★

Jacket and tie required
Street parking
AE, CB, DC
Full bar
Reservations required

Dinner: Nightly 6:00PM-11:00PM
Brunch: Sun. 11:30AM-3:30PM

Spartan in its simplicity, this much-in-vogue new restaurant boasts a kitchen manned by chef Jay Trubee, a consummate cucina Italiana artist. The bill of fare leans toward northern cookery, but you'll find refreshing southern touches shining through.

ELAINE'S 9

1703 2nd Avenue
New York, NY
(212) 534-8114

Italian

F ★ ★ ½
S ★ ★ ★
A ★ ★ ★
P ★ ★

No dress restrictions
Street parking
AE
Full bar
Reservations required

Lunch: Mon.-Fri. 12:00PM-3:00PM
Dinner: Nightly 6:00PM-2:00AM

Owner Elaine Kauffman has used posters and pictures of actors, actresses, and sports luminaries to decorate her clubby, entertainment-oriented establishment that attracts an intellectual and artistic crowd. You'll find osso buco featured, plus all the traditional dishes that comprise hearty authentic Italian fare.

EL RINCÓN DE ESPAÑA 121

226 Thompson Street
New York, NY
(212) 475-9891/260-4950/344-5228

Spanish/Continental

F ★ ★ ★ ½
S ★ ★ ★ ½
A ★ ★ ★
P ★ ★ ★

Jacket preferred
Street parking
All major credit cards
Full bar
Reservations required

Lunch: Mon.-Fri. 12:00PM-3:00PM
Dinner: Mon.-Thurs. 5:00PM-11:00PM
Fri. & Sat. 5:00PM-12:00AM
Closed Sunday

Small, dimly lit, and with a rustic Spanish tavern ambiance that seems right at home in Greenwich Village, you'll find good Spanish cooking and a selection of continental entrées featured here. Clams, mussels, shrimp, lobster, and scallops are offered in a variety of combinations. A robust paella is served by the potful.

ELIO'S 6

1621 2nd Avenue
New York, NY
(212) 772-2242

Italian

F ★ ★ ★
S ★ ★ ★ ½
A ★ ★ ★
P ★ ★ ★

Good taste in dress required
Street parking
AE
Full bar
Reservations required

Dinner: Nightly 5:30PM-12:00AM

This bustling, popular pub-café is the brainchild of owner Elio Guaitolini. It lures an illustrious celebrity crowd who mingle with the hoi polloi waiting for such savory enticements as fried calamari, Cornish hen al mattone, and veal cutlet Milanese. Grilled gamberoni (those behemoth red Spanish shrimp) is a house specialty.

THE FOUR SEASONS 74

99 East 52nd Street
New York, NY
(212) 754-9494

American

F ★ ★ ★ ★
S ★ ★ ★ ★
A ★ ★ ★ ★
P ★ ★ ★ ★

Jacket and tie required
Valet parking after 6:00PM
All major credit cards
Full bar
Reservations required

Lunch: Mon.-Sat. 12:00PM-2:30PM
Dinner: Mon.-Sat. 5:00PM-11:30PM
Closed Sunday

A world-class restaurant whose success stems from uncompromising quality and the personal supervision of owners Paul Kovi and Tom Margittai. Always in a state of flux, with seasonally changing décor and menu, the service, inspired food, and atmosphere are reliably constant.

GAGE & TOLLNER 116

372 Fulton Street
Brooklyn, NY
(718) 875-5181

American

F ★ ★ ★
S ★ ★ ★
A ★ ★ ★
P ★ ★ ★

Good taste in dress required
Street parking
All major credit cards
Full bar
Reservations not required

Lunch/
Dinner: Mon.-Fri. 12:00PM-9:30PM
Sat. 4:00PM-10:30PM
Closed Sunday

You'll find more than a touch of nostalgia at Gage & Tollner, where the original décor, extant since 1889, includes gas chandeliers that are lit every night. The hard-to-find heritage American cooking emphasizes fresh seafoods and steaks.

GALLAGHER'S STEAK HOUSE   37

228 West 52nd Street
New York, NY
(212) 245-5336

American

F ★ ★ ★
S ★ ★ ★ ★
A ★ ★ ★ ★
P ★ ★ ★ ½

Good taste in dress required
Street parking
All major credit cards
Full bar
Reservations required

Lunch/
Dinner: Mon.-Sun. 12:00PM-12:00AM

This Broadway area landmark has lured the sports, theatrical, and political famous for 52 years. The New York cut steak was born here, and over 500 sirloin strips are on view in the glass ageing box. A bustling, colorful, informal eatery.

GIAMBELLI 50TH   76

46 East 50th Street
New York, NY
(212) 688-2760

Italian

F ★ ★ ★
S ★ ★ ★ ½
A ★ ★ ★ ½
P ★ ★ ★ ★

Jacket preferred
Valet parking
All major credit cards
Full bar
Reservations required

Lunch/
Dinner: Mon.-Sat. 12:00PM-12:00AM
          Closed Sunday

In this classic, three-floor Italian eatery you'll find handsome paintings, dim lights, and friendly formal service to backdrop the Northern Italian cuisine. House specialties offered may include such dishes as Pollo Cacciatora, Fettuccine ala Giambelli, and shrimp crêpes.

GIAN MARINO   70

221 East 58th Street
New York, NY
(212) 752-1696

Italian

F ★ ★ ★
S ★ ★ ★
A ★ ★ ★
P ★ ★ ½

Jacket required
Garage parking across the street
All major credit cards
Full bar
Reservations not required

Lunch/
Dinner: Tues.-Fri. 12:00PM-12:00AM
          Sat. 4:00PM-12:00AM
          Sun. 1:00PM-11:00PM
          Closed Monday

Appreciated for its warm, friendly atmosphere and regional Italian dishes, Gian Marino has kept customers happily coming back for more for over 40 years. Among the house specialties you will find are Chicken Sofia Loren, and pasta with broccoli and zucchini.

THE GIBBON   4

24 East 80th Street
New York, NY
(212) 861-4001

Japanese/Continental

F ★ ★ ★
S ★ ★ ★
A ★ ★ ★
P ★ ★ ★ ★

Jacket required
Street parking
All major credit cards
Full bar
Reservations required

Lunch: Mon.-Fri. 12:00PM-2:30PM
Dinner: Mon.-Sat. 5:45PM-10:00PM
Closed Sunday

The blending of Japanese and continental cuisines succeeds admirably in this quiet, comfortable clublike establishment that has become a haven for art dealers and their associates. The appetizers are works of art and the entrées such as kamo-hasamiyaki (roasted slices of duck breast layered with Oriental vegetables) are eminently satisfying.

GIRAFE   68

208 East 58th Street
New York, NY
(212) 752-3054

Italian

F ★ ★ ★
S ★ ★ ★
A ★ ★ ★
P ★ ★ ★ ★

Jacket required
Street parking
All major credit cards
Full bar
Reservations required

Lunch: Mon.-Fri. 12:00PM-3:00PM
Dinner: Mon.-Sat. 5:30PM-10:45PM
Closed Sunday

Paintings of wildlife on the African plains, candles, and flowers decorate this two-tiered supper-club featuring Northern Italian cuisine. The portions here are generous and you'll find all the food, from the blissful antipasto through the al dente pastas, to the heavenly zabaglione, is exceptionally well prepared.

GLOUCESTER HOUSE   59

37 East 50th Street
New York, NY
(212) 755-7394

Seafood

F ★ ★ ★
S ★ ★ ★
A ★ ★ ½
P ★ ★ ★ ★

Jacket and tie required
Street parking
All major credit cards
Full bar
Reservations required

Lunch: Daily 12:00PM-2:30PM
Dinner: Nightly 5:30PM-10:30PM

A favorite of gourmets for more than 50 years, Gloucester House lets you savor Maine lobsters and seasonally fresh seafoods in a setting replicating a New England seaport, complete with a miniature boat display.

GOTHAM BAR & GRILL   111

12 East 12th Street
New York, NY
(212) 620-4020

American

F ★ ★ ★
S ★ ★ ★
A ★ ★ ★
P ★ ★ ★

No dress restrictions
Lot and street parking
All major credit cards
Full bar
Reservations required

Lunch: Mon.-Sat. 12:00PM-3:00PM
Dinner: Sun.-Thurs. 5:00PM-12:00AM
Fri. & Sat. 5:00PM-1:00AM
Brunch: Sun. 11:30AM-3:30PM

This glitzy, glittering new brasserie has captured the imagination of the trendy set who flock here to enjoy some of the most eclectic food in the city. You'll discover a menu of such diversity it boggles the mind. You will also find some classic favorites if your mood is less than adventuresome. The wine list is solid and the service is great.

GREENE STREET RESTAURANT   119

101 Greene Street
New York, NY
(212) 925-2415

French/Continental/American

F ★ ★ ★ ½
S ★ ★ ★
A ★ ★ ★ ★
P ★ ★ ★ ½

Good taste in dress required
Street parking
All major credit cards
Full bar
Reservations required

Dinner: Mon.-Thurs. 5:00PM-11:30PM
          Fri. & Sat. 5:00PM-1:00AM
          Sun. 5:30PM-9:30PM
Brunch: Sun. 11:30AM-3:30PM

Sited in a former warehouse, with arched brick walls soaring to a 35-foot ceiling, you'll find large potted trees, a muraled wall, and wicker furnishings creating a city-square café ambiance. The eclectic menu offered in this theatrical setting is accompanied by live jazz. The staff is welcoming and friendly, the food up to epicurean standards.

HATSUHANA   64

17 East 48th Street
New York, NY
(212) 355-3345

Japanese

F ★ ★ ★
S ★ ★ ★ ½
A ★ ★ ★
P ★ ★ ★ ★

Good taste in dress required
Street parking
All major credit cards
Full bar
Reservations required

Lunch: Mon.-Fri. 11:45AM-2:30PM
Dinner: Mon.-Fri. 5:30PM-9:30PM
          Sat. & Sun. 5:00PM-9:30PM

Hatsuhana lets you enjoy sushi, sashimi, and other Japanese dishes in an austere contemporary atmosphere, where the effort is concentrated on preparing and presenting the featured cuisine with consummate skill and artistry.

HUNAM   95

845 Second Avenue
New York, NY
(212) 687-7471

Chinese

F ★ ★ ★
S ★ ★ ★
A ★ ★ ½
P ★ ★ ½

Good taste in dress required
Lot parking
AE, CB, DC
Full bar
Reservations required

Lunch/
Dinner: Sun.-Thurs. 12:00PM-10:45PM
          Fri. & Sat. 12:00PM-11:45PM

Hidden behind dim lighting and a somewhat uninspired Oriental décor you will find exceptionally good Chinese cuisine served here. Reflecting the cooking style of its namesake province, the dishes are often hot and peppery. House specialties include fillet of sea bass with shrimp roe sauce, moo shu pork, and lobster Hunam style.

IL CANTINORI 113

32 East 10th Street
New York, NY
(212) 673-6044

Tuscan

F ★ ★ ★
S ★ ★ ★
A ★ ★ ½
P ★ ★ ★

No dress restrictions
Street parking
AE, DC
Full bar
Reservations required

Lunch: Mon.-Fri. 12:00PM-3:00PM
Dinner: Mon.-Thurs. 6:00PM-11:30PM
Fri. & Sat. 6:00PM-12:00AM
Sun. 5:00PM-11:00PM

This antique-furnished rustic retreat with its cozy terrace, terra cotta floors, and display of old farm tools, puts you in the perfect frame of mind for the hearty Tuscan cooking featured here. Game meats, fresh fish from Italy, imported truffles, and specials such as quail with polenta, add gusto to the bounty of standard menu fare.

IL CORTILE 127

125 Mulberry Street
New York, NY
(212) 226-6060

Italian

F ★ ★ ★
S ★ ★ ★ ½
A ★ ★ ★
P ★ ★ ★ ½

Good taste in dress required
Street parking
All major credit cards
Full bar
Reservations required

Lunch/
Dinner: Mon.-Thurs. 12:00PM-12:00AM
Fri. & Sat. 12:00PM-1:00AM
Sun. 1:00PM-12:00AM

Your choice of three dining rooms are available in this lovely spot with its wood and brick décor and skylighted enclosed garden. From the kitchen come palate-pleasing dishes in the Northern Italian style, with such specialties as Sardinian-style eel, Bouillabaisse Marinaro, and Chicken du Cordonnier.

IL MENESTRELLO 49

14 East 52nd Street
New York, NY
(212) 421-7588

Italian

F ★ ★ ★
S ★ ★ ★
A ★ ★ ★
P ★ ★ ★ ½

Jacket required
Street parking
AE, DC, MC, V
Full bar
Reservations required

Lunch/
Dinner: Mon.-Thurs. 12:00PM-11:00PM
Fri. & Sat. 12:00PM-12:00AM

Oak, brass, pictures, and an overall posh atmosphere are the staging for the Northern Italian meals served here. Interesting appetizers, robust soups, and your choice of 45 entrées are standard fare. The capelli d'angelo Il Menestrello has been lauded by critics, as has the tortellini alla panna.

IL MONELLO 17

1460 2nd Avenue
New York, NY
(212) 535-9310

Italian

F ★ ★ ★
S ★ ★ ★ ½
A ★ ★ ★
P ★ ★ ★ ★

Jacket required
Street parking
All major credit cards
Full bar
Reservations required

Lunch: Mon.-Sat. 12:00PM-3:00PM
Dinner: Mon.-Sat. 5:00PM-12:00AM
Closed Sunday

Like a well-composed painting, this restaurant holds the attention of its patrons. The setting is plush and elegant, the service quick and smooth, and the cuisine excellent. Owner Adi Giovannetti offers an extensive menu featuring Italian classics and specialties.

IL NIDO   71

251 East 53rd Street
New York, NY
(212) 753-8450

Italian

F ★ ★ ★
S ★ ★ ★ ½
A ★ ★ ★
P ★ ★ ★ ½

Jacket required
Street parking
All major credit cards
Full bar
Reservations required

Lunch: Mon.-Sat. 12:00PM-2:15PM
Dinner: Mon.-Sat. 5:30PM-10:15PM
Closed Sunday

Gracious and inviting, this intimate establishment is filled with colorful flowers and patient customers. The Northern Italian cuisine is nearly faultless and the service is excellent. The menu is diverse and includes many uncommon entrées. The wine list has been carefully compiled.

JAMS   13

154 East 79th Street
New York, NY
(212) 772-6800

American

F ★ ★ ★ ½
S ★ ★ ★ ½
A ★ ★ ★ ½
P ★ ★ ★ ★

Jacket required
Street parking
AE, DC
Full bar
Reservations required

Lunch: Tues.-Fri. 12:00PM-2:15PM
Dinner: Mon.-Sat. 6:00PM-11:15PM
Closed Sunday

This cheerful, California-style restaurant represents the creative genius of Melvyn Master and Jonathan Waxman. Here you'll find free-range chicken, spicy blackened swordfish, lamb, and game cooked over mesquite in an open kitchen. The wine list is impressive and the desserts downright delectable.

JEAN LAFITTE   38

68 West 58th Street
New York, NY
(212) 751-2323

French

F ★ ★ ★
S ★ ★ ★
A ★ ★ ★
P ★ ★ ★

No dress restrictions
Street parking
AE, DC, MC, V
Full bar
Reservations required

Lunch: Mon.-Fri. 12:00PM-3:00PM
Dinner: Nightly 6:00PM-12:00AM

Fresh fish, veal, beef, pasta, and foie gras, the nucleus of French cuisine, seem to be reenergized in the bourgeois bistro fare served here. The atmosphere may seem somewhat cliché, but the phalanx of contented customers seem to like it just that way.

JOE & ROSE RESTAURANT 89

747 Third Avenue
New York, NY
(212) 980-3985

Italian/American

F ★ ★ ★
S ★ ★ ★ ★
A ★ ★ ★
P ★ ★ ★ ½

No dress restrictions
Street parking
AE, CB, DC
Full bar
Reservations required

Lunch: Mon.-Fri. 12:00PM-3:00PM
Dinner: Mon.-Sat. 5:30PM-10:00PM
         Closed Sunday

A family-run restaurant in continuous operation since 1913, Joe & Rose carried on business as usual while a 38-story office building sprung up over and around them. The homemade pastas are excellent; the meat dishes and seafood of highest caliber.

JOHN CLANCY'S   109
RESTAURANT

181 West 10th Street
New York, NY
(212) 242-7350

Seafood

F ★ ★ ★
S ★ ★ ★
A ★ ★ ★
P ★ ★ ★ ½

Jacket required
Lot and street parking
All major credit cards
Full bar
Reservations required

Dinner: Mon.-Sat. 6:00PM-11:00PM
         Sun. 4:00PM-10:00PM

The pearl gray and white color scheme is a perfect setting for this gem of a restaurant devoted to seafood. Owner John Clancy is a renowned chef/author/teacher who has put his talents on the line here. The fish and shellfish specialties are of international scope, and a mesquite grill is the featured cooking method.

KEEN'S   91

72 West 36th Street
New York, NY
(212) 947-3636

American

F ★ ★ ★
S ★ ★ ★
A ★ ★ ★
P ★ ★ ★ ½

No dress restrictions
Lot parking
All major credit cards
Full bar
Reservations recommended

Lunch: Mon.-Fri. 11:45AM-3:00PM
Dinner: Mon.-Fri. 5:30PM-11:00PM
         Sat. 5:00PM-11:00PM
         Closed Sunday

Established 100 years ago, this clubby haunt of illuminaries is a living legend, decorated with historic memorabilia and a clay pipe collection of thousands of pieces displayed hanging from the ceiling. The setting is like taking a sentimental journey backward through time. The menu is diverse, and the fist-sized succulent mutton chops for which this restaurant has always been rightly famed are still a favorite entrée.

LA CARAVELLE   43

33 West 55th Street
New York, NY
(212) 586-4252

French

F ★ ★ ★
S ★ ★ ★ ★
A ★ ★ ★ ★
P ★ ★ ★ ★

Jacket and tie required
Street parking
All major credit cards
Full bar
Reservations required

Lunch: Mon.-Sat. 12:15PM-2:30PM
Dinner: Mon.-Sat. 6:00PM-10:30PM
          Closed Sunday

The darling of New York society for 25
years, La Caravelle projects an image of
understated elegance and classic good
taste. Specialties include such savory delights as Quenelles de Brochet Homardine,
Côte de Veau Normande, and Soufflé
Glacé au Praline.

LA COLOMBE D'OR   97

134 East 26th Street
New York, NY
(212) 689-0666

French

F ★ ★ ★
S ★ ★ ★
A ★ ★ ★
P ★ ★ ★

No dress restrictions
Street parking
AE, DC, MC, V
Full bar
Reservations required

Lunch: Mon.-Fri. 12:00PM-2:30PM
Dinner: Mon.-Sun. 6:00PM-11:00PM

You'll find southern French cooking, with
its emphasis on garlic, featured in this restaurant with its refreshing French country
setting. The bouillabaisse is hearty and
full-flavored. Other highly touted entrées
are Mignonnettes d'Agneau, and an elaborately prepared Poulet Maison.

LA CÔTE BASQUE   45

5 East 55th Street
New York, NY
(212) 688-6525

French

F ★ ★ ★ ★
S ★ ★ ★ ★
A ★ ★ ★ ★
P ★ ★ ★ ★

Jacket and tie required
Street parking
All major credit cards
Full bar
Reservations required

Lunch: Mon.-Sat. 12:00PM-2:30PM
Dinner: Mon.-Fri. 6:00PM-10:30PM
          Sat. 6:00PM-11:00PM
          Closed Sunday

Jean Jacques Rachou, owner, chef, and
impressario of this illustrious success
story, utilizes murals of Basque scenes and
opulent floral arrangements to add a sense
of grandeur to this fashionable eatery. The
cuisine is impeccable, the service marvelous, and the wine list above reproach.

LA GRENOUILLE   63

3 East 52nd Street
New York, NY
(212) 752-1495

French

F ★ ★ ★ ½
S ★ ★ ★ ½
A ★ ★ ★ ½
P ★ ★ ★ ★

Jacket required
Street parking
AE, CB, DC
Full bar
Reservations required

Lunch: Mon.-Sat. 12:00PM-2:30PM
Dinner: Mon.-Sat. 6:00PM-10:30PM
         Closed Sunday

For two and a half decades this regal establishment has reigned as one of New York's supreme deities of French cuisine. Now under the direction of Gisèle and Charles Masson, the ambiance, exquisite floral arrangements, and service level have lost none of their lustre. The menu, as always, offers a select, well balanced compendium of enticing specialties.

LA RESERVE   62

4 West 49th Street
New York, NY
(212) 247-2993

French

F ★ ★ ★
S ★ ★ ★ ★
A ★ ★ ★ ★
P ★ ★ ★ ★

Jacket required
Lot parking
All major credit cards
Full bar
Reservations required

Lunch: Daily 12:00PM-3:00PM
Dinner: Nightly 5:30PM-11:00PM

La Reserve, with its unique decor emulating a wildlife refuge with touches of elegance, won the instant endorsement of sophisticated New York diners. The French cuisine is prepared in the haute nouvelle manner — with fresh, natural flavors predominating.

LA RIPAILLE   102

605 Hudson Street
New York, NY
(212) 255-4406

French

F ★ ★ ★ ★
S ★ ★ ★ ½
A ★ ★ ★
P ★ ★ ★

Good taste in dress required
Street parking
AE, DC, MC, V
Full bar
Reservations required

Dinner: Nightly 5:30PM-11:30PM

You will find a friendly, congenial atmosphere at Patrick and Alain Laurent's country-style bistro. The menu changes daily and includes elements of nouvelle and traditional cuisines, with freshness of ingredients stressed.

LA TULIPE   108

104 West 13th Street
New York, NY
(212) 691-8860

French

F ★ ★ ★ ★
S ★ ★ ★ ½
A ★ ★ ★ ★
P ★ ★ ★ ★

Good taste in dress required
Street and public garage parking
All major credit cards
Full bar
Reservations recommended

Dinner: Tues.-Sun. 6:30PM-10:00PM
         Closed Monday

Small, intimate, and lovely, La Tulipe has a wonderful ambiance created by the owners, Sally (chef) and John (manager) Darr.

The service is friendly, the food fresh and light. Red Snapper en Papillote, Smoked Eel Mousse, and Apricot Soufflé are among the house specialties.

LAURENT   51

111 East 56th Street
New York, NY
(212) 753-2729

French

F ★ ★ ★
S ★ ★ ★ ½
A ★ ★ ★ ½
P ★ ★ ★ ½

Jacket and tie required
Lot and street parking
All major credit cards
Full bar
Reservations required

Lunch: Mon.-Fri. 12:00PM-3:00PM
Dinner: Sun.-Fri. 6:00PM-10:30PM
         Sat. 5:00PM-11:00PM

Celebrating its 34th year, Laurent Losa's restaurant offers a menu that changes daily, featuring prime seasonal specialties. The air-conditioned wine cellar keeps 36,000 bottles at their peak, with modest, great, and rare vintages on the award-winning list.

LE CHANTILLY   52

106 East 57th Street
New York, NY
(212) 751-2931

French

F ★ ★ ★ ½
S ★ ★ ★ ★
A ★ ★ ★ ½
P ★ ★ ★ ½

Jacket required and tie preferred
Garage parking
All major credit cards
Full bar
Reservations recommended

Lunch: Mon.-Sat. 12:00PM-3:30PM
Dinner: Mon.-Sat. 6:00PM-11:00PM
         Closed Sunday

Murals depicting chateau scenes from Chantilly give credence to the name of this picturesque French dining retreat. Classically elegant décor, silver service, jubilant fresh flowers, and a professional staff make dining here a pure delight. A daily special, created by executive chef Roland Chenus, augments the traditional French bill of fare.

LE CHERCHE-MIDI   84

936 First Avenue
New York, NY
(212) 355-4499

French

F ★ ★ ★ ½
S ★ ★ ★ ½
A ★ ★ ★ ½
P ★ ★ ★ ★

Good taste in dress required
Street parking
MC, V
Full bar
Reservations required

Lunch: Tues.-Fri. 12:00PM-2:30PM
Dinner: Mon.-Sat. 6:00PM-11:00PM
         Closed Sunday

This busy, bustling eatery, with its provincial country-style decor and petite back garden is the private domain of owner/chef Sally Scoville. Here you'll find a warm welcome, an obliging staff, and a meticulously contrived limited menu that pays homage to highest quality fresh ingredients, delicately prepared.

LE CIRQUE 20

58 East 65th Street
New York, NY
(212) 794-9292

French

```
F  ★  ★  ★  ½
S  ★  ★  ★  ½
A  ★  ★  ★  ★
P  ★  ★  ★  ★
```

Jacket and tie required
Street parking
AE, CB, DC
Full bar
Reservations required

Lunch: Mon.-Sat. 12:00PM-2:45PM
Dinner: Mon.-Sat. 6:00PM-10:30PM
         Closed Sunday
         Closed month of July

For the erudite diner who dotes on the trendy, Le Cirque couples old-school elegance and cuisine with character. Seviche of Red Snapper au Coriander, mussel salad, duck or rabbit pâté, feathery soufflés, and delectable crêpes typify the menu selections.

LE CYGNE 50

55 East 54th Street
New York, NY
(212) 759-5941

French

```
F  ★  ★  ★  ½
S  ★  ★  ★  ½
A  ★  ★  ★  ½
P  ★  ★  ★  ★
```

Jacket and tie required
Street parking
All major credit cards

Full bar
Reservations required

Lunch: Daily 12:00PM-2:30PM
Dinner: Sun.-Thurs. 6:00PM-10:00PM
         Fri.-Sat. 6:00PM-11:00PM

Intimate and chic, dining at Le Cygne offers you a choice of classic or light French cuisine, served in an elegant atmosphere. Fish specialties and whisper-light soufflés are both featured. The food pleases the eye and the palate.

LE LAVANDOU 23

134 East 61st Street
New York, NY
(212) 838-7987

French

```
F  ★  ★  ★
S  ★  ★  ★  ½
A  ★  ★  ★
P  ★  ★  ★  ★
```

Jacket and tie required
Street parking
AE
Beer/Wine
Reservations required

Lunch: Mon.-Sat. 12:00PM-2:30PM
Dinner: Mon.-Fri. 6:00PM-10:30PM
         Sat. 6:00PM-11:00PM
         Closed Sunday

This petite Basque auberge attracts a clientele of thoughtful people who come to savor the food and enjoy good company. Murals of Southern France coastal scenes are dominant in the décor. The food is classic, and served with the respect it deserves. The desserts are stellar.

LE PÉRIGORD 87

405 East 52nd Street
New York, NY
(212) 755-6244

French

F ★ ★ ★ ½
S ★ ★ ★
A ★ ★ ★ ½
P ★ ★ ★ ★

Jacket and tie required
Street parking
All major credit cards
Full bar
Reservations required

Lunch: Mon.-Fri. 12:00PM-3:00PM
Dinner: Mon.-Sat. 5:30PM-10:30PM
          Closed Sunday

This fashionable haven in the Sutton Place area, is named for a French Province renowned for its cooking. Cozy and quiet, with exceptionally good acoustics, Le Périgord invites intimate conversation, which can be a wonderful accompaniment to the well prepared and deftly served cuisine.

LE PÉRIGORD PARK   27

575 Park Avenue
New York, NY
(212) 752-0050/752-0051

French

F ★ ★ ★ ½
S ★ ★ ★ ½
A ★ ★ ★ ★
P ★ ★ ★ ½

Jacket required
Street parking
All major credit cards
Full bar
Reservations required

Lunch: Tues.-Fri. 12:00PM-3:00PM
Dinner: Mon.-Sat. 6:00PM-10:30PM
          Closed Sunday

There's a golden aura at this intimate spot, with its trompe l'oiel murals and fabulous floral displays. The menu offers a diversity of entrées, ranging from fish soufflé to peppered steaks. The magret of duck, served in two parts, is a favorite house specialty.

LE REFUGE   5

166 East 82nd Street
New York, NY
(212) 861-4505

French

F ★ ★ ★
S ★ ★ ★
A ★ ★ ★
P ★ ★ ★

Good taste in dress required
Street parking
Credit cards not accepted
Beer/Wine
Reservations required

Lunch: Mon.-Sat. 12:00PM-3:00PM
Dinner: Mon.-Sat. 6:00PM-11:00PM
          Closed Sunday

Enjoy relaxed dining in this rustic country inn setting with brick walls, beamed ceilings, and 17th century tapestries. The enticing cuisine includes such choices as Huitres Gratinée au Safran and Mousse aux Amandes Amères.

LE RÉGENCE   28

Hotel Plaza Athénée
37 East 64th Street
New York, NY
(212) 734-9100

French

F ★ ★ ★ ½
S ★ ★ ★ ½
A ★ ★ ★ ½
P ★ ★ ★ ★

Jacket and tie required
Street parking
All major credit cards
Full bar
Reservations required

Breakfast: Daily 7:00AM-10:00AM
Lunch: Daily 12:00PM-2:30PM
Dinner: Nightly 6:00PM-10:00PM

Designed in the grand Regency manner, this enchanting dining room has inspired touches such as the mural of the sky in the vaulted ceiling. The French cuisine is prepared by highly acclaimed chef Daniel Boulud, who effectively balances nouvelle touches with classic presentation.

LE RELAIS   24

712 Madison Avenue
New York, NY
(212) 751-5108

French

F ★ ★ ★ ½
S ★ ★ ★ ½
A ★ ★ ★ ½
P ★ ★ ★ ½

Good taste in dress required
Street parking
AE, MC, V
Full bar
Reservations required

Lunch: Mon.-Sat. 12:00PM-3:00PM
Dinner: Mon.-Fri. 6:30PM-11:00PM
          Sat. & Sun. 7:00PM-11:00PM
Brunch: Sun. 12:30PM-3:30PM

This mirrored miracle of haute cuisine attracts the European jet-setter crowd who dote on dining here in summer when the room extends out to embrace a sidewalk café. The service is friendly and correct, and the ever-changing menu has nouvelle overtones. The sweet finales are notable.

LE SAINT JEAN DES PRÉS   122

112 Duane Street
New York, NY
(212) 608-2332

Belgian

F ★ ★ ★
S ★ ★ ★
A ★ ★ ★
P ★ ★ ★

No dress restrictions
Lot parking
All major credit cards
Full bar
Reservations required

Lunch/
Dinner: Mon.-Fri. 12:00PM-12:00AM
          Sat. 6:00PM-12:00AM
          Closed Sunday

There's a sense of permanence and stature in this grand-scale restaurant that offers you such amenities as china from Belgium, service by French waitresses, and behemoth bouquets of flowers. Chef Pascal Fisette presents such Belgian delights as stuffed lobsters, veal kidney, and Belgian endives sautéed with North Sea shrimp.

LE STEAK   72

1089 2nd Avenue
New York, NY
(212) 421-9072

American

F ★ ★ ★
S ★ ★ ★
A ★ ★ ★
P ★ ★ ★

No dress restrictions
Lot parking
All major credit cards
Beer/Wine
Reservations required

Dinner: Nightly 5:30PM-11:00PM

Owner Monique Peridon adds French flair to this innovative, and highly personal eatery, that offers seating for 60 lucky souls. While the food is basically American, predominantly steaks and fish, the sauces and presentation are definitive, and Gallic in concept.

LE TRIANON 65

Helmsley Palace Hotel
455 Madison Avenue
New York, NY
(212) 888-7000

International

F ★ ★ ★ ★
S ★ ★ ★ ★
A ★ ★ ★ ★
P ★ ★ ★ ★

Jacket required
Hotel garage parking
All major credit cards
Full bar
Reservations recommended

Lunch: Mon.-Fri. 12:00PM-2:30PM
Dinner: Nightly 5:30PM-12:00AM
Brunch: Sat. & Sun. 12:00PM-2:30PM

This much respected restaurant occupies a historical mansion, and the dining rooms are chic and charming. The varied menu has wide appeal, and includes pan-fried filet of veal with Grand Marnier and green pepper sauce, and rack of lamb.

LE VEAU D'OR 29

129 East 60th Street
New York, NY
(212) 838-8133

French

F ★ ★ ★
S ★ ★ ★ ½
A ★ ★ ★ ★
P ★ ★ ★ ★

Jacket required
Street parking
AE
Full bar
Reservations required

Lunch: Mon.-Sat. 12:00PM-2:30PM
Dinner: Mon.-Sat. 6:00PM-10:15PM
         Closed Sunday

Transcending the vagaries of fashion, Le Veau d'Or has maintained an enthusiastic following for decades. The atmosphere is pure Parisian, the food delicious, and the service civilized. The cassoulets, onion soup, and salads are all excellent.

LE ZINC 123

139 Duane Street
New York, NY
(212) 732-1226

French

F ★ ★ ★
S ★ ★ ★
A ★ ★ ★
P ★ ★ ★ ★

No dress restrictions
Street parking
AE
Full bar
Reservations required

Dinner: Mon.-Thurs. 6:30PM-12:30AM
         Fri. & Sat. 6:30PM-1:00AM
         Sun. 6:30PM-11:30PM

The mirrors and zinc bar must be magnetized in this chic, sleek gargantuan bistro, for the whole appearance-conscious fashion world seems to be drawn here. Once a busy shoe factory, the kitchen that is now here turns out sole and other inventive dishes with a polished French accent.

LELLO RISTORANTE 53

65 East 54th Street
New York, NY
(212) 751-1555

Italian

F ★ ★ ★
S ★ ★ ★ ★
A ★ ★ ★ ★
P ★ ★ ★

Jacket required
Street parking
All major credit cards
Beer/Wine
Reservations required

Lunch: Mon.-Fri. 12:00PM-3:00PM
Dinner: Mon.-Thurs. 5:30PM-10:30PM
Fri. & Sat. 5:30PM-11:00PM
Closed Sunday

Lello's polished performance will delight aficionados of both Northern and Southern Italian cuisine. The menu offers a medley of cooking in a sophisticated setting. The selection of cheeses is outstanding, should you opt for a light dessert.

LES PLEIADES 18

20 East 76th Street
New York, NY
(212) 535-7230

French

F ★ ★ ★ ½
S ★ ★ ★ ½
A ★ ★ ★
P ★ ★ ★ ½

Jacket required
Street parking
All major credit cards
Full bar
Reservations required

Lunch: Daily 12:00PM-3:00PM
Dinner: Nightly 5:30PM-11:00PM

In the hub of Madison Avenue's art galleries and museums, this eatery has been a rendevous for artists, museum personnel, and art dealers for the past 15 years. Specialties include Le Steak au Poivre Des Iles Malgaches, and La Truite Fraiche.

LUTÈCE 82

249 East 50th Street
New York, NY
(212) 752-2225/26

French

F ★ ★ ★ ★
S ★ ★ ★ ★
A ★ ★ ★ ★
P ★ ★ ★ ★

Jacket and tie preferred
Street parking
AE, CB, DC
Full bar
Reservations required

Lunch: Tues.-Fri. 12:00PM-1:45PM
Dinner: Mon.-Sat. 6:00PM-9:30PM
Closed Sunday

This "grande dame" of French restaurants occupies an unpretentious brownstone, refurbished to portray a French scene. Chef/owner André Soltner prepares daily specialties with verve and imagination.

THE MAESTRO 10

58 West 65th Street
New York, NY
(212) 787-5990

American

F ★ ★ ★
S ★ ★ ★
A ★ ★ ★ ½
P ★ ★ ½

Good taste in dress required
Lot and street parking
All major credit cards
Full bar
Reservations required

Lunch: Daily 11:30AM-3:30PM
Dinner: Tues.-Thurs. 5:00PM-11:30PM
Sun. & Mon. 5:00PM-12:00AM
Fri. & Sat. 5:00PM-1:30AM
Supper: Mon.-Sun. 5:00PM-1:30AM

Lincoln Center's new haven for opera buffs occupies a renovated parking garage, and is as spacious and dramatic as the stage at the Met. Here you'll enjoy quality cuisine richly sauced with musical accompaniments. Co-owner Larry Woodard, singer-pianist, performs Tuesday through Saturday, and singer/guests and staff members add their talents to the impromptu fun.

MANHATTAN MARKET   81

1016 Second Avenue
New York, NY
(212) 752-1400

American

F ★ ★ ½
S ★ ★ ★ ½
A ★ ★ ★
P ★ ★ ★

No dress restrictions
Public garage parking
All major credit cards
Full bar
Reservations required

Lunch: Mon.-Fri. 11:45AM-3:00PM
Dinner: Mon.-Fri. 5:30PM-11:30PM
         Sat. 6:00PM-12:00AM
Brunch: Sun. 11:00AM-3:30PM

Polished and urbane, Manhattan Market's modernistic décor is romanced with a historic massive old bar, and a refreshing garden atrium. The service is pleasant, the cooking is innovative, and there is an excellent, reasonably priced wine list.

THE MANHATTAN   40
OCEAN CLUB

57 West 58th Street
New York, NY
(212) 371-7777

Seafood

F ★ ★ ★ ½
S ★ ★ ★ ½
A ★ ★ ½
P ★ ★ ★ ½

No dress restrictions
Street parking
All major credit cards

Full bar
Reservations recommended

Lunch/
Dinner: Mon.-Fri. 12:00PM-12:00AM
          Sat.& Sun. 5:00PM-12:00AM

The gourmet's catch of the season, The Manhattan Ocean Club is an ultra-sophisticated restaurant decorated with green marble, Picasso pottery, polished brass, and cast iron Grecian columns. The menu has magic touches, the service is adroit.

MAURICE   39

118 West 57th Street
New York, NY
(212) 245-5000

French

F ★ ★ ★
S ★ ★ ★ ½
A ★ ★ ★ ½
P ★ ★ ★ ★

Jacket and tie required
Valet parking
All major credit cards
Full bar
Reservations required

Breakfast: Daily 7:30AM-10:30AM
Lunch: Daily 12:00PM-2:15PM
Dinner: Nightly 6:00PM-10:45PM

The inventive genius of much-honored master chef Alain Sendenrens of L'Archestrate in Paris inspires the French menu offered here. Chef Christian Delouvrier's nouvelle interpretations often surpass the original. The décor is blithely beautiful, the stunning bouquets impressive, and the service pure delight.

MAXWELL'S PLUM   33

64th Street & First Avenue
New York, NY
(212) 628-2100

American/Continental

F ★ ★ ★
S ★ ★ ★ ★
A ★ ★ ★ ★
P ★ ★ ★

Good taste in dress required
Street parking
All major credit cards
Full bar
Reservations required

Lunch: Mon.-Sat. 12:00PM-5:00PM
Dinner: Sun.-Thurs. 5:00PM-12:30AM
         Fri.& Sat. 5:00PM-1:30AM
Brunch: Sun. 11:00AM-5:00PM

The exuberant décor with its famous Tiffany stained glass ceiling is as dramatic as the stage setting for an old-time extravaganza. The food is eclectic and skillfully prepared, the service is above reproach.

MORTIMER'S   14

1057 Lexington Avenue
New York, NY
(212) 861-2481

American

F ★ ★ ★
S ★ ★ ★
A ★ ★ ★
P ★ ★ ★

No dress restrictions
Street parking
All major credit cards
Full bar
Reservations required

Lunch/
Dinner: Sun. & Mon. 12:15PM-1:00AM
          Tues.-Sat. 12:00PM-2:30AM

There's a clubby elitism at this friendly, casual, brick-walled tavern-of-a-meeting place that attracts a highly loyal clientele. The menu offers an interesting array of light and heavy entrées running the gamut from sautéed calf liver to chicken paillard, to rack of lamb.

MR. CHOW   78

324 East 57th Street
New York, NY
(212) 751-9030

Chinese/Continental

F ★ ★ ★
S ★ ★ ★ ½
A ★ ★ ★ ½
P ★ ★ ★ ★

Good taste in dress required
Garage parking
AE, DC, MC, V
Full bar
Reservations required

Lunch: Mon.-Fri. 12:30PM-2:30PM
Dinner: Nightly 6:30PM-12:00AM

Sleek and uncluttered, this sophisticated purveyor of Peking cuisine caters to an international clientele in the art, film, and fashion worlds. The Chinese cookery is supplemented by continental dishes that include a variety of seafoods, and fresh handmade pastas. The Peking Duck is eternally popular and Mr. Chow's noodles should be given a try.

NANNI   88

146 East 46th Street
New York, NY
(212) 697-4161

Italian

F ★ ★ ★
S ★ ★ ★
A ★ ★ ★
P ★ ★ ★

Jacket required
Street parking
All major credit cards
Beer/Wine
Reservations required

Lunch: Mon.-Fri. 12:00PM-3:00PM
Dinner: Mon.-Sat. 5:30PM-11:00PM
         Closed Sunday

A hustling, bustling Italian bistro that thrives on conviviality and an extensive menu of Northern Italian dishes. The Capellini à la Nanni tops the list of superb entrées. Expect quick and friendly service.

NANNI AL VALLETTO 93

133 East 61st Street
New York, NY
(212) 838-3939

Italian

F ★ ★ ★
S ★ ★ ★
A ★ ★ ★ ½
P ★ ★ ★ ★

Jacket required
Street parking
All major credit cards
Full bar
Reservations required

Lunch: Mon.-Fri. 12:00PM-3:00PM
Dinner: Mon.-Sat. 5:30PM-12:00AM
         Closed Sunday

For more than a decade this beautiful restaurant has earned accolades from discerning New York diners. You'll find formal service and an air of grandeur here. The stable menu of Italian classics is augmented by daily changing specials utilizing fresh ingredients at their seasonal prime.

NICOLA PAONE 128

207 East 34th Street
New York, NY
(212) 889-3239

Italian

F ★ ★ ★ ★
S ★ ★ ★ ½
A ★ ★ ★ ½
P ★ ★ ★ ★

Jacket and tie required
Garage parking
AE, DC
Full bar
Reservations required

Lunch: Mon.-Fri. 12:00PM-1:30PM
Dinner: Mon.-Sat. 5:00PM-9:30PM
         Closed Sunday

Owner Nicola Paone is an absolute perfectionist, and personally supervises every facet of this operation. You'll find savory fish, beef, veal, and pasta dishes on the well rounded menu, with daily specialties also offered. The setting is opulent and Romanesque, arranged to emulate the Trojan market.

NIPPON 77

145 East 52nd Street
New York, NY
(212) 758-0226

Japanese

F ★ ★ ★
S ★ ★ ★
A ★ ★ ★
P ★ ★ ★ ½

Jacket required
Street parking
All major credit cards
Beer/Wine
Reservations required

Lunch: Mon.-Fri. 12:00PM-2:30PM
Dinner: Mon.-Thurs. 5:30PM-10:00PM
         Fri. & Sat. 5:30PM-10:30PM
         Closed Sunday

Nippon is as close to an authentic Japanese restaurant as one can get, without visiting Tokyo. You have a choice of tatami room or conventional seating and the sushi bar presents a kaleidoscope of tempting offerings. The menu features traditional Japanese cuisine, with dishes such as sukiyaki and shabu shabu cooked tableside.

ODEON 124

145 West Broadway
New York, NY
(212) 233-0507

French

F ★ ★ ★
S ★ ★ ★ ½
A ★ ★ ★ ½
P ★ ★ ★ ★

Good taste in dress required
Street parking
AE, MC, V
Full bar
Reservations recommended

Lunch: Mon.-Fri. 12:00PM-3:00PM
Dinner: Nightly 7:00PM-12:30AM
Late
Supper: Nightly 1:00AM-2:30AM
Brunch: Sun. 12:00PM-3:30PM

Dine here in the midst of delightful décor, that replicates Manhattan in the '30s. The atmosphere created by owner Keith Mc-Nally is relaxed, easy going, and just plain fun. Fish dishes highlight the broad menu that leans toward nouvelle French. The two to four daily specials attest to the resourcefulness of the chef.

OENOPHILIA 1

473 Columbus Avenue
New York, NY
(212) 580-8127

Continental

F ★ ★ ★
S ★ ★ ★
A ★ ★ ★
P ★ ★ ★ ½

No dress restrictions
Lot and street parking
All major credit cards
Full bar
Reservations not required

Lunch/
Brunch: Daily 11:30AM-3:00PM
Dinner: Mon.-Thurs. 6:00PM-11:00PM
Fri. & Sat. 5:30PM-11:30PM
Sun. 5:30PM-10:00PM

Each of the three dining rooms at Oenophilia has its own distinctive ambiance — so that you can select a setting attuned to your mood. The cuisine features fresh fish from all over the world, wild game, and superior meats.

ONE FIFTH AVENUE 112

One Fifth Avenue
New York, NY
(212) 260-3434

Continental

F ★ ★ ★
S ★ ★ ★
A ★ ★ ★
P ★ ★ ★

Good taste in dress required
Street parking
All major credit cards
Full bar
Reservations recommended

Lunch: Mon.-Fri. 12:00PM-3:00PM
Dinner: Sun.-Thurs. 6:00PM-12:30AM
Fri. & Sat. 6:30PM-1:30AM
Brunch: Sat. 12:00PM-4:00PM
Sun. 11:00PM-4:00PM

This brash, boisterous restaurant was created from the wreckage of art déco S.S. Caledonia, and even features "portholes" that offer you "ocean views." The cruise cuisine featured here is somewhat eclectic, and is generally well prepared.

OYSTER BAR & 92
RESTAURANT

Grand Central Station - Lower Level
New York, NY
(212) 490-6650

Seafood

F ★ ★ ★
S ★ ★ ½
A ★ ★ ½
P ★ ★ ★

Good taste in dress required
Street parking
All major credit cards
Full bar
Reservations required

Lunch/
Dinner: Daily 11:30AM-9:30PM

A favorite dining spot for seafood fanciers. The menu changes daily bringing you the freshest available fish and shellfish from Fulton Fish Market, or flown in from Florida, Canada, the West Coast, and Europe.

PALM   94

837 Second Avenue
New York, NY
(212) 687-2953

Italian/American

F ★ ★ ★ ½
S ★ ★ ★
A ★ ★ ½
P ★ ★ ★ ★

No dress restrictions
Street parking
All major credit cards
Full bar
Luncheon reservations required

Lunch/
Dinner: Daily 12:00PM to 12:00AM

An upbeat, casual, friendly tavern and steakhouse with cartoon-covered walls, and sawdust on the floors. Prime steaks and jumbo lobsters are long-time favorites; the Italian dishes have their own following of loyal devotees.

PALM II   94

840 Second Avenue
New York, NY
(212) 697-5198

Italian/American

F ★ ★ ★ ½
S ★ ★ ½
A ★ ★ ½
P ★ ★ ★ ★

No dress restrictions
Street parking
All major credit cards
Full bar
Luncheon reservation required

Lunch/
Dinner: Daily 12:00PM-12:00AM

Shuffle through the sawdust, enjoy the gallery of cartoons, and join the friendly habitués in this old speakeasy setting. A relaxed place to enjoy great steaks and huge lobsters.

PARI PASSU   46

147 East 60th Street
New York, NY
(212) 832-8972

French

F ★ ★ ★
S ★ ★ ★
A ★ ★ ★
P ★ ★ ★

No dress restrictions
Street parking
All major credit cards
Full bar
Reservations required

Lunch: Daily 12:00PM-3:00PM
Dinner: Nightly 5:30PM-10:30PM

An elegant restaurant, blessed with a beautiful summer/winter garden, Pari Passu offers a variety of fresh fish, veal, beef, and duck entrées and a renowned rack of lamb.

PARIOLI ROMANISSIMO   4

24 East 81st Street
New York, NY
(212) 288-2391

Italian

F ★ ★ ★
S ★ ★ ★ ★
A ★ ★ ★ ★
P ★ ★ ★ ★

Jacket and tie required
Street parking
AE, CB, DC
Full bar
Reservations required

Dinner: Tues.-Sat. 6:00PM-11:30PM
          Closed Sunday & Monday

Dine here in the rosy glow of dimmed lights in a renaissance town house with a chic and continental ambiance. White truffles and game in season can be had, among other house specialties. The pasta dishes reign supreme.

PATSY'S   34

236 West 56th Street
New York, NY
(212) 247-3491

Italian

F ★ ★ ★
S ★ ★ ★ ½
A ★ ★ ★ ½
P ★ ★ ★ ★

Jacket required
Street parking
AE, DC, MC, V
Full bar
Reservations required for 5 or more persons

Lunch/
Dinner: Tues.-Thurs. & Sun. 12:00PM-
          10:30PM
          Fri. & Sat. 12:00PM-11:30PM
          Closed Monday

Joseph and Salvatore Scognamillo, the third generation of the family who started this 42-year-old restaurant, are responsible for Patsy's success today. Hearty Neopolitan fare includes time-honored classics; perfectly prepared and served with gusto.

PETER LUGER   116
STEAKHOUSE

178 Broadway
Brooklyn, NY
(718) 387-7400

American

F ★ ★ ★
S ★ ★ ★
A ★ ★ ½
P ★ ★ ★

Jacket required
Street parking
Credit cards not accepted
Full bar
Reservations required

Lunch/
Dinner: Mon.-Thurs. 11:30AM-9:45PM
          Fri. & Sat. 11:00AM-10:45PM
          Sun. 1:00PM-9:45PM

Nearly a century old, this historic German tudor restaurant continues to serve grilled porterhouse, T-bone, and filet mignon steaks of the finest quality to a faithful Wall Street clientele. This is a cherished institution where discreet service, and the quality concept will always be esteemed.

PICCOLO MONDO   31
RISTORANTE

1269 1st Avenue
New York, NY
(212) 249-3141/2

Italian

F ★ ★ ★
S ★ ★ ★
A ★ ★ ★
P ★ ★ ★ ★

Jacket preferred
Lot parking
All major credit cards
Full bar
Reservations required

Lunch: Daily 12:00PM-3:00PM
Dinner: Nightly 5:00PM-12:00AM

Spacious and nicely appointed, this restaurant tempts your taste buds with such house specialties as Capellini d'Angelo Primavera, Fegato Veneziana con Polenta Fritta, and Costolette Divitello 'Monte Bianco.'

PIG HEAVEN   22

1540 Second Avenue
New York, NY
(212) 744-4333

Chinese

F ★ ★ ½
S ★ ★ ★
A ★ ★ ½
P ★ ★ ★

Good taste in dress required
Street parking
AE, DC
Full bar
Reservations required

Lunch/
Dinner: Sun.-Thurs. 12:00PM-12:00AM
         Fri. & Sat. 12:00PM-1:00AM

This porker's paradise has a personality all its own. White butcher paper tops yellow slicker tablecloths and the Chinese cuisine features roast meats with whole roast suckling pig as a highlight.

PIRANDELLO   118

7 Washington Place
New York, NY
(212) 260-3066

Italian

F ★ ★ ★
S ★ ★ ★
A ★ ★ ★
P ★ ★

Good taste in dress required
Street parking
AE
Full bar
Reservations required

Dinner: Mon.-Sat. 5:30PM-11:30PM
         Closed Sunday

The décor here is a pastiche of white walls, hanging plants, brass chandeliers, and curtains that conceal the corner windows. The mood is friendly and mellow. The bill of fare is standard Northern Italian, but you'll find a bevy of refreshing specials offered daily adding zest and zeal.

THE POST HOUSE   25

28 East 63rd Street
New York, NY
(212) 935-2888

American

F ★ ★ ★
S ★ ★ ★ ½
A ★ ★ ½
P ★ ★ ★ ½

No dress restrictions
Street parking
All major credit cards
Full bar
Reservations recommended

Lunch/
Dinner: Mon.-Thurs. 12:00PM-11:00PM
         Fri. 12:00PM-12:00AM
         Sat. 5:30PM-12:00AM
         Sun. 5:30PM-11:00PM

Large and attractive with a spicing of antiques in the décor, The Post House focuses on perfectly prepared quality steaks and chops, prime rib, and a limited selection of seafood. The service is dignified; the desserts classic American.

PRUNELLE   96

18 East 54th Street
New York, NY
(212) 759-6410

French

F ★ ★ ★
S ★ ★ ★ ½
A ★ ★ ★ ½
P ★ ★ ★ ★

Jacket and tie required
Garage parking
AE
Full bar
Reservations required

Lunch: Daily 12:00PM-3:00PM
Dinner: Nightly 5:30PM-11:00PM

This lovely gem of a restaurant works
burled maple wood and plum-colored
fabrics into a charming art déco design.
The combined talents of co-owners Jacky
Ruette, your host, and chef Pascal Dir-
ringer, make dining here a marvelous experience.

QUATORZE   104

240 West 14th Street
New York, NY
(212) 206-7006

French

F ★ ★ ★
S ★ ★ ★
A ★ ★ ½
P ★ ★ ½

No dress restrictions
Street parking
AE
Full bar
Reservations required

Lunch: Mon.-Fri. 12:00PM-2:30PM
Dinner: Nightly 6:00PM-12:00AM

French to the core, this bright bistro with
its tiled floor and marble top bar exudes
charm and self confidence. Choucroûte
garnie (cuts of pork and sausages over
sauerkraut), and hot bacon and chicory
salad typify the variety of French dishes
offered. The baked-on-the premises apple
tart leads the parade of sweet treats.

THE QUILTED GIRAFFE   83

955 2nd Avenue
New York, NY
(212) 753-5355

French

F ★ ★ ★ ★
S ★ ★ ★ ★
A ★ ★ ★ ★
P ★ ★ ★ ★

Jacket and tie required
Lot and street parking
All major credit cards
Full bar
Reservations required

Dinner: Mon.-Fri. 5:45PM-10:00PM
          Closed Saturday & Sunday

All the components that combine to make
dining a true delight come together with
seeming effortless ease here. The contemporary setting is mellowed by silver, china
and crystal. Well-served, innovative dishes
— caviar, truffles, foie gras — are complemented by a good selection of fine wines.

RAGA   61

57 West 48th Street
New York, NY
(212) 757-3450

Indian

F ★ ★ ★
S ★ ★ ★ ★
A ★ ★ ★ ½
P ★ ★ ★

Jacket required
Lot parking
All major credit cards

Full bar
Reservations required for dinner on
Saturday and Sunday

Lunch: Mon.-Fri. 12:00PM-3:00PM
Dinner: Nightly 5:30PM-11:00PM

You'll find hand carved teak walls, antique musical instruments and, authentic tandoori cooking (a clay oven barbecue) in this spacious dining room.

THE RAINBOW ROOM   58

30 Rockefeller Plaza
New York, NY
(212) 757-9090

French/Italian

F   ★ ★ ½
S   ★ ★ ★ ½
A   ★ ★ ★ ½
P   ★ ★ ★ ½

Jacket and tie required
Street parking
All major credit cards
Full bar
Reservations required

Dinner: Nightly 5:00PM-12:00AM

A sentimental New York tradition, the Rainbow Room affords you an incomparable view of the skyline, plus big band music for your listening and dancing pleasure. The menu offers specialties for every taste, served with quiet dignity.

RAOUL'S   120

180 Prince Street
New York, NY
(212) 966-3518

French

F   ★ ★ ★
S   ★ ★ ★ ★
A   ★ ★ ★
P   ★ ★ ★ ★

No dress restrictions
Street parking
AE, MC, V
Full bar
Reservations required

Dinner: Nightly 6:30PM-11:30PM

Guy and Serge Raoul have transformed an old saloon into an upbeat French bistro that serves highly acclaimed traditional French cuisine with precocious daily specials. You'll find Raoul's crowded, cheerful, and very 'in.'

RAPHAEL   55

33 West 54th Street
New York, NY
(212) 582-8993

French

F   ★ ★ ★
S   ★ ★ ★
A   ★ ★ ★ ½
P   ★ ★ ★ ★

Jacket required
Street parking
All major credit cards
Full bar
Reservations required

Lunch: Daily 12:00PM-2:00PM
Dinner: Nightly 6:00PM-9:30PM

Raphael gives you the feeling you are dining in your own chateau, complete with garden and fireplace. The contemporary cuisine features nouvelle touches in such dishes as: Fresh Tuna Carpaccio, St. Jacques au Beurre de Lavande, and Carré D'Agneau à la VaPeur de Thym.

RENÉ PUJOL   36

321 West 51st Street
New York, NY
(212) 246-3023

French

F ★ ★ ★
S ★ ★ ★ ½
A ★ ★ ★
P ★ ★ ★ ★

Jacket required
Street parking
All major credit cards
Full bar
Reservations required

Lunch: Mon.-Fri. 12:00PM-3:00PM
Dinner: Mon.-Sat. 5:00PM-11:30PM
         Closed Sunday

This cozy, warm, French provincial, family run restaurant uses its roaring fireplace for cooking in cool weather and offers you a good choice of wines to accompany the interesting array of authentically prepared French house specialties.

RISTORANTE PRIMAVERA   15

1578 1st Avenue
New York, NY
(212) 861-8608

Italian

F ★ ★ ★
S ★ ★ ★
A ★ ★ ★
P ★ ★ ★ ★

Jacket and tie required
Lot and street parking
AE
Full bar
Reservations required

Dinner: Nightly 5:30PM-12:00AM

At Ristorante Primavera you will find a discreetly elegant atmosphere, outstanding service, and well prepared pastas and other Italian specialties. Choice Italian wines and a good dessert menu round-out the pleasure of your evening.

THE RIVER CAFÉ   116

1 Water Street
Brooklyn, NY
(718) 522-5200

American

F ★ ★ ★
S ★ ★ ★ ½
A ★ ★ ★ ★
P ★ ★ ★ ★

Jacket required at dinner; tie preferred; no jeans or shorts
Valet parking
AE, CB, DC
Full bar
Reservations required

Lunch: Daily 12:00PM-3:00PM
Dinner: Nightly 6:30PM-11:00PM
         (7:00PM-11:30PM in summer)

The River Café offers you spectacular views of Manhattan, Hudson Bay, and the river traffic. The creative menu features ingredients such as buffalo and shark, prepared with the emphasis on nutritional nouvelle. The wine list is thoughtfully selected.

ROMEO SALTA   42

30 West 56th Street
Brooklyn, NY
(212) 246-5772

Italian

F ★ ★ ★
S ★ ★ ★ ½
A ★ ★ ★ ½
P ★ ★ ★ ½

Jacket required
Lot and street parking
AE
Full bar
Reservations required

Lunch/
Dinner: Daily 12:00PM-11:00PM

While the menu here emphasizes Northern Italian cooking, you will find an interesting selection of dishes from the central and southern provinces also featured. The atmosphere is one of pure old world charm.

ROXANNE'S   99

158 8th Avenue
New York, NY
(212) 741-2455

French/American

F ★ ★ ★
S ★ ★ ★
A ★ ★ ★
P ★ ★ ★

No dress restrictions
Street parking
AE, MC, V
Full bar
Reservations required

Dinner: Nightly 6:00PM-11:00PM

The seasonal menu featured in this intimate story-book eatery is guided by the inventive Richard Malanga, who melds new ideas with old successes. The two flower-filled dining rooms, and charming back garden are intimate and romantic, luring a leisurely, lingering clientele.

THE RUSSIAN TEA ROOM   35

150 West 57th Street
New York, NY
(212) 265-0947

Russian

F ★ ★ ★
S ★ ★ ★
A ★ ★ ★ ½
P ★ ★ ★ ½

Jacket preferred at lunch, required at dinner
Street parking
AE, DC, MC, V

Beer/Wine
Reservations recommended

Lunch/
Dinner: Sun.-Fri. 11:30AM-12:30AM
          Sat. 11:30AM-1:30AM

Jubilant and colorful, the Russian Tea Room with its rich paintings and samovars, attracts personalities from the theatrical, musical, and publishing worlds. Borscht, herrings, blini, pirojok, and chicken Kiev are among the many tempting offerings.

SALTA IN BOCCA   98

179 Madison Avenue
New York, NY
(212) 684-1757

Italian

F ★ ★ ★
S ★ ★ ★
A ★ ★ ★
P ★ ★ ★

Jacket and tie required
Street parking
All major credit cards
Full bar
Reservations required

Lunch: Mon.-Fri. 12:00PM-5:00PM
Dinner: Mon.-Thurs. 5:00PM-10:30PM
          Fri. 5:00PM-11:00PM
          Sat. 5:00PM-12:00AM
          Closed Sunday

A heavenly retreat, brightened by mosaic tiles, professional service, and culinary works of art such as tortelloni with sage and butter, or chicken with mushrooms in white wine sauce.

SANDRO'S   73

420 East 59th Street
New York, NY
(212) 355-5150

Italian

F ★ ★ ★ ½
S ★ ★ ★
A ★ ★ ★
P ★ ★ ★

No dress restrictions
Lot, street, and garage parking
All major credit cards
Full bar
Reservations required

Dinner: Nightly 5:00PM-12:00AM
Late
Supper: Nightly 12:00AM-3:00AM

Designed to resemble an elegant Italian inn, with tile floors and modern décor, this restaurant is the inspiration of owner, Sandro, formerly one of Italy's most illustrious chefs. You'll discover gustatory delights offered here, such as homemade pasta stuffed with a mixture of sea urchin roe and white fish, with a sauce of baby scallops.

SCARLATTI 66

34 East 52nd Street
New York, NY
(212) 753-2444

Italian

F ★ ★ ★
S ★ ★ ★
A ★ ★ ★ ★
P ★ ★ ★

Jacket required
Street parking
All major credit cards
Full bar
Reservations required

Lunch: Mon.-Sat. 12:00PM-3:00PM
Dinner: Mon.-Sat. 5:30PM-11:00PM
Closed Sunday

This sophisticated dining spot has won widespread acclaim for the fidelity of its regional Italian dishes and the new types of pasta made on the premises including malfatti, golosi, vele, and tortellacci.

SHUN LEE PALACE 75

155 East 55th Street
New York, NY
(212) 371-8844

Chinese

F ★ ★ ★ ½
S ★ ★ ★
A ★ ★ ★
P ★ ★ ★

Jacket required
Valet parking
AE, CB, DC
Full bar
Reservations required

Lunch/
Dinner: Daily 12:00PM-11:00PM

A staff of five chefs, under the direction of T.T. Wang, perform prodigious feats of culinary artistry at this elaborately decorated Oriental dining retreat. Specialties from the Mandarin, Szechwan, and Hunan provinces of China share starring roles.

SHUN LEE WEST 11

43 West 65th Street
New York, NY
(212) 598-8895

Chinese

F ★ ★ ★
S ★ ★ ★
A ★ ★ ★
P ★ ★ ½

Jacket required
Valet parking
All major credit cards
Full bar
Reservations required

Lunch/
Dinner: Daily 12:00PM-11:30PM

This palatial-sized establishment brings you the best of regional specialties from the provinces of Hunan, Szechwan, and

Peking, with the hot and spicy dishes so indicated on the highly original menu. This restaurant bespeaks of owner Michael Tong's sure hand at pleasing western tastes with classic Oriental cuisine.

SIGN OF THE DOVE 30

1110 Third Avenue
New York, NY
(212) 861-8080

Continental/French/Italian

F ★ ★ ★ ½
S ★ ★ ★ ½
A ★ ★ ★ ★
P ★ ★ ★ ½

Jacket required
Street parking
All major credit cards
Full bar
Reservations required

Lunch: Tues.-Sat. 12:00PM-3:00PM
Dinner: Nightly 6:00PM-12:00AM
Brunch: Sun. 11:45AM-4:00PM

Fresh flowers and lush plants enhance the 1900s brownstone garden setting, creating an elegant ambiance at this restaurant. The continental cuisine is eclectic with French nouvelle and Italian overtones. Splendid service and an in-house pastry chef contribute to diners' pleasure.

SMITH & WOLLENSKY 80

797 Third Avenue
New York, NY
(212) 753-1530

American

F ★ ★ ★
S ★ ★ ★ ½
A ★ ★ ★
P ★ ★ ★ ½

No dress restrictions
Street parking

All major credit cards
Full bar
Reservations recommended

Lunch/
Dinner: Mon.-Fri. 12:00PM-12:00AM
         Sat.& Sun. 5:00PM-12:00AM
Grill: Daily 11:30AM-2:00AM

The clublike atmosphere of this large restaurant that sprawls over two levels, echoes other enduring New York steakhouses. Here, the food ranks high — the portions are man-sized, and the service is cordial.

SPARKS STEAKHOUSE 90

210 East 46th Street
New York, NY
(212) 687-4855

American

F ★ ★ ★
S ★ ★ ★
A ★ ★ ★
P ★ ★ ★ ★

Jacket required
Street parking
All major credit cards
Full bar
Reservations required

Lunch/
Dinner: Mon.-Thurs. 12:00PM-11:00PM
         Fri. & Sat. 12:00PM-11:30PM
         Closed Sunday

An exuberant crowd of loyal diners are perfectly attuned to this spacious, publike steakhouse, and the type of food purveyed. Prime steaks, jumbo live lobsters, fresh fish, clams, and oysters are featured.

TAVERN ON THE GREEN 9

Central Park at West 67th Street
New York, NY
(212) 873-3200

Continental

F ★ ★ ★
S ★ ★ ★
A ★ ★ ★ ½
P ★ ★ ₊★ ½

Good taste in dress required
Lot parking
All major credit cards
Full bar
Reservations recommended

Lunch:　Mon.-Fri. 12:00PM-4:00PM
Dinner:　Mon.-Fri. 5:30PM-1:00AM
　　　　Sat. & Sun. 5:00PM-1:00AM
Brunch:　Sat. & Sun. 10:00AM-4:00PM

Enter a wonderland of sparkling chandeliers, mirrors, wood carvings, and brass, in this dining room that overlooks a beautifully landscaped terrace garden and Central Park. Catering to a celebrity clientele, Tavern on the Green offers entrées such as Dover Sole Meunière.

THE TERRACE　1

400 West 119th Street
New York, NY
(212) 666-9490

French

F ★ ★ ★ ½
S ★ ★ ★ ★
A ★ ★ ★ ★
P ★ ★ ★ ½

Jacket required
Valet parking
All major credit cards
Full bar
Reservations required

Lunch:　Tues.-Fri. 12:00PM-2:30PM
Dinner:　Tues.-Thurs. 6:00PM-10:00PM
　　　　Fri. & Sat. 6:00PM-10:30PM
　　　　Closed Sunday

This candlelit sanctuary, brimming with plants and flowers, offers you a dazzling view of the city skylines and George Washington Bridge. Lyrical harp music adds to the charm of the evening, as you dine on French haute cuisine.

TORTILLA FLATS　107

767 Washington Street
New York, NY
(212) 243-1053

Mexican

F ★ ★ ★
S ★ ★ ★
A ★ ★ ½
P ★ ★

No dress restrictions
Street parking
Credit cards not accepted
Full bar
Reservations not required

Lunch/
Dinner:　Mon.-Thurs. 12:00PM-12:00AM
　　　　Fri. 12:00PM-1:00AM
　　　　Sat. 5:00PM-1:00AM
　　　　Sun. 3:00PM-11:00PM

As jumping as a Mexican bean, this convivial, crowded little patch of New York real estate never quits. The décor is upbeat fifties, the service immaterial, the music rousing honky tonk, and the TexMex food adequately prepared. This is a fun, good feeling place to be, where the ''happy hour'' lasts as long as you are there.

TRATTORIA　103
DA ALFREDO

90 Bank Street
New York, NY
(212) 929-4400

Italian

F ★ ★ ★ ★
S ★ ★ ★ ½
A ★ ★ ★
P ★ ★ ★

Good taste in dress required
Street parking
Credit cards not accepted
Bring your own spirits
Reservations required

Lunch: Mon. & Wed.-Sat.
12:00PM-2:00PM
Dinner: Mon. & Wed.-Sat.
6:00PM-10:00PM
Sun. 5:00PM-9:00PM
Closed Tuesday

The food's the thing at this Greenwich Village eatery, and patrons have been clamoring for more of the same, since Alfredo Viazzi opened his trattoria more than ten years ago. You'll find a friendly, Mediterranean café atmosphere here, and some of the best pastas you will ever encounter.

TRE SCALINI   69

230 East 58th Street
New York, NY
(212) 688-6888

Italian

F ★ ★ ★
S ★ ★ ★ ★
A ★ ★ ★
P ★ ★ ★

Jacket required
Garage parking next door
All major credit cards
Beer/Wine
Reservations required

Lunch: Mon.-Fri. 12:00PM-3:00PM
Dinner: Mon.-Sat. 5:00PM-12:00AM
Closed Sunday

Dine in a contemporary Roman garden setting, lavished with murals, at Tre Scalini. The service is superior and the food exceptional. Specialties include Veal à la Tre Scalini, Pappellini Primavera, and Tartufo Gelato.

"21" CLUB   54

21 West 52nd Street
New York, NY
(212) 582-7200

Continental/American

F ★ ★ ★ ½
S ★ ★ ★ ½
A ★ ★ ★ ½
P ★ ★ ★ ★

Jacket and tie required
Street parking
All major credit cards
Full bar
Reservations recommended

Lunch/
Dinner: Mon.-Sat. 12:00PM-1:00AM
Closed Sunday

A glittering mecca for celebrities since 1930, "21" Club, renowned for its Remington art collection, has maintained its prestigious position regardless of changing fashions. There is a colorful bar and formal dining rooms. The menu is standard, the wine list extensive.

VANESSA   114

289 Bleeker Street
New York, NY
(212) 243-4225

American

F ★ ★ ★
S ★ ★ ★
A ★ ★ ★
P ★ ★ ★ ★

Jacket required
Street parking
AE
Full bar
Reservations required

Dinner: Nightly 6:00PM-12:00AM

Mellow and romantic, with art déco brass fixtures gleaming against purple walls, and a verdant display of tropical plants adding a softening element. Although the menu is American, the preparation methods are highly individualistic. The gazpacho, Omelette Basquaise, and warmed filet of chicken breast salad are highly touted choices.

VIENNA '79   26

35 East 60th Street
New York, NY
(212) 734-4700

Viennese/Continental

F ★ ★ ★
S ★ ★ ★ ½
A ★ ★ ★ ½
P ★ ★ ★ ★

Jacket required
Street parking
All major credit cards
Full bar
Reservations required

Lunch: Daily 12:00PM-3:00PM
Dinner: Nightly 5:30PM-11:00PM

In a warm, glowing, elegant décor, you
will be treated to cuisine that is constantly
evolving under the knowing guidance of
owner Peter Grunauer. Venison and other
game, Zwiebelrostbraten, and Tafelspitz
are among the house specialties.

WILKINSON'S   8
SEAFOOD CAFÉ

1573 York Avenue
New York, NY
(212) 535-5454

Seafood

F ★ ★ ★
S ★ ★ ★
A ★ ★ ½
P ★ ★ ★

Good taste in dress required
Street and garage parking
All major credit cards
Full bar
Reservations recommended

Dinner: Sun.-Thurs. 6:00PM-10:00PM
          Fri. & Sat. 6:00PM-11:00PM

Seascape murals by Ted Jacobs enhance
the art nouveau décor at this pleasant café,
that features seafood but also offers other
interesting entrées. Red snapper in Saki
and black bean sauce is an innovative
favorite; grilled quail, rack of lamb, and
peppercorn-coated filet mignon are other
noteworthy specialties.

WINDOWS ON   122
THE WORLD

1 World Trade Center
New York, NY
(212) 938-1111

International

F ★ ★ ★
S ★ ★ ★
A ★ ★ ★ ½
P ★ ★ ★

Jacket and tie required, no denims
Free lot parking
All major credit cards
Full bar
Reservations required, except for Sunday
Brunch

THE RESTAURANT

Dinner: Mon.-Sat. 5:00PM-10:00PM
Buffet: Sat. 12:00PM-3:00PM
          Sun. 12:00PM-7:30PM

Like an eagle's aerie, Windows on the
World is perched 107 stories high, giving
diners an incomparable view. Director
Alan Lewis provides both a table d'hôte
menu and à la carte selections. The service
is excellent — the wine list extraordinary.

THE HORS D'OEUVRERIE

Breakfast: Mon.-Fri. from 7:30AM
Drinks/
Hors d'oeuvre:Mon.-Sun. 3:00PM-1:00AM
Brunch: Sun. 12:00PM-3:00PM

Dining in the sky, 107 stories up, is an exhilarating experience. Here international
chefs prepare palate-pleasing appetizers of
every ethnic persuasion. There's music for
dancing, a served international Sunday
brunch, and Afternoon Tea.

Orlando

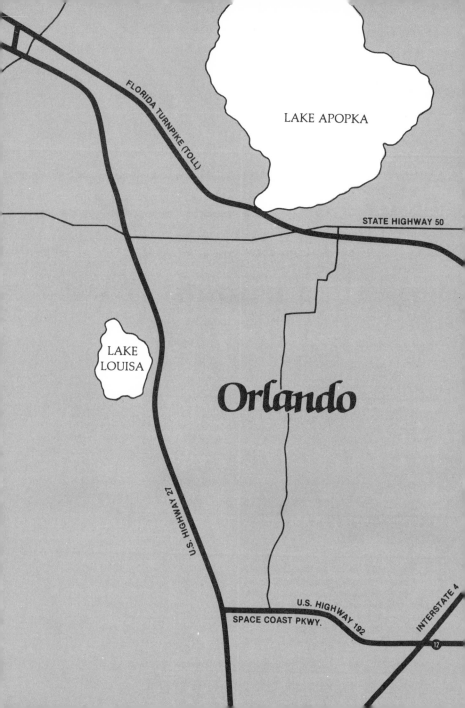

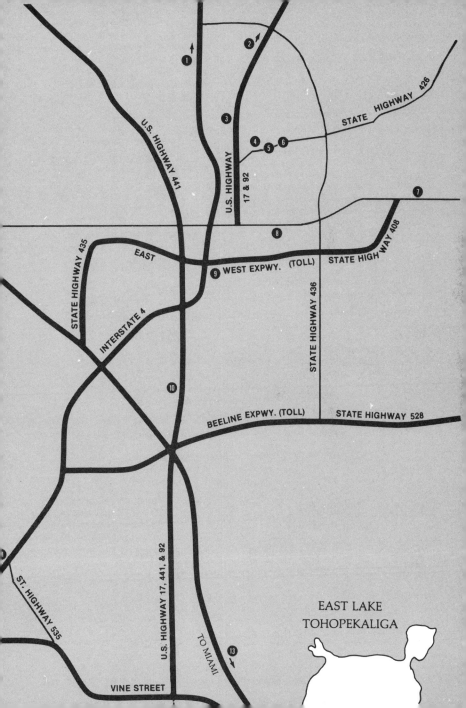

EMPRESS ROOM   11

Walt Disney World Shopping Village
Lake Buena Vista, FL
(305) 828-3900

French

F   ★ ★ ★
S   ★ ★ ★ ½
A   ★ ★ ★ ★
P   ★ ★ ★ ★

Jacket required
Valet and lot parking
AE, MC
Full bar
Reservations required

Dinner: Sun.-Thurs. 5:30PM-11:00PM
          Fri. & Sat. 6:00PM-9:30PM

Dine regally in the Empress Room, a sophisticated Louis XV setting that tops an anchored paddlewheeler. You'll discover tuxedoed waiters, a good wine list, and gourmet cuisine with such special dishes as sole with salmon mousse and medallions of wild boar being offered.

FREDDIE'S STEAK &   2
SEAFOOD HOUSE

U.S. Highway 17-92
Fern Park, FL
(305) 339-3265

Continental

F   ★ ★ ★
S   ★ ★ ★ ★
A   ★ ★ ★ ★
P   ★ ★ ★

Good taste in dress required
Valet parking
All major credit cards
Full bar
Reservations recommended

Dinner: Mon.-Sat. 4:30PM-1:30AM
          Closed Sunday

Freddie's has been dispensing warm hospitality in a congenial atmosphere for four decades. Owners Joseph Fried and Jerrod Zlatkiss take pride in personally greeting customers. You'll find smooth service at this award-winner, and specialties such as prime rib, steaks, duck, and fresh seafood.

LA CANTINA   7

4721 East Colonial Drive
Orlando, FL
(305) 894-4491

American/Italian

F   ★ ★ ★
S   ★ ★ ★
A   ★ ★
P   ★ ★

No dress restrictions
Lot parking
AE, MC, V
Full bar
Reservations not required

Dinner: Tues. 5:00PM-10:00PM
          Wed. & Thurs. 5:00PM-10:30PM
          Fri. & Sat. 5:00PM-11:00PM
          Closed Sunday and Monday

This lively, laid-back restaurant with its cozy fireplace, splashing fountain and sunken conversation pit, has been satisfying hefty appetites for nearly 40 years. The beef is aged and cut in house into man-sized T-bones, New York cuts and filet mignons. There is homemade lasagna and other pasta dishes, and well prepared veal.

LA NORMANDIE 8

2021 East Colonial Drive
Orlando, FL
(305) 896-9976

French

F ★ ★ ★ ½
S ★ ★ ★ ½
A ★ ★ ★
P ★ ★ ★

Good taste in dress required
Lot parking
All major credit cards
Full bar
Reservations recommended

Lunch: Mon.-Fri. 11:30AM-2:00PM
Dinner: Mon.-Sat. 5:30PM-10:00PM
          Closed Sunday

Chef Claude Melchiorri, formerly with Maxim's of Paris, transforms fresh ingredients into such marvels as Le Veau DuPecheur (cream of spinach topped with veal, scallops, shrimp, and white wine cream sauce) for discriminating patrons at this gem of a Gallic restaurant. You'll find French antiques, formal service, fresh flowers, and joie de vivre all adding to your pleasure here.

LA SCALA 1

203 Lorraine Drive
Altamonte Springs, FL
(305) 862-3257

Italian

F ★ ★ ★
S ★ ★ ★
A ★ ★ ★
P ★ ★ ½

Good taste in dress required
Lot parking
All major credit cards
Beer/Wine
Reservations required

Lunch: Mon.-Fri. 11:30AM-2:30PM
Dinner: Mon.-Thurs. 5:30PM-10:30PM
          Fri. & Sat. 5:30PM-11:00PM
          Closed Sunday

One might bill this restaurant as a "one man show," for chef/owner Joseph Del Vento, a former opera star, gives a stellar performance in the kitchen and treats guests to operatic arias. The smart décor is a perfect staging for the tableside service of many entrées. Osso buco, Fettuccine Alfredo, and homemade cheesecake are house specialties.

LE CORDON BLEU 4

537 West Fairbanks Avenue
Winter Park, FL
(305) 647-7575

French/Continental

F ★ ★ ★ ½
S ★ ★ ★
A ★ ★ ★
P ★ ★ ★ ½

Jacket and tie preferred
Valet parking
All major credit cards
Full bar
Reservations required

Lunch: Mon.-Fri. 11:30AM-3:00PM
Dinner: Mon.-Sat. 5:30PM-11:00PM
          Closed Sunday

Decorated in a turn-of-the-century Victorian motif, Le Cordon Bleu is a pleasant spot to enjoy excellent French/European cuisine. Owner/chef George Vogelbacher offers a large selection of fresh fish, beef, veal, and poultry dishes including bouillabaisse, Tournedos Rossini, Chateaubriand, and Duck à l'Orange.

LILI MARLENE'S 9
AVIATOR PUB

129 West Church Street
Orlando, FL
(305) 422-2434

American

F ★ ★ ★
S ★ ★ ★
A ★ ★ ★
P ★ ★ ★

No dress restrictions
Lot and street parking
AE, MC, V
Full bar
Reservations not required

Lunch/
Dinner: Daily 11:00AM-12:00AM

This sedate establishment is decorated with World War I and II flight memorabilia, and massive antiques, including the walnut fireplace and bookcases from Rothchild's Paris mansion, and Al Capone's dining room table. Prime rib, steaks, and seafood highlight the bill of fare. Dutch apple walnut cheesecake is everyone's favorite dessert.

LIMEY JIM'S 12
RESTAURANT

Hyatt Orlando Hotel
6375 Spacecoast Parkway
Kissimmee, FL
(305) 396-1234

Continental

F ★ ★ ★ ½
S ★ ★ ★ ½
A ★ ★ ★ ½
P ★ ★ ★ ½

Good taste in dress required
Lot parking

All major credit cards
Full bar
Reservations required

Dinner: Nightly 6:00PM-11:00PM

A bit of 18th century England seems to take form here, pleasantly modified by a fresh peach and green color scheme. You'll find bevies of fresh flowers, formal table service, and a wide range of continental cuisine. Entrées include prime rib and steak au poivre; Key lime pie is a highly praised dessert.

MAISON & JARDIN 1

430 South Wymore Road
Altamonte Springs, FL
(305) 862-4410

Continental

F ★ ★ ★ ½
S ★ ★ ★ ½
A ★ ★ ★ ½
P ★ ★ ★

Jacket preferred
Lot parking
All major credit cards
Full bar
Reservations recommended

Dinner: Tues.-Sun. 6:30PM-10:30PM
Brunch: Sun. 11:00AM-2:00PM
          Closed Monday

High on a hill, Maison & Jardin surrounds you with sylvan beauty as you dine leisurely in this elegant old home. Only fresh ingredients are used in the preparation of the continental cuisine; the menu changes daily. You'll find over 400 labels on the wine list at this award-winning restaurant.

PARK PLAZA GARDENS 6

319 Park Avenue South
Winter Park, FL
(305) 645-2475

Continental

F ★ ★ ★ ½
S ★ ★ ★
A ★ ★ ★ ½
P ★ ★ ★ ½

Good taste in dress required
Lot and street parking
All major credit cards
Full bar
Reservations required for dinner

Lunch: Daily 11:30AM-3:00PM
Dinner: Nightly 6:00PM-10:00PM

A glorious indoor-outdoor glass enclosed garden setting makes dining here a pure delight. Veal and beef dishes are served, as are tempting salad platters. The house specialty, however, is fresh seafood including Lobster Vanderbilt, fresh red snapper, Seafood Marinière, and Grouper Riche.

PICCADILLY   10

Gold Key Inn
7100 South Orange Blossom Trail
Orlando, FL
(305) 855-0050

Continental

F ★ ★ ★ ½
S ★ ★ ★
A ★ ★ ★
P ★ ★ ★

Good taste in dress required
Lot parking
All major credit cards
Full Bar
Reservations recommended

Lunch: Mon.-Sat. 11:15AM-1:30PM
Dinner: Nightly 6:00PM-10:30PM
Brunch: Sun. 11:00AM-2:00PM

Pewter plates and polished wood add a publike ambiance to this old English country inn setting, where you can dine on rack of lamb, roast beef with Yorkshire pudding, or a host of other continental savories. The service is prompt, and the wine list noteworthy.

SPINELLI'S   13

1200 Pennsylvania Avenue
Saint Cloud, FL
(305) 892-2435

Italian/Continental

F ★ ★ ★ ½
S ★ ★ ★ ½
A ★ ★ ★ ½
P ★ ★ ★

Jacket preferred
Lot parking
All major credit cards
Full bar
Reservations required

Lunch: Mon.-Fri. 11:30AM-2:00PM
Dinner: Mon.-Sat. 5:00PM-10:00PM
          Sun. 11:30AM-9:00PM

Spinelli's has earned many awards for the unfailing quality of the cuisine, and the Mediterranean ambiance. Old Italian favorites are enhanced with innovative touches. There are more than 100 entrées offered here, including a wide variety of continental dishes.

TWO FLIGHTS UP   5

329 Park Avenue South
Winter Park, FL
(305) 644-9868

Continental

F ★ ★ ★
S ★ ★ ★
A ★ ★ ½
P ★ ★ ½

Good taste in dress required;
  no shorts or T-shirts after 5PM
Lot and street parking
All major credit cards
Full bar
Reservations not required

Lunch/
Dinner: Mon.-Sat. 11:30AM-2:00AM
            Closed Sunday

This trendy New York style bistro, with its second floor location, offers you balcony seating with a view of a verdant, plant-laden atrium. Owned and operated by the Giovanna Esposito family, the menu stresses entrées prepared from signature recipes and featuring veal, pasta and fresh fish.

VILLA NOVA 3

839 North Orlando Avenue
Winter Park, FL
(305) 644-2060

Italian

F	★	★	★ ½
S	★	★	★
A	★	★	★
P	★	★	★

Good taste in dress required
Valet, lot, and street parking
All major credit cards
Full bar
Reservations required

Lunch: Mon.-Fri. 11:30AM-2:00PM
Dinner: Nightly 6:00PM-12:00AM

Since 1948 Villa Nova has been offering fine Northern Italian cuisine, steaks, and seafood, to an appreciative clientele. You have a choice of several formal dining rooms, in which to enjoy your selections from a wide range of gourmet dishes that are well prepared and adroitly served.

Philadelphia

Philadelphia

INTERSTATE 76

SCHUYLKILL EXPRESSWAY

LINCOLN HWY.

TOWNSHIP LINE ROAD

LANCASTER AVENUE

WEST CHESTER PIKE

CHESTNUT STREET

MARKET STREET

BROAD STREET

WALNUT ST.

SPRUCE STREET

LOMBARD STREET

SOUTH STREET

38TH ST.

6TH STREET

5TH STREET

INTERSTATE 13

ARTHUR'S STEAK HOUSE 5

1512 Walnut Street
Philadelphia, PA
(215) 735-2590

American

F ★ ★ ★
S ★ ★ ★
A ★ ★ ★
P ★ ★ ★

Good taste in dress required
Lot parking
All major credit cards
Full bar
Reservations required

Lunch: Mon.-Fri. 11:30AM-2:30PM
Dinner: Mon.-Fri. 5:00PM-10:00PM
Sat. 5:00PM-11:00PM
Closed Sunday

Since 1932, this restaurant has been renowned for serving great steaks and prime rib of beef. That tradition continues in this bright, congenial eatery, and you will also find interesting poultry, seafood, and veal dishes.

BOGART'S 8

The Latham Hotel
17th and Walnut Streets
Philadelphia, PA
(215) 563-9444

American/Continental

F ★ ★ ★
S ★ ★ ★
A ★ ★ ★ ½
P ★ ★ ½

Jacket preferred
Valet parking
All major credit cards
Full bar
Reservations required

Breakfast/
Lunch:
Dinner: Daily 7:00AM-12:00AM

Patterned after the restaurant in the movie "Casablanca," Bogart's ceiling fans and Moroccan décor recall another era. You won't hear "Play it again, Sam," but you will find excellent aged beef, and a large selection of seafood and veal dishes.

BOOKBINDER'S 14
OLD ORIGINAL

125 Walnut Street
Philadelphia, PA
(215) 925-7027

Seafood

F ★ ★ ★ ½
S ★ ★ ★
A ★ ★ ★
P ★ ★ ★ ★

Good taste in dress required
Valet parking
All major credit cards
Full bar
Reservations required

Lunch: Mon.-Fri. 11:45AM-2:45PM
Dinner: Nightly 3:00PM-10:00PM

Since 1865 this restaurant has been a favorite of the great and near great, and the walls are lined with fascinating bits and pieces of historical memorabilia. Dedicated to excellence, Bookbinder's reputation for serving only the choicest seafood, meats, vegetables, and fruit has won them national and international acclaim.

BOOKBINDER'S 29
SEAFOOD HOUSE

215 South 15th Street
Philadelphia, PA
(215) 545-1137

Seafood

F ★ ★ ★ ½
S ★ ★ ★
A ★ ★ ★
P ★ ★ ★

Good taste in dress required
Lot parking
All major credit cards
Full bar
Reservations not required

Lunch/
Dinner: Mon.-Fri. 11:30AM-11:00PM
            Sat. 4:00PM-12:00AM
            Sun. 12:00PM-10:00PM

Such seafood specialties as Snapper soup, Florida stone crabs, mushrooms stuffed with escargot, Imperial Baked Crab, and lobsters are served here by Richard and Samuel Bookbinder, 4th generation members to continue their family seafood restaurant tradition.

CAFÉ ROYAL   3

The Palace Hotel
18th & The Benjamin Franklin Parkway
Philadelphia, PA
(215) 963-2244

French

F ★ ★ ★ ½
S ★ ★ ★ ½
A ★ ★ ★ ½
P ★ ★ ★ ★

Jacket and tie required at dinner
Valet parking
All major credit cards
Full bar
Reservations recommended

Lunch: Mon.-Fri. 12:00PM-2:00PM
Dinner: Mon.-Sat. 6:00PM-10:00PM
         Sun. 6:00PM-8:30PM
Brunch: Sun. 11:30AM-2:30PM

Stunning in its elegant simplicity, this restaurant is considered the 'jewel' of the Palace Hotel. In this resplendent setting, with its inspiring view of the Parkway, chef Jean-Pierre Petit presents innovative translations of classic French cuisine. Prefixe dinners are accompanied by piano music, and feature entrées such as filet of lamb in puff pastry.

THE CITY TAVERN   13

Second Street near Walnut
Philadelphia, PA
(215) 923-6059

American

F ★ ★ ★
S ★ ★ ★
A ★ ★ ★
P ★ ★ ★ ½

Good taste in dress required
Lot and street parking
AE, MC, V
Full bar
Reservations recommended

Lunch: Daily 11:30AM-3:30PM
Dinner: Sun.-Thurs. 5:00PM-9:00PM
         Fri. & Sat. 5:00PM-10:00PM

When you visit this historic tavern, built in 1773, you'll find a costumed staff, harpsichord music in the evening, and an authentic 18th century atmosphere. Roasted meats and fresh fish are house specialties.

DANIEL'S AT THE   2
RIVERFRONT

Delaware River at Poplar Street
Philadelphia, PA
(215) 925-7000

Seafood

F ★ ★ ★
S ★ ★ ★
A ★ ★ ★
P ★ ★ ★

Jacket and tie preferred
Lot and street parking
All major credit cards
Full bar
Reservations recommended

Dinner: Tues.-Fri. 5:45PM-8:30PM
         Sat. 5:30PM-10:30PM
         Sun. 3:00PM-9:00PM

Every table at this handsome establishment has a sweeping view of the river rolling by. The décor is contemporary with brass accents and mirrored walls, and the house specializes in tableside service and cooking. You'll find a 25-foot salad bar laden with tempting tidbits, and a choice of fresh seafood, steaks, and chops for your entrée.

DÉJÀ-VU   32

1609 Pine Street
Philadelphia, PA
(215) 546-1190

French

```
F  ★ ★ ★ ½
S  ★ ★ ★ ½
A  ★ ★ ★ ½
P  ★ ★ ★ ★
```

Jacket and tie required
Lot and street parking
All major credit cards
Full bar
Reservations required

Dinner: Mon.-Sat. 6:00PM-9:00PM
          Closed Sunday

Tucked comfortably into a 19th century townhouse, this petite restaurant with its elegant Louis XIV décor features six-course, prix-fixe gourmet dinners. Owner/chef Salomon Montezinos presents such specialties as mustard-ginger lamb filets, loin of wild boar, herb sorbets, and pastries that are unique creations.

DEUX CHEMINÉES   21

251 South Camac Street
Philadelphia, PA
(215) 985-0367

French

```
F  ★ ★ ★ ½
S  ★ ★ ★
A  ★ ★ ★ ★
P  ★ ★ ★ ★
```

Good taste in dress required
Street parking
AE, MC, V
Full bar
Reservations required

Dinner: Mon.-Fri. 5:30PM-9:00PM
          Sat. 5:30PM-9:30PM
          Sun. 5:30PM-8:00PM

The elegant dining rooms of this restored 19th century townhouse with their working fireplaces and antique furnishings provide a luxe setting for chef/proprietor Fritz Blank's classic French cuisine.

ÉLAN   17

The Warwick
1701 Locust Street
Philadelphia, PA
(215) 546-8800

Continental/Italian

```
F  ★ ★ ★ ½
S  ★ ★ ★
A  ★ ★ ★
P  ★ ★ ★ ½
```

Good taste in dress required
Street parking
All major credit cards
Full bar
Reservations required

Dinner: Mon.-Sat. 7:00PM-12:00AM
Brunch: Sun. 10:00AM-2:30PM

Celebrities, businessmen, and professionals have made this chic private club a haven for the sophisticated epicurean. The cuisine is exceptional, featuring such house specialties as Fettuccine Élan.

THE FISH MARKET   7

124 South 18th Street
Philadelphia, PA
(215) 567-3559

Seafood

F ★ ★ ★ ½
S ★ ★ ★
A ★ ★ ★
P ★ ★ ★

No dress restrictions
Lot and street parking
All major credit cards
Full bar
Reservations recommended

Lunch: Mon.-Fri. 11:30AM-2:30PM
Dinner: Mon.-Sat. 5:00PM-10:00PM
Closed Sunday

A choice source of fresh seafood including seasonal and daily catches, this gourmand's sanctuary offers you five different dining rooms, a pleasant ambiance, and bustling service. Long-time chef Joseph O'Connor is picky about food preparation, and your meal here will never disappoint you.

THE FOUNTAIN 3
RESTAURANT

Four Seasons Hotel
1 Logan Square
Philadelphia, PA
(215) 963-1500

Continental

F ★ ★ ★ ½
S ★ ★ ★ ½
A ★ ★ ★ ½
P ★ ★ ★ ★

Jacket required
Valet, lot, and street parking
All major credit cards
Full bar
Reservations required

Breakfast/
Lunch/
Dinner: Daily 6:00AM-1:00AM

Enjoy the lovely view of Logan Square and the sense of total luxury this dining spot exudes. Lustrous wood paneling, crystal chandeliers, fabulous floral arrangements, formal service, and exquisite appointments are all found here. The continental menu is well balanced.

FRIDAY, SATURDAY, 26
SUNDAY

261 South 21st Street
Philadelphia, PA
(215) 546-4232

Continental

F ★ ★ ★ ½
S ★ ★ ★ ½
A ★ ★ ★ ½
P ★ ★ ★

No dress restrictions
Street parking
AE, DC, MC, V
Full bar
Reservations not required

Lunch: Mon.-Fri. 11:30AM-2:30PM
Dinner: Nightly 5:30PM-10:30PM

Tiny, and romantically inclined, here you'll find a blackboard menu detailing such carefully prepared dishes as rack of lamb, stuffed sea trout, and poached Norwegian salmon.

FROG 18

1524 Locust Street
Philadelphia, PA
(215) 735-8882

American/French/Thai

F ★ ★ ★ ½
S ★ ★ ★
A ★ ★ ★
P ★ ★ ★

Good taste in dress required
Lot and street parking
All major credit cards
Full bar
Reservations required on Friday
and Saturday

Dinner: Sun.-Thurs. 5:30PM-10:30PM
        Fri. & Sat. 5:30PM-11:30PM

Expect an upbeat interesting dining experience at Steven Poses' eatery which is a favorite of the media and fashion crowd. The décor is clean and elegant with a decided Eastern influence. The eclectic menu is in a constant state of flux.

THE GARDEN 28

1617 Spruce Street
Philadelphia, PA
(215) 546-4455

Continental/American

F ★ ★ ★ ½
S ★ ★ ★
A ★ ★ ★
P ★ ★ ★ ½

No dress restrictions
Lot parking
All major credit cards
Full bar
Reservations not required

Lunch: Mon.-Fri. 11:30AM-2:00PM
Dinner: Mon.-Sat. from 5:30PM
         Closed Sunday

Owner Kathleen Mulhern has transformed a historic Center City townhouse into an antique-filled, enchanting restaurant, with garden dining in the sunny season. There's an Oyster Bar, a fine wine cellar, and a menu featuring fresh seafood, steaks, game, and veal dishes.

HARRY'S BAR & GRILL 16

22 South 18th Street
Philadelphia, PA
(215) 561-5757

Italian/American

F ★ ★ ★
S ★ ★ ★
A ★ ★ ★
P ★ ★ ★

Jacket required
Lot parking
All major credit cards
Full bar
Reservations not required

Lunch: Mon.-Fri. 11:30AM-2:00PM
Dinner: Mon.-Fri. 5:30PM-9:30PM
         Closed Saturday and Sunday

Noted for its classic clublike atmosphere, quality wine list, and consistent cuisine, this restaurant lures a business-oriented clientele to its downstairs bar, and upstairs dining room.

HOFFMAN HOUSE 11

1214 Sansom Street
Philadelphia, PA
(215) 925-2772

German/Austrian

F ★ ★ ★
S ★ ★ ★
A ★ ★ ★
P ★ ★ ½

Good taste in dress required
Lot parking
All major credit cards
Full bar
Reservations recommended

Lunch: Tues.-Fri. 11:30AM-2:30PM
Dinner: Tues.-Sat. 5:00PM-9:00PM
         Closed Sunday and Monday

This centrally located restaurant has a warm, intimate old-world feeling with its wood-paneled walls, fresh floral bouquets, and crisp white table linens. Seasonal game such as venison, rabbit, and goose plus unusual seafood dishes are featured.

IL GALLO NERO 30

254 South 15th Street
Philadelphia, PA
(215) 546-8065

Italian

F ★ ★ ★ ½
S ★ ★ ★
A ★ ★ ½
P ★ ★ ½

Jacket preferred
Lot and street parking
All major credit cards
Full bar
Reservations not required

Lunch/
Dinner: Mon.-Thurs. 11:45AM-10:00PM
           Fri. 11:45AM-11:00PM
           Sat. 5:30PM-11:00PM
           Closed Sunday

Enzo and Carla Fusaro, owners, restored a century-old music school for their innovative restaurant that accommodates 85 guests in four rooms, each with a different décor. A favorite haunt of visiting musical celebrities who savor the glorious array of classic Italian dishes.

LA CAMARGUE   12

1119 Walnut Street
Philadelphia, PA
(215) 922-3148

French

F ★ ★ ★
S ★ ★ ★
A ★ ★ ★
P ★ ★ ★

Jacket and tie required
Street parking
All major credit cards
Full bar
Reservations required

Lunch: Mon.-Fri. 12:00PM-2:00PM
Dinner: Mon.-Sat. 5:30PM-11:00PM
          Closed Sunday

Let your host, Marcel Brossette, introduce you to the joys of haute cuisine, in his romantic restaurant with its lilting country charm. For your pleasure there is classical guitar music, a meritorious wine list, fresh flowers, and such superb dishes as filet of sole Dieppoise and Carré d'Agneau.

LA FAMAGLIA   23

8 South Front Street
Philadelphia, PA
(215) 922-2803

Italian

F ★ ★ ★ ½
S ★ ★ ★ ½
A ★ ★ ★ ½
P ★ ★ ★ ★

Jacket required
Lot parking
All major credit cards
Full bar
Reservations required

Lunch: Tues.-Sun. 12:00PM-2:00PM
Dinner: Tues.-Sun. 5:30PM-9:30PM
          Closed Monday

The concerted effort of the Sena family produces a heart-warming dining experience in this charming old-world restaurant with its antique art and marble columns. The gourmet Italian cuisine is prepared by "Mamma and Pappa" using recipes garnered in Italy.

LA TRUFFE   24

10 South Front Street
Philadelphia, PA
(215) 925-5062

French

F ★ ★ ★ ½
S ★ ★ ★ ½
A ★ ★ ★ ½
P ★ ★ ★ ½

Jacket required
Lot and street parking
All major credit cards
Full bar
Reservations required

Lunch: Tues.-Fri. 12:00PM-2:00PM
Dinner: Mon.-Sat. 6:00PM-11:00PM
Closed Sunday

Located by the waterfront in Old Philadelphia, here you will find candlelight, fresh flowers, fine service, and a selection of good wines to complement the standard-setting cuisine.

L'AIGLE D'OR 6

1920 Chestnut Street
Philadelphia, PA
(215) 567-0855

Continental

F ★ ★ ★ ½
S ★ ★ ★
A ★ ★ ★
P ★ ★ ★

Jacket preferred
Lot parking
All major credit cards
Full bar
Reservations recommended

Lunch: Mon.-Fri. 11:30AM-3:00PM
Dinner: Mon.-Thurs. 6:00PM-10:00PM
Fri. & Sat. 6:00PM-11:00PM
Closed Sunday

Here European-trained owner/chef Soren Arnoldi treats you to flights of culinary fancy. Menu offerings such as the duck liver pâté, Dover sole, individual rack of lamb, and veal dishes reflect French, German, and Italian influences.

LAUTREC 33

408 South 2nd Street
Philadelphia, PA
(215) 923-6660/574-0414

French

F ★ ★ ★ ½
S ★ ★ ★
A ★ ★ ★
P ★ ★ ★ ½

No dress restrictions
Lot and street parking
AE, DC, MC, V
Full bar
Reservations not required

Dinner: Tues.-Sat. 6:00PM-10:00PM
Sun. 6:00PM-1:00AM
Brunch: Sun. 12:00PM-4:00PM
Closed Monday

Toulouse Lautrec's brilliant works of art grace the walls of this intimate upstairs restaurant that offers you an ever-changing menu of classic French cuisine. There's also a left bank-style café downstairs serving desserts, cappuccino, and live jazz every night but Monday.

LE BEAU LIEU 27

The Barclay Hotel
On Rittenhouse Square
Philadelphia, PA
(215) 545-0300

Continental

F ★ ★ ★ ½
S ★ ★ ★ ½
A ★ ★ ★ ½
P ★ ★ ★ ½

Good taste in dress required
Valet and lot parking
All major credit cards
Full bar
Reservations recommended

Breakfast/
Lunch/
Dinner: Daily 7:00AM-10:00PM

Glittering and resplendent, this chic cosmopolitan dining room fairly shimmers with crystalline light reflecting in the mirrors. The décor is further enhanced by green brocade draperies and wall cover, that backdrop the gleaming golden service pieces and gold Lennox china. In the midst of this opulence, continental cuisine of epicurean quality is tastefully presented by career waiters.

LE BEC-FIN 9

1523 Walnut Street
Philadelphia, PA
(215) 567-1000

French

F ★ ★ ★ ★
S ★ ★ ★ ★
A ★ ★ ★ ★
P ★ ★ ★ ★

Good taste in dress required
Lot and street parking
AE, CB, DC
Full bar
Reservations required

Lunch: Mon.-Fri. 11:30AM-2:30PM
Dinner: Mon.-Sat. Seatings at
         6:00PM & 9:00PM
         Closed Sunday

Under the skilled guidance of chef and
host-owner Georges Perrier, this luxurious establishment is endowed with formal
Louis XV décor, glorious appointments,
impeccable service, an illustrious wine
list, and haute cuisine without peer.

LE CHAMPIGNON 34

122 Lombard Street
Philadelphia, PA
(215) 925-1106

French

F ★ ★ ★ ½
S ★ ★ ★ ½
A ★ ★ ★
P ★ ★ ★ ★

Jacket required
Lot and street parking
All major credit cards
Full bar
Reservations required

Lunch: Mon.-Fri. 12:00PM-2:30PM
Dinner: Mon.-Fri. 5:30PM-11:00PM
         Sat. 5:30PM-12:00AM
         Sun. 4:00PM-9:00PM

Beautifully displayed antique clocks, farm
implements, and 18th and 19th century
paintings, are the rich decorations of this
enchanting French country bistro restaurant. The cooking techniques meld hearty
country, haute cuisine, and nouvelle im-
provisations.

MARABELLA'S 19

1420 Locust Street
Philadelphia, PA
(215) 545-1845

Californian/Italian

F ★ ★ ★
S ★ ★ ★
A ★ ★
P ★ ½

Good taste in dress required
Street parking
AE, MC, V
Full bar
Reservations not required

Lunch/
Dinner: Mon.-Thurs. 11:30AM-11:00PM
         Fri. & Sat. 11:30AM-12:00AM
         Sun. 4:00PM-10:00PM

Here the Marabella family introduces you
to a trendy new culinary concept that
cross-pollinates nouvelle Californian cuisine with their Italian heritage.

MORGAN'S 15
RESTAURANT

135 South 24th Street
Philadelphia, PA
(215) 567-6066

French/Italian

F ★ ★ ★ ½
S ★ ★ ★
A ★ ★ ★
P ★ ★ ★

No dress restrictions
Lot parking
All major credit cards

Full bar
Reservations required

Lunch: Mon.-Fri. 11:45AM-2:00PM
Dinner: Mon.-Sat. 5:30PM-10:30PM
           Closed Sunday

Owners Alphonse and Anita Pignataro imbue this restaurant with their own enthusiasm and love of fine foods. The cuisine is subtle and personal, with touches of French, Northern Italian, and other Mediterranean countries shining through.

OCTOBER 25

26 South Front Street
Philadelphia, PA
(215) 925-4447

American

F ★ ★ ★ ½
S ★ ★ ★ ½
A ★ ★ ★ ½
P ★ ★ ★ ½

Jacket preferred
Lot and street parking
All major credit cards
Full bar
Reservations recommended

Lunch: Mon.-Fri. 11:30AM-2:30PM
Dinner: Mon.-Sat. 5:30PM-10:30PM
           Closed Sunday

Owners Gerry Poplar and Irv Chacker have garnered regional recipes from all over the U.S. to create the distinctive menu offered in this friendly intimate eatery. Here you can savor such gustatory delights as buffalo mignons, Louisiana redfish and jambalaya.

OSTERIA ROMANA 36

935 Ellsworth Street
Philadelphia, PA
(215) 271-9191

Italian

F ★ ★ ★ ½
S ★ ★ ★ ½
A ★ ★ ★ ½
P ★ ★ ★ ½

Good taste in dress required
Lot parking
AE, MC, V
Full bar
Reservations required

Dinner: Tues.-Thurs. 5:30PM-10:30PM
           Fri. & Sat. 5:30PM-11:00PM
           Sun. 3:00PM-9:30PM

The food served here is the heart of a wonderful dining experience. Chef/owner Ivana DiMarco offers Roman-style cuisine prepared with the sure hand of a master.

RESTAURANT 4
LA TERRASSE

3432 Sansom Street
Philadelphia, PA
(215) 387-3778

French

F ★ ★ ★
S ★ ★ ★ ½
A ★ ★ ★ ½
P ★ ★ ★

No dress restrictions
Lot and street parking
All major credit cards
Full bar
Reservations required

Lunch: Mon.-Fri. 11:30AM-2:30PM
Dinner: Tues.-Sat. 6:00PM-11:00PM
           Sun. & Mon. 5:30PM-10:00PM
Brunch: Sun. 11:30AM-3:00PM

Housed in a trio of brownstones with an open-air terrace (glassed in winter), trees growing through the roof, and a mini "rain forest" of hanging plants, this delightful dining spot has a relaxed atmosphere, and a friendly professional staff.

RISTORANTE DI LULLO   1

7955 Oxford Avenue
Philadelphia, PA
(215) 725-6000

Italian

```
F  ★ ★ ★
S  ★ ★ ★
A  ★ ★ ★
P  ★ ★ ½
```

Good taste in dress required
Lot and street parking
All major credit cards
Full bar
Reservations recommended

Dinner: Mon.-Sat. 5:00PM-12:00AM
          Sun. 4:00PM-11:00PM

High-tech Italian décor, with white tile, Italian marble, chrome, and shining mirrors, forms a chic setting at Joseph DiLullo's splendid dining establishment. You'll find such enticing entrées on the menu as Fegato alla Lizornese, Lomsbata Di Vitello Arrosto, and filet of beef.

SALOON   35

750 South 7th Street
Philadelphia, PA
(215) 627-1811

Italian

```
F  ★ ★ ★ ½
S  ★ ★ ★ ½
A  ★ ★ ★ ½
P  ★ ★ ★
```

No dress restrictions
Valet, lot, and street parking
Credit cards not accepted
Full bar
Reservations required

Lunch: Mon.-Fri. 11:30AM-2:00PM
Dinner: Mon.-Sat. 5:00PM-11:30PM
          Closed Sunday

Renowned for its beautiful historical furnishings, relaxed atmosphere, and the consistent quality and originality of its kitchen, this restaurant has been a trendsetter in Philadelphia's dining renaissance since 1967.

SARAH'S   20

The Hershey Philadelphia Hotel
Broad & Locust Streets
Philadelphia, PA
(215) 893-1600

Continental

```
F  ★ ★ ★
S  ★ ★ ★
A  ★ ★ ★ ½
P  ★ ★ ★
```

Jacket and tie required
Valet parking
All major credit cards
Full bar
Reservations recommended

Dinner: Nightly 5:30PM-11:00PM

This very uptown, elegant, art déco dining room is lavishly decorated with recessed murals and etched glass. There is an abundance of colorful fresh flowers, and extremely well done formal service stressing tableside food preparation.

SIVA'S RESTAURANT   22

34 South Front Street
Philadelphia, PA
(215) 925-2700

Indian

```
F  ★ ★ ★
S  ★ ★ ★
A  ★ ★ ★
P  ★ ★ ½
```

Jacket required
Lot and street parking
All major credit cards
Full bar
Reservations required

Lunch: Mon.-Fri. 12:00PM-2:00PM
Dinner: Nightly 5:30PM-10:30PM

Consistently judged one of Philadelphia's top-rated restaurants, owner Amar D. Bhalla has created a romantic setting decorated with ornate Indian tapestries in which to present authentic Northern Indian haute cuisine.

THE 20TH STREET CAFÉ 31

261 South 20th Street
Philadelphia, PA
(215) 546-6867

American

F ★ ★ ★
S ★ ★ ★
A ★ ★ ★
P ★ ★ ★

No dress restrictions
Street parking
All major credit cards
Full bar
Reservations not required

Lunch: Mon.-Fri. 11:30AM-2:30PM
Dinner: Mon.-Thurs. 5:00PM-10:00PM
         Fri. & Sat. 5:00PM-10:30PM
         Sun. 5:00PM-9:00PM
Brunch: Sun. 12:00PM-3:00PM

In the vanguard of the Philadelphia restaurant renaissance of the '70s, you'll find eclectic cuisine presented in an intimate environment of casual elegance, at this trendy café. Guests in jeans or tuxedoes savor dishes ranging from Chili Elizabeth Taylor to Breast of Duck Bigarade.

VERSAILLES 10

Bellevue Stratford Hotel
Broad at Walnut
Philadelphia, PA
(215) 893-1880

French

F ★ ★ ★ ½
S ★ ★ ★ ½
A ★ ★ ★ ½
P ★ ★ ★ ★

Jacket required, no jeans
Valet and lot parking
All major credit cards
Full bar
Reservations required

Dinner: Mon.-Sat. 5:30PM-10:30PM
         Closed Sunday

This elegant gourmet restaurant, decorated in a contemporary manner, caters to discerning epicures. The country French cooking featured here is nicely blended with nouvelle touches, and there is a wine list with 250 selections.

WILDFLOWERS 34

514 South Fifth Street
Philadelphia, PA
(215) 923-6708

French/American

F ★ ★ ★
S ★ ★ ★ ½
A ★ ★ ★
P ★ ★ ★

No dress restrictions
Lot and street parking
AE, MC, V
Full bar
Reservations recommended

Dinner: Mon.-Thurs. 5:00PM-11:00PM
         Fri. & Sat. 5:00PM-12:00AM
         Sun. 5:00PM-10:00PM
Brunch: Sun. 11:00AM-3:00PM

Exposed brick, beamed ceilings, hardwood tables, antique stained glass, and a plethora of green plants creates a beautiful ambiance at this 12-year-old restaurant. You'll enjoy fresh seafood and meats grilled over mesquite wood, an award-winning salad buffet, and specialties such as Moscovy duck breast and rack of lamb.

Phoenix

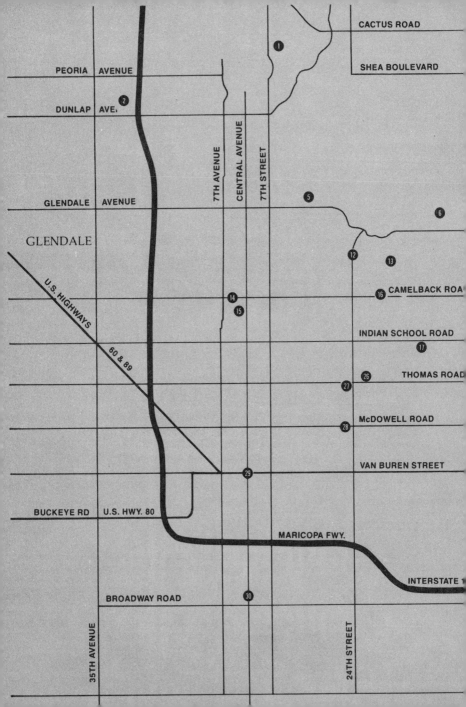

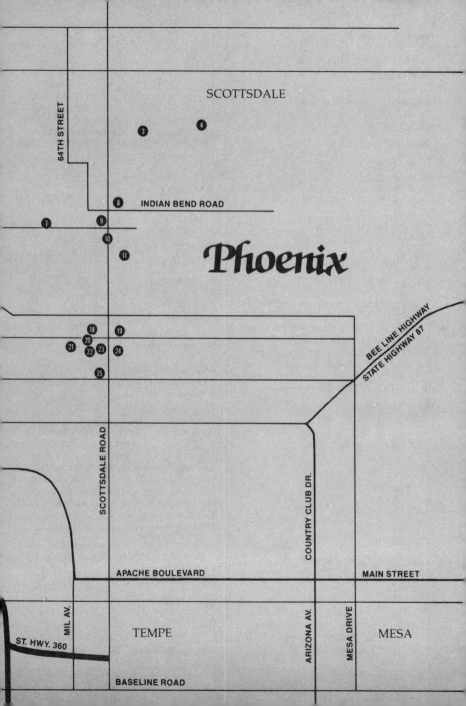

ARMENIA STEAK   20
& KABOB

7055 East Indian School Road
Scottsdale, AZ
(602) 994-4717

Armenian/Middle Eastern

F ★ ★ ★
S ★ ★ ★
A ★ ★ ★
P ★ ★ ★

Good taste in dress required
Lot parking
AE, MC, V
Full bar
Reservations required

Dinner: Nightly 5:00PM-10:30PM

Take a gourmet's magic carpet ride and
explore the rich heritage of fine Middle
Eastern fare at George Mardirossian's
unique establishment. Family recipes that
date back a thousand years are the basis of
the cuisine served here that encompasses
Armenian, Arabian, Bulgarian, Greek,
Jewish, Persian, and Turkish dishes.

ASIA HOUSE   28

2310 East Mc Dowell
Phoenix, AZ
(602) 267-7461

Chinese/Japanese/Mongolian

F ★ ★ ★ ½
S ★ ★ ★
A ★ ★ ★
P ★ ★ ½

Good taste in dress required
Lot parking
All major credit cards
Full bar
Reservations recommended

Dinner: Tues.-Sat. 6:00PM-10:00PM
          Sun. 5:30PM-9:30PM
          Closed Monday

This family owned and operated restaurant lets you enjoy your choice of three
types of Oriental cookery, each served in
its own appropriately decorated room. A
seven-course Cantonese dinner is served
in the main dining room; Japanese sukiyaki is featured in the tatami rooms, and
the Mongolian room specialty is Genghis
Khan barbecue.

AVANTI   26

2728 East Thomas Road
Phoenix, AZ
(602) 956-0900

Continental/Italian

F ★ ★ ★ ½
S ★ ★ ★ ½
A ★ ★ ★
P ★ ★ ★

Good taste in dress required
Valet and lot parking
AE, MC, V
Full bar
Reservations required

Lunch: Mon.-Fri. 11:30AM-3:00PM
Dinner: Nightly 5:30PM-10:00PM

An innovative quartette of restaurateurs:
Angelo, Benito, Franco, and Ramon, are
responsible for creating this award-
winning showplace with its candlelit
gardenlike setting, soft music, glorious
fresh flowers, and attentive formal
service. The diverse menu features fresh
fish daily, beef, and special entrées. The
chocolate mousse cake is unforgettable.

AVANTI'S OF   25
SCOTTSDALE

3102 North Scottsdale Road
Scottsdale, AZ
(602) 949-8333

Continental/Italian

F ★ ★ ★ ½
S ★ ★ ★ ½
A ★ ★ ★
P ★ ★ ★

Good taste in dress required
Valet and lot parking
AE, MC, V
Full bar
Reservations recommended

Dinner: Nightly 5:30PM-1:00AM

Contemporary décor, beautiful background music, and superb continental cuisine with Northern Italian accent notes, create a refreshing dining experience at this chic restaurant. You can watch the pastas being made, and indulge in your choice of a wide range of entrées.

BEEF EATERS   14

300 West Camelback Road
Phoenix, AZ
(602) 264-3838

Continental

F ★ ★ ★
S ★ ★ ★
A ★ ★ ★
P ★ ★ ½

Good taste in dress required
Valet and lot parking
All major credit cards
Full bar
Reservations recommended

Lunch/
Dinner: Mon.-Sat. 11:30AM-11:30PM
Sun. 11:30AM-10:30PM

Traditional Old English décor enhanced with antiques and memorabilia, creates a clubby feeling at Jay Newton's popular eatery. The continental menu features short ribs and prime ribs among the enticing entrées. Freshly baked breads and desserts have a loyal following. The Black Forest Cake is a temptress worth succumbing to.

BESIDE THE POINTE   5

The Pointe at Squaw Peak
7677 North 16th Street
Phoenix, AZ
(602) 997-2626

American/Italian/Mexican

F ★ ★ ★ ½
S ★ ★ ★ ½
A ★ ★ ★ ½
P ★ ★

Good taste in dress required
Lot parking
All major credit cards
Full bar
Reservations recommended

Breakfast/
Lunch/
Dinner: Sun.-Thurs. 6:00AM-1:00AM
Fri. & Sat. 6:00AM-3:00AM

Like a cool, refreshing oasis, this garden-like restaurant with its plentiful plants, and light airy feeling delights the eye as well as the taste buds. Italian and Mexican specialties join with American dishes in a menu offering 150 distinctive items ranging from chicken wings with barbecue sauce to baby back pork ribs; pizza to chimichangas to steak tournedos.

CHAPARRAL   6

5402 East Lincoln Drive
Scottsdale, AZ
(602) 948-6644

Continental

F ★ ★ ★ ½
S ★ ★ ★
A ★ ★ ★
P ★ ★ ★

Jacket preferred
Valet and lot parking
All major credit cards
Full bar
Reservations required

Dinner: Sun.-Thurs. 6:00PM-10:00PM
Fri. & Sat. 6:00PM-11:00PM

Here you can enjoy a dramatic view of Camelback mountain, warm southwestern hospitality, and smooth continental service. The wine cellar has been carefully planned to complement the menu, which offers you a wide variety of interesting choices. Individual rack of lamb, duck, veal, and pepper steak are among the featured entrées.

CHEZ LOUIS 24

7363 Scottsdale Mall
Scottsdale, AZ
(602) 946-1431/945-3303

French/International

F ★ ★ ★ ½
S ★ ★ ★ ½
A ★ ★ ★ ½
P ★ ★ ★ ½

Jacket and tie preferred
Valet parking
AE, DC, MC, V
Full bar
Reservations required

Lunch: Mon.-Sat. 11:30AM-3:00PM
Dinner: Mon.-Sat. 5:00PM-11:00PM
Closed Sunday

Soft music, a lovely view, a choice of three beautifully decorated dining rooms, gourmet quality food, and a fine wine list have earned an enviable reputation for this romantic restaurant, since its opening in 1958. Specialties include rack of lamb, lobster, veal, and wild game.

COMPASS 30

Hyatt Regency
122 North 2nd Street
Phoenix, AZ
(602) 257-1110

Continental

F ★ ★ ★
S ★ ★ ★
A ★ ★ ★
P ★ ★ ★

Good taste in dress required
Lot and street parking
All major credit cards
Full bar
Reservations recommended

Lunch: Mon.-Sat. 11:30AM-2:30PM
Dinner: Nightly 5:30PM-9:30PM
Brunch: Sun. 10:30AM-2:30PM

Perched atop a high rise hotel, an incomparable 360° view of Phoenix and the distant horizons awaits you in this luxurious dining spot that features sofas instead of chairs. Among the entrées you will find Roast Duckling Regency, twin lobster tails, and succulent prime rib.

EL CHORRO 7

5550 East Lincoln Drive
Scottsdale, AZ
(602) 948-5170

American

F ★ ★ ★
S ★ ★ ★
A ★ ★ ★
P ★ ★ ★

Good taste in dress required
Valet parking
All major credit cards
Full bar
Reservations required

Breakfast: Daily 9:00AM-11:30AM
Lunch: Daily 11:30AM-2:30PM
Dinner: Nightly 6:00PM-11:30PM

Since 1937 this remarkable establishment has been luring celebrities and locals to dine 'neath the stars on the fireplace-warmed patio, or in the gracious indoor dining rooms, with their rustic Western art décor. Chateaubriand and rack of lamb are long-time traditional favorites.

ERNESTO'S BACKSTREET 17

3603 East Indian School
Phoenix, AZ
(602) 957-0303

Continental

F ★ ★ ★ ½
S ★ ★ ★ ½
A ★ ★ ★
P ★ ★ ★

Good taste in dress required
Valet parking
All major credit cards
Full bar
Reservations required

Lunch: Mon.-Fri. 11:00AM-3:30PM
Dinner: Nightly 5:00PM-12:00AM

Very chic and elegant, this restaurant combines classic good taste with polished service and an extraordinary range of cuisine. Specialties of the house that highlight the 8-page menu are veal dishes, fresh seafood entrées, and a good selection of well prepared pastas.

ETIENNE'S DIFFERENT 1
POINTE OF VIEW

11111 North 7th Street
Phoenix, AZ
(602) 866-7500

French/Continental

F ★ ★ ★ ½
S ★ ★ ★ ★
A ★ ★ ★
P ★ ★ ★ ★

Jacket required in dining room
Valet parking
All major credit cards
Full bar
Reservations required

Dinner: Mon.-Thurs. 6:00PM-10:00PM
          Fri. & Sat. 6:00PM-11:00PM
Brunch: Sun. 11:30AM-3:30PM

Chauffeured limosines depart from The Pointe resort to bring diners to this mountain top retreat dedicated to gourmet cuisine, flawless service, and live entertainment. The panoramic view of the city is like a magnificent mirage; the high tech décor is dazzling; and the food and wine exemplary and award-winning.

GARCIA'S 19

7633 East Indian School Road
Scottsdale, AZ
(602) 945-1647

Mexican

F ★ ★ ★ ½
S ★ ★ ★ ½
A ★ ★ ★
P ★ ★

Good taste in dress required
Lot parking
AE, MC, V
Full bar
Reservations not required

Lunch/
Dinner: Sun.-Thurs. 11:00AM-10:00PM
          Fri. & Sat. 11:00AM-11:00PM

The first of a now burgeoning restaurant chain operating in 10 states, you will find this charming establishment run with the same friendly efficiency it was noted for when it opened as a small family-run eatery. There are refreshing, icy Margaritas, and such spicy house specialties as chimichangas, fajitas, and combination platters. Fried ice cream and flan are popular desserts.

THE GLASS DOOR 22

6939 Main Street
Scottsdale, AZ
(602) 994-5303

Continental

F ★ ★ ★ ★
S ★ ★ ★
A ★ ★ ★
P ★ ★ ½

Good taste in dress required
Valet, lot, and street parking
AE, MC, V
Full bar
Reservations recommended

Lunch: Mon.-Sat. 11:30AM-3:00PM
Dinner: Mon.-Sat. 5:30PM-11:00PM
Closed Sunday

Comfortably cosmopolitan, this art déco room features etched glass and chrome in a flattering peach and moss green color scheme. Owner Lou Mastella offers you a well balanced menu of continental cuisine with such choice entrées as Veal Port o' Prince, and a house lamb specialty.

GOLD ROOM   12

Arizona Biltmore
24th Street and Missouri
Phoenix, AZ
(602) 954-2504

Continental

F ★ ★ ★ ½
S ★ ★ ★ ½
A ★ ★ ★ ½
P ★ ★ ★ ½

Jacket required at dinner
Valet parking
All major credit cards
Full bar
Reservations not required

Breakfast: Daily 6:30AM-10:30AM
Lunch: Daily 11:30AM-2:30PM
Dinner: Nightly 6:30PM-10:30PM
Brunch: Sun. 11:15AM-3:00PM

This vintage restaurant has served as the main dining room of the prestigious and historic Arizona Biltmore since its opening in 1929. The expansive gold-leafed ceiling for which it is named has lost none of its splendor, nor has the view of the beautiful grounds diminished one whit. Dining here remains an event of significance.

THE GOLDEN EAGLE   29

North Central at Van Buren
Phoenix, AZ
(602) 257-7700

Continental

F ★ ★ ★ ½
S ★ ★ ★ ½
A ★ ★ ★ ½
P ★ ★ ★ ½

Jacket required
Lot parking
All major credit cards
Full bar
Reservations recommended

Lunch: Mon.-Fri. 11:30AM-2:00PM
Dinner: Mon.-Sat. 6:00PM-10:00PM
Closed Sunday

Nested 37-stories high atop the tallest building in Arizona, this restaurant is designed with windows 2-stories high on three sides, for expansive viewing. The food, service, and wine list are all exceptional.

GREGORY'S PENTHOUSE   27

2333 East Thomas Road
Phoenix, AZ
(602) 956-8740

American

F ★ ★ ★ ½
S ★ ★ ★ ½
A ★ ★ ★
P ★ ★ ★

No dress restrictions
Lot parking
AE, MC, V
Full bar
Reservations recommended

Lunch: Mon.-Fri. 11:30AM-3:00PM
Dinner: Mon.-Thurs. 5:30PM-10:00PM
Fri. & Sat. 5:30PM-11:00PM
Closed Sunday

This smart, Victorian-style dining room surrounds you with luxury and gives you a marvelous view of the city. The American menu is graced with well prepared classics such as Shrimp Provencal.

IANUZZI 16

2650 East Camelback Road
Phoenix, AZ
(602) 957-6888

Italian

F ★ ★ ★ ½
S ★ ★ ★ ½
A ★ ★ ★ ½
P ★ ★ ★ ½

Good taste in dress required
Lot parking
All major credit cards
Full bar
Reservations recommended

Dinner: Mon.-Sat. from 5:30PM
Closed Sunday

Owner Angelo Ianuzzi, a 5th generation restaurateur, has created a jewel-like setting in which to present exquisite Italian cuisine and vintage Italian wines. House specialties include fresh crustaceans, Fileto di Manza, and homemade desserts.

LA CHAMPAGNE 8

The Registry Resort
7171 North Scottsdale Road
Scottsdale, AZ
(602) 991-3800

French/American

F ★ ★ ★ ★
S ★ ★ ★ ★
A ★ ★ ★ ½
P ★ ★ ★ ★

Jacket required
Valet and lot parking
All major credit cards
Full bar
Reservations required

Dinner: Nightly 6:30PM-10:00PM

Beautiful appointments and a regal blue and pink color scheme create a romantic aura in this opulent dining room. You'll find an abundance of fresh flowers, fresh Beluga caviar, an award-winning wine list, and entrées such as veal medallions with green peppercorn sauce.

LA CHAUMIERE 18

6910 East Main Street
Scottsdale, AZ
(602) 946-5115

French

F ★ ★ ★ ½
S ★ ★ ★ ½
A ★ ★ ★
P ★ ★ ★ ★

Good taste in dress required
Valet and street parking
All major credit cards
Full bar
Reservations recommended

Dinner: Mon.-Sat. 5:30PM-9:30PM
Closed Sunday

An old home has been converted to resemble a thatched-roof Brittany cottage by chef/owner Claude Musguin as a companionable setting for his French country cuisine. Rack of lamb for two, fresh seafood, beef, poultry, and a bevy of other entrées are cooked to order.

LA FONTANELLA 21

4231 East Indian School Road
Phoenix, AZ
(602) 955-1213

Italian

F ★ ★ ★ ½
S ★ ★ ★
A ★ ★ ★
P ★ ★ ½

Good taste in dress required
Lot parking
AE, MC, V
Full bar
Reservations required

Lunch: Mon.-Fri. 11:00AM-2:00PM
Dinner: Nightly 4:30PM-10:00PM

This restaurant is a transplant from Chicago, now ensconced in a romantic setting in Phoenix with a villa-like décor. The staff is friendly and efficient; the Italian cuisine emphasizes Northern-style cooking.

LE BISTRO   23

7131 Main Street
Scottsdale, AZ
(602) 947-6042

Continental

F ★ ★ ★
S ★ ★ ★
A ★ ★ ★
P ★ ★ ★

Good taste in dress required
Lot and street parking
All major credit cards
Full bar
Reservations recommended

Lunch: Mon.-Sat. 11:30AM-2:30PM
Dinner: Tues.-Thurs. & Sun.
5:30PM-10:30PM
Fri. & Sat. 5:30PM-11:00PM

Nestled in the art and antique galleries of old Scottsdale, Stephen R. Slansky's intimate eatery offers attentive service, a warm atmosphere, and excellent continental cuisine sparked with country French touches. Among your entrée choices are Quenelles of Scallops, imported Dover Sole Bonne Femme, and Ris de Veau aux Chantrelles.

MANCUSO'S   10

6166 North Scottsdale Road
Scottsdale, AZ
(602) 948-9988

Italian/French

F ★ ★ ★ ½
S ★ ★ ★ ½
A ★ ★ ★
P ★ ★ ★

Good taste in dress required
Valet parking
All major credit cards
Full bar
Reservations required

Dinner: Nightly 5:30PM-10:30PM

This often-honored restaurant was opened in 1969 by Frank Mancuso, and offers you a unique castlelike, elegant ambiance. Black-tie service and a kitchen that produces Northern Italian and French specialties with true artistry make dining here a gourmet's delight.

ORANGERIE   13

Arizona Biltmore Hotel
24th Street and Missouri
Phoenix, AZ
(602) 955-6600

Continental

F ★ ★ ★ ½
S ★ ★ ★ ½
A ★ ★ ★ ★
P ★ ★ ★ ★

Jacket and tie required
Valet and lot parking
All major credit cards
Full bar
Reservations recommended

Lunch: Daily 11:30AM-2:30PM
Dinner: Nightly 6:00PM-11:00PM

The royal treatment is yours to enjoy at Orangerie, where you will dine in splendor 'neath a canopy of green plants and crystal chandeliers. The quality wine list reflects this establishment's well-deserved reputation for superbly prepared and presented gourmet food.

THE OTHER PLACE   9

Smoke Tree Resort
7101 East Lincoln Drive
Scottsdale, AZ
(602) 948-7910

American

F ★ ★ ★ ½
S ★ ★ ★
A ★ ★ ★ ½
P ★ ★ ½

No dress restrictions
Valet (dinner only) and lot parking
All major credit cards
Full bar
Reservations not required

Lunch: Mon.-Fri. 11:00AM-3:00PM
Dinner: Mon.-Thurs. 5:00PM-10:30PM
         Fri. & Sat. 5:00PM-11:30PM
         Sun. 4:00PM-10:30PM

This friendly, relaxed restaurant with its Spanish style hacienda setting lures a loyal clientele with house specialties such as fresh fish dishes and succulent prime rib. Here you can cozy up to the fireplaces, or dine in spacious patios depending on the weather and your whim.

THE PALM COURT   4

Scottsdale Conference Resort
7700 East McCormick Parkway
Scottsdale, AZ
(602) 991-3400

French/Russian

F ★ ★ ★ ★
S ★ ★ ★ ★
A ★ ★ ★ ★
P ★ ★ ★ ★

Jacket and tie required
Valet parking
All major credit cards
Full bar
Reservations required

Dinner: Nightly 5:00PM-10:00PM

One of only 35 restaurants in the world to be honored with Cartier's "Elegance in Dining" Gold Plate Award, this gourmet dining room features superb cuisine prepared tableside with highly dramatic au flambé presentation. The extensive wine list includes domestic and imported fine vintages.

POINTE OF VIEW   5

The Pointe at Squaw Peak
7677 North 16th Street
Phoenix, AZ
(602) 997-2626

Continental

F ★ ★ ★
S ★ ★ ★
A ★ ★ ★
P ★ ★ ★

Good taste in dress required
Valet and lot parking
All major credit cards
Full bar
Reservations recommended

Dinner: Nightly 5:30PM-11:30PM

Low key Spanish/Mediterranean décor with cool white walls and blue tablecloths sets the stage for casually elegant dining here. The continental cuisine has innovative nouvelle touches.

RICK'S CAFÉ AMERICANA   3

8320 North Hayden Road
Scottsdale, AZ
(602) 991-2233

Continental

F ★ ★ ★ ½
S ★ ★ ★
A ★ ★ ★ ½
P ★ ★ ★

No dress restrictions
Valet parking
AE, DC, MC, V
Full bar
Reservations recommended

Lunch: Daily from 11:30AM
Dinner: Nightly from 5:00PM

Shades of Casablanca! This restaurant deserves an Oscar for its real life performance in a setting straight from Bogart's classic film. The menu features continental favorites.

TRUMP'S   2

Hotel Westcourt
10220 North Metro Parkway
Phoenix, AZ
(602) 997-5900

American/Continental

F ★ ★ ★
S ★ ★ ★
A ★ ★ ★
P ★ ★ ★

Good taste in dress required
Lot parking
All major credit cards
Full bar
Reservations recommended

Dinner: Sun.-Thurs. 6:30PM-10:00PM
           Fri. & Sat. 6:30PM-11:00PM

Blackened redfish, rack of lamb, and whole Maine lobsters are among the many entrées on the continental and American menu featured at this attractive eatery.

VICTOR'S   15

21 West Camelback Road
Phoenix, AZ
(602) 265-1091

Continental

F ★ ★ ★ ½
S ★ ★ ★
A ★ ★ ★
P ★ ★ ★

Good taste in dress required
Valet, lot, and street parking
AE, MC, V
Full bar
Reservations required

Lunch: Mon.-Fri. 11:30AM-2:30PM
Dinner: Mon.-Sat. 5:30PM-10:30PM
           Closed Sunday

Soft classical music filters through the rooms in this hospitable Spanish style adobe restaurant. The menu is a mélange of Northern Italian, Greek, continental, and American specialties.

VOLTAIRE   11

8340 East McDonald Drive
Scottsdale, AZ
(602) 948-1005

French

F ★ ★ ★ ½
S ★ ★ ★ ½
A ★ ★ ★ ½
P ★ ★ ★

Jacket required
Lot parking
AE, MC, V
Full bar
Reservations required

Dinner: Tues.-Sat. 5:30PM-10:00PM
           Closed Sunday and Monday,
           and closed during July, August,
           and September

Chef/owners Claude Boucaud and Michel Bache have created this sophisticated sanctuary for devotees of authentic French cooking. The atmosphere is friendly, the appointments perfection. Specialties range from a hearty soupe à l'oignon Parisienne to calf sweetbreads sautéed in lemon butter with capers.

Pittsburgh

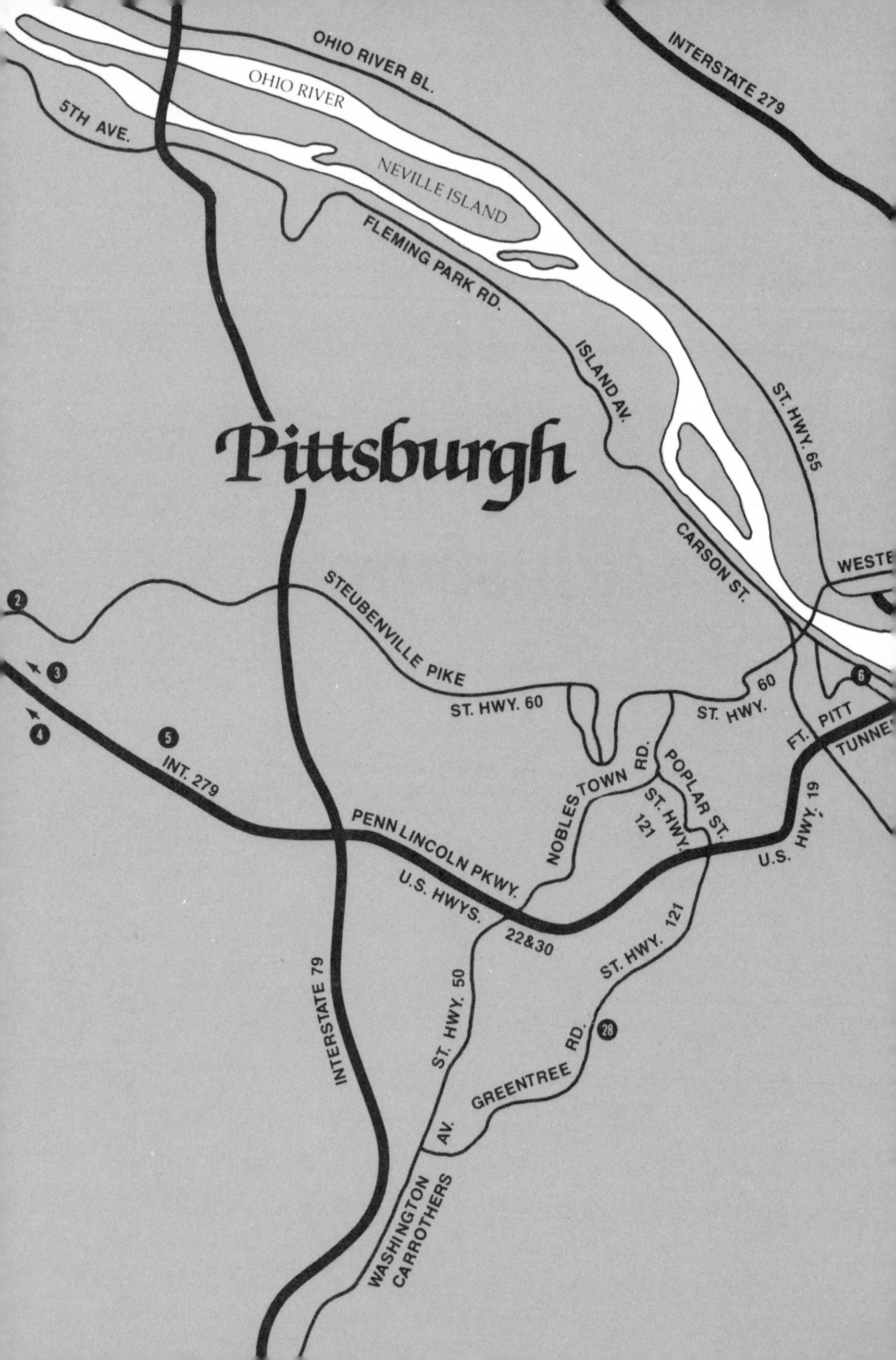

OHIO RIVER BL.
INTERSTATE 279
OHIO RIVER
5TH AVE.
NEVILLE ISLAND
FLEMING PARK RD.
ISLAND AV.
ST. HWY. 65
Pittsburgh
CARSON ST.
WESTE
STEUBENVILLE PIKE
2
3
4
5
6
ST. HWY. 60
60
ST. HWY.
FT. PITT
TUNNE
INT. 279
NOBLES TOWN RD.
POPLAR ST.
ST. HWY. 121
U.S. HWY. 19
PENN LINCOLN PKWY.
U.S. HWYS. 22&30
ST. HWY. 121
ST. HWY. 50
INTERSTATE 79
28
GREENTREE RD.
AV.
WASHINGTON
CARROTHERS

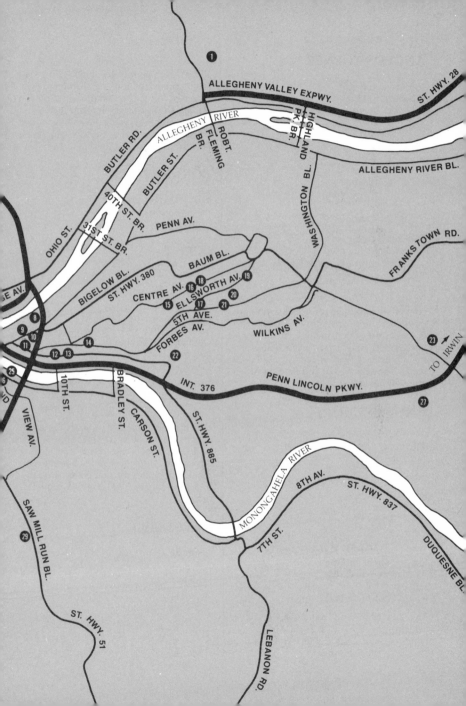

ANGEL'S CORNER 22

405 Atwood Street
Pittsburgh, PA
(412) 682-1879

Continental

F ★ ★ ★
S ★ ★ ★
A ★ ★ ★
P ★ ★ ½

Good taste in dress required
Lot parking
AE, MC, V
Full bar
Reservations required

Dinner: Mon.-Sat. 5:00PM-10:00PM
         Closed Sunday

Housed in a century-old corner church converted into a charming, elegantly appointed dining spot, this romantic restaurant offers continental cuisine prepared with only fresh ingredients. The menu changes twice a year. You'll find a well selected wine list and flaming Angel after-dinner coffees.

ARTHUR'S 13

209 Fourth Avenue
Pittsburgh, PA
(412) 566-1735

Continental

F ★ ★ ★ ½
S ★ ★ ★ ½
A ★ ★ ★ ½
P ★ ★ ½

Jacket required
Lot and street parking
All major credit cards
Full bar
Reservations required

Breakfast: Mon.-Sat. 7:00AM-9:30AM
Lunch: Mon.-Sat. 11:30AM-2:30PM
Dinner: Mon.-Sat. 5:30PM-11:30PM
         Closed Sunday

Sited in the oldest office building in the city, circa 1836, this delightful dining spot is comprised of four small rooms, each with two fireplaces, and rife with Colonial Williamsburg charm. Smoked meats and fish are highly acclaimed (smoking is done on the premises) as is the German Onion Beer soup.

BORN FREE 19

5899 Ellsworth Avenue
Pittsburgh, PA
(412) 362-1645

African

F ★ ★ ★
S ★ ★ ★
A ★ ★ ★
P ★ ★ ½

Good taste in dress required
Street parking
Credit cards not accepted
Full bar
Reservations required

Dinner: Tues.-Thurs. 5:00PM-11:00PM
         Fri. & Sat. 5:00PM-1:00AM
         Closed Sunday and Monday

This unique restaurant captures the unfettered spirit of the African continent with brilliant colors, African art, and stirring African music. The menu is based on regional specialties including entrées native to Mozambique, Ethiopia, and South Africa.

CHESTERFIELD'S 23

12119 Route 30, Irwin
Pittsburgh, PA
(412) 863-7450

American

F ★ ★ ★
S ★ ★ ★
A ★ ★ ½
P ★ ★

Good taste in dress required
Lot parking
All major credit cards
Full bar
Reservations not required

Lunch/
Dinner: Mon.-Sat. 11:00AM-1:00AM
Sun. 10:00AM-8:00PM

Warm brown tones backdrop classic English décor in this attractive traditional establishment with its clublike following of loyal devotees. Here you will experience dignified dining on generous portions of steaks, seafood, and prime rib, all properly embellished and pleasantly served. The ice cream torte is a favorite dessert.

CHRISTOPHER'S 6

1411 Grandview Avenue
Pittsburgh, PA
(412) 381-4500

Continental

F ★ ★ ★ ½
S ★ ★ ★
A ★ ★ ★
P ★ ★ ★

Jacket required
Valet parking
All major credit cards
Full bar
Reservations not required

Dinner: Mon.-Thurs. 5:00PM-11:00PM
Fri. & Sat. 5:00PM-12:00AM
Closed Sunday

This award winning restaurant pays tribute to the backbone industries upon which this city was founded. The décor blends steel, glass, aluminum, and a wall made of coal into a proud, elegant image. You'll find a glittering city view, strolling violins, and excellent continental cuisine featuring such specialties as Shrimp Barzac, rainbow trout stuffed with crab meat, and roast rack of lamb.

COLONY 28

Greentree & Cochran Roads
Pittsburgh, PA
(412) 561-2060

American

F ★ ★ ★ ★
S ★ ★ ★ ★
A ★ ★ ★ ½
P ★ ★ ★ ★

Jacket required
Valet parking
All major credit cards
Full bar
Reservations required on weekends, recommended on week days

Dinner: Mon.-Thurs. 5:00PM-10:30PM
Fri. & Sat. 5:00PM-11:00PM
Closed Sunday

Judged the local favorite for American cuisine, this sophisticated eatery has an open hearth grill for a focal point, jaunty fresh flowers, formal service, and pleasant piano music. Renowned for prime steaks, seafood specialties, and a great grilled veal T-bone. Fresh pastries and seasonal fruit are tempting finales.

THE COMMON PLEA 12 RESTAURANT

308 Ross Street
Pittsburgh, PA
(412) 281-5140

Continental

F ★ ★ ★
S ★ ★ ★ ★
A ★ ★ ★
P ★ ★ ★

Good taste in dress required
Lot and street parking
AE, MC, V
Full bar
Reservations not required

Lunch: Mon.-Fri. 11:30AM-2:30PM
Dinner: Mon.-Sat. 4:30PM-10:00PM
         Closed Sunday

For 15 years this restaurant has attracted its legal and political neighbors, Pittsburgh natives, and visiting businessmen with its award-winning food and superlative service. Seafood and veal dishes are house specialties; the homemade desserts sinfully delicious.

CROSS KEYS INN   1

599 Dorseyville Road
Pittsburgh, PA
(412) 963-8717

Continental

F ★ ★ ★
S ★ ★ ★
A ★ ★ ★ ½
P ★ ★ ½

No dress restrictions
Lot parking
MC, V
Full bar
Reservations not required

Lunch/
Dinner: Mon.-Fri. 11:30AM-10:00PM
         Sat. 5:00PM-11:00PM
         Sun. 4:00PM-9:00PM
Brunch: Sun. 11:00AM-2:30PM

This historic landmark was once a stagecoach stop, welcoming guests more than a century ago. Beautifully restored, you'll now find a cheerful, relaxing country inn ambiance, and an extensive continental menu including veal, pasta, seafood, and prime steaks.

DE FORO RESTAURANT   8

428 Forbes Avenue
Lawyers Building
Pittsburgh, PA
(412) 391-8873/391-8874

French/Italian

F ★ ★ ★ ½
S ★ ★ ★ ½
A ★ ★ ★
P ★ ★ ★

No dress restrictions
Lot parking
All major credit cards
Full bar
Reservations not required

Lunch: Mon.-Fri. 11:30AM-2:30PM
Dinner: Tues.-Sat. 5:30PM-10:30PM
         Closed Sunday

Distinguished cuisine prepared by French-trained chefs is the hallmark of this dining spot. The menu features French and Italian specialties with many veal dishes, Tournedos Rossini, and chateaubriand among the favorites offered. Daily seasonal chef's specialties might include whole sea bass, or poached fresh salmon.

GRAND CONCOURSE   25
RESTAURANT

One Station Square
Pittsburgh, PA
(412) 261-1717

Continental

F ★ ★ ★ ½
S ★ ★ ★ ½
A ★ ★ ★ ½
P ★ ★ ★

No dress restrictions
Lot parking
All major credit cards

Full bar
Reservations not required

Lunch: Mon.-Fri. 11:30AM-2:30PM
Dinner: Mon.-Thurs. 5:00PM-10:00PM
Fri. & Sat. 5:00PM-11:00PM
Sun. 5:00PM-9:00PM
Brunch: Sun. 10:00AM-2:30PM

Downtown Pittsburgh's rail terminal building is a fabulous historical landmark that has been restored to its former glory as a setting for this unique restaurant. Here you may dine on fresh seafood expressed in from North American waters, beef and poultry dishes, and a variety of dishes created with pastas made fresh daily.

HUGO'S ROTISSERIE 14

Hyatt Pittsburgh
Chatham Center
Pittsburgh, PA
(412) 471-1234

Continental

F ★ ★ ★
S ★ ★ ★
A ★ ★ ★
P ★ ★ ★

Good taste in dress required
Garage parking
All major credit cards
Full bar
Reservations recommended

Lunch: Mon.-Fri. 11:30AM-2:30PM
Dinner: Nightly 5:30PM-11:00PM
Brunch: Sun. 11:30AM-2:00PM

A favorite spot for Sunday brunch or quiet romantic dinners, this award-winner lets you watch your fowl or choice of meat cook to perfection on the spit, while you enjoy the seasonal bounty of the well stocked salad bar. Dessert is almost mandatory for the chocolate cheesecake topped with homemade truffles is in a class by itself.

HYEHOLDE RESTAURANT 4

190 Hyeholde Drive
Coraopolis, PA
(412) 264-3116

Continental

F ★ ★ ★ ½
S ★ ★ ★ ½
A ★ ★ ★ ★
P ★ ★ ★ ★

Good taste in dress required
Valet parking
All major credit cards
Full bar
Reservations required

Lunch: Mon.-Fri. 11:30AM-2:00PM
Dinner: Mon.-Sat. 5:00PM-10:00PM
Closed Sunday

Deemed one of the last of the great country inns, this bastion of gentility is famed for its lovingly assembled wine cellar, garden-grown flowers, and food prepared from scratch. Owners Patrick and Carol Foy present a well balanced menu brightened with changes in tune with the season. The merits of this unique establishment have received high acclaim.

JIMMY TSANG'S CHINESE 18 RESTAURANT

5700 Centre Avenue
Pittsburgh, PA
(412) 661-4226

Chinese

F ★ ★ ★
S ★ ★ ½
A ★ ★ ½
P ★ ★

Good taste in dress required
Lot and street parking
AE, MC, V
Full bar
Reservations required

Lunch/
Dinner: Mon.-Thurs. 11:30AM-10:00PM
           Fri. & Sat. 11:30AM-11:00PM
           Sun. 3:30PM-9:30PM

As Chinese as a fortune cookie, this beautiful Oriental dining spot prepares classic regional specialties such as E-Shon chicken, Peking duck, and honey shrimp; reflecting Shanghai, Cantonese, Mandarin, Hunan, and Szechwan cooking techniques and seasonings. The diverse menu offers choices to please every palate.

JOHNNY LOUNDERS   2

6380 Steubenville Pike (Rt. 60)
Pittsburgh, PA
(412) 787-5200

American

F ★ ★ ★ ½
S ★ ★ ★ ½
A ★ ★ ★ ½
P ★ ★ ★ ½

Jacket preferred
Lot parking
All major credit cards
Full bar
Reservations not required

Lunch/
Dinner: Daily 11:30AM-10:00PM

Here, owner John A. Lounder has created a westside haven for discriminating diners that has been winning accolades since 1970. The setting is elegant, the tableside service deftly done, and the veal, seafood, lobster, and steak specialties excellent. Flambé desserts are dramatic and delicious.

KABUKI   27

635 Brown Avenue
Turtle Creek, PA
(412) 823-0750

Japanese

F ★ ★ ★
S ★ ★ ★
A ★ ★ ★ ½
P ★ ★ ★

No dress restrictions
Lot parking
All major credit cards
Full bar
Reservations not required

Lunch: Mon.-Fri. 11:30AM-2:30PM
Dinner: Mon.-Sat. 5:00PM-10:00PM
           Closed Sunday

Experience the ritualistic feeling of dining in time-honored authentic Japanese style in the placid tatami room you will find here. The service is polite and quietly rendered. The menu includes sushi, shabu-shabu, and tempura; and introduces you to other less familiar foods and Oriental culinary techniques.

KLEIN'S   9

330 4th Avenue
Pittsburgh, PA
(412) 232-3312

Seafood

F ★ ★ ★
S ★ ★ ★
A ★ ★ ★
P ★ ★ ½

No dress restrictions
Lot parking
All major credit cards
Full bar
Reservations recommended

Lunch/
Dinner: Mon.-Fri. 11:00AM-10:00PM
           Sat. 4:30PM-10:00PM
           Closed Sunday

This vintage restaurant has been in business since the turn of the century and is a venerated Pittsburgh institution. The nautical décor adds extra zest to such entrées as imperial crab, shrimp, pan blackened redfish, and live Maine lobster. A haven for hearty eaters with a yen for well prepared fruits of the sea.

LA NORMANDE   16

5030 Centre Avenue
Pittsburgh, PA
(412) 621-0744

French

F ★ ★ ★ ★
S ★ ★ ★ ½
A ★ ★ ★ ½
P ★ ★ ★ ½

Jacket required
Valet parking
All major credit cards
Full bar
Reservations required

Dinner: Mon.-Thurs. 6:00PM-10:00PM
Fri. & Sat. 6:00PM-11:00PM
Closed Sunday

This much-honored restaurant turns the ritual of dining into a triumphant experience. Owner Reuben Katz welcomes guests into his world, where classical and modern French cuisine are creatively blended to produce a daily handwritten menu offering dishes of distinction. The list of French wines is exemplary.

LA PLUME   11

Westin William Penn Hotel
530 William Penn Place
Pittsburgh, PA
(412) 553-5065

Continental

F ★ ★ ★ ½
S ★ ★ ★
A ★ ★ ★
P ★ ★

No dress restrictions
Lot and street parking
AE, DC, MC, V

Full bar
Reservations not required

Lunch: Mon.-Fri. 11:00AM-2:00PM
Closed Saturday and Sunday

The main dining room of an historical landmark hotel, built in 1916, here you will be treated to an elegant ambiance, professional service, and quality continental cuisine. The menu offers beef, veal, chicken, and fresh seafood entrées; plus locally renowned Maurice Salad, and mouth-watering William Penn cheesecake.

LE MONT   24

1114 Grandview Avenue
Pittsburgh, PA
(412) 431-3100

Continental

F ★ ★ ★ ½
S ★ ★ ★ ½
A ★ ★ ★ ½
P ★ ★ ★ ½

Jacket required
Valet parking
All major credit cards
Full bar
Reservations required

Dinner: Nightly 5:00PM-11:00PM

A view site and thoughtful design (three glass walls and one all mirrored) affords every guest a panorama of the city's glittering lights. The setting is opulent, the service polished, and the continental cuisine prepared and presented with consummate skill.

LE PETIT CAFÉ   21

809 Bellefonte Street
Pittsburgh, PA
(412) 621-9000

French

F ★ ★ ★
S ★ ★ ★
A ★ ★ ★
P ★ ★ ★

Good taste in dress required
Lot and street parking
AE, MC, V
Full bar
Reservations required for 5 or more
on weekends

Lunch: Tues.-Sat. 11:30AM-4:00PM
Dinner: Tues.-Sat. 6:00PM-10:30PM
         Sun. 6:00PM-9:00PM
Brunch: Sun. 12:00PM-3:00PM

The décor is modern, but the mood is provencial French at this smart café where the daily changing menu is recited by the knowledgeable staff. The cuisine is strongly slanted toward nouvelle French, but the basic ingredients of each entrée are enhanced with culinary skill. Count on having dessert—the offerings are as good as they sound.

LOUIS TAMBELLINI'S 29

860 Saw Mill Run Boulevard
Pittsburgh, PA
(412) 481-1118

American

F ★ ★ ★ ½
S ★ ★ ★ ½
A ★ ★ ★
P ★ ★ ★

Good taste in dress required
Valet and lot parking
AE, MC, V
Full bar
Reservations not required

Lunch/
Dinner: Mon.-Sat. 11:30AM-12:00AM
         Closed Sunday

Seafood reigns supreme in this large, elegant restaurant, but you will also find classic Italian dishes, steaks, rack of lamb,

and a variety of veal entrées offered on the menu. Here the Tambellinis have orchestrated a dining experience that appeals to many tastes.

NINO'S 17

214 North Craig Street
Pittsburgh, PA
(412) 621-2700

Continental

F ★ ★ ★ ½
S ★ ★ ★
A ★ ★ ★
P ★ ★ ★

Jacket required
Valet parking
All major credit cards
Full bar
Reservations required

Lunch: Mon.-Sat. 11:30AM-3:00PM
Dinner: Mon.-Thurs. 5:00PM-10:00PM
         Fri. 5:00PM-11:00PM
         Sat. 5:00PM-12:00AM
         Closed Sunday

Reflecting a Mediterranean heritage feeling with handsome antiques creating a baroque atmosphere, this restaurant focuses on presenting fine cuisine with continental flair. Among the outstanding entrées you will find filet mignon with mushroom caps, Veal Romano, and Scallops Barsac ala Nino.

PARK SCHENLEY 15

3955 Dithridge Street
Pittsburgh, PA
(412) 681-0800

Continental

F ★ ★ ★
S ★ ★ ★
A ★ ★ ★
P ★ ★ ★

Jacket required
Valet parking
All major credit cards
Full bar
Reservations recommended

Lunch: Mon.-Sat. 11:00AM-3:00PM
Dinner: Mon. 5:00PM-10:00PM
Tues.-Sat. 5:00PM-11:00PM
Sun. 4:00PM-9:00PM

The décor is handsome and early '30s in Frank Blandi's renowned restaurant where he has been featuring French-accented continental specialties for nearly three decades. Here you can savor such comestibles as steak au poivre, crab meat almondine with lemon, and superb chateaubriand. Desserts are rich and innovative.

SGRO'S RESTAURANT   5

4400 Campbells Run Road
Pittsburgh, PA
(412) 787-1234

American

F ★ ★ ★ ½
S ★ ★ ★ ½
A ★ ★ ★
P ★ ★ ★ ½

Jacket required for dinner
Valet parking
All major credit cards
Full bar
Reservations not required

Lunch: Mon.-Sat. 11:30AM-2:30PM
Dinner: Mon.-Fri. 5:00PM-10:00PM
Sat. 5:00PM-10:30PM
Closed Sunday

This comfortable, family-owned restaurant with its interesting Spanish décor, overlooks a sylvan wooded setting. The kitchen's reputation has been built on uncompromising quality, and you'll find the eclectic menu offers you such choices as fish, lobster, steak, and lamb.

TIN ANGEL   26

1204 Grandview Avenue
Mt. Washington, PA
(412) 381-1919

American

F ★ ★ ★ ½
S ★ ★ ★
A ★ ★ ★
P ★ ★ ★ ★

Jacket and tie required
Lot parking
All major credit cards
Full bar
Reservations required

Dinner: Mon.-Sat. 6:00PM-11:00PM
Closed Sunday

From this elegant glassed-in room, diners have a birds-eye view of the Pittsburgh area and its dazzling light display. The service is formal and the cuisine imaginative. Tempting entrées include New York strip steak, lobster tail with drawn butter, and filet of sole baked in white wine.

TOP OF THE TRIANGLE   10

600 Grant Street, 62nd Floor
Pittsburgh, PA
(412) 471-4100

Continental

F ★ ★ ★
S ★ ★ ½
A ★ ★ ★
P ★ ★ ★

Jacket and tie preferred, no jeans
Lot parking
All major credit cards
Full bar
Reservations required

Lunch/
Dinner: Mon.-Fri. 11:30AM-10:00PM
Sat. 12:00PM-12:00AM
Closed Sunday

A cloud-high view of the city and surrounding countryside makes the 62-story elevator trip worthwhile. So does the extensive wine list, and the continental cuisine with chef's choice featured daily specials, and tableside preparation of many items.

UPSTAIRS AT BRENDAN'S   20

5505 Walnut Street
Pittsburgh, PA
(412) 683-5661/683-5662

Continental

F ★ ★ ★ ½
S ★ ★ ★
A ★ ★ ★
P ★ ★ ★ ½

Jacket required at dinner
Street parking
All major credit cards
Full bar
Reservations recommended

Lunch: Tues.-Sat. 11:30AM-2:30PM
Dinner: Tues.-Sat. 6:00PM-11:00PM
          Closed Sunday and Monday

The philosophy of this restaurant is "good eating is spoken here." You'll find an atmosphere that invites you to linger and indulge in good conversation, good food, and good wine. The continental cuisine is a symphony of epicurean delights reflecting high standards of culinary quality.

THE WINE RESTAURANT   7

One Oxford Centre
Grant Street
Pittsburgh, PA
(412) 288-9463

American

F ★ ★ ★
S ★ ★ ★
A ★ ★ ★
P ★ ★ ★

Good taste in dress required
Street parking
All major credit cards
Full bar
Reservations recommended

Lunch/
Dinner: Mon.-Thurs. 11:30AM-10:00PM
          Fri. & Sat. 11:30AM-12:00AM
          Closed Sunday

Sleekly modern high tech décor forms a suitable backdrop for the avant American cuisine you will find served here. You can sample wines of the world by the taste, glass, or bottle, and savor such extravagant entrées as spicy shrimp smothered with mushrooms, rack of lamb with green peppercorn sauce, and Southhampton duckling with black current sauce.

WOODEN ANGEL   3

West Bridgewater Street
Beaver, PA
(412) 774-7880

American

F ★ ★ ★ ½
S ★ ★ ★
A ★ ★ ★ ½
P ★ ★ ★

Jacket preferred
Lot parking
All major credit cards
Full bar
Reservations recommended

Dinner: Tues.-Sat. 5:00PM-11:00PM
          Closed Sunday & Monday

Owner/chef Alex Sebastian is a master of improvisation, and the menu he devises changes daily to accommodate seasonal plenty. Your waiter will first introduce you to innovative appetizers then describe the fresh fish, shellfish, veal, beef, lamb, and vegetable offerings of the day. Desserts are a house specialty and there is an all-American vintage wine list.

St. Louis

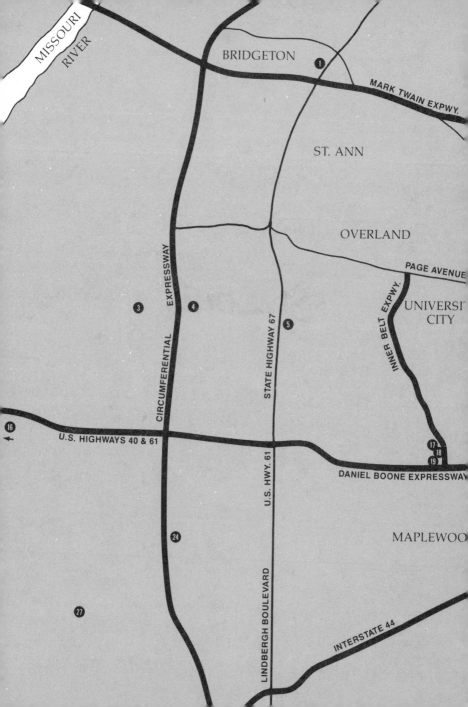

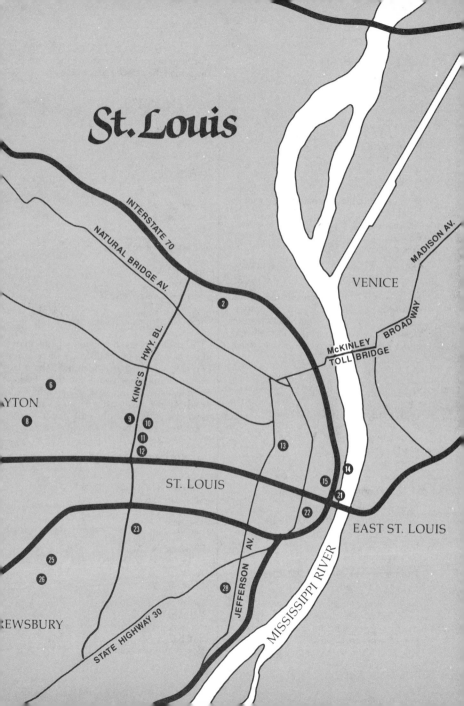

AL BAKER'S 18

8101 Clayton Road
St. Louis, MO
(314) 863-8878

Italian/Continental

F ★ ★ ★
S ★ ★ ★
A ★ ★ ★
P ★ ★ ★

Jacket required in the main dining room
Valet parking
All major credit cards
Full bar
Reservations recommended

Dinner: Mon.-Sat. 5:00PM-12:00AM
Closed Sunday

Host/owner Al Baker has created an aura of old-world elegance in his much-awarded restaurant. The house features fresh fish flown in from all over the world, and is renowned for its extensive wine list.

AL'S 21

1200 North Main Street
St. Louis, MO
(314) 421-6399

Italian/Continental

F ★ ★ ★ ½
S ★ ★ ★ ½
A ★ ★ ★ ½
P ★ ★ ★ ★

Jacket and tie required
Valet parking
MC, V
Full bar
Reservations not required

Dinner: Mon.-Sat. 5:00PM-12:00AM
Closed Sunday

At the same location for 60 years, you'll now find owner Albert Barroni carrying on the family tradition for dining excellence. Here the maitre d' presents the day's available meats and seafoods on a silver platter for your selection, describing the methods by which they can be prepared.

ANTHONY'S 15

10 South Broadway
St. Louis, MO
(314) 231-2434

French

F ★ ★ ★ ½
S ★ ★ ★ ½
A ★ ★ ★ ½
P ★ ★ ★ ½

Jacket and tie required
Valet parking
AE, MC, V
Full bar
Reservations required

Dinner: Mon.-Sat. 5:30PM-10:30PM
Closed Sunday

The sleek modern décor you will discover here is a perfect backdrop for the classic French cuisine that is featured. The à la carte menu gives you a choice of traditional dishes, fresh seafood, a variety of grilled meats, and entrées such as sweetbreads in light dill sauce with chanterelle mushrooms.

BENEDETTO'S 24

12240 East Manchester Road
St. Louis, MO
(314) 821-2555

Italian

F ★ ★ ★
S ★ ★ ★
A ★ ★ ★
P ★ ★ ½

Jacket and tie required
Lot parking
All major credit cards
Full bar
Reservations recommended

Dinner: Tues.-Sat. 4:00PM-11:00PM
Sun. 4:30PM-9:00PM
Closed Monday

This bright, light, and cheerful eatery couples handsome contemporary décor with crisp formal service to create a delightful dining experience. The menu offerings include pastas, beef, veal, and seafood entrées, and innovative specialties.

BOBBY'S CREOLE 6

6307 Delmar
St. Louis, MO
(314) 725-6985

Creole

F ★ ★ ★ ½
S ★ ★ ★
A ★ ★ ★
P ★ ★ ½

Good taste in dress required
Lot and street parking
MC, V
Full bar
Reservations not required

Dinner: Tues.-Thurs. 5:30PM-10:00PM
Fri. & Sat. 5:30PM-11:00PM
Closed Sunday and Monday

Bob and Barbara Suberi's restaurant specializes in fresh gulf seafood and authentic Creole/Cajun cuisine, served in a New Orleans-style dining room that opens up to a courtyard and bayou scene.

BRISTOL BAR & GRILL 4

11801 Olive Street Road
Creve Coeur, MO
(314) 567-0272

American

F ★ ★ ★ ½
S ★ ★ ★
A ★ ★ ★
P ★ ★ ½

No dress restrictions
Lot parking

All major credit cards
Full bar
Reservations not required

Lunch: Mon.-Sat. 11:00AM-2:30PM
Dinner: Mon.-Thurs. 5:00PM-11:00PM
Fri. & Sat. 5:00PM-12:00AM
Brunch: Sun. 10:00AM-3:00PM

As the name suggests, this restaurant has an English seacoast atmosphere, and specializes in live Maine lobsters and fresh seafood flown in daily from the Pacific, Atlantic, and Gulf coasts, prepared over mesquite wood broilers.

CAFÉ BALABAN 11

405 North Euclid
St. Louis, MO
(314) 361-8085

French/Continental

F ★ ★ ★ ½
S ★ ★ ★
A ★ ★ ★
P ★ ★ ★

No dress restrictions
Lot and street parking
AE, MC, V
Full bar
Reservations not required

Dinner: Mon.-Thurs. 6:00PM-10:40PM
Fri. & Sat. 6:00PM-11:15PM

Join the eclectic clientele enjoying relaxed dining in this cosmopolitan establishment with its turn-of-the-century ambiance. Beef Wellington, fresh fish, lobster, and veal sweetbreads are house specialties of the main dining room. The sidewalk café serves breakfast through after-theatre treats, and is open on Sunday.

CAFÉ DE FRANCE 22

410 Olive Street
St. Louis, MO
(314) 231-2204

French

```
F  ★ ★ ★ ★
S  ★ ★ ★ ★
A  ★ ★ ★ ★
P  ★ ★ ★ ★
```

Jacket and tie required
Valet parking
All major credit cards
Full bar
Reservations required

Lunch: Mon.-Fri. 11:30AM-2:00PM
Dinner: Mon.-Thurs. 5:30PM-10:30PM
         Fri. & Sat. 5:30PM-11:30PM
         Closed Sunday

French haute and nouvelle cuisine are presented in the grand manner by formally attired waiters in this classically elegant restaurant. You'll find three-course prix-fixe luncheons, and four-course gourmet dinners with five entrée and six dessert choices.

CHESHIRE INN   20

7036 Clayton Road
St. Louis, MO
(314) 647-7300

American

```
F  ★ ★ ★ ½
S  ★ ★ ★
A  ★ ★ ★ ½
P  ★ ★ ★
```

Good taste in dress required
Valet, lot, and garage parking
All major credit cards
Full bar
Reservations recommended

Lunch: Mon.-Fri. 11:00AM-3:00PM
         Sat. 11:30AM-3:00PM
Dinner: Mon.-Fri. 5:30PM-10:00PM
         Sat. 5:00PM-12:00AM
         Sun. 5:00PM-10:00PM
Brunch: Mon.-Fri. 7:00AM-10:00AM
         Sat. 7:30AM-11:30AM
         Sun. 8:30AM-2:00PM

Suits of armor, antiques, statues, and paintings add credence to the Merry Olde England pub atmosphere at this illustrious inn. Prime rib, veal, fresh seafood, and steaks share the honors on the bill of fare. For dessert you'll find great English trifle included in the offerings.

CHEZ LOUIS   11

26 North Meramec
St. Louis, MO
(314) 863-8400

French

```
F  ★ ★ ★ ★
S  ★ ★ ★ ½
A  ★ ★ ★ ½
P  ★ ★ ★
```

No dress restrictions
Valet parking
All major credit cards
Full bar
Reservations not required

Lunch: Mon.-Fri. 11:30AM-2:00PM
Dinner: Mon.-Sat. 6:00PM-11:00PM
         Closed Sunday

With the mien of a chic Parisian bistro, Bernard Douteau's contemporary eatery is graced with a marvelous collection of artwork and posters. The menu changes weekly and is built around creative cuisine utilizing fresh ingredients. The wine list complements the food and includes more than 100 labels.

CUNETTO HOUSE   26
OF PASTA

5453 Magnolia Avenue
St. Louis, MO
(314) 781-1135

Italian

```
F  ★ ★ ★ ½
S  ★ ★ ★
A  ★ ★
P  ★ ★
```

Good taste in dress required
Lot and street parking
All major credit cards
Full bar
Reservations not required

Lunch: Mon.-Thurs. 11:00AM-2:00PM
Dinner: Mon.-Thurs. 5:00PM-10:30PM
         Fri. & Sat. 5:00PM-12:00AM
         Closed Sunday

Owners Vincent J. and Frank C. Cunetto make you feel very much at home in their establishment, with its pleasant turn-of-the-century décor. The menu consists of 25 pasta dishes including gourmet veal, chicken, steak, and fish entrées. Linguini Tutto Mare is a favored specialty of the house.

DOMINIC'S   23

5101 Wilson Avenue
St. Louis, MO
(314) 771-1632

Italian

F ★ ★ ★ ½
S ★ ★ ★ ½
A ★ ★ ★ ½
P ★ ★ ★ ½

Jacket and tie required
Valet parking
All major credit cards
Full bar
Reservations required

Dinner: Tues.-Thurs. 5:00PM-11:00PM
         Fri. & Sat. 5:00PM-12:00AM
         Closed Sunday

Mr. & Mrs. Giovanni D. Galati have created this award-winning restaurant that sets high standards for the preparation and formal presentation of fine Italian cuisine. Luxurious décor and tableside service accent the excellence of the veal, lamb, homemade pastas, fresh vegetables, and homemade desserts that are yours to savor here.

FIO'S LA FOURCHETTE   17

1013 South Brentwood Boulevard
St. Louis, MO
(314) 863-6866

French

F ★ ★ ★ ½
S ★ ★ ★
A ★ ★ ½
P ★ ★ ★

Good taste in dress required
Lot parking
AE, MC, V
Full bar
Reservations recommended

Dinner: Mon.-Sat. 6:00PM-11:00PM
         Closed Sunday

Open, airy, and very contemporary with lush tropical plants and pale peach walls, this new entry into the St. Louis French restaurant scene features formal service and nouvelle haute cuisine. Such imaginative touches as onion soup served in a jumbo, hollowed-out onion are earning rave reviews.

GIOVANNI'S   12
ON THE HILL

5201 Shaw Avenue
St. Louis, MO
(314) 772-5958

Italian

F ★ ★ ★ ½
S ★ ★ ★ ½
A ★ ★ ½
P ★ ★ ★

Jacket and tie required
Valet parking
AE, DC, MC, V
Full bar
Reservations required

Dinner: Tues.-Sat. 5:30PM-11:00PM
         Closed Sunday and Monday

Giovanni Gabriele brings a new sense of sophistication to Italian cuisine in his beautifully designed, intimate restaurant. The recipient of many honors, the food served here is primarily Northern Italian, but each dish has its own innovative flair. Homemade pastas, veal dishes, and a daily fresh fish entrée are featured.

HACK'S TENDERLOIN ROOM 9

212 North Kings Highway
St. Louis, MO
(314) 361-1414

American

F ★ ★ ★ ½
S ★ ★ ★ ½
A ★ ★ ★ ½
P ★ ★ ★

Jacket required after 5:00PM
Valet parking
AE, DC, MC, V
Full bar
Reservations recommended

Lunch:　Mon.-Fri. 11:30AM-2:00PM
Dinner:　Mon.-Fri. 5:30PM-10:30PM
　　　　　Sat. 5:30PM-12:00AM
　　　　　Sun. 5:30PM-10:30PM

Here you'll be greeted by Maître d' "Hack" Ulrich, and seated in the midst of intimately lit Victorian elegance. Select your entrée from such house specialties as charcoal grilled prime cut steaks, Maine lobster, and fresh seafoods. The wine list is extensive and there's a dessert cart filled with irresistible goodies.

HANNEGAN'S 14

719 North 2nd
St. Louis, MO
(314) 241-8877

Continental

F ★ ★ ★
S ★ ★ ★ ½
A ★ ★ ★ ½
P ★ ★ ½

No dress restrictions
Lot and street parking
AE, MC, V
Full bar
Reservations not required

Lunch/
Dinner:　Mon.-Sat. 11:00AM-1:00AM
　　　　　Sun. 12:00PM-12:00AM

This politically oriented restaurant replicates a Senate dining room of the '30s, and has a decidedly masculine feeling. Stuffed double-rib pork chops are the house specialty, other highly touted entrées include veal Marsala, shrimp scampi, steaks, and Alaskan crab legs.

HENRY VIII 1

4690 North Lindbergh Boulevard
Bridgeton, MO
(314) 731-4888

American

F ★ ★ ★
S ★ ★ ★
A ★ ★ ★
P ★ ★ ★

Good taste in dress required
Lot parking
All major credit cards
Full bar
Reservations recommended

Breakfast/
Lunch/
Dinner:　Daily 6:00AM-11:00PM

This award-winning establishment honors its namesake with décor and paintings. The wine list is choice and the food is hearty. Prime rib, steak, and fresh seafood are mainstays of the bill of fare. Flambé desserts are featured, served tableside with proper flair.

JOHN MINEO'S 27

13490 Clayton Road
St. Louis, MO
(314) 434-5244

Italian

F ★ ★ ★ ½
S ★ ★ ★
A ★ ★ ★
P ★ ★ ★

Jacket required
Lot parking
Credit cards not accepted
Full bar
Reservations required

Dinner: Tues.-Sat. 5:00PM-12:00AM
          Closed Sunday and Monday

In a setting resplendent with crystal chandeliers, statuary, and oil paintings, owner John Mineo offers you warm hospitality, tableside service, and marvelous Northern Italian food. You'll find a variety of pastas, and such dishes as Veal Alla Panna and Filet Trifolato.

KEMOLL'S 2

4201 North Grand
St. Louis, MO
(314) 534-2705

Italian

F ★ ★ ★ ½
S ★ ★ ★ ½
A ★ ★ ½
P ★ ★ ★

Jacket preferred
Valet and lot parking
All major credit cards
Full bar
Reservations required

Lunch/
Dinner: Mon.-Sat. 11:15AM-10:00PM
          Closed Sunday

Opened in 1927, this long-time favorite of Italian food lovers is now run by 4th generation Kemoll family members. The tradition for using only fresh ingredients, preparing all food on the premises, and providing friendly service continue to draw plaudits from a loyal clientele.

LE BISTRO 16

14430 South Outer Road
Chesterfield, MO
(314) 434-3133

French

F ★ ★ ★ ★
S ★ ★ ★ ½
A ★ ★ ★
P ★ ★ ★ ½

Jacket required
Lot parking
AE, MC, V
Full bar
Reservations recommended

Dinner: Mon.-Sat. 5:00PM-10:30PM
          Closed Sunday

An adventure in dining awaits you at Gilbert and Simone Andujar's elegant restaurant, where their Marseille origin is much in evidence. You'll find such delights featured as wild game in season, filet of salmon with sorrel sauce, Canard a l'Abricot, bouillabaisse (southern French style), and Chocolate and Grand Marnier soufflé.

PORT ST. LOUIS 8

15 North Central Avenue
St. Louis, MO
(314) 727-1142

Seafood

F ★ ★ ★ ½
S ★ ★ ★ ½
A ★ ★ ★ ½
P ★ ★ ★ ½

Jacket preferred
Valet parking
All major credit cards
Full bar
Reservations recommended

Dinner: Nightly 5:00PM-12:00AM

For two and a half decades this delightful Victorian restaurant has been offering fastidious diners fresh fish and seafood flown in daily from all over the world. The ever-changing menu is augmented with prime steaks.

RICHARD PERRY   28

3265 South Jefferson Avenue
St. Louis, MO
(314) 771-4100

American

F ★ ★ ★ ½
S ★ ★ ★
A ★ ★ ★
P ★ ★ ★ ½

Good taste in dress required
Valet and street parking
All major credit cards
Full bar
Reservations recommended

Lunch: Mon.-Fri. 11:30AM-2:00PM
Dinner: Sun.-Thurs. 6:00PM-10:00PM
          Fri. & Sat. 6:00PM-12:00AM
Brunch: Sun. 10:00AM-2:00PM

Owner Richard Perry has transformed a turn-of-the-century Victorian building into a small restaurant with great charm where you can savor such delicacies as sole stuffed with lobster mousse with green herb sauce, and grilled lamb chops basted with red currant sauce.

TONY'S   8

826 North Broadway
St. Louis, MO
(314) 231-7007

Italian/Continental

F ★ ★ ★ ★
S ★ ★ ★ ★
A ★ ★ ★ ★
P ★ ★ ★ ½

Jacket required, tie preferred
Valet parking
All major credit cards
Full bar
Reservations not required

Dinner: Tues.-Sat. 5:00PM-12:00AM
          Closed Sunday and Monday

Established in 1948, this restaurant has earned distinguished awards repeatedly, and is a much-loved St. Louis dining "institution." Fresh seafood, prime veal, and prime beef are featured, and there is a full wine cellar. The tableside service is courteous and adroit; the food consistently of the highest quality.

WADE'S   5
A GATHERING PLACE

611 North Lindbergh
St. Louis, MO
(314) 997-5151

American

F ★ ★ ★
S ★ ★ ★ ½
A ★ ★ ★
P ★ ★ ★

Jacket required
Valet parking
All major credit cards
Full bar
Reservations recommended

Dinner: Mon.-Sat. 5:00PM-11:00PM
          Sun. 4:30PM-10:00PM

Step into the light, airy atmosphere of this greenhouse dining room, and enjoy the casual beauty of the verdant foliage canopy formed by hanging plants. Steakhouse food highlights the menu, with steak, seafood, chicken, and veal offered.

Salt Lake City

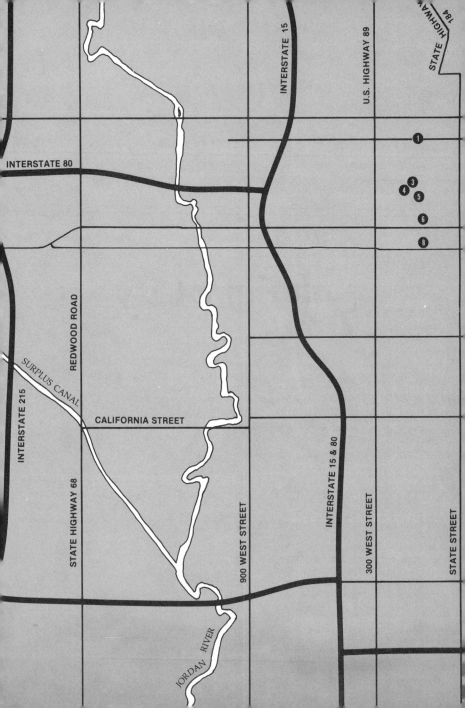

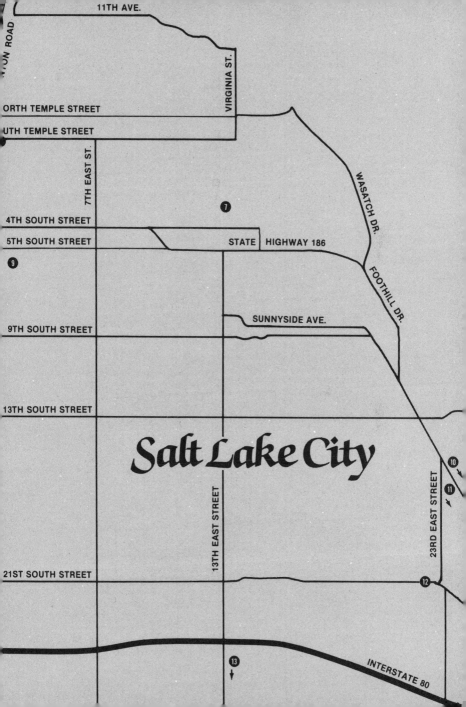

BENIHANA OF TOKYO 4

Arrow Press Square
165 South West Temple Street
Salt Lake City, UT
(801) 322-2421

Japanese

F ★ ★ ★
S ★ ★ ★
A ★ ★ ★ ½
P ★ ★ ★

Good taste in dress required
Lot parking
All major credit cards
Full bar
Reservations recommended

Lunch: Mon.-Fri. 11:30AM-2:00PM
Dinner: Mon.-Thurs. 5:30PM-10:30PM
Fri. & Sat. 5:30PM-11:30PM
Sun. 5:00PM-10:00PM

Deft as a surgeon, your skillful chef performs nimbly with knife and cleaver, transforming myriad ingredients into tempting morsels served sizzling from the hibachi at this authentic Japanese eatery. The décor is delightful, and you might nibble blissfully on lobster tails, steak, chicken, or shrimp.

THE HEATHER 13

6200 South Holliday Boulevard
Salt Lake City, UT
(801) 272-4468

Continental

F ★ ★ ★
S ★ ★ ★
A ★ ★ ★ ½
P ★ ★ ½

No dress restrictions
Lot parking
AE, MC, V
Full bar
Reservations required

Lunch: Tues.-Sat. 11:30AM-3:30PM
Dinner: Tues.-Thurs. 5:30PM-10:00PM
Fri. & Sat. 5:30PM-11:00PM
Brunch: Sun. 10:30AM-4:30PM
Closed Monday

Patterned after a Scottish hunting lodge, you'll find priceless paintings, fine antiques, and Highland bagpipers and dancers adding to your pleasure here. The cuisine is continental, but Scottish touches can often be discerned. 'Tis a bonnie place to bide a wee.

HIBACHI TEPPAN-YAKI, 2 SUKI-YAKI HOUSE

238 East South Temple
Salt Lake City, UT
(801) 364-5456

Japanese

F ★ ★ ★
S ★ ★ ★
A ★ ★ ★
P ★ ★ ★

Good taste in dress required
Valet parking
AE, DC, MC, V
Full bar
Reservations required

Dinner: Mon.-Sat. 6:00PM-10:30PM
Closed Sunday

The name of this restaurant summarizes beautifully what you will find here. The décor is artful, understated, and graced with splendid examples of Japanese art. Hibachi-style cooking produces a bevy of enticing entrées featuring chicken, beef, and seafood prepared in different but traditional ways.

LA CAILLE AT QUAIL RUN 11

9565 Wasatch Boulevard
Salt Lake City, UT
(801) 942-1751

French

F ★ ★ ★ ½
S ★ ★ ★
A ★ ★ ★ ½
P ★ ★ ★ ★

No dress restrictions
Valet parking
All major credit cards
Full bar
Reservations required

Dinner: Nightly 6:00PM-10:00PM
Brunch: Sun. 10:00AM-1:00PM

Leave your cares behind you and enter the magic world of this 18th century French chateau with its magnificent garden setting, and antique enhanced interior. The country French cuisine is prepared with great finesse and includes an interesting array of enticing entrées including duck, lamb, and veal specialties.

LA FLEUR DE LYS   3

165 South West Temple
Salt Lake City, UT
(801) 359-5753

French

F ★ ★ ★
S ★ ★ ★
A ★ ★ ★ ★
P ★ ★ ★

No dress restrictions
Lot and street parking
All major credit cards
Full bar
Reservations recommended

Dinner: Nightly 5:30PM-10:00PM

Meticulously decorated in 18th century splendor, this family operated restaurant is beautifully appointed and run with pride and care. The French fare produced by chef Roman Gales is presented with flourish on Royal Doulton china; in fact every detail combines to make dining here a special affair.

LOG HAVEN   10

Wasatch Boulevard and 3800 South
Salt Lake City, UT
(801) 272-8255

American

F ★ ★ ★
S ★ ★ ★
A ★ ★ ★
P ★ ★ ★

Good taste in dress required
Valet parking
All major credit cards
Full bar
Reservations required

Dinner: Wed.-Sat. 6:00PM-10:00PM
Brunch: Sun. 9:00AM-2:00PM
          Closed Monday & Tuesday

This sylvan sanctuary occupies a rustic log cabin mansion surrounded by 40 acres of private land with a view of Millcreek Canyon. Here you will discover a beautifully appointed dining room with formal service featuring a menu including prime rib, steaks, live Maine lobster, baked stuffed shrimp, "catch of the day," Millcreek mud pie, and baked Alaska.

MARKET STREET BROILER   7

260 South 1300 East
Salt Lake City, UT
(801) 583-8808

Seafood

F ★ ★ ★
S ★ ★ ★
A ★ ★ ½
P ★ ½

No dress restrictions
Lot and street parking
AE, MC, V
Spirits/Wine available for purchase
Reservations not required

Lunch: Mon.-Sat. 11:30AM-2:30PM
Dinner: Mon.-Fri. 5:00PM-10:00PM
          Sat. 5:00PM-10:30PM
          Sun. 4:00PM-9:00PM

This refurbished fire station is dedicated to a new kind of fire: mesquite coals. In a pristine white interior with a casual ambiance you'll find dining room, patio, and counter service and a menu that includes fresh fish and seafood flown in daily from around the world, barbecued ribs, clam chowder, sandwiches, salads, and luscious desserts made in house.

MARKET STREET GRILL   6

50 Post Office Place
Salt Lake City, UT
(801) 322-4668

American

F ★ ★ ★
S ★ ★ ★
A ★ ★ ½
P ★ ½

No dress restrictions
Lot and street parking
AE, MC, V
Spirits/Wine available for purchase
Reservations not required

Breakfast: Mon.-Fri. 6:30AM-11:30AM
           Sat. 7:30AM-11:00AM
Lunch: Mon.-Sat. 11:30AM-3:30PM
Dinner: Nightly from 4:00PM
Brunch: Sun. 9:30AM-3:30PM

Patterned after old-time grills with chefs in white and aproned waiters, you'll feel you've returned to days of yore when you visit here. The menu features fish and seafood flown in fresh from all over the world, but prime rib, chicken, chops, steaks, and pastas are also available. There's a special children's menu, and premise-made desserts galore.

MIKADO   5

67 West 1st South
Salt Lake City, UT
(801) 328-0929

Japanese

F ★ ★ ★
S ★ ★ ★
A ★ ★ ★ ★
P ★ ★ ★

No dress restrictions
Street parking
All major credit cards
Spirits/Wine available for purchase
Reservations required

Dinner: Mon.-Thurs. 6:00PM-9:30PM
          Fri. & Sat. 6:00PM-10:30PM
          Closed Sunday

Here you'll find owner Jerry Tsuyuki has staged an enchanting and authentic setting for the Japanese enticements he offers. Dine in the privacy of your own Zashiki room, on such delights as shrimp tempura, steak teriyaki, crab Mikado, plus a host of other traditional dishes.

RINO'S ITALIAN   12
RISTORANTE

2302 Parley's Way
Salt Lake City, UT
(801) 466-4614

Italian/Continental

F ★ ★ ★ ½
S ★ ★ ★
A ★ ★ ★
P ★ ★ ★

Good taste in dress required
Lot parking
AE, MC, V
Full bar
Reservations required

Dinner: Sun.-Thurs. 6:00PM-10:00PM
          Fri. & Sat. 5:30PM-10:30PM

Elegant dining in the tradition of old world splendor awaits you when you visit Rino Di Meo's handsome establishment. The menu is broad, offering you such choices as Tournedos Oscar, Beef Wellington, rack of lamb, milk fed veal, shrimp, lobster, linguine with seafood, fettuccine carbonara, cannelloni, and ravioli.

RISTORANTE DELLA FONTANA   9

336 South 4th East
Salt Lake City, UT
(801) 328-4243

Italian

F ★ ★ ★
S ★ ★ ★
A ★ ★ ★
P ★ ★

Good taste in dress required
Lot parking
All major credit cards
Spirits/Wine available for purchase
Reservations not required

Lunch/
Dinner: Mon.-Sat. 11:30AM-10:00PM
          Closed Sunday

A church with beautiful stained glass windows has been converted into this charming dining spot that features a waterfall cascading from the ceiling. Three-course luncheons, and six-course dinners are served, with a melding of Italian and American dishes featured. Casseroles are popular specialties of the house.

THE ROOF   1

Hotel Utah
South Temple & Main Streets
Salt Lake City, UT
(801) 531-1000

Continental

F ★ ★ ★ ½
S ★ ★ ★ ½
A ★ ★ ★ ½
P ★ ★ ★ ½

Good taste in dress required
Lot parking
All major credit cards
Spirits/Wine available for purchase
Reservations recommended

Lunch: Mon.-Fri. 12:00PM-2:00PM
Dinner: Nightly 6:00PM-10:30PM

This smart, cosmopolitan restaurant overlooks the Mormon Temple square. You'll find formal service, an air of understated elegance, and fine continental cuisine featuring entrées such as Veal Marsala, and fresh filets of salmon baked with white wine and dill butter, or poached with Hollandaise. Don't overlook the pastry cart—it's laden with goodies.

TOWNE HALL   8

Hilton Hotel
150 West 500 South Street
Salt Lake City, UT
(801) 532-3344

American

F ★ ★ ★
S ★ ★ ★
A ★ ★ ★
P ★ ★ ½

Good taste in dress required
Valet parking
All major credit cards
Spirits/Wine available for purchase
Reservations recommended

Buffet/
Lunch: Mon.-Sat. 11:30AM-2:00PM
Dinner: Mon.-Sat. 5:00PM-11:00PM
          Closed Sunday

On the agenda here is casually elegant dining by candlelight, with formal service and an expansive menu. Favored entrées include New York steak, lobster tails, fresh pastas, excellent salads, and Steak Diane (cooked and served tableside). Premise-baked desserts include cheesecake and fresh fruit cakes. The buffet luncheon offers a wide range of savory enticements and is as popular with locals as it is with hotel guests.

San Diego

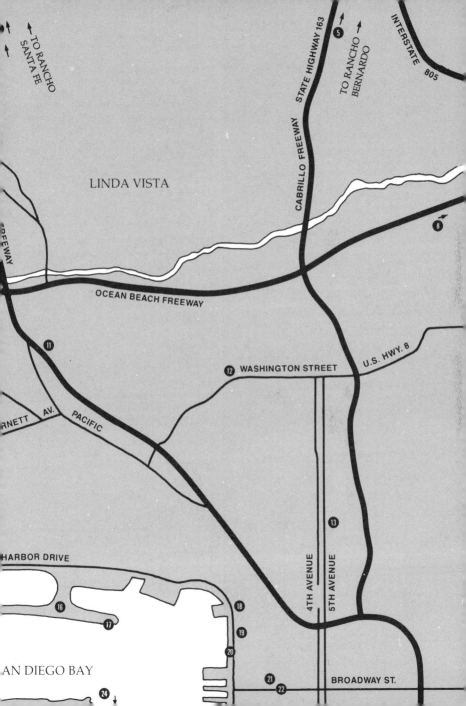

ANTHONY'S STAR OF THE SEA ROOM   20

1360 Harbor Drive
San Diego, CA
(619) 232-7408

Seafood

F ★ ★ ★ ½
S ★ ★ ★ ½
A ★ ★ ★
P ★ ★ ★ ½

Jacket and tie required
Street parking
AE, MC, V
Full bar
Reservations required

Dinner: Nightly 5:30PM-10:30PM

Locals and tourists cherish this handsome eatery with its elegant décor and glorious bay view. All varieties of seafood are featured here, with emphasis on local catches. The food preparation has gourmet flourish and the flaming cart service can be spectacular.

ATLANTIS RESTAURANT   7

2595 Ingraham Street
San Diego, CA
(619) 226-3888

Continental

F ★ ★ ★ ½
S ★ ★ ★ ½
A ★ ★ ★
P ★ ★ ★

No dress restrictions
Valet and lot parking
All major credit cards
Full bar
Reservations recommended

Lunch/
Dinner: Mon.-Thurs. 11:30AM-10:00PM
         Fri.-Sun. 11:30AM-11:00PM

Set in the midst of aquatic ponds at the water's edge, this restaurant is an imaginative tribute to the lost continent of Atlantis. The fruits of the sea are featured, together with beef, veal, poultry, salads, and other enticing entrées.

AVANTI'S   1

875 Prospect Street
La Jolla, CA
(619) 454-4288

Italian/Continental

F ★ ★ ★ ½
S ★ ★ ★
A ★ ★ ★
P ★ ★ ★

Good taste in dress required
Garage parking
AE, MC, V
Full bar
Reservations not required

Lunch: Mon.-Fri. 11:30AM-3:00PM
Dinner: Nightly 5:30PM-10:30PM

Art déco, and all sleek, shine, and sparkle, this restaurant offers bright banks of flowers, formal table service, and a menu with specialties such as paella, Osso Buco Milanese, and zabaglione.

BACI'S   3

1955 Morena Boulevard
San Diego, CA
(619) 275-2094

Italian

F ★ ★ ★
S ★ ★ ★
A ★ ★ ★
P ★ ★ ★

Good taste in dress required
Valet parking
All major credit cards
Full bar
Reservations recommended

Lunch: Mon.-Fri. 11:30AM-2:30PM
Dinner: Mon.-Sat. 5:30PM-10:00PM
Closed Sunday

Homemade pasta, scampi, lobster filet, and veal dishes lure lovers of Northern Italian cuisine to this intimate restaurant with its candle light, soft music and quiet air of romantic elegance.

BOAT HOUSE 15

2040 Harbor Island Drive
San Diego, CA
(619) 291-8010

American

F ★ ★ ★
S ★ ★ ★
A ★ ★ ★
P ★ ★ ★

No dress restrictions
Lot parking
AE, MC, V
Full bar
Reservations recommended

Lunch: Mon.-Sat. 11:30AM-2:30PM
Dinner: Mon.-Thurs. 5:30PM-10:30PM
Fri. & Sat. 5:00PM-11:00PM
Sun. 5:00PM-10:30PM
Brunch: Sun. 10:00AM-2:30PM

Combination dinners mating fresh seafood (prepared every way imaginable) and red meats are specialties of this neat, nautical establishment. The menu is inventive, and the service above par.

CAFÉ PACIFICA 11

2414 San Diego Avenue
San Diego, CA
(619) 291-6666

Seafood

F ★ ★ ★
S ★ ★ ★
A ★ ★ ★
P ★ ★ ★

Good taste in dress required
Valet, lot, and street parking
All major credit cards
Beer/Wine
Reservations recommended

Lunch: Mon.-Fri. 11:30AM-2:30PM
Dinner: Nightly 6:00PM-10:00PM

Twinkling lights and their mirrored reflections create a casually elegant setting for the presentation of fresh seafood in this popular eatery. You'll find a vast array of entrée choices, and cooking techniques.

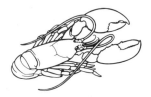

DI CANTI 1

5721 La Jolla Boulevard
La Jolla, CA
(619) 454-1177

Italian

F ★ ★ ★ ½
S ★ ★ ★ ½
A ★ ★ ★
P ★ ★ ★ ★

Jacket required
Lot and street parking
All major credit cards
Full bar
Reservations required

Dinner: Nightly 5:30PM-11:30PM

Owner Joe Cantisani makes frequent trips to Italy, bringing back new recipes that keep the menu fresh and contemporary. For example, you'll find a unique Scalone Adriana (scallops and abalone with lemon butter, capers, and white wine) among the house specialties. The atmosphere is warm and caring; the service pleasant and adroit.

DOBSON'S BAR &   22
RESTAURANT

956 Second Avenue
San Diego, CA
(619) 231-6771

Continental

F ★ ★ ★
S ★ ★ ★
A ★ ★ ★
P ★ ★ ★

Good taste in dress required
Garage parking
AE, MC, V
Full bar
Reservations recommended

Lunch: Mon.-Fri. 11:30AM-3:00PM
Dinner: Mon.-Thurs. 5:30PM-10:00PM
         Fri. & Sat. 5:30PM-12:00AM
         Closed Sunday

This restored turn-of-the-century pub has
an open kitchen and a warm, clubby ambiance. International and seafood
specialties are prepared under the guidance of chef Craig Brown. The menu
changes daily; veal, fresh fish, and poultry
are the mainstays.

EL BIZOCHO ROOM   5

Rancho Bernardo Inn
17550 Bernardo Oaks Drive
San Diego, CA
(619) 487-1611

French

F ★ ★ ★ ½
S ★ ★ ★
A ★ ★ ★
P ★ ★ ★

Jacket required
Valet and lot parking
All major credit cards
Full bar
Reservations required

Dinner: Sun.-Thurs. 6:00PM-10:00PM
          Fri. & Sat. 6:00PM-10:30PM

This early California ranch style room
overlooking the golf course has a welcoming air of ageless splendor. There is an
exemplary wine list, and superbly prepared and presented specialties such as
roasted duckling with green peppercorns,
tournedos au Zinfandel, and lobster salad
with asparagus.

EL CHALAN   1

5621 La Jolla Boulevard
La Jolla, CA
(619) 459-7707

Peruvian

F ★ ★ ★ ½
S ★ ★ ★
A ★ ★ ★
P ★ ★ ½

Good taste in dress required
Street parking
AE, MC, V
Full bar
Reservations not required

Dinner: Sun.-Thurs. 5:30PM-10:00PM
          Fri. & Sat. 5:30PM-11:00PM

Resembling a fine restaurant in Lima,
Peru, this establishment is decorated with
red tablecloths, alpaca rugs, and Inca
paintings. Here you can sample Peruvian
appetizers and Peru's national drink, a
Pisco sour. You'll find a choice of beef,
seafood, lamb, and chicken dishes, including the chef's specialty, pescado El
Chalan (fresh fish with a scallop, clam,
and shrimp sauce topping).

EL CRAB CATCHER   1

1298 Prospect Street
La Jolla, CA
(619) 454-9587

Seafood

F ★ ★ ★ ½
S ★ ★ ½
A ★ ★ ★
P ★ ★ ★

Good taste in dress required
Garage parking
AE, MC, V
Full bar
Reservations recommended

Lunch: Mon.-Sat. 11:30AM-3:00PM
Dinner: Mon.-Thurs. 5:30PM-10:00PM
          Fri. & Sat. 5:30PM-11:00PM
Brunch: Sun. 10:30AM-3:00PM

A dazzling view, patio dining, and great food are the main attractions at this Hawaiian transplant. You'll find five to six different fresh fish offered daily plus sautéed scampi, king crab, and a host of other savory seafood dishes.

ELARIO'S RESTAURANT   1

Summer House Inn
7955 La Jolla Shores Drive
La Jolla, CA
(619) 459-0261

French

F ★ ★ ★ ½
S ★ ★ ★ ½
A ★ ★ ★ ★
P ★ ★ ★ ½

Jacket and tie preferred
Lot parking
All major credit cards
Full bar
Reservations recommended

Breakfast: Daily 7:00AM-11:00AM
Lunch: Daily 11:30AM-2:00PM
Dinner: Nightly 6:00PM-10:30PM

A sweeping view of the Pacific shoreline entrances guests at this cosmopolitan restaurant. The French cuisine is prepared in the nouvelle manner and features daily specials and innovative entrées. The award-winning wine list has both depth and stature.

GUSTAF ANDERS   1

2182 Avenida de la Playa
La Jolla Shores, CA
(619) 459-4499

Continental

F ★ ★ ★ ½
S ★ ★ ★ ½
A ★ ★ ★
P ★ ★ ★ ★

Jacket required
Street parking
AE, MC, V
Full bar
Reservations required

Lunch/
Dinner: Daily 11:00AM-12:00AM

You'll always find something new at this lovely local favorite. There is an ever-changing art show, and a spontaneous menu built around the best and freshest in-season foods prepared in the continental manner with touches of Scandinavian finesse.

HOTEL DEL CORONADO   24

1500 Orange Avenue
San Diego, CA
(619) 435-6611

American/Continental

F ★ ★ ★
S ★ ★ ★
A ★ ★ ★ ½
P ★ ★ ½

Jacket required
Valet and lot parking
All major credit cards
Full bar
Reservations required

Breakfast/
Lunch/
Dinner: Daily 7:00AM-10:30PM

This ageless Victorian beauty has held court to the world's great since its debut, way back when. The cuisine tends to the traditional and is always of the highest quality. You've a choice of several rooms—all resplendent and impressive.

HUMPHREYS   23

2241 Shelter Island Drive
San Diego, CA
(619) 224-3577

Continental

F ★ ★ ★
S ★ ★
A ★ ★ ★
P ★ ★ ★

No shorts, T-shirts, sandals in dining room at dinner
Lot parking
All major credit cards
Full bar
Reservations not required

Breakfast: Mon.-Sat. 7:00AM-11:30AM
            Sun. 7:00AM-10:00AM
Lunch: Mon.-Sat. 11:30AM-3:30PM
Dinner: Mon.-Thurs. 5:30PM-10:00PM
            Fri. & Sat. 5:30PM-11:00PM
            Sun. 5:30PM-9:00PM
Brunch: Sun. 10:00AM-2:00PM

This pleasant retreat on Shelter Island affords you a view of the busy harbor from a plant-filled tropical setting. (You can dine outdoors if you wish.) The continental menu leans to fresh seafood, and features live Maine lobster.

LA CHAUMINE   2

1466 Garnet Avenue
San Diego, CA
(619) 272-8540

French

F ★ ★ ★ ½
S ★ ★ ★ ½
A ★ ★ ★
P ★ ★ ★ ½

Jacket preferred
Lot and street parking
All major credit cards
Full bar
Reservations required

Dinner: Tues.-Sun. 6:00PM-11:00PM
            Closed Monday

Chef/owner/host Roland Chassang's Parisian establishment is a consistent winner of international awards. The cuisine is lively and exciting, with provincial flavoring touches. There is a well thought out wine list, excellent service, and stunning desserts.

LE FONTAINEBLEAU   21

The Westgate Hotel
1055 Second Avenue
San Diego, CA
(619) 238-1818

French/Continental

F ★ ★ ★ ½
S ★ ★ ★ ½
A ★ ★ ★ ½
P ★ ★ ★ ½

Jacket and tie required
Valet parking
All major credit cards
Full bar
Reservations required

Lunch: Mon.-Fri. 11:45AM-2:00PM
Dinner: Nightly 6:30PM-10:00PM
Brunch: Sun. 10:00AM-2:00PM

The stately elegance of an 18th century European salon is the image projected here, where formally attired waiters perform white-gloved service. You'll hear harp or piano music in the background as you focus your attention on the continental bill of fare with its interesting French accents.

LEHRS GREENHOUSE 8
RESTAURANT AND FLORIST

2828 Camino Del Rio South
San Diego, CA
(619) 299-2828

American

F ★ ★ ★
S ★ ★ ★ ½
A ★ ★ ★ ½
P ★ ★ ★

No dress restrictions
Lot and street parking
AE, MC, V
Full bar
Reservations recommended

Lunch: Mon.-Sat. 11:30AM-3:30PM
Dinner: Mon.-Thurs. 5:00PM-9:30PM
Fri. & Sat. 5:00PM-10:30PM
Sun. 4:30PM-9:30PM
Brunch: Sun. 9:30AM-2:30PM

In a greenhouse that spans a full acre, Murray and Dean D. Lehr, a father and son team, have created a tropical garden paradise where you will dine in private white wicker gazebos tucked among the plants and statuary. Fresh regional seafood broiled over mesquite is the specialty; there is an imposing 60-item salad bar.

LUBACH'S 19

2101 North Harbor Drive
San Diego, CA
(619) 232-5129

Continental

F ★ ★ ★ ½
S ★ ★ ★ ½
A ★ ★ ★
P ★ ★ ★

Jacket required; tie preferred at dinner
Valet parking
AE, MC, V
Full bar
Reservations required

Lunch/
Dinner: Mon.-Fri. 11:30AM-12:00AM
Sat. 4:00PM-12:00AM
Closed Sunday

This prestigious restaurant has been earning accolades for three decades. Family-owned with a harbor view, you'll find fresh roses on linen-topped tables, highly professional service, and a well contrived menu of continental cuisine, emphasizing seafood.

MANDARIN HOUSE 1

6765 La Jolla Boulevard
La Jolla, CA
(619) 454-2555

Chinese

F ★ ★ ★
S ★ ★ ★
A ★ ★ ½
P ★ ★

No dress restrictions
Street parking
All major credit cards
Full bar
Reservations required

Lunch: Mon.-Sat. 11:30AM-2:30PM
Dinner: Sun.-Thurs. 2:30PM-10:00PM
Fri. & Sat. 2:30PM-11:00PM

Aglow with oriental splendor with intricately carved room dividers and lotus lamps, here you can enjoy a choice of Mandarin, Peking, and Szechwan cooking styles, with seasonings tailored to your taste.

MARINE ROOM 1

2000 Spindrift Drive
La Jolla, CA
(619) 459-7222

Continental

F ★ ★ ★
S ★ ★ ★
A ★ ★ ★ ½
P ★ ★ ★

Jacket required
Lot parking
All major credit cards
Full bar
Reservations required

Lunch: Mon.-Sat. 11:30AM-2:30PM
Dinner: Sun.-Fri. 6:00PM-10:00PM
         Sat. 6:00PM-11:00PM
Brunch: Sun. 10:30AM-2:30PM

Nestled on the sand, with an ocean view from every table, this La Jolla institution features seafood, steak, and veal dishes in a candlelit, flower-filled setting that is charming and romantic. You'll also find live music, and dancing nightly.

MILLE FLEURS   6

6009 Paseo Delicias
Rancho Santa Fe, CA
(619) 756-3085

French

F ★ ★ ★ ½
S ★ ★ ★
A ★ ★ ★ ½
P ★ ★ ★ ★

Jacket required
Street parking
AE, MC, V
Full bar
Reservations required

Lunch: Mon.-Fri. 11:30AM-2:30PM
Dinner: Nightly 6:00PM-9:30PM
Brunch: Sun. 10:30AM-2:00PM

This romantic restaurant with its patios, enclosed terrace, fireplaces, plants, and multi-dining rooms is patterned after a famous dining spot in Portugal. The cuisine is impeccable and includes such specialties as mustard soup and home-smoked salmon.

MISTER A'S   13

Fifth Avenue Financial Centre
5th and Laurel
San Diego, CA
(619) 286-9601

Continental

F ★ ★ ★ ½
S ★ ★ ★ ½
A ★ ★ ★ ½
P ★ ★ ★ ½

Jacket required
Valet and street parking
All major credit cards
Full bar
Reservations required

Lunch/
Dinner: Mon.-Fri. 11:30AM-2:00AM
         Sat. & Sun. 5:30PM-2:00AM

From its lofty perch atop the Fifth Avenue Financial Centre, Mister A's offers you a 360° view of the city, harbor, and bay. Here you'll find consistently good service and an ambitious continental menu featuring Beef Wellington, Veal Oskar, and numerous seafood entrées. The wine list is diverse and interesting.

NINO'S   9

4501 Mission Bay Drive
San Diego, CA
(619) 274-3141

Italian

F ★ ★ ★ ½
S ★ ★ ★
A ★ ★ ½
P ★ ★ ★

Good taste in dress required
Lot and street parking
All major credit cards
Full bar
Reservations recommended

Lunch: Tues.-Sat. 12:00PM-2:00PM
Dinner: Tues.-Sat. 5:00PM-10:30PM
        Closed Sunday & Monday

This family owned eatery has a plushy, romantic air and a low-key profile. Milk-fed veal stars in entrées such as Veal Florentina; other enticements include scampi, chicken livers, and fresh fish prepared in the Northern Italian manner.

OLD TRIESTE 4

2335 Morena Boulevard
San Diego, CA
(619) 276-1841

Italian

F ★ ★ ★
S ★ ★ ★
A ★ ★ ★
P ★ ★ ★

Jacket required at dinner, no jeans
Lot parking
All major credit cards
Full bar
Reservations required

Lunch: Tues.-Fri. 12:00PM-2:30PM
Dinner: Tues.-Sat. 5:00PM-10:30PM
        Closed Sunday and Monday

For more than 20 years the clubby ambiance and high quality Italian cuisine have kept this small dining room filled with happy people. Eastern veal, fresh fish, cannelloni, sautéed chicken livers, calamari, scampi, and great fried zucchini are popular menu highlights.

PAPAGAYO 18

Seaport Village
861 West Harbor Drive
San Diego, CA
(619) 232-7581

Seafood

F ★ ★ ★ ½
S ★ ★ ★
A ★ ★ ★
P ★ ★ ★

Good taste in dress required
Lot parking
All major credit cards
Full bar
Reservations recommended

Lunch: Mon.-Sat. 11:30AM-2:30PM
Dinner: Mon.-Thurs. 5:30PM-10:00PM
        Fri. & Sat. 5:00PM-11:00PM
        Sun. 5:00PM-10:00PM
Brunch: Sun. 10:30AM-3:00PM

This seaside establishment weds superb views, tasteful décor, a good wine list, and cuisine called "Seafood Latino," prepared by chef John Borg. The freshest seafoods are enhanced with tantalizing sauces to produce award-winning entrées such as Corvina Cabo San Lucas.

PAX 1

1025 Prospect Street
La Jolla, CA
(619) 454-9711

Italian

F ★ ★ ★
S ★ ★ ★
A ★ ★ ★
P ★ ★ ★

Good taste in dress required
Garage parking
AE, MC, V
Full bar
Reservations recommended

Lunch/
Dinner: Mon.-Thurs. 11:30AM-10:30PM
        Fri. & Sat. 6:00PM-10:30PM
        Closed Sunday

The culinary concept here combines California's native ingredients with Northern Italian cooking techniques. The menu includes mesquite-grilled entrées, pastas, and a succulent roast served tableside from a silver cart. The atmosphere is pleasantly European.

PIRET'S   12

902 West Washington Street
San Diego, CA
(619) 297-2993

French

F ★ ★ ★ ½
S ★ ★ ★ ½
A ★ ★ ★
P ★ ★ ½

No dress restrictions
Street parking
All major credit cards
Beer/Wine
Reservations not required

Breakfast/
Lunch/
Dinner: Sun.-Thurs. 9:00AM-9:30PM
          Fri. & Sat. 9:00AM-10:30PM

The original location of a rapidly expanding chain, this French-style bistro has a verdant atrium setting, in the heart of the banking district. Famous for their cassoulet (bean stew with duck, lamb, pork, and sausages) and the best French pastries in town.

REUBEN E. LEE   17
STERNWHEELER
RESTAURANT &
SEAFOOD RESTAURANT

880 East Harbor Island Drive
San Diego, CA
(619) 291-1870

American/Seafood

F ★ ★ ★
S ★ ★ ★
A ★ ★ ★
P ★ ★ ½

No dress restrictions
Lot parking
AE, DC, MC, V
Full bar
Reservations not required

Sternwheeler:
Lunch: Mon.-Fri. 11:30AM-2:00PM
Dinner: Sun.-Thurs. 5:30PM-11:00PM
          Fri. & Sat. 5:30PM-12:00AM
Seafood Restaurant:
Lunch: Mon.-Sat. 11:30AM-4:00PM
Dinner: Sun.-Thurs. 4:00PM-11:00PM
          Fri. & Sat. 4:00PM-12:00AM
Brunch: Sun. 10:00AM-2:00PM

Mark Twain would have loved this authentic replica of an 1800s Mississippi riverboat tied up on the east end of Harbor Island! The view is spectacular and you can dine on American cuisine in the Sternwheeler, or sample some of this region's finest fresh seafoods in the congenial Seafood room.

SHEPPARD'S   16

Sheraton Harbor Island East
1380 Harbor Island Drive
San Diego, CA
(619) 692-2255

Californian

F ★ ★ ★ ½
S ★ ★ ★ ½
A ★ ★ ★ ½
P ★ ★ ★

Jacket required, no jeans or shorts
Valet parking
All major credit cards
Full bar
Reservations not required

Dinner: Tues.-Sun. from 6:00PM
          Closed Monday

West Coast regional cuisine, with a soupcon of French country flair, is featured at this distinctive Harbor Island restaurant. You'll find interesting appetizers and dinner entrées including veal medallions, duckling, loin of lamb, and fresh salmon. Freshness of ingredients and local bounty reflect in the menu.

SKY ROOM 1

La Valencia Hotel
1132 Prospect Street
La Jolla, CA
(619) 454-0771

Continental

F ★ ★ ★ ½
S ★ ★ ★
A ★ ★ ★ ½
P ★ ★ ★ ★

Jacket required
Valet and street parking
AE, MC, V
Full bar
Reservations required

Lunch: Mon.-Fri. 11:30AM-3:00PM
Dinner: Mon.-Sat. 6:00PM-9:30PM
         Closed Sunday

This beautiful hotel-topper offers an ocean view, tuxedoed service, and a handsome marble bar in the center of the room. The continental cuisine, ambiance, and wine list reflect the finest traditions of pleasurable dining.

SU CASA 1

6738 La Jolla Boulevard
La Jolla, CA
(619) 459-0549

Seafood

F ★ ★ ★
S ★ ★ ½
A ★ ★ ★
P ★ ★ ½

Good taste in dress required
Lot parking
All major credit cards
Full bar
Reservations not required

Lunch/
Dinner: Daily 11:30AM-10:30PM

This lovely old 18th century beachside hacienda, embellished with lush plants, an aviary, salt water aquariums, stained glass, and fountains has housed this much-honored restaurant for 21 years. There's an oyster bar, world-class Margaritas, and an impressive menu devoted to fresh seafood.

THEE BUNGALOW 10

4996 West Point Loma Boulevard
San Diego, CA
(619) 224-2884

Continental

F ★ ★ ★ ½
S ★ ★ ★ ½
A ★ ★ ★
P ★ ★ ★ ½

Good taste in dress required
Lot parking
All major credit cards
Beer/Wine
Reservations required

Dinner: Wed.-Sun. 6:00PM-11:00PM
         Closed Monday & Tuesday

Chef/owner Siegfried Heil has converted an Ocean Beach house into a romantic rendezvous that earns critic's praise and honorary awards on an on-going basis. There's an extensive wine list, chef's daily specials, and intriguing interpretations of continental cuisine. The service is crisp and the desserts are all homemade.

TOM HAM'S   14
LIGHTHOUSE

2150 Harbor Island Drive
San Diego, CA
(619) 291-9110

Continental

F ★ ★ ★
S ★ ★ ½
A ★ ★ ★
P ★ ★ ½

Good taste in dress required
Lot parking
All major credit cards
Full bar
Reservations not required

Lunch/
Dinner: Mon.-Fri. 11:15AM-1:00AM
          Sat. 5:00PM-1:00AM
          Sun. 10:00AM-12:00AM

What could be more logical than utilizing an authentic lighthouse for a bayside dining room? There's a view of the city and the harbor from this snug haven with its nostalgic early California décor. The bill of fare features a large variety of continental entrées and some choice Mexican specialties.

TOP O' THE COVE   1

1216 Prospect Street
La Jolla, CA
(619) 454-7779

French

F ★ ★ ★
S ★ ★ ★
A ★ ★ ★
P ★ ★ ★ ★

Jacket required
Street parking
All major credit cards
Full bar
Reservations required

Lunch: Mon.-Sat. 11:30AM-2:30PM
Dinner: Mon.-Sat. 5:30PM-10:30PM
Brunch: Sun. 10:00AM-2:00PM

Dine here in a picturesque 19th century cottage overlooking La Jolla Cove, on authentic French cuisine, accompanied by selections from the award-winning wine cellar. There's a romantic courtyard and a menu featuring classic dishes, daily specials, hot and cold hors d'oeuvres, and downy light soufflés.

San Francisco

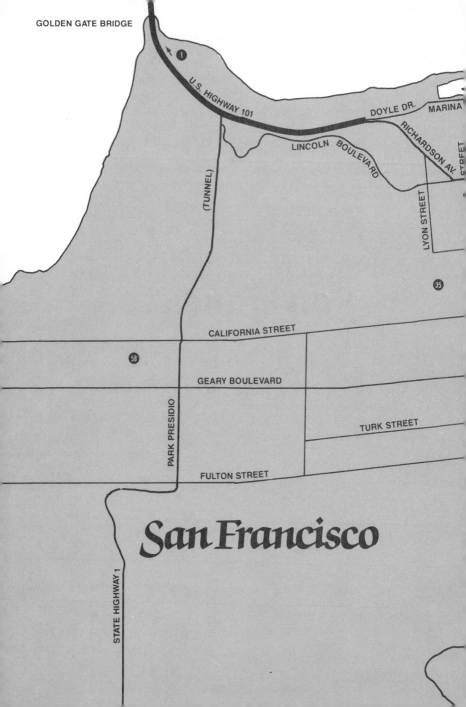

SAN FRANCISCO BAY

ALEJANDRO'S SOCIEDAD GASTRONOMICA   58

1840 Clement Street
San Francisco, CA
(415) 668-1184

Spanish/Peruvian/Mexican

F ★ ★ ★
S ★ ★ ★ ½
A ★ ★ ★
P ★ ★

Good taste in dress required
Street parking
All major credit cards
Full bar
Reservations recommended

Dinner: Mon.-Fri. 5:00PM-11:00PM
           Sat. 5:00PM-12:00AM
           Sun. 4:00PM-11:00PM

If the thought of paella triggers your taste buds, this colorful, exuberant restaurant with its medley of ethnic cuisines is for you. Chef/owner Alejandro, and Ruriko Espinosa concentrate on seafood and shellfish dishes, such as Zarvuela de Mariscos.

ALFRED'S   23

886 Broadway
San Francisco, CA
(415) 781-7058

Continental

F ★ ★ ★
S ★ ★ ★ ½
A ★ ★ ★
P ★ ★ ★ ½

Jacket preferred
Valet parking
All major credit cards
Full bar
Reservations recommended

Dinner: Nightly 5:30PM-10:30PM

Renowned since 1928 for superlative steaks, this elegant old San Francisco establishment continues to feature prime cuts of Eastern corn-fed beef, aged in house, and cooked precisely to your order over a hot mesquite fire. Seafood, chicken, rack of lamb, and veal are also available, but here, the steak is king.

ANNABEL'S   55

Orchard Hotel
566 Sutter Street
San Francisco, CA
(415) 433-4434

French/Italian

F ★ ★ ★ ½
S ★ ★ ★
A ★ ★ ★
P ★ ★ ★

Good taste in dress required
Valet and garage parking
All major credit cards
Full bar
Reservations required

Breakfast: Mon.-Sat. 7:00AM-10:00AM
Lunch: Mon.-Sat. 11:30AM-2:30PM
Dinner: Nightly 6:00PM-10:00PM

Picture pretty, this charming dining room with its floral décor and burgundy and pink color scheme has a warm, welcoming ambiance. The menu is a mélange of French, Italian, and California-style cuisine, and changes weekly to take advantage of seasonal ingredients.

BLUE BOAR INN   10

1713 Lombard Street
San Francisco, CA
(415) 567-8424

French

F ★ ★ ★ ½
S ★ ★ ★ ½
A ★ ★ ★ ½
P ★ ★ ★

Good taste in dress required
Valet parking
All major credit cards
Full bar
Reservations required

Dinner: Mon.-Sat. 6:00PM-1:00AM
           Sun. 5:00PM-11:00PM

An idealized version of a "little bit of England," this two-story restaurant is richly adorned with British memorabilia. The classic French cuisine is enriched with country-fresh produce from Sonoma.

BLUE FOX   32

659 Merchant Street
San Francisco, CA
(415) 981-1177

Continental

F ★ ★ ★ ½
S ★ ★ ★ ½
A ★ ★ ★ ½
P ★ ★ ★ ★

Jacket and tie required
Valet parking
All major credit cards
Full bar
Reservations recommended

Dinner: Mon.-Sat. 6:00PM-11:00PM
           Closed Sunday

Considered one of San Francisco's most prestigious restaurants, the Blue Fox is a rendevous for celebrities. Owner Mario Mondin has maintained high standards of service and cuisine for over 40 years.

CADILLAC BAR   67

1 Holland Court
San Francisco, CA
(415) 543-8226

Mexican

F ★ ★ ★ ½
S ★ ★ ★
A ★ ★ ★
P ★ ★

No dress restrictions
Lot parking
All major credit cards
Full bar
Reservations not required

Lunch/
Dinner: Mon.-Thurs. 11:00AM-11:00PM
           Fri. 11:00AM-12:00AM
           Sat. 5:00PM-12:00AM
           Closed Sunday

Housed in a huge converted warehouse, with an 18-foot ceiling, this restaurant gives you the feeling of entering a small border town. In this setting you can watch the chef through glass windows as gourmet Mexican cuisine is grilled over mesquite. Seafood is a specialty, and the Botana Platter (1/2 chicken, steak, carnita, queso flameado) is highly touted.

CAFÉ MOZART   56

708 Bush Street
San Francisco, CA
(415) 391-8480

French

F ★ ★ ★ ½
S ★ ★ ★ ½
A ★ ★ ★ ½
P ★ ★ ★ ★

Jacket and tie preferred
Street parking
AE, MC, V
Beer/Wine
Reservations required

Dinner: Nightly 6:00PM-12:00AM

Flower-graced and with an open fireplace, Karl Kaussen's Café Mozart is warm, intimate, and inviting. The food is light with naturally reduced sauces, attesting to the skill of Chef Pierre-Jean Lefour.

CAFFE SPORT   18

357 Green Street
San Francisco, CA
(415) 981-1251

Sicilian/Italian

F ★ ★ ★ ★
S ★ ★ ★
A ★ ★ ★
P ★ ★ ★

Good taste in dress required
Street parking
Credit cards not accepted
Beer/Wine
Reservations only for four or more

Lunch: Tues.-Sat. 12:00PM-2:00PM
Dinner: Tues.-Sat. Seatings at
          6:30PM, 8:30PM, 10:30PM
          Closed Sunday and Monday

You'll find garlic, cheese, and hams hanging from the ceiling in this informal, family style Sicilian restaurant. The daily specials revolve around available seafood, which the chef, Antonio, prepares with consummate skill.

CAMPTON PLACE   11
RESTAURANT

Campton Place Hotel
340 Stockton Street
San Francisco, CA
(415) 781-5155

American

F ★ ★ ★ ½
S ★ ★ ★
A ★ ★ ★
P ★ ★ ★ ★   .

Jacket required at lunch; jacket and tie required for dinner
Valet and garage parking
All major credit cards
Full bar
Reservations required

Breakfast: Mon.-Fri. 7:00AM-11:00AM
           Sat. 8:00AM-11:00AM
           Sun. 8:00AM-10:30AM
Lunch: Mon.-Sat. 11:30AM-2:30PM
Dinner: Nightly 5:30PM-10:30PM
Brunch: Sun. 10:30AM-2:30PM

The salmon and taupe color scheme featured here creates a setting of subtle elegance. Chef Bradley Ogden's flexible menu is based on heritage recipes modernized to take advantage of the availability of fresh fish, meats, and other ingredients.

CANLIS   48

Fairmont Hotel
950 Mason Street
San Francisco, CA
(415) 392-0113

American

F ★ ★ ★ ½
S ★ ★ ★ ½
A ★ ★ ★
P ★ ★ ★ ½

Jacket required
Street parking
All major credit cards
Full bar
Reservations recommended

Dinner: Nightly 6:00PM-11:15PM

Warm and intimate, with an air of genteel elegance, this restaurant offers you broiled steaks, swordfish, salmon, and other fresh seafoods, cooked to perfection over Hawaiian mesquite charcoal.

CARAVANSARY   8

2263 Chestnut Street
San Francisco, CA
(415) 921-3466

Mediterrean

F ★ ★ ★
S ★ ★ ★
A ★ ★ ★
P ★ ★ ½

Good taste in dress required
Street parking
All major credit cards
Beer/Wine
Reservations recommended

Lunch: Mon.-Sat. 11:00AM-3:00PM
Dinner: Mon.-Sat. 5:00PM-10:00PM
         Closed Sunday

This browsers' paradise offers an intriguing array of gourmet goodies, including cookware, plus a café and restaurant that blend together and a small espresso bar serving sandwiches and tasty homemade sweets.

CARAVANSARY   51

310 Sutter Street
San Francisco, CA
(415) 362-4640

Mediterrean

F ★ ★ ★
S ★ ★ ★
A ★ ★ ★
P ★ ★ ½

Good taste in dress required
Street parking
All major credit cards
Full bar
Reservations recommended

Lunch: Mon.-Sat. 11:00AM-3:00PM
Dinner: Mon.-Sat. 5:00PM-10:00PM
         Closed Sunday

More formal and sedate than its Chestnut Street sister, here you will find a separate espresso bar, a retail section devoted to gourmet items, and a dining room that serves such entrées as rack of lamb marinated in pomegranate juice and presented with a pomegranate sauce, and daily fresh fish specialties.

CARNELIAN ROOM   44

Bank of America Center
555 California Street
San Francisco, CA
(415) 433-7500

American

F ★ ★ ★
S ★ ★ ★
A ★ ★ ★ ½
P ★ ★ ★ ½

Jacket and tie required
Building garage parking
All major credit cards
Full bar
Reservations required

Dinner: Nightly 6:00PM-11:00PM
Brunch: Sun. 10:00AM-3:00PM

A full circle view of the bay area and a regal setting decorated with Louis XV and XVI antiques, draws a loyal clientele to The Carnelian Room. The wine list is exemplary and the menu changes with each equinox.

CHEZ MICHEL   5

804 North Point
San Francisco, CA
(415) 771-6077

French

F ★ ★ ★ ½
S ★ ★ ★ ½
A ★ ★ ★
P ★ ★ ★ ½

Jacket required
Street parking
MC, V
Full bar
Reservations recommended

Dinner: Tues.-Sun. 6:00PM-12:30AM
         Closed Monday

Here you will feel as if owner Michel El-kaim was welcoming you into his home.

The food preparation leans toward nouvelle, with specialties such as medallions of beef, and fresh seafood.

CHEZ PANISSE 72

1517 Shattuck Avenue
Berkeley, CA
(415) 548-5525

French/Californian

F ★ ★ ★ ½
S ★ ★ ★
A ★ ★ ★
P ★ ★ ★

No dress restrictions
Street parking
Credit cards not accepted
Beer/Wine
Reservations required in restaurant

Restaurant:
Dinner: Tues.-Sat. 6:00PM-12:00AM
          Closed Sunday & Monday
Cafe:
Lunch/
Dinner: Mon.-Sat. 11:30AM-11:30PM
          Closed Sunday

Alice Waters' two-tiered triumph serves à la carte French country cuisine in the upstairs café, and prix fixe-five-course dinners in the downstairs dining room, where you might find leg of lamb, charcoal-grilled salmon, or quail on the daily changing menu.

DONATELLO 65
RISTORANTE

Pacific Plaza Hotel
501 Post Street
San Francisco, CA
(415) 441-7182

Italian

F ★ ★ ★ ½
S ★ ★ ★ ½
A ★ ★ ★ ½
P ★ ★ ★ ½

Jacket and tie required
Valet parking
All major credit cards
Full bar
Reservations required

Breakfast: Daily 7:00AM-10:30AM
Lunch: Daily 11:30AM-2:30PM
Dinner: Nightly 6:00PM-10:30PM

Comprised of two beautifully decorated intimate rooms, Donatello's offers you a lovely setting for a joyous dining experience. The pastas and other entrées are carefully prepared — the service is unobtrusive and friendly.

DORO'S 28

714 Montgomery Street
San Francisco, CA
(415) 397-6822

Continental

F ★ ★ ★ ½
S ★ ★ ★ ½
A ★ ★ ★ ½
P ★ ★ ★ ★

Jacket and tie required
Valet and garage parking
All major credit cards
Full bar
Reservations recommended

Lunch: Mon.-Fri. 11:30AM-2:30PM
Dinner: Mon.-Sat. 6:00PM-10:30PM
          Closed Sunday

This much-honored restaurant, in the same location for 30 years, continues to shine. The wine cellar is considered one of the ten best in the U.S., and the consistent quality of the cuisine has placed owner Don Dianda in the Restaurant Hall of Fame.

EMPRESS OF CHINA 31

838 Grant Avenue
San Francisco,CA
(415) 434-1345

Chinese

F ★ ★ ★
S ★ ★ ★
A ★ ★ ★
P ★ ★ ★

Jacket and tie required at dinner
Street and garage parking
AE,DC, MC, V
Full bar
Reservations required

Lunch: Daily 11:30AM-3:00PM
Dinner: Nightly 5:00PM-11:00PM

The Empress of China is an exquisite roof garden restaurant located in a high-rise, with superb views of the bay and city. You may choose gourmet dishes from all regions of China when you dine here, in a setting of oriental splendor.

ENGLISH GRILL   57

Westin St. Francis Hotel
335 Powell Street
San Francisco, CA
(415) 774-0223

American

F ★ ★ ★ ½
S ★ ★ ★
A ★ ★ ★
P ★ ★ ½

Good taste in dress required
Valet and lot parking
All major credit cards
Full bar
Reservations recommended

Lunch: Mon.-Sat. 11:30AM-2:30PM
Dinner: Mon.-Sat. 6:00PM-11:00PM
          Closed Sunday

A carved Mahogany ceiling and an air of Old World grandeur distinguish this handsome establishment that is noted for its wide range of specialties. You'll find a crab buffet bar, seven fish selections, a brochette of the day, and a daily fresh fish feature.

ERNIE'S   47

847 Montgomery Street
San Francisco, CA
(415) 397-5969

French

F ★ ★ ★ ★
S ★ ★ ★ ★
A ★ ★ ★ ½
P ★ ★ ★ ★

Jacket and tie required
Valet parking
All major credit cards
Full bar
Reservations required

Dinner: Nightly 6:30PM-10:30PM

Lush, plush, turn-of-the-century décor, complete with antiques and crystal chandeliers give Ernie's a lustre that is untarnished with time. This 50-year old success story now adds nouvelle touches to their handsomely presented cuisine.

FLEUR DE LYS   37

777 Sutter Street
San Francisco, CA
(415) 673-7779

French

F ★ ★ ★
S ★ ★ ★
A ★ ★ ★ ★
P ★ ★ ★

Jacket and tie required
Valet parking
AE
Full bar
Reservations required

Dinner: Tues.-Sun 6:00PM-11:00PM
          Closed Monday

A triumph of elegant good taste, Maurice Rouas' Fleur de Lys serves haute cuisine to dedicated diners, with great élan. The place to go for Magret of Duck Massena, Tournedos of Boeuf Brigette, and Escalope de Veau en Champagne.

FOURNOU'S OVENS   41

Stanford Court Hotel
905 California Street
San Francisco, CA
(415) 989-1910

Continental

F   ★ ★ ★ ½
S   ★ ★ ★ ½
A   ★ ★ ★ ½
P   ★ ★ ★ ★

Jacket required
Valet parking
All major credit cards
Full bar
Reservations recommended

Lunch: Mon.-Fri. 11:30AM-2:30PM
Dinner: Nightly 5:30PM-11:00PM

Located in the Stanford Court, multi-leveled Fournou's Ovens uses huge working ovens, faced with Provincial tile, to roast to perfection savory duckling, rack of lamb, filets of beef, and pork. The ambiance is light and cheerful — the staff friendly and capable

FRANCISCAN   7

Pier 43 1/2, The Embarcadero
San Francisco, CA
(415) 362-7733

Seafood

F   ★ ★ ★ ½
S   ★ ★ ★
A   ★ ★ ★
P   ★ ★ ★

No dress restrictions
Lot parking
AE, DC, MC, V
Full bar
Reservations not required

Lunch/
Dinner: Daily 11:00AM-11:00PM

This finely tuned Fisherman's Wharf restaurant, with its three-tiered dining room, provides you with a scenic panorama of the bay, and a wide selection of fresh seafoods, prepared with a master's hand.

FRENCH ROOM   63

Four Seasons Clift Hotel
495 Geary Street
San Francisco, CA
(415) 775-4700

Continental

F   ★ ★ ★ ★
S   ★ ★ ★ ★
A   ★ ★ ★ ★
P   ★ ★ ★ ★

Jacket and tie required at dinner
Valet parking
All major credit cards
Full bar
Reservations recommended

Breakfast: Daily 7:00AM-11:00AM
Lunch: Mon.-Sat. 12:00PM-2:00PM
Dinner: Nightly 6:00PM-11:00PM

Posh and impressive with high ceilings, a trio of grand chandeliers, large palm trees, and exquisite old French décor, dining here is a splendid experience. The wine list is exemplary, the cuisine offers such choices as prime rib and a different seafood specialty nightly.

GAYLORD INDIA   3
RESTAURANT

Ghirardelli Square
900 North Point Street
San Francisco, CA
(415) 771-8822

Indian

F ★ ★ ★ ½
S ★ ★ ★
A ★ ★ ★
P ★ ★ ★

No dress restrictions
Lot parking
All major credit cards
Full bar
Reservations not required

Lunch: Daily 12:00PM-2:00PM
Dinner: Nightly 5:00PM-11:00PM
Brunch: Sun. 12:00PM-3:00PM

You'll dine in sumptuous comfort at Gaylord's, while enjoying an inspiring view of the bay. Manager/chef Kishore Kripalani's tandoori cooking lets the finest Indian spices meld gently with the basic ingredients with splendid result.

GREENS 2

Building A of Fort Mason
San Francisco, CA
(415) 771-6222

Vegetarian

F ★ ★ ★ ½
S ★ ★ ★
A ★ ★ ★
P ★ ★ ★

No dress restrictions
Lot parking
MC, V
Wine with meals only
Reservations required for dinner,
recommended for lunch

Lunch: Tues.-Sat. 11:30AM-2:15PM
Dinner: Tues.-Sat. from 6:00PM
Brunch: Sun. 10:30AM-1:45PM

Greens has turned meatless cooking into a new form of culinary art. Both café-style and fixed menu service is offered in this spacious restaurant that provides you with a great view of the Golden Gate Bridge. Pastas and pizzas are luncheon features; soufflés, crêpes, and cannelloni among the dinner specialties.

HAYES STREET GRILL 70

320 Hayes Street
San Francisco, CA
(415) 863-5545

Seafood

F ★ ★ ★ ½
S ★ ★ ★
A ★ ★ ½
P ★ ★ ★

No dress restrictions
Street parking
MC, V
Beer/Wine
Reservations recommended

Lunch: Mon.-Fri. 11:30AM-3:00PM
Dinner: Mon.-Fri. 5:00PM-10:00PM
          Sat. 6:00PM-11:00PM
          Closed Sunday

Nostalgically decorated in the old San Francisco manner, this busy restaurant, located near the performing arts complex, serves "daily-catch" fresh fish, meats, and house-made sausages, grilled over mesquite coals.

HOUSE OF PRIME RIB 21

1906 Van Ness Avenue
San Francisco, CA
(415) 885-4605

English

F ★ ★ ★ ½
S ★ ★ ★
A ★ ★ ½
P ★ ★ ★

Good taste in dress required, no shorts
Lot and street parking
All major credit cards
Full bar
Reservations not required

Dinner: Nightly 5:15PM-10:00PM

This pub-style restaurant is heaven to a large contingent of "meat and potatoes" fanciers. Buttery-tender prime rib, served from a cart is the only entrée offered. A crisp salad, creamed spinach, Yorkshire pudding, your choice of baked or mashed potatoes, and homemade desserts round out the menu.

HUGO'S MARKET   73

1333 Bayshore Highway
Burlingame, CA
(415) 342-7741

Continental

F ★ ★ ★
S ★ ★ ★
A ★ ★ ★
P ★ ★ ★

No dress restrictions
Lot parking
All major credit cards
Full bar
Reservations not required excepting for Sunday brunch

Lunch: Mon.-Fri. 11:30AM-2:30PM
Dinner: Nightly 5:30PM-10:30PM
Brunch: Sun. 10:30AM-2:30PM

Festive and lively, Hugo's Market has won acclaim for its outstanding salad bar, fresh seafood, prime rib, veal, lamb, and steaks — all prepared with a knowing hand. You'll find prompt, courteous service and an ambiance that is upbeat and contemporary.

IMPERIAL PALACE   27

919 Grant Avenue
San Francisco, CA
(415) 982-4440

Chinese

F ★ ★ ★ ½
S ★ ★ ★
A ★ ★ ★
P ★ ★ ★

Jacket and tie required
Lot parking

All major credit cards
Full bar
Reservations required

Lunch/
Dinner: Daily 11:30AM-1:00AM

Grandiose and superbly appointed, you'll find the Chinese cuisine served here tends to the traditional. Peking Duck, minced, squab, chicken salad, barbecued lamb, and Lobster Imperial (prepared with Maine lobster) are among the classic dishes that are perennial favorites.

JACK'S RESTAURANT   33

615 Sacramento Street
San Francisco, CA
(415) 986-9854/421-7355

French

F ★ ★ ★
S ★ ★ ★
A ★ ★ ★
P ★ ★ ★

Jacket and tie required
Lot and street parking
Credit cards not accepted
Full bar
Reservations recommended

Lunch/
Dinner: Mon.-Fri. 11:30AM-9:30PM
          Sat. & Sun. 5:00PM-9:30PM

An official San Francisco landmark, Jack's was established in 1864 and rebuilt on the original site after the 1906 earthquake. Noteworthy specialties include Filet of Sole Marguery, Chicken Sauté Sec, Broiled English Mutton Chop, and Sweetbreads Sauté.

JULIUS CASTLE   16

1541 Montgomery Street
San Francisco, CA
(415) 362-3042

Continental/Italian/French

F ★ ★ ★ ½
S ★ ★ ★ ½
A ★ ★ ★ ★
P ★ ★ ★ ½

Jacket required at dinner, no jeans
Valet parking
All major credit cards
Full bar
Reservations required

Lunch: Mon.-Fri. 11:30AM-3:00PM
Dinner: Nightly 5:30PM-9:30PM

Occupying a historic home on Telegraph Hill, diners at this view-oriented restaurant have watched a veritable parade of change roll by since it opened in 1933. The cuisine you'll find is consistently excellent, matched by efficient service. A most congenial spot for leisurely dining.

KANS 43

708 Grant Avenue
San Francisco, CA
(415) 982-2388

Chinese

F ★ ★ ★ ½
S ★ ★ ★
A ★ ★ ★
P ★ ★

Good taste in dress required
Street parking
All major credit cards
Full bar
Reservations recommended

Lunch/
Dinner: Mon.-Fri. 12:00PM-10:00PM
Sat. 4:30PM-11:00PM
Sun. 4:30PM-10:00PM

This family owned restaurant has a 40 years history of delighting customers with their meticulously prepared Cantonese cuisine. Owner Guy Wong offers such succulent specialties as Prawns à la Kan's (sautéed in a black bean sauce) and Peking Beef.

KEE JOON'S CUISINE OF 73
CHINA PENTHOUSE

433 Airport Boulevard
Burlingame, CA
(415) 348-1122

Chinese

F ★ ★ ★ ½
S ★ ★ ★ ½
A ★ ★ ★ ½
P ★ ★ ★ ★

Jacket required
Lot parking
AE, MC, V
Full bar
Reservations required for 4 or more

Lunch: Mon.-Fri. 11:30AM-2:00PM
Dinner: Nightly 5:00PM-10:30PM

Here you can overlook the golden San Francisco Bay while dining in an atmosphere replicating the splendor of the Sung Dynasty. Honored with awards since it opened in 1976, this restaurant offers you such winning dishes as Mongolian Lamb and Manchurian Beef.

LA BOURGOGNE 62

330 Mason Street
San Francisco, CA
(415) 362-7352

French

F ★ ★ ★ ½
S ★ ★ ★ ½
A ★ ★ ★ ★
P ★ ★ ★ ★

Jacket and tie required
Valet parking
All major credit cards
Full bar
Reservations not required

Dinner: Mon.-Sat. 5:30PM-11:45PM
Closed Sunday

The rich, royal blue and gold décor, muted background music, and quality cuisine have made La Bourgogne a long-time favorite of San Francisco sophisticates. The à la carte menu of classic French cuisine is nicely accented by a well selected wine cellar.

LA MERE DUQUESNE   61

101 Shannon Alley
San Francisco, CA
(415) 776-7600

French

```
F  ★ ★ ★ ½
S  ★ ★ ★ ½
A  ★ ★ ★ ½
P  ★ ★ ★
```

No dress restrictions
Lot parking
AE, MC, V
Full bar
Reservations recommended

Lunch: Mon.-Sat. 11:30AM-2:30PM
Dinner: Nightly from 5:30PM

Zesty French country cuisine is presented here in a setting with the warm ambiance of a hospitable French manor home. The house specialties at this family owned and operated restaurant include Veau de Pecheur and a delicate, delicious Grand Marnier soufflé.

LA MIRABELLE   17

1326 Powell Street
San Francisco, CA
(415) 421-3374

French/Continental

```
F  ★ ★ ★ ½
S  ★ ★ ★ ½
A  ★ ★ ★
P  ★ ★ ★
```

Jacket preferred
Valet parking

All major credit cards
Full bar
Reservations recommended

Dinner: Tues.-Sun. 5:30PM-10:30PM
Closed Monday

Decorated in rich burgundy tones with lovely antique French furnishings, this restaurant surrounds you with a sense of opulence and luxurious ease. The menu features a rich blend of continental cuisine and classic French cookery and offers you a choice of unusual specialties.

LA PERGOLA   8

2060 Chestnut Street
San Francisco, CA
(415) 563-4500

Italian

```
F  ★ ★ ★ ½
S  ★ ★ ★ ½
A  ★ ★ ★
P  ★ ★ ½
```

No dress restrictions
Street parking
MC, V
Beer/Wine
Reservations required

Dinner: Mon.-Sat. 5:00PM-10:30PM
Closed Sunday

This petite restaurant specializes in cuisine from Tuscany, a northern Italian region where many fresh herbs are used in food preparation. Owner Angelo Piccinini offers fresh fish, seasonal dishes, and such specialties as Lombata of Veal (oven-roasted with rosemary and garlic).

LA TRAVIATA   75

2854 Mission Street
San Francisco, CA
(415) 282-0500

Italian

F ★ ★ ★
S ★ ★ ★
A ★ ★ ★ ½
P ★ ★ ½

Good taste in dress required
Street parking
MC, V
Beer/Wine
Reservations recommended

Dinner: Tues.-Sun. 4:00PM-10:30PM
Closed Monday

If you are attuned to opera and relish Italian food, dining here should be on your "must do" list. The motif is operatic, as is the background music, and the ambiance is warm and friendly. Chicken Beverly Sills, Scampi à la Domingo, and Veal Traviata are among the house specialties.

LAS MANANITAS 26

850 Montgomery Street
San Francisco, CA
(415) 434-2088

Mexican/Continental

F ★ ★ ★ ½
S ★ ★ ★
A ★ ★ ★
P ★ ★ ½

Jacket preferred
Valet parking for dinner
All major credit cards
Full bar
Reservations recommended

Lunch/
Dinner: Mon.-Fri. 11:00AM-12:00AM
Sat. & Sun. 5:00PM-12:00AM

Created in the image of an elegant Mexico City style restaurant, here you will find a colorful outdoor dining area, and lively Mariachi music in the evening. Polle en Mole fresh cerviche, and Huachinango Vera Cruz typify the cosmopolitan menu offerings.

LE CASTEL 35

3235 Sacramento Street
San Francisco, CA
(415) 921-7115

French

F ★ ★ ★ ½
S ★ ★ ★ ½
A ★ ★ ★ ½
P ★ ★ ★ ½

Jacket required
Valet parking
All major credit cards
Beer/Wine
Reservations required

Dinner: Mon.-Sat. 6:00PM-10:00PM
Closed Sunday

An aristocratic Victorian home has been converted into this romantic, flower-filled restaurant where you'll find the service as faultless as the décor. Owner-chef Fritz Frankel offers his inspired version of traditional French and Alsatian cuisine.

LE CENTRAL 46

453 Bush Street
San Francisco, CA
(415) 391-2233

French

F ★ ★ ★
S ★ ★ ★ ½
A ★ ★ ★
P ★ ★ ★

No dress restrictions
Street parking
AE, DC, MC, V
Full bar
Reservations required

Lunch: Mon.-Fri. 11:45AM-3:30PM
Dinner: Mon.-Sat. 5:30PM-10:30PM
Closed Sunday

Le Central is like a transplanted Parisian bistro brasserie — chic, informal, and fun. House specialties include Leeks Vinaigrette, Saucissou Chaud, Cassoulet, Choucroûte, and Fresh Salmon Nantais.

LE CLUB   34

1250 Jones Street
San Francisco, CA
(415) 771-5400

French

F ★ ★ ★ ½
S ★ ★ ★ ★
A ★ ★ ★ ½
P ★ ★ ★ ★

Jacket and tie required
Valet parking
All major credit cards
Full bar
Reservations required

Dinner: Mon.-Sat. 5:30PM-11:30PM
           Closed Sunday

Two luxe dining rooms, one with French Provencial décor, the other plushy red, and Victorian, highly personal service, and a sense of quiet intimacy, has earned this spot an enviable reputation. This Nob Hill haven offers classic French cuisine and epicurean specialties.

LEHR'S GREENHOUSE   54

740 Sutter Street
San Francisco, CA
(415) 474-6478

Continental

F ★ ★ ★
S ★ ★ ★
A ★ ★ ★ ½
P ★ ★ ½

Good taste in dress required
Lot parking
AE, MC, V
Full bar
Reservations recommended

Lunch: Mon.-Sat. 11:30AM-4:00PM
Dinner: Nightly 5:00PM-11:00PM
Brunch: Sun. 9:30AM-2:30PM

This imaginative setting is an actual greenhouse, brimming with garden plants in colorful bloom. Here you'll find such entrées as "Three Star Duckling" with your choice of plum, citrus, or ginger sauce; rack of New Zealand lamb; and game specialties such as boar, venison, and buffalo stew.

L'ETOILE   66

Huntington Hotel
1075 California Street
San Francisco, CA
(415) 771-1529

French

F ★ ★ ★ ½
S ★ ★ ★ ½
A ★ ★ ★ ★
P ★ ★ ★ ★

Jacket and tie required
Valet and lot parking
All major credit cards
Full bar
Reservations required

Dinner: Mon.-Sat. 6:00PM-10:30PM
           Closed Sunday

You'll join San Francisco's social elite when you dine in the dignified splendor of L'Etoile. There is quiet good taste in décor and service; and you'll find a grand Les Quenelles Cardinal, prepared daily with available fresh fish, and served with a light lobster sauce.

THE LIPIZZANER   12

2223 Union Street
San Francisco, CA
(415) 921-3424

French/Viennese

F ★ ★ ★ ½
S ★ ★ ★
A ★ ★ ★
P ★ ★ ½

No dress restrictions
Street parking
MC, V
Beer/Wine
Reservations required

Dinner: Mon.-Sat. 5:30PM-10:00PM
Closed Sunday

The flicker of candles, French cottage windows, and light-toned walls imbue this petite dining room with a warm, intimate feeling. There is an extensive à la carte menu from which to choose and daily specials, such as fresh Dover sole.

MAC ARTHUR PARK 30

607 Front Street
San Francisco, CA
(415) 398-5700

Continental

F ★ ★ ★ ½
S ★ ★ ★
A ★ ★ ★
P ★ ★ ½

No dress restrictions
Street parking for lunch
Valet parking for dinner
AE, MC, V
Full bar
Reservations recommended

Lunch: Mon.-Fri. 11:30AM-2:30PM
Dinner: Mon.-Sat. 5:00PM-10:30PM
Sun. 5:00PM-10:00PM

The old brick and glass décor, open, airy feeling, verdant plants and trees, and easy-going fun atmosphere add up to a restaurant that is rustic with pizazz. Baby back pork ribs, smoked in an oakwood smoker—then broiled over mesquite, live Maine lobster, fresh fish, and juicy steaks are specialties that lure a lively crowd.

MAMA'S OF 38
SAN FRANCISCO

1177 California Street
San Francisco, CA
(415) 928-1004

Continental

F ★ ★ ★ ½
S ★ ★ ★ ½
A ★ ★ ★ ½
P ★ ★ ★

Good taste in dress required
Lot parking
AE, MC, V
Full bar
Reservations recommended

Breakfast/
Lunch: Mon.-Fri. 8:30AM-3:00PM
Sat.& Sun. 8:30AM-5:30PM
Dinner: Sun.-Thurs. 5:30PM-10:30PM
Fri.& Sat. 5:30PM-11:00PM

Revel in the fresh, cheerful ambiance created by colorful flowers, lattice-work gazebos, and Mexican floor tiles at Mama's. Michael Sanchez, owner, carries on the family tradition for superb omelettes; with steaks, veal dishes, and fish sharing honors on the menu.

THE MANDARIN 4

Ghirardelli Square
900 North Point Street
San Francisco, CA
(415) 673-8812

Chinese

F ★ ★ ★ ½
S ★ ★ ★ ½
A ★ ★ ★
P ★ ★ ★

Good taste in dress required
Lot parking
All major credit cards
Full bar
Reservations required

Lunch/
Dinner: Daily 12:00PM-11:00PM

Overlooking the bay, The Mandarin has luxurious appointments and contemporary oriental décor. Owner Mme. Cecelia Chiang offers specialties such as smoked tea duck, Peking duck, minced squab, and sweet and sour fish — dishes from the provinces of Szechwan and Hunan.

MARRAKECH PALACE   39

417 O'Farrell Street
San Francisco, CA
(415) 776-6717

Moroccan

F ★ ★ ★ ½
S ★ ★ ★ ½
A ★ ★ ★
P ★ ★ ★

Good taste in dress required
Valet parking
All major credit cards
Full bar
Reservations required

Dinner: Mon.-Sat. 6:00PM-11:00PM
              Closed Sunday

Plan on devoting your evening to dining like a sultan when you visit Marrakech. Lounge in the midst of palatial splendor on comfortable cushions and relish the multi-course Moroccan feast served by costumed waiters. A not-to-be-hurried, unique dining experience.

MASA'S   49

648 Bush Street
San Francisco, CA
(415) 989-7154

French

F ★ ★ ★ ★
S ★ ★ ★ ★
A ★ ★ ★ ½
P ★ ★ ★ ★

Jacket required
Valet parking
AE, MC, V
Full bar
Reservations required

Dinner: Tues.-Sat. 6:00-9:00PM
              Closed Sunday and Monday

French-trained chef/owner, Masataka Kobayashi, cooks with supreme self-confidence and innate sensitivity in his small, elegant domain. Daily prix fixe or à la carte offerings include pasta with truffles, lobster sausage, pheasant with morels, and iced hazelnut soufflé.

MAURICE ET   1
CHARLES BISTROT

901 Lincoln Avenue
San Rafael, CA
(415) 456-2010

French

F ★ ★ ★ ½
S ★ ★ ★
A ★ ★ ★
P ★ ★ ★

Good taste in dress required
Lot parking
All major credit cards
Beer/Wine
Reservations required

Dinner: Tues.-Sat. 6:30PM-10:30PM
              Closed Sunday and Monday

In a casual setting enhanced with charming floral paintings, bouquets of fresh flowers, and flickering candles, you'll find exceptionally good French cuisine offered here with many dishes reflecting the cooking style of Lyon. Seasonal and local products are featured, keeping the menu and method of preparation in a continuous state of evolvement.

MAXWELL'S PLUM   4

Ghirardelli Square
900 North Point Street
San Francisco, CA
(415) 441-1161

Continental/American

F ★ ★ ★
S ★ ★ ★
A ★ ★ ★
P ★ ★ ★

No dress restrictions
Garage parking
All major credit cards
Full bar
Reservations required

Lunch/
Dinner: Daily 11:30AM-11:30PM

Considered the "showplace" of Ghirardelli Square, Maxwell's Plum serves everything from hamburgers to chateaubriand — excellent seafood, pastas, and sumptuous desserts.

MODESTO LANZONE'S   68

601 Van Ness Avenue
San Francisco, CA
(415) 928-0400

Italian

F ★ ★ ★
S ★ ★ ★
A ★ ★ ★
P ★ ★ ★ ★

Jacket required
Valet parking
All major credit cards
Full bar
Reservations required

Lunch/
Dinner: Daily 11:30AM-12:00AM

Spacious and meticulously planned, this restaurant serves as a modern art gallery, with owner Modesto Lanzone's private art collection on display, and as a showcase for beautifully presented Italian food. The pastas are above reproach, and the Chicken Cacciatore highly praised.

NARSAI'S   74

385 Colusa Avenue
Kensington, CA
(415) 527-7900

French/Mediterranean

F ★ ★ ★ ★
S ★ ★ ★ ½
A ★ ★ ★
P ★ ★ ★ ½

No dress restrictions
Lot and street parking
All major credit cards
Full bar
Reservations recommended

Dinner: Sun.-Thurs. 5:00PM-10:00PM
           Fri. & Sat. 5:00PM-11:00PM
Brunch: Sun. 10:00AM-2:00PM

Situated in a quiet neighborhood in North Berkeley, Narsai's offers relaxed dining in the warm glow of California redwood and an original art display. The wine list is world-class, and the menu offers a wide range of full-course epicurean dinners.

NORTH BEACH   19
RESTAURANT

1512 Stockton Street
San Francisco, CA
(415) 392-1700

Italian

F ★ ★ ★ ½
S ★ ★ ★ ½
A ★ ★ ★
P ★ ★ ½

No dress restrictions
Valet parking
All major credit cards
Full bar
Reservations recommended

Lunch/
Dinner: Daily 11:30AM-11:30PM

Lorenzo Petroni and chef Bruno Orsi endeavor to bring you the finest Cucina Toscana possible here. They buy only the finest meats, vegetables, cheese, and fish (often from their own boat); make fresh pasta daily; cure their own prosciutto hams; and taste and serve the finest of California and foreign wines. The service is congenial and the atmosphere appealing.

OLD POODLE DOG   53
RESTAURANT

161 Sutter Street
San Francisco, CA
(415) 392-0353

French

F ★ ★ ★ ½
S ★ ★ ★
A ★ ★ ★
P ★ ★ ★ ½

Jacket required
Garage parking
AE, DC, MC, V
Full bar
Reservations recommended

Lunch: Mon.-Fri. 11:00AM-2:30PM
Dinner: Tues.-Sat. 6:00PM-9:30PM
Closed Sunday

Here you'll find décor reminiscent of Paris in the '30s, with the ceiling used to create a lovely homage to Matisse. The French cuisine served here is modified with contemporary touches. Specialties of the house include rack of lamb and veal medallions. Pastries and ice cream, made in house, are pure caloric poetry.

ORSI   52

375 Bush Street
San Francisco, CA
(415) 981-6535

Italian

F ★ ★ ★ ½
S ★ ★ ★ ½
A ★ ★ ★
P ★ ★ ★

Jacket required
Street parking
All major credit cards
Full bar
Reservations recommended

Lunch/
Dinner: Mon.-Fri. 11:30AM-11:30PM
Sat. 5:30PM-11:30PM
Closed Sunday

In the grand tradition, Orsi's dining room is lavish and ornate. Lovers of Northern Italian cooking will appreciate the heritage recipes, in the family for generations, responsible for such specialties as Veal alla Valdostana, Lamb du Medici and Beef alla Orsi, included in the menu.

PAPRIKAS FONO   4

Ghirardelli Square
900 North Point Street
San Francisco, CA
(415) 441-1223

Hungarian

F ★ ★ ★ ½
S ★ ★ ★ ½
A ★ ★ ★
P ★ ★ ½

Good taste in dress required
Garage parking
AE, MC, V
Full bar
Reservations recommended

Lunch/
Dinner: Mon.-Thurs. 11:30AM-11:00PM
Fri. & Sat. 11:30AM-12:00AM
Sun. 11:30AM-10:30PM

Decorated with charming Hungarian folk art and hand-painted furniture, this restaurant brings a Budapest ambiance to a great location that offers enclosed terrace dining overlooking the bay. Veal Paprikash, Transylvanian Cabbage Gulyas, and pork, lamb, prawn and seafood dishes, treat your palate to Hungarian-style cooking.

PASHA 22

1516 Broadway
San Francisco, CA
(415) 885-4477

Moroccan

F ★ ★ ★ ½
S ★ ★ ★ ½
A ★ ★ ★ ½
P ★ ★ ★

No dress restrictions
Valet parking
All major credit cards
Full bar
Reservations required

Dinner: Tues.-Sun. 6:00PM-1:00AM
         Closed Monday

Escape to the world of "a thousand and one nights," and feast at Pasha's in an opulent sheik's tent. The exotic Middle Eastern cuisine is ordered from an à la carte menu, and served to the lively accompaniment of harem dancers.

PHIL LEHR'S STEAKERY 69

Hilton Hotel Tower
330 Taylor Street
San Francisco, CA
(415) 673-6800

American

F ★ ★ ★ ½
S ★ ★ ½
A ★ ★ ★ ½
P ★ ★ ★

Jacket required
Valet parking

All major credit cards
Full bar
Reservations recommended

Dinner: Nightly 5:00PM-12:00AM

Pleasantly posh, this bustling establishment features steak cut to your order in the dining room by tuxedoed butchers. Chicken, lamb, lobster, and fresh fish entrées are also available. Try the unique San Francisco "Fog" desserts, a popular house specialty.

PREGO 13

2000 Union Street
San Francisco, CA
(415) 563-3305

Italian

F ★ ★ ★
S ★ ★ ★ ½
A ★ ★ ★
P ★ ★ ½

No dress restrictions
Street parking
AE, MC, V
Full bar
Reservations not required

Lunch/
Dinner: Daily 11:30AM-12:00AM

A neighborhood gathering spot for informal dining in a casual, though sophisticated atmosphere. You'll find homemade pasta, and an oak-burning brick pizza oven. Grilled fish, meats, and poultry entrées are well prepared, and the service is prompt and friendly.

RENE VERDON 59
LE TRIANON

242 O'Farrell Street
San Francisco, CA
(415) 982-9353

French

F ★ ★ ★ ★
S ★ ★ ★ ½
A ★ ★ ★
P ★ ★ ★ ★

Jacket and tie required
Paid parking by customer
All major credit cards
Full bar
Reservations required

Dinner: Mon.-Sat. 6:00PM-10:00PM
          Closed Sunday

Compliments to owner-chef Rene Verdon, and his wife Yvette, your gracious hostess, for orchestrating a triumphant dining experience. The Louis XV décor, classic and contemporary French cuisine, and smooth service by the international staff all contribute to your evening's total enjoyment.

SAM'S GRILL   50

374 Bush Street
San Francisco, CA
(415) 421-0594

Seafood

F ★ ★ ★ ½
S ★ ★ ★
A ★ ★ ★
P ★ ★ ½

No dress restrictions
Street parking
MC, V
Full bar
Reservations accepted for parties of 6 or more

Lunch/
Dinner: Mon.-Fri. 11:00AM-8:30PM
          Closed Saturday and Sunday

Founded in 1867, Sam's Grill is an old-style San Francisco fish restaurant with an open kitchen, mahogany walls, and service by tuxedoed waiters. Fresh Pacific Coast seafood is the specialty of the house, although steaks, chops, and chicken share the bill of fare.

SANTA FE BAR AND GRILL   72

1310 University Avenue
Berkeley, CA
(415) 841-4740

Californian

F ★ ★ ★ ½
S ★ ★ ★
A ★ ★ ★
P ★ ★ ★

Good taste in dress required
Lot parking
AE, MC, V
Full bar
Reservations recommended

Lunch: Daily 11:30AM-2:30PM
Dinner: Sun.-Thurs. 5:30PM-10:00PM
          Fri. & Sat. 5:30PM-11:00PM

The unique décor and ambiance you will find here is inspired by the building's history as a train station for the Santa Fe Superchief. Chef Jeremiah Tower's trademarks include fresh local ingredients prepared in simple, though imaginative ways, and grilling over mesquite charcoal.

SCOMA'S   6

Pier 47
San Francisco, CA
(415) 771-4383

Italian-style Seafood

F ★ ★ ★ ½
S ★ ★ ★
A ★ ★ ★
P ★ ★ ★ ½

Good taste in dress required
Valet parking
All major credit cards
Full bar
Reservations not required

Lunch/
Dinner: Daily 11:30AM-11:00PM

Scoma's is at the end of Fish Alley on Pier 47. Identical lunch and dinner menus feature fresh fish (often from their own boat) cooked-to-order, Italian style. This can be a lengthy process, but you'll discover it is well worth the wait.

SCOTT'S SEAFOOD GRILL   9

2400 Lombard Street
San Francisco, CA
(415) 563-8988

Seafood

F ★ ★ ★ ½
S ★ ★ ★
A ★ ★ ★ ½
P ★ ★ ★

Good taste in dress required
Valet parking
All major credit cards
Full bar
Reservations not required

Lunch/
Dinner: Daily 11:00AM-11:00PM

Scott's provides a congenial atmosphere in which to indulge in the freshest possible seafoods, garnered from all over the world. The fisherman's stew has a loyal following — daily specials revolve around market availability, and "the catch of the day."

THE SHADOWS   15

1349 Montgomery Street
San Francisco, CA
(415) 982-5536

German

F ★ ★ ★ ½
S ★ ★ ★
A ★ ★ ★ ★
P ★ ★ ★

Good taste in dress required
Street parking

All major credit cards
Full bar
Reservations not required

Dinner: Nightly 5:00PM-10:30PM

Occupying a century old loft on Telegraph Hill, this distinguished restaurant has delighted three generations of diners with its wonderful view, cozy ambiance, and classic German cooking. You'll find conventional American entrées also included on the menu.

SPENGER'S FISH   72
GROTTO

1919 4th Street
Berkeley, CA
(415) 845-7771

Seafood

F ★ ★ ★ ½
S ★ ★ ★
A ★ ★ ½
P ★ ★

Good taste in dress required
Lot parking
All major credit cards
Full bar
Reservations not required

Breakfast/
Lunch/
Dinner: Daily 8:00AM-12:00AM

Two generations of Spengers continue the family tradition for fine seafood started here at the turn of the century. Fish from their own boats and from all parts of the world are offered. The atmosphere is low-key and congenial.

SQUARE ONE   29

190 Pacific
San Francisco, CA
(415) 788-1110

International/Mediterranean

F ★ ★ ★
S ★ ★ ★
A ★ ★ ★
P ★ ★ ★

Good taste in dress required
Valet and street parking
MC, V
Full bar
Reservations required

Lunch: Mon.-Fri. 11:30AM-2:30PM
Dinner: Mon.-Thurs. 5:30PM-10:30PM
         Fri. & Sat. 5:30PM-11:30PM
         Closed Sunday

This aesthetically pleasing sleek, modern eatery is large, open, and airy. Here owner Joyce Goldstein focuses on serving ever-changing cuisine in the international and Mediterranean manner, that reflects the current availability of fresh, quality ingredients, using seasonal bounty for her menu mainstays.

SQUIRE RESTAURANT   40

Fairmont Hotel
950 Mason Street
San Francisco, CA
(415) 772-5211

Continental

F ★ ★ ★ ½
S ★ ★ ★ ½
A ★ ★ ★ ½
P ★ ★ ★ ½

Jacket and tie required
Valet and lot parking
All major credit cards
Full bar
Reservations recommended

Lunch: Mon.-Fri. 11:30AM-2:30PM
Dinner: Nightly 6:00PM-11:00PM

This domed Victorian dining room sparkles with mirrors, glass, and chandeliers. Against this dazzling background excellent cuisine is served with aplomb. The wine list features California boutique vintners, and the menu includes daily chef selections.

STARS   71

150 Redwood Alley
San Francisco, CA
(415) 861-7827

Californian

F ★ ★ ★
S ★ ★ ★
A ★ ★ ★
P ★ ★ ½

No dress restrictions
Street parking
AE, MC, V
Full bar
Reservations recommended

Lunch: Mon.-Sat. 11:30AM-2:30PM
Dinner: Mon.-Sat. 5:30PM-10:30PM
         Sun. 5:00PM-10:00PM
Brunch: Sun. 11:30AM-2:30PM

The sure hand of chef Jeremiah Tower, an acknowledged leader in the resurgence of American cuisine, is much in evidence here. The décor is light, modern and casual with gleaming brass and redwood featured. From the open kitchen comes such specialties as oysters with spicy lamb sausage and mesquite grilled steaks and fish. Homemade desserts include James Beard's apple pie.

TADICH GRILL   45

240 California Street
San Francisco, CA
(415) 391-2373

Seafood

F ★ ★ ★ ½
S ★ ★ ★
A ★ ★ ½
P ★ ★ ★

Good taste in dress required
Street parking
Credit cards not accepted
Full bar
Reservations not required

Lunch/
Dinner: Mon.-Sat. 11:30AM-8:30PM
Closed Sunday

This historic restaurant dates back to 1849, and its high ceilings, booths, long bar, and counter reflect its early San Francisco heritage. Charcoal broiled seafood and meats, and other house specialties, plus scrumptious desserts, keep a large clientele happy.

TRADER VIC'S 60

20 Cosmo Place
San Francisco, CA
(415) 776-2232

Continental/Polynesian

F ★ ★ ★ ½
S ★ ★ ★
A ★ ★ ★
P ★ ★ ★ ½

Jacket and tie required, no jeans
Valet parking
All major credit cards
Full bar
Reservations required

Lunch: Mon.-Fri. 11:30AM-2:30PM
Dinner: Mon.-Sat. 5:00PM-12:00AM
Sun. 4:30PM-11:00PM

Trader Vic's, celebrating its 50th anniversary year, now has 20 sister-restaurants in America, Europe, and the Far East. The wide variety of entrées include Chinese barbecued meats, fish, and poultry; Indonesian lamb roast; and South Seas specialties. The exotic décor is pure Polynesian.

VANESSI'S 25

498 Broadway
San Francisco, CA
(415) 421-0890

Italian/Continental

F ★ ★ ★ ½
S ★ ★ ★ ½
A ★ ★ ½
P ★ ★ ½

Good taste in dress required
Lot parking
All major credit cards
Full bar
Reservations recommended

Lunch/
Dinner: Mon.-Sat. 11:30AM-1:00AM
Sun. 4:30PM-1:00AM

Opened in 1936, this restaurant has prospered and endured by consistently setting high standards for the basic quality of the food. Daily specials, fresh fish, a wide range of veal entrées, and fresh-made daily pastas augment the broad and varied menu. The fish stew and minestrone soup are hearty classics with a loyal following.

VICTOR'S 64

Westin St. Francis Hotel
335 Powell Street
San Francisco, CA
(415) 774-0154

Californian

F ★ ★ ★ ½
S ★ ★ ★ ½
A ★ ★ ★ ★
P ★ ★ ★ ★

Jacket preferred
Valet and lot parking
All major credit cards
Full bar
Reservations recommended

Dinner: Nightly 6:00PM-11:00PM

This grandiose restaurant, with its inspiring city and bay area view and 50,000 bottle wine cellar, lets you sample the seasonal delights of the region as prepared by chef Joel Rambaud. Experience such marvels as rabbit filet and veal liver with honey and caraway, or the fresh fish of the day.

YAMATO   42

717 California Street
San Francisco, CA
(415) 397-3456

Japanese

F ★ ★ ★
S ★ ★ ★
A ★ ★ ★ ½
P ★ ★ ★

Good taste in dress required
Street and garage parking
All major credit cards
Full bar
Reservations recommended

Lunch: Tues.-Fri. 11:45AM-2:00PM
Dinner: Tues.-Sun. 5:00PM-10:00PM
          Closed Monday

The oldest Japanese restaurant on the West Coast, Yamato is a long-time award-winner. The cuisine includes crisp shrimp, seafood and vegetable tempuras, steak teriyaki, and sukiyaki prepared at the table, plus a busy sushi bar. A Uguisu Bari bridge, pond, and diminutive gardens create a lovely ambiance.

YOSHIDA-YA   14

2909 Webster Street
San Francisco, CA
(415) 346-3431

Japanese

F ★ ★ ★ ½
S ★ ★ ★
A ★ ★ ★
P ★ ★ ★

Jacket required, no shorts or jogging suits
Street parking
All major credit cards
Full bar
Reservations required

Dinner: Sun.-Thurs. 5:30PM-10:30PM
          Fri. & Sat. 5:30PM-11:00PM

Expect an unusually rewarding adventure in dining at the beautifully decorated, award-winning Yoshida-Ya. Specialties include yakitori, kushi-katsu, Seafood Fantasia, Prawn-Lovers' Special, sushi, and an Omakase dinner that is chef's choice.

ZOLA'S   36

1722 Sacramento Street
San Francisco, CA
(415) 775-3311

French

F ★ ★ ★ ½
S ★ ★ ★ ½
A ★ ★ ★ ½
P ★ ★ ★

No dress restrictions
Lot parking
AE, DC, MC
Beer/Wine
Reservations required

Dinner: Tues.-Sat. 6:00PM-11:00PM
          Sun. 5:30PM-10:00PM
          Closed Monday

Zola's has a personality all its own. The small dining room is understated and restrained, featuring a dramatic central bouquet of fresh flowers as its focal point. Catherine Pantsios, owner/chef, offers her interpretation of country French cuisine, offering aromatic, savory, deeply satisfying dishes.

Seattle

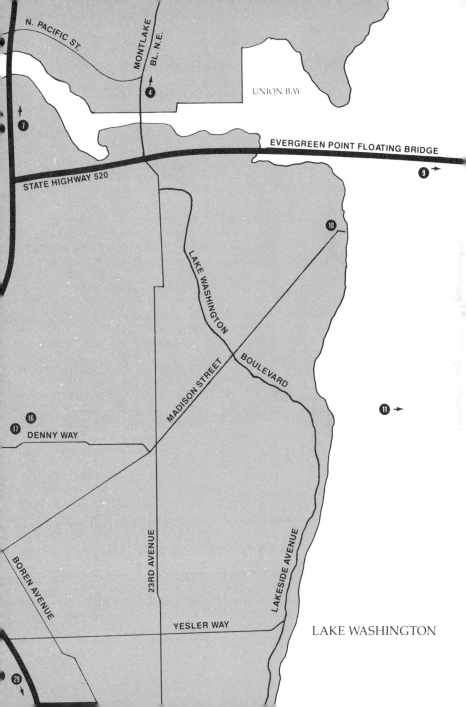

ALEXIS RESTAURANT   24

1007 First Avenue at Madison
Seattle, WA
(206) 624-4844

French

F ★ ★ ★
S ★ ★ ★
A ★ ★ ★
P ★ ★ ★

Good taste in dress required
Valet, lot, and street parking
All major credit cards
Full bar
Reservations recommended

Breakfast/
Lunch/
Dinner: Daily 6:30AM-10:30PM

The ambiance you will find in this restored
classic 19th century art déco building
echoes the mood of fine restaurants in
small European hotels. The French cuisine
blends classic with nouvelle cooking styles
and is based on using the freshest possible
Pacific Northwest meat, fish, and fowl.

AMERICA'S CUP   5

1900 North Northlake Way
Seattle, WA
(206) 633-0161

American

F ★ ★ ★ ½
S ★ ★ ★
A ★ ★ ★
P ★ ★ ½

Good taste in dress required
Lot and street parking
AE, MC, V
Full bar
Reservations recommended

Lunch: Mon.-Sat. 11:30AM-2:30PM
Dinner: Mon.-Sat. 5:00PM-10:30PM
          Sun. 4:00PM-10:30PM
Brunch: Sun. 9:30AM-2:30PM

Sleek and trim with a beautiful bay window view of the gasworks, park, Union
Bay, the Space Needle, and the lights of
Seattle, this winning restaurant focuses
on dishes featuring varieties of fresh
Northwest fish. Other equally well prepared American classics are also available.

BAFFERT'S   16
NORTHWEST CUISINE

314 Broadway East
Seattle, WA
(206) 323-1990

American/Continental

F ★ ★ ★
S ★ ★ ★
A ★ ★ ★
P ★ ★ ½

No dress restrictions
Valet parking
AE, DC, MC, V
Full bar
Reservations not required

Lunch: Mon.-Sat. 11:30AM-2:30PM
Dinner: Nightly 5:30PM-11:00PM
Brunch: Sun. 9:00AM-2:30PM

Fresh seafood is the hallmark of this smart
downtown restaurant where you will find
at least six fresh fish specials nightly, using seafood from the Northwest and
around the world. The menu is rife with
imaginative dishes of both American and
continental background.

BRASSERIE PITTSBOURG   26

602 1st Avenue
Seattle, WA
(206) 623-4167

French

F ★ ★ ★
S ★ ★ ★
A ★ ★ ★
P ★ ★ ½

Good taste in dress required
Valet, lot, and street parking
AE, DC, MC, V
Full bar
Reservations not required

Lunch: Mon.-Sat. 11:30AM-2:30PM
Dinner: Mon.-Sat. 5:30PM-10:30PM
         Closed Sunday

This is Seattle's oldest continuously operating restaurant, and it has been flourishing with undiminished style since 1892. The original pressed tin ceilings and marble counters are still part of the pleasantly informal décor. Parisian-trained chef Francois, and Julia Kissel, the current owners, present classic French cuisine enhanced with specialties based on the Northwest's seasonal provender.

CANLIS RESTAURANT   8

2576 Aurora Avenue North
Seattle, WA
(206) 283-3313

American

F ★ ★ ★ ½
S ★ ★ ★ ½
A ★ ★ ★
P ★ ★ ★

Jacket required
Valet parking
All major credit cards
Full bar
Reservations required

Dinner: Mon.-Sat. 5:30PM-1:00AM
         Closed Sunday

For 30 years patrons have been happily endorsing the renowned copper broiler cooking method used here to produce grilled steaks and fresh seafood, the specialties of the house. The tradition of the Canlis family for using heavy linens, sterling, and fine china continues, as does the warmth with which you are greeted, and the friendly uncompromising service.

THE CARVERY   28

SeaTac International Airport
Seattle, WA
(206) 433-5622

Continental

F ★ ★ ★
S ★ ★ ★
A ★ ★ ★ ½
P ★ ★ ½

Shoes and shirt required
Lot parking
AE, MC, V
Full bar
Reservations not required

Breakfast/
Lunch/
Dinner: Daily 6:00AM-10:00PM

As posh and sedate as an elite English men's club, this restaurant with its gleaming dark wood and Oriental carpets brings a sense of old world elegance to a very modern setting. Here you will enjoy spectacular views of the SeaTac runways and the Olympic mountain range while dining on fine continental cuisine and Northwest regional specialties.

CHEZ CLAUDE   2

419 Main Street
Edmonds, WA
(206) 778-9888

French

F ★ ★ ★
S ★ ★ ★
A ★ ★ ★
P ★ ★ ★

Good taste in dress required
Street parking
All major credit cards
Full bar
Reservations required

Dinner: Tues.-Sun. 5:30PM-10:30PM
Closed Monday

The "house that Claude built" teems with French provincial charm and is the perfect setting to display the culinary expertise of owner/chef Claude Faure, a third generation French chef. The menu boasts such delicacies as pheasant, veal, fresh salmon, and rack of lamb.

DOMINIQUE'S PLACE   10

1927 43rd Avenue East
Seattle, WA
(206) 329-6620

French

F ★ ★ ★
S ★ ★ ★
A ★ ★ ★
P ★ ★ ★

Good taste in dress required
Lot and street parking
All major credit cards
Beer/Wine
Reservations recommended

Lunch/
Dinner: Mon.-Thurs. 11:30AM-10:00PM
Fri. & Sat. 11:30AM-11:30PM
Brunch/
Dinner: Sun. 10:30AM-10:00PM

As sure-handed with décor as he is with subtle flavors, owner Dominique Place, presents superb French cuisine in a beautifully appointed country French setting. You'll enjoy formal service, fresh flowers, and entrées such as pepper steak, fresh venison, smoked duck salad with orange dressing, and fresh young rabbit salad.

EL GAUCHO   21

624 Olive Way
Seattle, WA
(206) 682-3202

Argentine

F ★ ★ ★ ½
S ★ ★ ★ ½
A ★ ★ ★
P ★ ★ ★

Good taste in dress required
Valet (weekends only) and street parking
AE, DC, MC, V
Full bar
Reservations required

Lunch: Mon.-Fri. 11:00AM-3:00PM
Dinner: Mon.-Fri. 5:00PM-12:00AM
Sat. 5:00PM-11:00PM
Hunt's
Breakfast: Sat. 11:00AM-2:00PM
Closed Sunday

You'll find a wealth of luxury touches in this elegant establishment. There are mink-lined and purple velvet booths, large paintings, and an attitude that implies you, the guest, deserve nothing but the best. Owner Don Rose specializes in seafood and choice aged steaks.

GERARD'S RELAIS   7
DE LYON

17121 Bothell Way, N.E.
Bothell, WA
(206) 485-7600

French

F ★ ★ ★ ★
S ★ ★ ★ ★
A ★ ★ ★ ½
P ★ ★ ★ ½

No dress restrictions
Lot parking
AE, DC, MC, V
Full bar
Reservations required

Dinner: Tues.-Sun. 5:00PM-11:00PM
Closed Monday

Chef/owner Gérard Parrat's "Bocuse" training is evidenced in the triumphant entrées emerging from the kitchen of this restful country home turned chic French eatery. Here the freshest ingredients are imaginatively blended into such specialties as Saumon en Croûte, and Veal Ciboulette.

THE GREEN LAKE GRILL 6

7200 East Greenlake Drive North
Seattle, WA
(206) 524-0365

American

F ★ ★ ★
S ★ ★ ★
A ★ ★ ★
P ★ ★ ½

No dress restrictions
Street parking
AE, MC, V
Full bar
Reservations not required

Lunch: Mon.-Fri. 11:30AM-2:30PM
Dinner: Nightly 6:00PM-11:00PM

Karl Beckley, owner/chef, established this restaurant to combine the finest Pacific Northwest ingredients with nouvelle cooking techniques. The resulting cuisine brings a new dimension to dining options in Seattle and freshness and finest quality are the key elements of its success. The nightly specials offer the season's best, and there is a broad list of imported and domestic wines.

HENRY'S OFF BROADWAY   17

1705 East Olive Way
Seattle, WA
(206) 329-8063

Continental/American

F ★ ★ ★ ½
S ★ ★ ★ ½
A ★ ★ ★
P ★ ★ ★

No dress restrictions
Valet parking

All major credit cards
Full bar
Reservations not required

Lunch: Mon.-Fri. 11:30AM-2:00PM
Dinner: Mon.-Thurs. 5:30PM-10:00PM
          Fri. & Sat. 5:30PM-11:00PM
          Sun. 5:00PM-10:00PM

The recipient of many awards, this '30s-themed restaurant features cuisine based on continental and American dishes utilizing regional ingredients. House specialties include fresh fish, aged steaks, rack of lamb Dijon, and seafood fettuccine. There's a dining terrace, and an Oyster Bar lounge, in addition to the dining rooms.

IVAR'S INDIAN   3
SALMON HOUSE

401 N.E. Northlake Way
Seattle, WA
(206) 632-0767

American

F ★ ★ ★
S ★ ★ ★
A ★ ★ ★
P ★ ★ ½

No dress restrictions
Lot and street parking
AE, MC, V
Full bar
Reservations not required

Lunch: Mon.-Fri. 11:30AM-2:00PM
Dinner: Mon.-Fri. 5:00PM-10:00PM
          Sat. & Sun. 4:00PM-10:00PM
Brunch: Sun. 10:00AM-2:00PM

This unique establishment with its striking architecture and all-cedar construction hugs the North Shore of Lake Union providing guests with a dramatic Seattle skyline view and an endless boat parade. The Salmon House has become a mecca for local and tourist gourmands who relish the Indian style alder-smoked salmon, cod, and other native seafood specialties.

JAKE O'SHAUGHNESSEY'S 12

100 Mercer
Seattle, WA
(206) 285-1897

American

F ★ ★ ★ ½
S ★ ★ ★
A ★ ★ ★
P ★ ★ ½

Good taste in dress required
Lot and street parking
AE, MC, V
Full bar
Reservations recommended

Dinner: Sun. & Mon. 5:00PM-10:00PM
          Tues.-Sat. 5:00PM-11:00PM

Diner's favorites at this legendary Seattle establishment are fresh salmon roasted over riverbed alder and saloon beef (prime rib roasted in a cast of roasting salt). Of course, the kitchen also offers a full complement of fresh water fish and shellfish.

JONAH & THE WHALE 11

Holiday Inn Bellevue
11211 Main Street
Bellevue, WA
(206) 455-5240

Continental

F ★ ★ ★ ½
S ★ ★ ★ ½
A ★ ★ ★
P ★ ★ ★ ½

Good taste in dress required
Lot parking
All major credit cards
Full bar
Reservations recommended

Lunch: Mon.-Fri. 11:30AM-2:00PM
Dinner: Mon.-Thurs. 6:00PM-10:30PM
          Fri. & Sat. 6:00PM-11:00PM
          Closed Sunday

This three-tiered establishment sports a huge whale, rendered in copper and brass, occupying the ceiling. The aura is intimate and romantic, with attentive tableside service of many entrées.

LE PROVENCAL 9 RESTAURANT FRANÇAIS

212 Central Way
Kirkland, WA
(206) 827-3300

French

F ★ ★ ★ ½
S ★ ★ ★
A ★ ★ ★
P ★ ★ ½

Good taste in dress required
Street parking
All major credit cards
Full bar
Reservations required

Dinner: Mon.-Sat. 5:30PM-11:00PM
          Closed Sunday

Experience the warm intimacy of French countryside dining at this rustic restaurant. The expertise owner/chef Philippe Gayte garnered in his parent's restaurant in Avignon, France, is evident in every phase of this operation.

LE TASTEVIN 14

19 West Harrison
Seattle, WA
(206) 283-0991

French

F ★ ★ ★ ½
S ★ ★ ★ ½
A ★ ★ ★
P ★ ★ ★

No dress restrictions
Lot parking
AE, MC, V

Full bar
Reservations not required

Lunch: Mon.-Fri. 11:30AM-2:30PM
Dinner: Mon.-Sat. 5:00PM-11:30PM
Closed Sunday

The combined ideas of owners Emile Ninaud and Jacques Boiroux blend to form a remarkable French dining experience here. The ambiance is warm, the water and mountain view inspiring, the service flawless, the wine list award-winning, and the cuisine consistently delicious.

MAXI'S 29

Red Lion Inn/Sea-Tac
18740 Pacific Highway South
Seattle, WA
(206) 246-8600

Continental

F ★ ★ ★ ½
S ★ ★ ★ ½
A ★ ★ ★ ½
P ★ ★ ★

Good taste in dress required
Lot parking
All major credit cards
Full bar
Reservations recommended

Lunch: Mon.-Fri. 11:30AM-1:30PM
Dinner: Nightly 5:30PM-10:00PM
Brunch: Sun. 9:00AM-2:00PM

Posh and formal with a view of the airport and regal Mt. Rainier, here you'll enjoy tableside service, band music for dancing nightly, and excellent continental cuisine. Traditional favorites such as Steak Diane and scampi are offered.

MIKADO 27

514 South Jackson Street
Seattle, WA
(206) 622-5206

Japanese

F ★ ★ ★ ½
S ★ ★ ★
A ★ ★ ★
P ★ ★ ★

No dress restrictions
Lot parking
AE, DC, MC, V
Full bar
Reservations recommended

Dinner: Mon.-Sat. 5:30PM-10:00PM
Closed Sunday

East greets West with welcoming formality at this authentic Japanese dining establishment. You may opt for Japanese-style seating in the private tatami rooms, or dine with conventional seating. You'll find sushi and sashimi plus a full range of exquisite entrées such as Beef Mikado, King Crab Batayaki, and Salmon Teriyaki.

MIRABEAU 23

46th Floor, 1001 4th Avenue
Seattle, WA
(206) 624-4550

Continental

F ★ ★ ★ ½
S ★ ★ ★ ½
A ★ ★ ★ ½
P ★ ★ ★

No dress restrictions
Lot parking
All major credit cards
Full bar
Reservations recommended

Lunch: Mon.-Fri. 11:30AM-2:00PM
Dinner: Mon.-Sat. 5:30PM-10:00PM
Closed Sunday

Poised serenely on its lofty niche 729 feet high, this restaurant affords you an unparalleled view of Seattle and its sylvan environs. A dazzling success story since its opening in 1969, the wine list and cuisine continue to delight discerning diners.

1904 RESTAURANT   20

1904 4th Avenue
Seattle, WA
(206) 682-4142

French/Italian

F ★ ★ ★
S ★ ★ ★
A ★ ★ ★
P ★ ★

No dress restrictions
Street parking
AE, DC, MC, V
Full bar
Reservations not required

Lunch/
Dinner: Mon.-Sat. 11:30AM-2:00AM
          Closed Sunday

This downtown haven offers you French and Italian favorites in a sophisticated setting. Savor homemade pâtés and carpaccio while considering your entrée choice. Fresh fish, fresh pastas, beef, chicken, and lamb dishes are all there to tempt you.

THE PALM COURT   18

The Westin Hotel, Seattle
1900 Fifth Avenue
Seattle, WA
(206) 728-1000

Continental

F ★ ★ ★ ½
S ★ ★ ★ ★
A ★ ★ ★ ½
P ★ ★ ★ ½

Jacket and tie required
Valet parking
All major credit cards
Full bar
Reservations recommended

Lunch: Mon.-Fri. 11:30AM-2:00PM
Dinner: Mon.-Thurs. 6:00PM-9:30PM
          Fri. & Sat. 6:00PM-10:30PM
          Closed Sunday

As alluring as a glimmering oasis, this restaurant with its Tivoli lights, crystal chandeliers, and glass pavilion dining room with twinkling city lights overhead, is an elegant setting for gourmet delights.

RAY'S BOATHOUSE   23

6049 Seaview Avenue N.W.
Seattle, WA
(206) 789-4130

Seafood

F ★ ★ ★ ½
S ★ ★ ★
A ★ ★ ★
P ★ ★ ½

No dress restrictions
Lot parking
All major credit cards
Full bar
Reservations recommended

Lunch: Daily 11:30AM-2:45PM
Dinner: Nightly 5:00PM-10:00PM

Located on the waterfront at Shilshole Bay, this stellar dining spot lets you watch the boats go by, and see the sunset behind the towering Olympic mountains. In this placid setting you will find simply prepared Northwest seafood.

RAY'S DOWNTOWN   25

2nd & Marion Streets
Seattle, WA
(206) 623-7999

Seafood

F ★ ★ ★ ½
S ★ ★ ★
A ★ ★ ★
P ★ ★ ½

No dress restrictions
Garage parking
All major credit cards
Full bar
Reservations recommended

Lunch: Mon.-Fri. 11:00AM-2:45PM
Dinner: Nightly 5:00PM-10:00PM

The food served here echoes the menu of its Boathouse sibling: Simply prepared Northwest seafood, with king salmon, Olympia oysters, dungeness crab, and spot shrimp featured. Here the family resemblance ends, however, for this Ray's is highly sophisticated with Northwest art setting the tone of the décor.

RISTORANTE SALUTE 4

3410 N.E. 55th Street
Seattle, WA
(206) 527-8600

Italian

F ★ ★ ★
S ★ ★ ★
A ★ ★
P ★ ½

No dress restrictions
Lot and street parking
MC, V
Beer/Wine
Reservations not required

Dinner: Tues.-Sun. 5:00PM-10:00PM
Closed Monday

This newly launched entry in the Seattle restaurant scene features the culinary artistry of Raffaele Calise who brings Neapolitan know-how to the kitchen. Small in size but grandiose in cuisine, you will find such delicacies as fettuccine with smoked salmon, peas, shallots, brandy, and cream; 10 original pizza combinations, and triumphant desserts.

ROSELLINI'S FOUR-10 4

Fourth and Wall Streets
Seattle, WA
(206) 624-5464

Continental/American

F ★ ★ ★ ½
S ★ ★ ★ ½
A ★ ★ ★ ½
P ★ ★ ★

Good taste in dress required
Valet parking
All major credit cards
Full bar
Reservations recommended

Lunch/
Dinner: Mon.-Fri. 11:00AM-12:00AM
Sat. 5:00PM-12:00AM
Closed Sunday

Winner of fine dining awards for 28 consecutive years, this illustrious restaurant moves smoothly ahead under the personal supervision of owner Victor Rosellini. You'll find tapestried walls, crisp linens, and a broad menu ranging from sweetbreads to chicken Kiev, and from fish and seafood dishes to Italian specialties.

ROSELLINI'S 22
OTHER PLACE

319 Union Street
Seattle, WA
(206) 623-7340

French

F ★ ★ ★ ½
S ★ ★ ★ ½
A ★ ★ ★ ½
P ★ ★ ★ ½

No dress restrictions
Lot parking
All major credit cards
Full bar
Reservations recommended

Lunch/
Dinner: Mon.-Fri. 11:00AM-11:00PM
Sat. 5:00PM-12:00AM
Closed Sunday

Homage is paid to the prolific bounty of the Northwest region here, where the kitchen transforms the freshest of local ingredients into epicurean French cuisine. During the decade the Other Place has been in business, close connections have been established with many farms, ensuring patrons of a wide range of unusually enticing items on the ever-changing menu.

SIMON'S   29

17401 Southcenter Parkway
Seattle, WA
(206) 575-3500

American/Continental

F ★ ★ ★ ½
S ★ ★ ★ ½
A ★ ★ ★ ★
P ★ ★ ★ ½

Good taste in dress required
Lot parking
All major credit cards
Full bar
Reservations recommended

Lunch: Mon.-Fri. 11:00AM-2:30PM
Dinner: Nightly 5:30PM-10:30PM

Open and airy, with a sense of modern grandeur, this atrium setting projects a great sense of joie de vivre. Here you can sample such delicacies as brandied dungeness crab legs, duckling caraway, veal roquefort, fresh Northwest salmon noir and a host of other inventive dishes. The service is silky smooth and the wine list intelligently assembled.

THIRTEEN COINS   15 & 29
RESTAURANTS

125 Boren Avenue North
Seattle, WA
(206) 682-2513

18000 Pacific Hiway South
Seattle, WA
(206) 243-9500

American

F ★ ★ ★ ½
S ★ ★ ★
A ★ ★ ★
P ★ ★ ★

Good taste in dress required
Lot parking
All major credit cards
Full bar
Reservations not required

Breakfast/
Lunch/
Dinner: Open 24 hours every day

Perfect for spur-of-the-moment gourmet dining, any hour of the day, you can dine intimately in a secluded spot, or enjoy watching the chefs at work from the handsome counter seats. Both locations offer over 120 entrées and the entire menu is served around the clock.

TRADER VIC'S   19

The Westin Hotel, Seattle
1900 Fifth Avenue
Seattle, WA
(206) 728-1000

Polynesian

F ★ ★ ★ ½
S ★ ★ ★
A ★ ★ ★ ½
P ★ ★ ★ ½

Jacket and tie required
Valet parking
All major credit cards
Full bar
Reservations recommended

Lunch: Mon.-Fri. 11:30AM-2:30PM
Dinner: Nightly 5:30PM-10:45PM

This treasure chest of South Seas exotica is the Seattle link in a world-renowned chain. The menu couples continental favorites with authentic Chinese and Polynesian fare. Dining here is a fun experience, and to add to your joy there are more than 77 potent tropical drinks for adventuresome imbibers.

Washington, D.C.

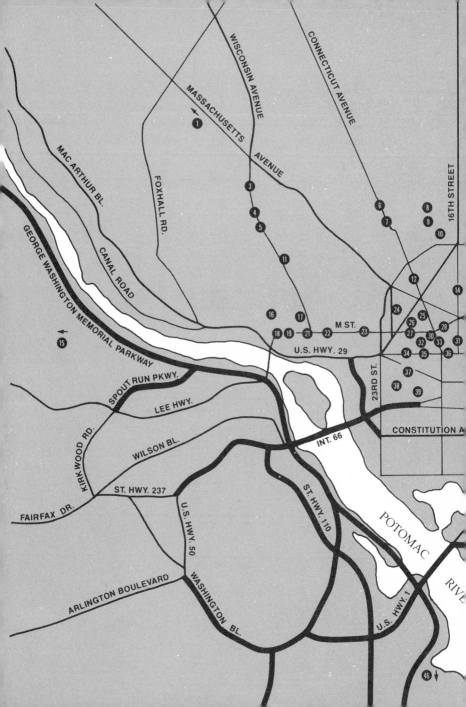

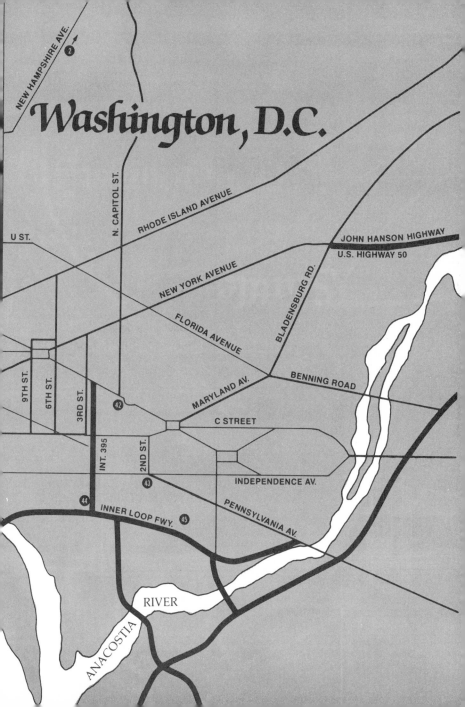

APANA   22

3066 M Street, N.W.
Washington, D.C.
(202) 965-3040

Indian

F ★ ★ ★ ½
S ★ ★ ★
A ★ ★ ★
P ★ ★ ★

No dress restrictions
Street parking
All major credit cards
Full bar
Reservations recommended

Dinner: Sun.-Thurs. 6:00PM-1:00AM
          Fri. & Sat. 6:00PM-12:00AM

Quiet and dimly lit, this intimate rendez-vous has been serving award-winning In-dian cuisine to knowledgeable diners for more than a decade. The tantalizing food is authentic, but mellowed for American tastes.

AUX BEAUX CHAMPS   23

Four Seasons Hotel
2800 Pennsylvania Avenue, N.W.
Washington, D.C.
(202) 342-0810

French

F ★ ★ ★ ★
S ★ ★ ★ ★
A ★ ★ ★ ½
P ★ ★ ★ ★

No dress restrictions
Valet and street parking
All major credit cards
Full bar
Reservations recommended

Breakfast: Daily 7:00AM-11:00AM
Lunch: Daily 12:00PM-2:30PM
Dinner: Nightly 6:30PM-10:30PM

Spacious and luxurious, with regal fresh flower arrangements, this restaurant is dappled with sun light by day, and glow-ing with candles at night. Here you will dine on artfully prepared cuisine, while viewing the sylvan beauty of Rock Creek Park.

THE BROKER   45

713 8th Street, S.E.
Washington, D.C.
(202) 546-8300

Swiss

F ★ ★ ★
S ★ ★ ★
A ★ ★ ★
P ★ ★ ★

Jacket required
Valet parking
AE, MC, V
Full bar
Reservations required

Lunch: Mon.-Fri. 11:30AM-2:30PM
Dinner: Mon.-Thurs. 5:30PM-10:00PM
         Fri. & Sat. 6:00PM-11:00PM
         Sun. 5:00PM-9:00PM
Brunch: Sun. 11:00AM-3:00PM

Open and contemporary in feeling, with exposed brick walls, light woods, skylights, and bright fresh flowers, this Capitol Hill establishment features continental cuisine, rich fondues and "Raclette," a Swiss spe-cialty.

CANTINA D'ITALIA   28

1214 A 18th Street, N.W.
Washington, D.C.
(202) 659-1830

Italian

F ★ ★ ★ ★
S ★ ★ ★ ½
A ★ ★ ★
P ★ ★ ★ ½

Jacket and tie required
Street parking

All major credit cards
Beer/Wine
Reservations required

Lunch: Mon.-Fri. 12:00PM-2:30PM
Dinner: Mon.-Fri. 6:00PM-12:30AM
         Closed Saturday and Sunday

The acknowledged champion of Italian cuisine in Washington, there's Italian art and music in the background, a fine choice of imported wine, pastas made fresh daily, and an ever-changing menu that reflects the seasons.

CLYDE'S   19

3236 M Street, N.W.
Washington, D.C.
(202) 333-9180

American

F ★ ★ ★ ½
S ★ ★ ★ ½
A ★ ★ ★
P ★ ★

No tank tops
Lot and street parking
All major credit cards
Full bar
Reservations not required

Breakfast: Mon.-Fri. 7:30AM-11:30AM
Lunch: Mon.-Fri. 11:00AM-5:00PM
Dinner: Mon.-Sun. 5:00PM-12:00AM
Brunch: Sat. & Sun. 9:00AM-4:00PM

This Georgetown landmark is a pub of great renown. The leafy atrium and the omelette room are lovely places to meet and eat. The menu runs the gamut from homemade soups and chili to burgers, salads, omelettes, and beef and seafood entrées.

DOMINIQUE'S   37

1900 Pennsylvania Avenue, N.W.
Washington, D.C.
(202) 452-1126

French

F ★ ★ ★ ½
S ★ ★ ★ ½
A ★ ★ ★ ½
P ★ ★ ★

Jacket required
Valet and lot parking
All major credit cards
Full bar
Reservations required

Lunch: Mon.-Fri. 11:30AM-2:30PM
Dinner: Mon.-Thurs. 5:30PM-12:00AM
         Fri. & Sat. 5:30PM-1:00AM
         Closed Sunday

Four distinctively decorated dining rooms and a menu of legendary length that encompasses such exotica as ostrich and rattlesnake as well as more traditional entrées, have earned this elegant establishment an illustrious following. The dessert prepared especially for Elizabeth Taylor: chocolate truffles on a plate of whipped cream, drizzled with chocolate sauce and topped with almonds, is now everyone's favorite.

EL BODEGÓN   14
RESTAURANT

1637 R Street, N.W.
Washington, D.C.
(202) 667-1710

Spanish

F ★ ★ ★ ½
S ★ ★ ★ ½
A ★ ★ ★
P ★ ★ ½

Good taste in dress required
Valet parking
All major credit cards
Full bar
Reservations recommended

Lunch: Mon.-Fri. 12:00PM-2:30PM
Dinner: Mon.-Thurs. 5:30PM-10:30PM
         Fri. & Sat. 5:30PM-11:00PM
         Closed Sunday

Washingtonians have been enjoying the "El Bodegón experience" for more than two decades. There's a lively Flamenco show nightly, Spanish wine served guests from the "porrón" bottle, and cuisine reflecting cooking styles from all the regions of Spain.

EL CARIBE 9

1828 Columbia Road, N.W.
Washington, D.C.
(202) 234-6969

South American

F ★ ★ ★ ½
S ★ ★ ★
A ★ ★ ½
P ★ ★

No dress restrictions
Street parking
All major credit cards
Full bar
Reservations required

Lunch/
Dinner: Mon.-Thurs. 11:30AM-11:00PM
Fri. 11:30AM-11:30PM
Sat. 1:00PM-11:30PM
Sun. 1:00PM-11:00PM

Pint-sized and crowded, but full of Latin American charm, this bustling eatery serves savory specialties from Spain and many South American countries. Hearty stews with pork, rabbit, or seafood bases are house specialties.

EL CARIBE (Georgetown) 18

3288 M Street, N.W.
Washington, D.C.
(202) 338-3121

Spanish

F ★ ★ ★ ½
S ★ ★ ★
A ★ ★ ½
P ★ ★

No dress restrictions
Lot parking

All major credit cards
Full bar
Reservations recommended

Lunch/
Dinner: Daily 11:30AM-11:30PM

Winner of blue-ribbon awards since 1977, this local favorite serves Spanish cuisine flavored with Latin American accents. House specialties are paellas, pork roasted with pineapple juice, and hearty mariscadas. Seafood, steaks, lamb, and rabbit are menu mainstays.

FOURWAYS 12

1701 20th Street, N.W.
Washington, D.C.
(202) 483-3200

French

F ★ ★ ★ ½
S ★ ★ ★ ½
A ★ ★ ★ ★
P ★ ★ ★ ½

Jacket and tie required
Valet parking
All major credit cards
Full bar
Reservations required

Lunch: Mon.-Fri. 12:00PM-2:30PM
Dinner: Nightly 6:00PM-10:30PM
Brunch: Sun. 11:30AM-3:00PM

Sited in a restored 19th century Washington mansion in the Embassy Row area, Fourways presents dining in the grand manner. You'll find high, ornate ceilings, 14 fireplaces, a choice of many rooms, and European-style service. The classic French cuisine is often graced with imaginative nouvelle touches.

GARY'S 30

1800 M Street, N.W.
Washington, D.C.
(202) 463-6470

American

F ★ ★ ★
S ★ ★ ★ ★
A ★ ★ ★
P ★ ★ ★

No dress restrictions
Lot parking
All major credit cards
Full bar
Reservations required

Lunch/
Dinner: Mon.-Fri. 11:30AM-10:00PM
Sat. 6:00PM-10:30PM
Closed Sunday

This is probably one of the plushiest steak houses extant. The atmosphere is sedate and stately, and the service is as smooth as silk. The menu is quite diverse, but critics recommend the steak and roast beef, grilled seafoods, veal, and rack of lamb or pork.

GERMAINE'S ASIAN CUISINE 5

2400 Wisconsin Avenue, N.W.
Washington, D.C.
(202) 965-1185

Pan-Asian

F ★ ★ ★ ½
S ★ ★ ★ ½
A ★ ★ ★ ½
P ★ ★ ★ ½

Jacket required
Street parking
All major credit cards
Full bar
Reservations required

Lunch: Mon.-Fri. 12:00PM-2:30PM
Dinner: Sun.-Thurs. 6:00PM-10:00PM
Fri. & Sat. 6:00PM-11:00PM

Owners Dick and chef Germaine Swanson have created a high fashion establishment that pays tribute to the exotic cuisines of eight southeast Asian countries. Here you can sample such enticing items as Vietnamese spring rolls, Korean kim chi, Thai basil beef, Japanese teriyaki, Indonesian sates, and Peking Duck, all at one sitting.

HARVEY'S 35

1001 18th Street, N.W.
Washington, D.C.
(202) 833-1858

American

F ★ ★ ★ ½
S ★ ★ ★ ½
A ★ ★ ★ ½
P ★ ★ ★ ½

Good taste in dress required
Valet and lot parking
All major credit cards
Full bar
Reservations recommended

Lunch/
Dinner: Mon.-Fri. 11:30AM-10:30PM
Sat. & Sun. 5:00PM-11:00PM

Founded in 1858, this restaurant has been lauded for its superb seafood by a historic roster of loyal patrons ever since. Crab Imperial was created here and continues to be an all time favorite. Other popular entrées include crab cakes, sautéed softshells, and grilled fresh fish.

IL GIARDINO 27

1110 21st Street, N.W.
Washington, D.C.
(202) 223-4555

Italian

F ★ ★ ★ ½
S ★ ★ ★ ½
A ★ ★ ★ ½
P ★ ★ ★

Jacket and tie required
Lot and street parking
All major credit cards
Full bar
Reservations required

Lunch: Mon.-Fri. 12:00PM-2:30PM
Dinner: Nightly 6:00PM-10:30PM

With the calm, restful ambiance of a pleasant patio, this restaurant also offers you a gallery of art, and a party room with a garden view. Linguine with truffles, rockfish with herbs, and a wide variety of milk fed veal and lamb dishes are house specialties. Owner Mario Fazio is a stickler for detail, and proud of the thoughtful service.

J. PAUL'S 21

3218 M Street, N.W.
Washington, D.C.
(202) 333-3450

American

F ★ ★ ★
S ★ ★ ★
A ★ ★ ½
P ★ ½

Good taste in dress required
Street parking
All major credit cards
Full bar
Reservations not required

Lunch/
Dinner: Mon.-Thurs. 11:30AM-11:30PM
Fri. & Sat. 11:30AM-12:00AM
Sun. 10:30AM-11:30PM

Handsome and clubby, sporting a 100-year-old wood and brass bar salvaged from a former Chicago stockyard pub, here you'll find an aura of the early '20s, and good hearty food. Try the "Chicups" (chicken and scallops sautéed with white pasta), the barbecued ribs, or the crab cakes. Grasshopper pie is a favorite dessert.

JACQUELINE'S 26

1990 M Street, N.W.
Washington, D.C.
(202) 785-8877

French

F ★ ★ ★ ½
S ★ ★ ★
A ★ ★ ★
P ★ ★ ★

Good taste in dress required, no jeans
Valet parking
All major credit cards
Full bar
Reservations recommended

Lunch: Mon.-Fri. 12:00PM-2:30PM
Dinner: Mon.-Sat. 6:00PM-10:30PM
Closed Sunday

Carved woods, stained glass windows, a romantic color scheme, fresh flowers, and formal table service combine to make dining here a thoroughly French experience. Owner Jacqueline Rodier presents classic French cuisine prepared with sure handed artistry.

JAPAN INN 11

1715 Wisconsin Avenue, N.W.
Washington, D.C.
(202) 337-3400

Japanese

F ★ ★ ★ ½
S ★ ★ ★
A ★ ★ ★
P ★ ★

No dress restrictions
Lot parking
All major credit cards
Full bar
Reservations required

Lunch: Mon.-Fri. 12:00PM-2:00PM
Dinner: Mon.-Thurs. 6:00PM-10:00PM
Fri. & Sat. 6:00PM-10:30PM
Sun. 5:00PM-9:00PM

Owner Izumi Yoshimoto has composed a trio of marvelous dining experiences at his

Georgetown inn. There's an authentic sushi bar; Teppan-Yaki second-floor room, where chef's deftly concoct scallop, shrimp, steak, and chicken grill-cooked delicacies at the table; and a Tatami Room, with low-table seating for such enticements as sukiyaki and shabu shabu prepared by your kimonoed waitress.

JEAN LOUIS   2

2650 Virginia Avenue, N.W.
Washington, D.C.
(202) 298-4488

French

F ★ ★ ★ ★
S ★ ★ ★ ½
A ★ ★ ★ ½
P ★ ★ ★ ★

Jacket and tie preferred
Valet parking
All major credit cards
Full bar
Reservations required

Lunch: Mon.-Fri. 12:00PM-2:00PM
Dinner: Mon.-Sat. 6:30PM-9:30PM
         Closed Sunday

Inventive use of ingredients and a succession of seasonal surprises await diners at this enchanting, intimate, beautifully decorated restaurant. Multi-coursed prix fixe meals are orchestrated by much-honored chef Jean Louis Palladin. The desserts served here are legendary.

JEAN-PIERRE   32

1835 K Street
Washington, D.C.
(202) 466-2022

French

F ★ ★ ★ ½
S ★ ★ ★ ½
A ★ ★ ★ ½
P ★ ★ ★ ½

Jacket and tie required
Valet parking
All major credit cards
Full bar
Reservations required

Lunch: Mon.-Fri. 12:00PM-2:00PM
Dinner: Mon.-Sat. 6:00PM-10:00PM
         Closed Sunday

Sparkling after a recent renovation, this fine restaurant, personally supervised by owner Jean-Pierre Farret, continues to serve classic French cuisine to an appreciative clientele. Award-winning chef Gerard Vettraino of Lyon, balances the menu with imaginative ingredients and nouvelle expertise. The wine list is meticulously assembled to complement the food.

THE JOCKEY CLUB   1

2100 Massachusetts Avenue, N.W.
Washington, D.C.
(202) 293-2100

French

F ★ ★ ★ ½
S ★ ★ ★
A ★ ★ ★
P ★ ★ ★ ★

Jacket and tie required
Valet parking
All major credit cards
Full bar
Reservations required

Lunch: Daily 12:00PM-2:30PM
Dinner: Nightly 6:00PM-11:30PM

This Washington institution with its club-like décor of dark wood, leather banquettes, and spacious tables offers its illustrious clientele old-world service and classic French cuisine. Renowned for crab cakes and fresh seafood.

LA BERGERIE 46

218 North Lee Street (Old Town)
Alexandria, VA
(703) 683-1007

French

F ★ ★ ★
S ★ ★ ★
A ★ ★ ★
P ★ ★ ½

Jacket required, no jeans
Lot parking
All major credit cards
Full bar
Reservations required

Lunch: Daily 11:30AM-2:30PM
Dinner: Nightly 6:00PM-10:30PM

You'll find variety of succulent Basque dishes and interesting daily specials augmenting the French cuisine offered in this elegant "Old Town" establishment. The atmosphere is pleasant and comfortable and the lighting is soft and flattering.

LA COLLINE 42

400 North Capitol Street, N.W.
Washington, D.C.
(202) 737-0400

French

F ★ ★ ★ ½
S ★ ★ ★ ½
A ★ ★ ★
P ★ ★ ½

Good taste in dress required
Garage parking
All major credit cards
Full bar
Reservations not required

Breakfast: Mon.-Fri. 7:00AM-10:00AM
Lunch: Mon.-Fri. 11:30AM-3:00PM
Dinner: Mon.-Sat. 6:00PM-10:00PM
          Closed Sunday

This refreshing country-style brasserie is comfortable, casual, and very "in." Co-owner/chef Robert Gréault, a member of L'Academie Culinaire of France, reigns in the kitchen with great aplomb producing a good range of award-winning French cuisine.

LA NIÇOISE 5

1721 Wisconsin Avenue, N.W.
Washington, D.C.
(202) 965-9300

French

F ★ ★ ★
S ★ ★ ★
A ★ ★ ★
P ★ ★ ★

Jacket required
Street parking
All major credit cards
Full bar
Reservations required

Dinner: Nightly 5:30PM-10:30PM

This entertaining establishment subscribes to the theory that dining should be a fun, light-hearted occasion. You'll find a lively cabaret show nightly, put on by the staff, and quick, smooth service performed by roller skating waiters. The bill of fare is primarily French.

L'AUBERGE CHEZ FRANÇOIS 15

332 Springvale Road
Great Falls, VA
(703) 759-3800

French

F ★ ★ ★ ½
S ★ ★ ★ ½
A ★ ★ ★ ½
P ★ ★ ★ ½

Jacket and tie preferred
Lot parking

AE, MC, V
Full bar
Reservations required

Dinner: Tues.-Sat. 5:00PM-9:00PM
Sun. 2:30PM-8:00PM
Closed Monday

Nestled in Virginia's rolling hills, this pleasant French country inn lures gastronomes from nearby Washington, D.C. with its daily changing menu and ever popular house specialties such as Le Salmon Soufflé.

LE GAULOIS 38

2133 Pennsylvania Avenue, N.W.
Washington, D.C.
(202) 466-3232

French

F ★ ★ ★
S ★ ★ ★
A ★ ★ ½
P ★ ★

Good taste in dress required
Lot and street parking
AE, MC, V
Full bar
Reservations recommended

Lunch: Mon.-Fri. 11:30AM-2:30PM
Dinner: Mon.-Thurs. 5:30PM-11:00PM
Fri. & Sat. 5:30PM-12:00AM
Closed Sunday

Bernard and Darinka Baudrand's busy eatery is casual, friendly, and award-winning. The kitchen produces a long list of daily specials to add depth to the Gallic menu. Zucchini spaghetti with seafood and homemade fruit tarts are customer favorites.

LE LION D'OR 31

1150 Connecticut Avenue, N.W.
Washington, D.C.
(202) 296-7972

French

F ★ ★ ★ ½
S ★ ★ ★ ½
A ★ ★ ★ ½
P ★ ★ ★ ★

Jacket and tie required, no jeans
Lot parking
All major credit cards
Full bar
Reservations required

Lunch: Mon.-Fri. 12:00PM-2:00PM
Dinner: Mon.-Sat. 6:00PM-10:00PM
Closed Sunday

Chef/owner Jean Pierre Goyenvalle attributes the critic's unanimous praise of the consistent quality of the food served here to the fact that only fresh seasonal and local products are used in the food preparation. Both classic and nouvelle French dishes share billing on the menu.

LE PAVILLON 33

1050 Connecticut Avenue, N.W.
Washington, D.C.
(202) 833-3846

French

F ★ ★ ★ ½
S ★ ★ ★ ½
A ★ ★ ★ ½
P ★ ★ ★ ★

Jacket and tie required
Valet parking
AE, DC, MC, V
Full bar
Reservations required

Lunch: Mon.-Fri. from 11:45AM
Dinner: Mon.-Sat. from 6:45PM
Closed Sunday

Designed around a Lalique table, this lovely dining room reflects the character of Janet and chef Yannik Cam, the owners. The daily prix fixe menu is based upon seasonal bounty, and this food is prepared with artistry and imagination.

MAISON BLANCHE 39

1725 F Street, N.W.
Washington, D.C.
(202) 842-0070

French

F ★ ★ ★ ½
S ★ ★ ★ ½
A ★ ★ ★ ½
P ★ ★ ★ ½

Jacket required
Valet parking
All major credit cards
Full bar
Reservations recommended

Lunch: Mon.-Fri. 11:45AM-2:30PM
Dinner: Mon.-Fri. 6:00PM-11:00PM
         Sat. 6:00PM-11:30PM
         Closed Sunday

This sedate and spacious restaurant offers you a sense of peace and privacy. The appointments are elegant and the service is quiet and smooth. The classic French menu is supplemented by a long list of specials.

MARKET INN 44

200 E Street, S.W.
Washington, D.C.
(202) 554-2100

American

F ★ ★ ★
S ★ ★ ★
A ★ ★ ★
P ★ ★ ★

Good taste in dress required
Valet parking
All major credit cards
Full bar
Reservations recommended

Lunch/
Dinner: Mon.-Fri. 11:00AM-2:00AM
         Fri. & Sat. 11:00AM-3:00AM
         Sun. 4:00PM-12:00AM

Known as the "lobster house of Washington," this bustling restaurant has been attracting seafood lovers for a quarter of a century. You'll find a choice of more than 85 seafood and beef entrées from which to choose.

MEL KRUPIN'S 36

1120 Connecticut Avenue, N.W.
Washington, D.C.
(202) 331-7000

American

F ★ ★ ★ ½
S ★ ★ ★
A ★ ★ ★
P ★ ★ ★

Jacket required
Valet parking
All major credit cards
Full bar
Reservations required

Lunch/
Dinner: Mon.-Sat. 11:30AM-11:00PM
         Closed Sunday

Blessed with a loyal following of politicians, lawyers, sports figures, journalists, and other gentry with good appetites, this eatery purveys liberal portions of New York City style fare such as chopped liver, matzoh ball soup, crab cakes, herring, and boiled beef.

MONTEPELIER 29

Madison Hotel
1177 15th Street, N.W.
Washington, D.C.
(202) 862-1600

French

F ★ ★ ★ ½
S ★ ★ ★ ½
A ★ ★ ★ ½
P ★ ★ ★

Jacket and tie required
Valet parking

All major credit cards
Full bar
Reservations required

Lunch: Mon.-Fri. 12:00PM-3:00PM
Dinner: Mon.-Sat. 6:00PM-10:30PM
          Closed Sunday

This subdued and elegant restaurant is lavished with antiques and paintings and projects a polished, formal image. Here you will be treated to impeccably prepared French cuisine including such entrées as duck, rack of lamb, and a variety of daily fresh fish specials.

MORTON'S OF CHICAGO   17

3251 Prospect Street, N.W.
Washington, D.C.
(202) 342-6258

American

F ★ ★ ★ ½
S ★ ★ ★ ½
A ★ ★ ★
P ★ ★ ★

Jacket and tie preferred
Lot and street parking
All major credit cards
Full bar
Reservations not required

Dinner: Mon.-Sat. 5:30PM-11:00PM
          Closed Sunday

Prime dry-aged steaks and whole Maine lobsters are the chief attractions at this stalwart establishment, rated among the top favorites by Washingtonians. The setting is clublike and elegant, the service meticulous, and the food fresh and of the highest quality.

THE NEW ORLEANS   8
EMPORIUM

2477 18th Street, N.W.
Washington, D.C.
(202) 328-3421

Creole/Cajun

F ★ ★ ★
S ★ ★ ★
A ★ ★ ½
P ★ ★ ★

Good taste in dress required
Lot parking
All major credit cards
Full bar
Reservations recommended

Lunch: Mon.-Fri. 11:30AM-2:30PM
Dinner: Sun.-Thurs. 5:30PM-11:00PM
          Fri. & Sat. 5:30PM-12:00AM
Brunch: Sat. & Sun. 11:30AM-3:00PM

Spreading the joys of New Orleans style cookery, this bustling establishment provides a friendly, comfortable setting in which to savor barbecued shrimp, blackened redfish, inventive crawfish dishes, bread pudding with brandy sauce, and a host of other mouth-watering house specialties.

OLD EBBITT GRILL   40

675 15th Street, N.W.
Washington, D.C.
(202) 347-4801

American

F ★ ★ ★
S ★ ★ ★
A ★ ★ ★ ½
P ★ ★

No dress restrictions
Lot and street parking
AE, DC, MC, V
Full bar
Reservations recommended

Breakfast/
Lunch/
Dinner: Mon.-Fri. 7:30AM-2:00AM
          Sat. 8:00AM-2:00AM
          Sun. 10:00AM-2:00AM

This Washington landmark, originally established in 1856, has been refurbished to reflect proudly on its Victorian heritage.

Here you will find 60 gaslights, plush velvet booths, and an air of ageless gentility. The menu changes daily and features seasonal abundance. There's a popular oyster bar, and a bevy of rich premise-made desserts.

OLD EUROPE   3

2434 Wisconsin Avenue, N.W.
Washington, D.C.
(202) 333-7600

German

F ★ ★ ★
S ★ ★ ★
A ★ ★ ½
P ★ ★ ½

Good taste in dress required
Street parking
All major credit cards
Full bar
Reservations required

Lunch: Mon.-Sat. 11:30AM-3:00PM
Dinner: Mon.-Thurs. 5:00PM-10:30PM
          Fri. & Sat. 5:00PM-12:00AM
Lunch/
Dinner: Sun. 12:30PM-10:00PM

This establishment is legendary for its unending round of festivals and good-time feeling. Antique steins and grandiose oil paintings add charm to the décor. If you miss the Oktoberfest, there's always the May Wine Fest and the game season festival! The German fare is hearty and there are specialties tied-in with the festival occasions.

PETITTO'S RISTORANTE   6
D'ITALIA

2653 Connecticut Avenue, N.W.
Washington, D.C.
(202) 667-5350

Italian

F ★ ★ ★
S ★ ★ ★ ½
A ★ ★ ★ ½
P ★ ★ ★

Jacket and tie preferred
Street parking
All major credit cards
Full bar
Reservations required

Lunch: Mon.-Fri. 11:30AM-2:30PM
Dinner: Mon.-Sat. 6:00PM-10:30PM
          Closed Sunday

This chic restaurant, located in a vintage townhouse, boasts a candlelit private dining room, fireplaces in all four eating areas, and a sidewalk café in the summer season. Pastas with more than 30 meat, seafood, and vegetable sauces are the menu mainstays. Fresh veal and fish dishes and homemade desserts are specialties of the house.

PICCOLO MONDO   10

1835 K Street, N.W.
Washington, D.C.
(202) 223-6661

Italian

F ★ ★ ★ ½
S ★ ★ ★ ½
A ★ ★ ★ ½
P ★ ★ ★

Good taste in dress required, no jeans
Lot parking
AE, DC, MC, V
Full bar
Reservations required

Lunch/
Dinner: Mon.-Fri. 12:00PM-10:30PM
          Sat. 6:00PM-10:30PM
          Closed Sunday

Step down the art déco stairway into the lavish, formal underground world of this distinctive multi-roomed eatery. The cuisine is a celebration of the best of Northern Italian dishes.

THE PRIME RIB   34

2020 K Street, N.W.
Washington, D.C.
(202) 466-8811

American

F ★ ★ ★ ½
S ★ ★ ★ ½
A ★ ★ ★ ½
P ★ ★ ★

Jacket and tie required
Valet parking
All major credit cards
Full bar
Reservations not required

Lunch: Mon.-Fri. 11:30AM-3:00PM
Dinner: Mon.-Sat. 5:30PM-12:00AM
         Closed Sunday

A sleek art déco setting, with gilt trimmed black walls and a collection of Icart prints, makes this a very chic restaurant. There's entertainment nightly, and quality food, including fresh Chesapeake Bay seafood.

1789   16

1226 36th Street, N.W.
Washington, D.C.
(202) 965-1789

French

F ★ ★ ★ ½
S ★ ★ ★
A ★ ★ ★ ½
P ★ ★ ★ ½

Jacket required
Valet parking
All major credit cards
Full bar
Reservations required

Dinner: Mon.-Thurs. 6:30PM-11:00PM
         Fri. & Sat. 6:30PM-12:00AM
         Closed Sunday

Richard McCooey's Georgetown master-piece occupies a 18th century house with an historic federal period atmosphere. Widely acclaimed by critics for its wine list, food, and service, you'll find a wide menu here, sparked with daily specials such as Wellfleet oysters in puff pastry.

TWO CONTINENTS   41

1420 F Street, N.W.
Washington, D.C.
(202) 347-4499

Continental

F ★ ★ ★ ½
S ★ ★ ★
A ★ ★ ★ ½
P ★ ★ ★ ★

Jacket and tie required
Lot parking
All major credit cards
Full bar
Reservations required

Dinner: Mon.-Fri. 6:00PM-10:30PM
         Sat. & Sun. 5:00PM-10:30PM

Resplendent and romantic, this dining spot sparkles with crystal chandeliers, fresh flower arrangements, and an aura of complete self assurance. The menu is a marvel of continental favorites, all presented with artistic precision.

209½   43

209½ Pennsyliania Avenue, S.E.
Washington, D.C.
(202) 544-6352

American

F ★ ★ ★ ½
S ★ ★ ★ ½
A ★ ★ ★
P ★ ★ ★ ½

No dress restrictions
Street parking
All major credit cards
Full bar
Reservations recommended

Lunch: Mon.-Fri. 11:30AM-2:30PM
Dinner: Mon.-Fri. 6:00PM-10:30PM
         Sat. 6:00PM-11:00PM
         Closed Sunday

New American cuisine, prepared in exciting, innovative ways using the finest ingredients obtainable, has earned national acclaim for this intimate eatery with its masses of fresh flowers and welcoming air. The menu changes with the seasons; always displays an exuberance of imaginative flair.

VIET CHATEAU   7

2637 Connecticut Avenue, N.W.
Washington, D.C.
(202) 232-6464

Vietnamese/French

F   ★ ★ ★
S   ★ ★ ★
A   ★ ★ ½
P   ★ ★ ½

Good taste in dress required
Lot parking
All major credit cards
Beer/Wine
Reservations required

Lunch: Mon.-Fri. 11:00AM-3:00PM
Dinner: Nightly 5:30PM-11:00PM

This modern restaurant is an amalgam of East and West offering you a totally unique dining experience. In the open air setting with its lairae bar and pavilionlike main dining room you may sample Vietnamese sushi, and a fabulous array of other tempting foods.

VINCENZO   24

1606 20th Street, N.W.
Washington, D.C.
(202) 667-0047

Italian-style Seafood

F   ★ ★ ★ ½
S   ★ ★ ★
A   ★ ★ ★
P   ★ ★ ★ ½

Jacket required
Street parking
AE, MC, V
Full Bar
Reservations required

Lunch: Mon.-Fri. 12:00PM-2:00PM
Dinner: Mon.-Fri. 6:00PM-10:00PM
         Sat. 5:30PM-10:00PM
         Closed Sunday

This restaurant focuses on doing one thing extremely well, and that is serving the finest fresh fish and seafood prepared in the Italian manner. You'll find grilled Mediterranean sea bass, and marvelous fish, shellfish, and pasta combinations.

WASHINGTON PALM   25

1225 19th Street, N.W.
Washington, D.C.
(202) 293-9091

American

F   ★ ★ ★ ★
S   ★ ★ ★
A   ★ ★ ★
P   ★ ★ ★ ★

No dress restrictions
Valet parking
All major credit cards
Full bar
Reservations required

Lunch/
Dinner: Mon.-Fri. 11:45AM-10:30PM
         Sat. 6:00PM-10:00PM
         Closed Sunday

This offshoot of the famous New York City Palm restaurant is headed by Walter Ganzi, Jr. and Bruce Bozzi, third generation members of the families who opened the NYC Palm during the roaring '20s. This haven for hearty eaters features prime aged beef and jumbo lobsters.

Appendix

VINTAGE	59	60	61	62	63	64	65	66
France								
Bordeaux — Red	9	4	10	7	1	5-6	0	8
Sauternes	9	2	8	9	0	6	3	7
Red Burgundy	9	2	9	7	3	7	2	7-8
White Burgundy	9	2	10	8-9	3	7	2	6
Rhone	9	10	9	7	3	8	2	7
Alsace	8	—	8	5	—	9	—	4
Champagne	—	—	—	—	—	8	—	—
Germany	8	3	6	5	3	6	2	6
Italy								
Barolo, Barbaresco Piedmont	4	4	9	6	5	10	7	3
Brunello di Montalcino, Chianti Riserva Tuscany	4	5	7	2	4	8	4	4
Portugal								
Port	—	—	—	—	10	NV	NV	7
California								
Cabernet Sauvignon, Pinot Noir, Zinfandel				7	7	5-6	4	8
Sauvignon Blanc, Chardonnay								

10=the best   0=not worth drinking

67	68	69	70	71	72	73	74	75	76	77	78	79	80	81	82	83	84
5-6	2	2	8	7	2	4	4	9	7	6	8	7	5	8	10	8	5
8	1	3	8	8	5	4	5	9	8	5	7	5	7	8	7	8	5
5	3	7-8	6-7	8	6-7	4	4	2	8	4	8	5	5	5-6	5-6	8	2-3
6	2	8-9	7-8	7-8	6	7	5	4-5	8	5	8	7	5	7	8	9	4-5
6	3	8	8	6	8	6	6	4	8	5	10	6	7	6	7	8	7
—	—	—	5	9	5	7	6	7	9	4	7	7	6	7	7	7	5
—	—	9	8	9	NV	7	NV	9	9	NV	NV	8	7	8	8	NV	NV
7	4	7	6	10	2	7	5	8	9	5	5	6	2	6	2	9	2
6	4	4	8	9	3	5	8	2	5	5	10	8	6	6	9	7	6
7	8	7	8	10	4	4	8	7	2	8	9	6	7-8	9	8	8	7-8
7	NV	14	8	NV	7	NV	NV	6	NV	10	6	NV	6	—	—	—	—
7	10	4	10	7	7-8	9-10	9-10	7	9-10	7	9	7	9-10	7	8	7	7
		4	7	7	7	8-9	8-9	8	7	8	9	8	9	7	7-8	7	7

Note: Ratings are effective as of 1984 and subject to revision as the wines evolve.

abaisse (Fr.) piece of rolled dough used for pies, tarts and pastries
abbacchio (It.) lamb
à blanc (Fr.) meat boiled until it just turns color
abricôts (Fr.) apricots
affumicato (It.) smoked
aglio (It.) garlic
agneau (Fr.) lamb as: carré d'agneau, rack of lamb; couronne d'agneau, the two racks shaped as a crown and roasted; côtes d'agneau, lamb chops; noisette d'agneau, center part of the lamb chop—no bone; selle d'agneau, saddle of lamb.
agnellotti (It.) small filled pasta circles
ai ferri (It.) grilled, broiled
aigre (Fr.) sour
aiguillettes (Fr.) thin long slices of meat carved on each side of the breast of a duck or goose
ail (Fr.) garlic
aioli (Fr.) garlic-flavored mayonnaise
ajo (Sp.) garlic
à l; à la, au, aux (Fr.) in the style of
a la, (Sp.) in the style of
al, al, alla (It.) in the style of
à la broche (Fr.) on skewers
à la carte (Fr.) priced by the dish; opposite of table d'hôte
à la francaise (Fr.) with little peas, lettuce, pieces of lard, small onions
à la mode (Fr.) in the particular style
à la paysanne (Fr.) country style
à la vapeur (Fr.) steamed
albicocca (It.) apricot
al burro (It.) with butter
alcachofes (Sp.) artichokes
al dente (It.) not overcooked, a little chewy
al forno (It.) baked
al horno (Sp.) baked
à l'huile (Fr.) in oil, as a l'huile d'olive, in olive oil
alla cacciatore (It.) hunter's style
alla marinara (It.) seaman's style, meatless sauce: tomatoes, olives, garlic, herbs
alla matriciana (It.) country style
allumettes (Fr.) food cut in strips
almejas (Sp.) clams
amande (Fr.) almond, as amandine
ananas (Fr.) pineapple
ananasso (It.) pineapple
anatra (It.) duck
anchois (Fr.) anchovies
andouille (Fr.) pork sausage
animelle (It.) sweetbreads
antipasto (It.) hors d'oeuvre
apfel (Ger.) apple
apfelkuchen (Ger.) sliced apples baked in thin cake dough
apfelsinen (Ger.) oranges as apfelsinensaft, orange juice
aragosta (It.) lobster
argenteuil (Fr.) with asparagus
arroser (Fr.) to baste
arrosto (It.) roast
arroz (Sp.) rice
asparago (It.) asparagus
asperge (Fr.) asparagus
aubergine (Fr.) eggplant
au beurre noir (Fr.) browned butter
au bleu (Fr.) fish stewed in wine or vinegar and water

au gratin (Fr.) sprinkled with breadcrumbs and cheese, baked in oven to form a light brown crust
au jus (Fr.) in natural juices
au naturel (Fr.) simply cooked
au sec (Fr.) cooked tightly covered without added water
aux champignons (Fr.) with mushrooms

baba (Fr.) round yeast cake
baguette (Fr.) long loaf of bread
ballottine (Fr.) boned meat roll
barquettes (Fr.) boat shaped pastries
bavaroise (Fr.) a rich custard
bearnaise sauce (Fr.) egg yolks beaten, mixed with melted butter, tarragon, lemon juice
bechamel (Fr.) flour cooked with butter and made into a white sauce by adding milk
beignet (Fr.) a puffed pastry fritter
bercy (Fr.) brown sauce with white wine and parsley
berenjenas (Sp.) eggplants
beurre (Fr.) butter as: à l'ail, with garlic; fondue, melted; maitre d'hotel, spices lemon and parsley; manié, flour and butter used for thickening sauces; meuniere, lightly browned butter; noir, darkly browned butter; noisette, melted to nut-like color and flavor
bifteck (Fr.) steak
bigarde (Fr.) brown sauce of orange juice and peel, and liqueur
bisque (Fr.) fish, shellfish, chicken or game soup
bistecca (It.) steak
blanchir (Fr.) to plunge food into boiling water until it is partially cooked
blancmange (Fr.) a milky pudding
blumenkohl (Ger.) cauliflower
blutwurst (Ger.) sausage with bacon and pork's blood
boeuf (Fr.) beef
boeuf bourguignon (Fr.) beef stew, vegetables in burgundy wine
bolitto (It.) boiled beef as bollito misto, boiled mixed meats
bombe (Fr.) dessert of ices, whipped cream, fruits
bonne-femme (Fr.) white sauce of fish stock, onions or shallots, egg yolk and lemon juice
bordelaise sauce (Fr.) brown stock, red wine, shallots, beef marrow
borscht (Fr.) clear broth with beet juice, minced beef and beets
bouillabaisse (Fr.) fish and shellfish chowder
bouilli (Fr.) boiled; boiled beef
bouquetiere (Fr.) assorted vegetables
braten (Ger.) roast, grill, fry as hackbraten, meat loaf
bratwurst (Ger.) pork sausage
bretonne (Fr.) white beans, chopped onions, tomato sauce, fines herbes
brochette de boeuf (Fr.) chunks of beef on skewer, broiled
brochet (Fr.) pike
brunoise (Fr.) vegetables, finely diced
bue (It.) beef

cacciucco (It.) seafood stew
caille (Fr.) quail
calamares (Sp.) small squid
caldo (Sp.) broth

callos (Sp.) tripe
camerón (Sp.) shrimp
campesina (Sp.) farmer, country
canard (Fr.) duck
cannelloni (It.) filled rolls of pasta
cappalletti (It.) stuffed pasta squares
caracoles (Sp.) snails
carbonnade (Fr.) meat grilled over charcoal
carciofi (It.) artichokes
carne (Sp.) meat
casseruola (It.) casserole
cassoulet (Fr.) a stew with white beans, pork, bacon, mutton
caviar (Fr.) roe of the sturgeon
cebolla (Sp.) onion
ceci (It.) chick peas or garbonzo beans
cèpes (Fr.) large wild mushrooms
cerises (Fr.) cherries
cervelles (Fr.) brains

champignons (Fr.) mushrooms
charcuteries (Fr.) cold cuts
chasseur à la (Fr.) hunter's style
chateaubriand (Fr.) broiled double filet sliced at your table

chevreuil (Fr.) deer
chiles (Sp.) peppers
chorizos (Sp.) sausages
choron sauce (Fr.) bearnaise with mashed tomatoes
choucroute (Fr.) sauerkraut
choux (Fr.) cabbage
choux de bruxelles (Fr.) brussels sprouts
choux fleur (Fr.) cauliflower
chuletas (Sp.) chops, cutlets as chuletas de cordero, lamb chops
cochino (Sp.) pig
cochon (Fr.) pig
cocido (Sp.) stew of beef, pork, ham, bacon, cabbage, chick peas, etc.
concombres (Fr.) cucumbers
coniglio (It.) rabbit
consommé (Fr.) clear broth of various vegetables with either poultry, game, beef or veal
coquillages (Fr.) oysters, scallops or mussels
coquille (Fr.) a shell for seafood
coreille de fruit (Fr.) fruit bowl
costato (It.) rib steaks
costillas de cerdo (Sp.) pork spareribs
costole di maiale (It.) spareribs
costoletta, cotoletta (It.) chop, cutlet
côte (Fr.) rib
côtelette de veau (Fr.) veal chop
coupes (Fr.) ice cream, sherbet or both with fruit sauce or nuts
courgette (Fr.) zucchini
cozza (It.) mussel
crecy (Fr.) cream of carrot soup
crème (Fr.) cream; crème fraiche, a combination of sour and sweet cream
crème caramel (Fr.) caramel custard
crème chantilly (Fr.) whipped cream with sugar added
crêpe (Fr.) thin pancake rolled around various fillings
cresson (Fr.) watercress
crevettes (Fr.) shrimp
crochette (It.) croquettes

croustades (Fr.) fried and hollowed dough filled with food in sauce
croûte (Fr.) crust, en croûte, covered with pastry
cuisses de grenouilles (Fr.) froglegs

dampfnudeln (Ger.) sweet dessert dumplings
darne (Fr.) slice of a large size fish; darne, de saumon - salmon steak
degraisser (Fr.) to remove excess fat
demi-deuil (Fr.) white sauce of chicken stock and truffles
deutsches beefsteak (Ger.) hamburgers, German style
diable (Fr.) any food coated with mustard and lightly breaded
diable sauce (Fr.) brown stock, shallots, red wine, Worcestershire sauce, mustard
dieppoise (Fr.) mussels, shrimp with white sauce
dolci (It.) sweets
doria (Fr.) with cucumber
du barry (Fr.) cream of cauliflower soup
dugleré (Fr.) bechamel with fish stock and stewed tomatoes

éclair (Fr.) pastry, puffed with whipped cream or custard filling
écrevisse (Fr.) crayfish
ei (Ger.) egg
eierpflanze (Ger.) eggplant
eisbein (Ger.) pig's knuckles
en gelée (Fr.) jellied
ensalada (Sp.) salad
entrecôte (Fr.) rib steak
entrée (Fr.) usually main course
entremeses (Sp.) hors d'oeuvre
épaule (Fr.) shoulder
épice (Fr.) spice
épinard (Fr.) spinach
erbse (Ger.) pea, as erbsensuppe, pea soup
erdbeere (Ger.) strawberry as erdbeerentorte, strawberry cake
escallopes (Fr.) boneless slices of meat, flattened
escargot (Fr.) snail
espárrago (Sp.) asparagus
espinaca (Sp.) spinach
estofado (Sp.) meat stew
estouffat catalán (Fr.) beef pot roast with white beans
estragon (Fr.) tarragon
étuvée (Fr.) stew

fabada (Sp.) stew
fagiano (It.) pheasant
fagioli (It.) dried white beans
faisan (Fr.) pheasant, faisandé, gamey
farci (Fr.) stuffed
fasan (Ger.) pheasant
fava (It.) bean
fedelini (It.) fine pasta
fegato (It.) liver
feijoada (Br.) Brazilian stew of black beans, rice & meats
fettuccine (It.) thin, flat pasta
filet (Fr.) fillet of meat, chicken, fish

filet de boeuf Wellington (Fr.) beef in pastry
filete (Sp.) fillet
filetto (It.) fillet
fines herbes (Fr.) mixed fresh herbs
finocchio (It.) fennel
flageolet (Fr.) small green kidney bean
flambé (Fr.) flamed
flan (Fr., Sp.) custard
fleisch (Ger.) meat
fleischsalat (Ger.) salad of cold meats
florentine (Fr.) with spinach
flûte (Fr.) slender loaf of crusty bread
foie (Fr.) liver as foie de canard, duck liver
foie d'oie (Fr.) goose liver
foie gras (Fr.) goose liver as pâté de foie gras, poached goose liver
fond blanc (Fr.) white stock made from fish or white meat, such as poultry or veal
fond brun (Fr.) brown stock made from red meat, mainly beef
fondua (It.) casserole of cheese and truffles
fondue (Fr.) melted cheese and wine
forelle (Ger.) trout
forestière (Fr.) with mushrooms, bacon, diced potatoes
formaggio (It.) cheese
four, fourné (Fr.) oven, baked
fourré (Fr.) filled
fra diavolo (It.) spicy tomato and herb sauce
fragola (It.) strawberry
fraise (Fr.) strawberry
framboise (Fr.) raspberry
frappé (Fr.) iced
fresa (Sp.) strawberry
fricandelles (Fr.) chopped meat in patties or balls, fried and braised
fricasé (Sp.) fricassee
fricassée (Fr.) stew of poultry or other meats in a light sauce
frijoles (Sp.) beans
frite (Fr.) fried
frito, fritas (Sp.) fried
frittata (It.) omelet
fritto misto (It.) meat, fish, vegetables, cut small and deep-fried in batter
froid (Fr.) cold
fromage (Fr.) cheese
fruits de mer (Fr.) seafood
frutti de mare (It.) shellfish
funghi (It.) mushrooms

galantine (Fr.) boned poultry or game stuffed and pressed into symmetrical shape. Truffles are usually added. Served cold.
galette (Fr.) broad, flat cake, seabiscuit
gallina (Sp.) hen
gamberetto di mare (It.) shrimp
gans (Ger.) goose
ganso (Sp.) goose
garbure (Fr.) bacon and vegetable soup
gazpacho (Sp.) cold raw vegetable soup
gebacken (Ger.) fried
gedämpft (Ger.) stewed
gefüllt (Ger.) stuffed

gekocht (Ger.) boiled
gelato (It.) ice cream
gelée (Fr.) jellied
gemüse (Ger.) vegetables
gerstensuppe (Ger.) thick barley soup
gervais (Fr.) double cream cheese
geschmort (Ger.) stewed
gibelotte (Fr.) rabbit stew
gibier (Fr.) game
gigot (Fr.) leg of lamb
glacé (Fr.) iced, frozen, candied, glazed
glacer (Fr.) to give a brown glaze to a sauce dish either in the oven or under the broiler
gnocchi (It.) potato or puff paste dumplings
gorgonzola (It.) blue-veined cheese
grand veneur (Fr.) sauce of brown stock, blood of game, red wine
granita (It.) ices
gratine (Fr.) same as "au gratin"
gribiche (Fr.) cold sauce of egg yolks, oil, vinegar, mustard, capers, herbs
grissini (It.) breadsticks
guisado (Sp.) stew
gulasch (Ger.) beef, pork, or veal cubes, stewed with paprika and onions

habas (Sp.) broad bean
haché (Fr.) minced
hackbraten (Ger.) meatloaf
hamburger kümmelfleisch (Ger.) lamb with onions, cabbage, potatoes and caraway seeds
hareng (Fr.) herring
haricots (Fr.) beans
haricots verts (Fr.) green beans
hase (Ger.) hare, rabbit
hasenpfeffer (Ger.) hare or rabbit braised in red win and spices
helado (Sp.) ice cream
Henry IV (Fr.) a clear soup with pieces of vegetable, chicken giblets, croutons and cheese
hielo (Sp.) ice
hollandaise (Fr.) egg yolks, beaten, mixed with melted butter, lemon juice
holsteiner schnitzel (Ger.) breaded veal cutlets with fried eggs and anchovies
homard (Fr.) lobster
honig (Ger.) honey
hörnchen (Ger.) crescent-shaped rolls
hors d'oeuvre (Fr.) appetizer or canape served before entree
huevos (Sp.) eggs
huevos revueltos (Sp.) scrambled eggs
huile (Fr.) oil as huile d'olive, olive oil
huîtres (Fr.) oysters
hummer (Ger.) lobster
hussarde (Fr.) garnish of tomato with onion, potato, horseradish filling

ile flottante (Fr.) floating island, custard dessert with meringue
insalata (It.) salad
involto (It.) "bundle" as involto di Vitello, rolled veal

jambon (Fr.) ham
jardin (Fr.) garden
jardinière (Fr.) mixed vegetables
jorbküse (Ger.) white cheese
julienne (Fr.) food cut in strips

kaffee (Ger.) coffee, as kaffee mit sahne, coffee with
    whipped cream
kaffee mit schalagobers (Ger.) Viennese coffee with
    heavy whipped cream topping
kalb (Ger.) calf
kalbshaxe (Ger.) veal shanks
kartoffel (Ger.) potato as kartoffelklösse, potato
    dumplings
kipfel (Ger.) crescent-shaped rolls
klops (Ger.) meatballs
knockwurst (Ger.) thick frankfurters
knödel (Ger.) dumpling
kohl (Ger.) cabbage
kotelett (Ger.) chop, cutlet as schweinkoteletten, pork
    chops
krabben (Ger.) shrimp
kraut (Ger.) herb, cabbage
kuchen (Ger.) cake
kümmel (Ger.) caraway

lachs (Ger.) salmon
lait (Fr.) milk
laitue (Fr.) lettuce
lamm (Ger.) lamb
lammauflauf (Ger.) Austrian lamb and veal loaf
langosta (Sp.) lobster
langostinos (Sp.) shrimp or crawfish
langouste, (Fr.) crawfish
langoustine (Fr.) prawn or baby crawfish
langue (Fr.) tongue
lapereau (Fr.) young rabbit as lapereau à la Normand
lapin (Fr.) rabbit
lasagne (It.) broad noodles, layered with chopped meat,
    mozzarella and ricotta cheese, tomatoes and sausage
latte (It.) milk
lattuga (It.) lettuce
lausch (Ger.) leek
leber (Ger.) liver
leberknödel (Ger.) liver dumpling
leberwurst (Ger.) liverwurst
leche (Sp.) milk
lechuga (Sp.) lettuce
legumbre (Sp.) vegetable
légume (Fr.) vegetable
legumi (It.) vegetables
lendenbraten (Ger.) roast beef
lengua (Sp.) tongue
lenguado (Sp.) sole
lenticchie (It.) lentils
lepre (It.) hare
lièvre (Fr.) hare
limande (Fr.) flounder

macaron (Fr.) macaroon
macarrón (Sp.) macaroon

maccheroni (It.) macaroni
macédoine (Fr.) cut-up fruit or vegetables
macedonia (It.) fruit salad
madeleine (Fr.) small buttery cakes
madrilène (Fr.) tomato-flavored clear soup, sometimes
    jellied
maiale (It.) pork
maionese (It.) mayonnaise
mais (Fr.) corn
maître d'hôtel beurre (Fr.) seasoned butter
maíz (Sp.) corn
makrele (Ger.) mackerel
mandarine (Fr.) tangerine
mandarino (It.) tangerine
mandeln (Ger.) almonds
manicotti (It.) large, hollow tubes of delicate pasta suffed
    with ricotta cheese
manzana (Sp.) apple
manzo (It.) beef
maquereau (Fr.) mackerel
mariné (Fr.) pickled
marinière (Fr.) sauce of white wine, fines herbes,
    shallots, fish stock
marron (Fr.) chestnut
maultasche (Ger.) similar to ravioli with meat filling
medaillons (Fr.) round or oval shaped slices of fish,
    poultry or meat decorated and glazed with gelatin
mehl (Ger.) flour
mejillón (Sp.) mussel
melanzana (It.) eggplant
melocotón (Sp.) peach
meuniere (Fr.) browned butter with lemon juice
mexicaine (Fr.) sauteed tomatoes and onions with
    grilled pepper
mille-feuille (Fr.) usually many leaves of very thin flaky
    pastry
minceur (Fr.) slenderness
minestra (It.) soup
minestrone (It.) vegetable soup
mirabeau (Fr.) garnish of olives, tarragon, anchovies
mirepoix (Fr.) diced mixture of carrots, onions, celery
    with herbs, sometimes bacon
moletas, mollejas (Sp.) sweetbreads
mornay (Fr.) sauce of bechamel, egg yolks, grated cheese
moule (Fr.) mussel
mousse (Fr.) flavored custard
mousseline (Fr.) sauce of hollandaise with whipped
    cream added
mousseux (Fr.) sparkling
moutarde (Fr.) mustard
mouton (Fr.) mutton (sheep)
mozzarella (It.) mild white cheese
mulligatawny (Fr.) cream of poultry soup with curry,
    minced apple, minced chicken (served cold)
muschein (Ger.) mussels, shellfish

nantua (Fr.) white sauce, crawfish, butter, brandy
nasello (It.) whiting
nature (Fr.) plain, natural
navarin (Fr.) lamb or mutton stew
navet (Fr.) turnip
neroli (Fr.) orange-blossom extract and almond pastries
neufchâtel (Fr.) soft white creamy cheese

niçoise, à la (Fr.) garnish with anchovies, tomatoes, olives, capers, string beans, potatoes
nieren (Ger.) kidneys
nivernaise, à la (Fr.) garnished with small glazed onions and carrots
noce (It.) walnut
nockerl (Ger.) dumplings
noisette (Fr.) hazelnut, shaped like hazelnuts, as potatoes or meat rounds
noques (Fr.) Alsatian dumplings
normande (Fr.) white sauce with cider, wine
nudel (Ger.) noodle
nuss (Ger.) nut as nusstorte, nut cake

oblaten (Ger.) thin, wafflelike wafers, slightly sweetened
obst (Ger.) fruit, as obsttorte, fruit tart
ochsenbraten (Ger.) beefsteak
oeuf (Fr.) egg, as à la coque, boiled eggs; au plat, shirred eggs; brouillés, scrambled eggs; cuits dur, hard cooked eggs; frits, fried eggs; mollets, soft boiled eggs; pochés, poached eggs
oeufs à la neige (Fr.) a custard base dessert topped with poached meringues
oie (Fr.) goose
oignon (Fr.) onion
oiseau (Fr.) bird, as oiseaux de veau sans tête, veal cutlets, stuffed and rolled to make "veal birds"
ostras (Sp.) oysters

paella (Sp.) a rice and chicken, vegetables, sausage, meat, seafood dish, and/or paella valenciana, seafood variety containing clams, lobster, chicken, sausage, peas, garlic and saffron rice
pain (Fr.) bread
paloise (Fr.) bearnaise sauce with mint instead of tarragon
palourde (Fr.) clam
pamplemousse (Fr.) grapefruit
pan (Sp.) bread
panache (Fr.) mixed
pancetta affumicata (It.) bacon
pane (It.) bread, also appears in names of cakes and pastries as panettone, spiced yeast cake with raisins and citron
pane (Fr.) breaded
panino (It.) bread roll
panna (It.) whipped cream
pannequets (Fr.) thin pancakes filled with jam, meat, seafood, or mushrooms
papas (Sp.) potatoes
papillote, en (Fr.) fish or meat baked in parchment, aluminum foil or paper
paprikahuhn (Ger.) braised paprika chicken and sour cream
parfait (Fr.) ice cream
parmentier (Fr.) potato soup
parmigiana, alla (It.) with mozzarella and tomato
parmigiano (It.) parmesan cheese
pasta (It.) generic name for noodles and macaronis
pasticceria (It.) pastry
patata (Sp.) potato
pâté (Fr.) mixture of meat, liver, poultry, fish or vegetables, sliced and served cold

patisseries (Fr.) pastries
pato (Sp.) duck
paupiette (Fr.) stuffed and rolled slice of meat
pavo (Sp.) turkey
pêches (Fr.) peaches
pecorino (It.) sheep's milk cheese
pepe (It.) pepper
peperone (It.) pepper, green, yellow, or red
pepino (Sp.) cucumber
pepitas (Sp.) pumpkin seeds
pepitoria (Sp.) fricassee
perigourdine, à la (Fr.) sauces with pâté de foie gras and truffles
persil (Fr.) parsley
pesca (It.) peach
pescado (Sp.) fish
pesce (It.) fish
pesto (It.) basil and garlic sauce
petite marmite (Fr.) consomme of lean beef, chicken, vegetables, marrow, croutons with cheese
petit pois (Fr.) little peas
petits fours (Fr.) small fancy cakes
pfannkuchen (Ger.) thin dessert pancake filled with jam
pflaume (Ger.) plum as pflaumenkuchen, halved pitted plums baked in thin cake dough
picadillo (Sp.) minced meat
picante (Sp.) spicy
piccata (It.) thinly sliced meat
pieds de cochon (Fr.) pig's feet as pieds de cochon diable, deviled pig's feet
pikant (Ger.) spicy
pilze (Ger.) mushrooms
piquante (Fr.) chopped onions sauteed, vinegar, brown stock with tomato, chopped cornichons
pizza (It.) flat, baked pielike dishes
platanos (Sp.) bananas
Plateau de fromages (Fr.) cheese tray
poche (Fr.) poached
poire (Fr.) pear
poireau (Fr.) leek
pois (Fr.) pea
poisson (Fr.) fish
poitrine (Fr.) breast
poivrade (Fr.) peppery sauce
poivre (Fr.) pepper
poivrons (Fr.) peppers
polenta (It.) cornmeal pudding
polipi (It.) squid
pollitos (Sp.) squabs or young chickens
pollo (It., Sp.) chicken
polpette (It.) meatballs
polpettone (It.) meat loaf
pomme (Fr.) apple
pomme de terre (Fr.) potato
pommes (Fr.) as: pommes Anna, raw sliced potatoes, molded, baked brown; pommes boulangères, scalloped potatoes, sliced onions, broth, oven baked; pommes duchèsse, mashed potatoes with eggs, shaped into a mound, oven baked; pommes Parisiennes, small round roasted potatoes; pommes paille, fried shoe string potatoes; pommes persillées, parsley potatoes; pommes purée, mashed potatoes; pommes vapeur, steamed potatoes
pomodoro (It.) tomato

pont l'eveque (Fr.) table cheese
porc (Fr.) pork as côtelette de porc, pork chop
potage (Fr.) soup
pot au feu (Fr.) boiled beef with vegetables
pots de crème (Fr.) chilled dessert of flavored cream, very rich
poularde (Fr.) usually a good size hen, braised or poached
poule (Fr.) chicken, as poule au pot, stuffed chicken, vegetables
poulet (Fr.) young chicken
poulette (Fr.) white sauce of mushrooms, egg yolks, cream, parsley, lemon juice
printanier (Fr.) made of spring vegetables
profiterole (Fr.) small cream puffs with chocolate frosting
prosciutto (It.) ham sliced very thin
provençal (Fr.) with tomatoes, garlic, oil
provola (It.) soft cheese, like mozzarella
provolone (It.) hard cheese
pruneaux (Fr.) prunes
puchero (Sp.) meat and vegetable stew
puerco (Sp.) pork
purée (Fr.) mashed

quadrucci (It.) pasta squares
quatre-épices (Fr.) four spices used for pâtés and terrines
quenelle (Fr.) finely chopped and seasoned meat or fish dumplings
quesillo (Sp.) custard
queso (Sp.) cheese
queue (Fr.) tail, as queue de boeuf, oxtail
quiche (Fr.) filled, unsweetened egg-based tart or pie
quignon (Fr.) pie-shaped piece of bread
quisquilla (Sp.) shrimp

rábano fuerte (Sp.) horseradish
rafano (It.) horseradish
rafraichi (Fr.) cooled, chilled
ragôut (Fr.) stew
ragù (Sp.) stew
rahm (Ger.) cream
raifort (Fr.) horseradish
rana (Sp.) frog
ratatouille (Fr.) eggplant mixture with zucchini, tomatoes, olive oil
ravigote (Fr.) cold sauce of oil, vinegar, capers, herbs
ravioli (It.) square of dough stuffed with spinach, chopped meat and cheese or with ricotta and boiled or fried
reis (Ger.) rice
relleno (Sp.) stuffed
remoulade (Fr.) mayonnaise with mustard, capers, chopped gherkins
ribes (It.) currants
ricotta (It.) white fresh soft cheese
rind, rindfleisch (Ger.) beef as rinderrouladen, rolled, stuffed slices of beef
riñones (Sp.) kidneys
ripieno (It.) stuffed
ris de veau (Fr.) veal sweetbreads
riso (It.) rice, as risotto, boiled or steamed rice with sauce and parmesan cheese; rice-based dishes
riz (Fr.) rice
rognon (Fr.) kidney

rognone (It.) kidney
roh (Ger.) raw, rare
rostbraten (Ger.) roast beef
róti (Fr.) roast
rotoli (It.) rolled and stuffed fillets of beef
rotkraut (Ger.) red cabbage
rouille (Fr.) sauce of pimiento and garlic
rouladen (Ger.) rolled fillets, as rinderrouladen, rolled beef fillets
royale (Fr.) with pieces of egg custard
rührei (Ger.) scrambled egg

sacher torte (Ger.) chocolate cake with apricot jam filling
sahne (Ger.) cream, as sauer sahne, sour cream
saison, en (Fr.) in season
sal (Sp.) salt, as sal y pimienta, salt and pepper; salado, salty
salade (Fr.) salad
salat (Ger.) salad
salchicha (Sp.) sausage
salé (Fr.) salted
salmón (Sp.) salmon, as salmón ahumado, smoked salmon
salmone (It.) salmon, as salmone affumicato, smoked salmon
salsa (It., Sp.) sauce, gravy
salsiccia (It.) sausage
saltimbocca (It.) little rolls of thinly sliced veal stuffed with prosciutto, cheese
salz (Ger.) salt, as salz und pfeffer, salt and pepper, salzig, salty
saucisse (Fr.) sausage
sauer (Ger.) sour
sauerbraten (Ger.) spiced pot roast
saumon (Fr.) salmon, as saumon fumé, smoked salmon
sauté (Fr.) fried lightly in butter
scaloppa (It.) breaded slice of meat
scaloppine (It.) thinly sliced meat, usually veal
scarola (It.) escarole
schichttorte (Ger.) layercake
schinken (Ger.) ham
schnapps (Ger.) various strong, distilled liquors
schnitz (Ger.) sliced, dried fruit
schnitzel (Ger.) veal cutlet, literally, small slice
schwein (Ger.) pork, as schweinebraten, roast pork
scungilli (It.) a seafood extracted from a conch and served with a hot sauce
sel (Fr.) salt, as du sel et du poivre, salt and pepper; sel blanc, table salt
selle (Fr.) saddle, as selle d'agneau
senf (Ger.) mustard
smitane (Fr.) sauce of sauteed onion, white wine, sour cream
sogliola (It.) sole or flounder, filetto di sogliola, fillet of sole
sole (Fr.) sole, as filet de sole à la bonne femme, "plain" fillet of sole
sorbet (Fr.) sherbet
sorbo (Ger.) sauce, gravy
soubise (Fr.) sauce of sauteed onions, bechamel and chicken stock
soufflé (Fr.) light, fluffy baked mixture of foods with beaten egg whites, dessert or main course, as soufflé au jambon, ham soufflé

soupe (Fr.) soup, as soupe à l'oignon, onion soup with Gruyere cheese over toast

spargel (Ger.) asparagus

spätzle (Ger.) egg and flour dumplings dipped into boiling water or soup

spiedini (It.) mozzarella between slices of bread with anchovies, baked

spumone (It.) a variety of Italian ice cream

stracchino (It.) Milanese soft creamy cheese

stracciatella (It.) Roman egg-drop soup

streuselkuchen (Ger.) crumb cake

strudel (Ger.) sheet of paper-thin dough rolled up with various fillings and baked as apfelstrudel, apple strudel

stufatino (It.) stew, as stufatino firenze, florentine veal stew

stufato (It.) stewed meat, pot roast

succo (It.) juice

sucra, sucré (Fr.) sugared, sweet, as sucreries, sweets

suprême (Fr.) white sauce of chicken with mushrooms, cream and lemon juice

suprême de volaille (Fr.) breast of chicken or game birds without skin or bone

süss (Ger.) sweet, as süsser wein, sweet wine

tacchino (It.) turkey

tagliatelle (It.) noodles as tagliatelle in brodo, noodles in broth

talleyrand (Fr.) white sauce of chicken stock, cream, madeira, truffles, tongue

tartare (Fr.) cold mayonnaise, chopped pickles, chives; also an uncooked chopped beefsteak with raw egg yolks, capers, seasonings

tartelettes (Fr.) miniature pies

tartufi (It.) truffles

taschenkrebs (Ger.) crabs

té (Sp.) tea, as té débil, weak tea; té forte, strong tea; té helado, iced tea

tè (It.) tea, as tè debole, weak tea; tè forte, strong tea; tè in ghiaccio, iced tea

tee (Ger.) tea, as schwacher tee, weak tea; starker tee, strong tee; eistee, ice tea

ternera (Sp.) veal, as ternera con verenjenas, baked veal with eggplant

terrine (Fr.) potted meat, named for the earthenware pot in which it is cooked

thé (Fr.) tea, as thé faible, weak tea; thé forte, strong tea; thé glacé, iced tea

thunfisch (Ger.) tuna

timbale (Fr.) steamed, molded custard

tisane (Fr.) infusion of herbs, herb tea

tonno (It.) tuna

torrijas (Sp.) bread slices soaked in milk or wine, fried and covered with sugar and cinnamon, like American french toast

torta (It.) pie, as torta di Prosciutto, ham pie; also cake, torta di crema, layer cake

torte (Ger.) cake, as schwarzwälder kirschtorte, a chocolate cake with sherry and whipped cream filling; esp. Black Forest

tortellini (It.) shell of dough filled with meat

torticas (Sp.) small rum cakes; esp. Seville

tortilla (Sp.) a round, thin cake of unleavened cornmeal bread

tournedos (Fr.) small filet mignon, should be wrapped with bacon

tourte (Fr.) raised pie with fish, meat or fruit inside, as tourte Lorraine, veal-pork pie

tourtière (Fr.) pie dish; French Canadian pork pie

tranche (Fr.) slice as tranche de veau et cocombres, veal slices with cucumbers

tripe (Fr.) tripe, as tripe à la mode caen, stuffed mutton tripe; esp. Provence

trippa (It.) tripe, as trippa alla Fiorentina, tripe in meat sauce

trota (It.) trout

trucha (Sp.) trout

trufas (Sp.) truffles

truffe (Fr.) small black wild growing fungus that grows underground and is valued as a table delicacy

truite (Fr.) trout, as truite en bleu, trout in vinegar

truthuhn (Ger.) turkey

uccelletti (It.) strips of rolled, stuffed veal

uovo (It.) egg as uova fritte, fried eggs

valencienne (Fr.) dish served with rice

veau (Fr.) veal

velouté (Fr.) smooth white sauce, based on chicken or veal stock

venaison (Fr.) venison

verdura (It., Sp.) vegetables

véronique (Fr.) white sauce of fish stock, white grapes, white wine

vert-pré (Fr.) grilled meat served with potatoes and watercress

viandes (Fr.) meats

vichyssoise (Fr.) leek and potato soup, served cold

vin (Fr.) wine, as vin blanc, vin rouge, white wine, red wine

vinaigre (Fr.) vinegar as vinaigrette dressing for salads, cooked vegetables, grilled meats

vitello (It.) veal

viveurs (Fr.) soup with beet juice, pieces of beets and minced chicken or beef

volailles (Fr.) poultry

weinbergschnecken (Ger.) snails

weinsuppe (Ger.) name of soups with wine as ingredient

weintrauben (Ger.) grapes

westfälischer schinken (Ger.) Westphalian ham, cured and sliced thin, served cold

wiener schnitzel (Ger.) viennese-style breaded veal cutlets

zabaione, zabaglione (It.) warm eggnog dessert

zingara (Fr.) julienne of ham, truffles, mushrooms, tongue, brown sauce with tomatoes

zitrone (Ger.) lemon

zucchero (It.) sugar

zucchino (It.) zucchini squash as zucchini ripieni, stuffed zucchini

zumo (Sp.) juice

zunge (Ger.) tongue

zuppa (It.) soup

zuppa inglese (It.) soft, rich, Roman cake and custard

zwetschgenknödel (Ger.) broiled or steamed dumplings with a plum in the center, a dessert

ABOUT THE VERY BEST

To enhance your dining pleasure, we have indicated by an asterisk those restaurants considered to be The Very Best by our readers and frequent fliers. These restaurants were given Four Star ratings in the categories of food, service, and ambiance and therefore merit the phrase "the very best."